History, Religion and Spiritual Democracy
Essays in Honor of Joseph L. Blau

HISTORY, RELIGION, and SPIRITUAL DEMOCRACY

ESSAYS IN HONOR OF JOSEPH L. BLAU

MAURICE WOHLGELERNTER
Editor

James A. Martin, Jr.　　　　Peter H. Hare
David R. Blumenthal　　　　Howard B. Radest
Co-Editors

NEW YORK　COLUMBIA UNIVERSITY PRESS　1980

Library of Congress Cataloging in Publication Data
Main entry under title:

History, religion, and spiritual democracy.

Bibliography: p.
1. Religion—Philosophy—Addresses, essays,
lectures. 2. Philosophy, American—History—
Addresses, essays, lectures. 3. Political
science—Addresses, essays, lectures. 4. Judaism
—Addresses, essays, lectures. 5. Philosophy,
Jewish—History—Addresses, essays, lectures.
6. Blau, Joseph Leon, 1909- —Addresses,
essays, lectures. I. Blau, Joseph Leon, 1909–
II. Wohlgelernter, Maurice.
BL51.H58   191   79-23234
ISBN 0–231–04624–3

Columbia University Press
New York   Guildford, Surrey

Contents

Preface

THIS JUBILEE VOLUME is a labor of love. Wishing to express their love, a group of former teachers, colleagues and students of Joseph L. Blau felt that the written word would best reveal and confirm it. Hence, what all the participants in this volume have to say—each one uniquely expressing thoughts inspired in some tangible way by the person this book honors—is the very committed and permanent expression of that love.

Furthermore, the participants—especially the editors—were motivated to publish this *Festschrift* for yet another reason. Reviewing Professor Blau's three decades and some at Columbia University prior to his recent retirement, they concluded, as did other editors on another occasion, that "too often, distinguished academic careers pass virtually unnoticed into the waves of time. Ironically, the fault—if that word can be used—is the professor's: he performs his duties so well for so long that consistent excellence is taken for granted." The editors of this *Festschrift* simply refused to take that excellence for granted. Always aware that, in the life of a man, especially an academician, there can be no more painful—nay, frightening—moment than when, after a long and distinguished career, he walks out of the halls of his university for the last time, too often unsung, unheralded, and unaccompanied by either students or colleagues, much less teachers, and thus terribly alone, the editors intend this volume to serve as a reminder to this scholar that his splendid accomplishments have not been "washed away by the waves of time." On the contrary, they are lastingly recorded here so that he need never again feel the particular loneliness that often takes over the end of a distinguished academic career.

In fact, the idea of publishing this volume occurred at the very moment of Dr. Blau's greatest loneliness. When, in the summer of 1977, he underwent major surgery and was, naturally, deeply perturbed about its outcome, we thought that nothing could possibly add as much encouragement to his recovery as a jubilee collection, a promising reminder that all of us do indeed care. Whether this decision added anything to his subsequent recovery can hardly be argued with any certainty. What is, however, certain is that it helped immeasurably in persuading him that, because others, too, shared his anxieties, he was not—nor need ever be—starkly alone.

Soon after that difficult summer, a small group—James A. Martin, Jr., David R. Blumenthal, Peter H. Hare, Howard B. Radest, and I—met to refine the plan and content of this work. Together, we confirmed three basic decisions. First, the volume would be so arranged that its parts would reflect, in some measure, the four major areas of Blau's scholarly concern: the philosophy of religion, the history and philosophy of Judaism, American philosophy, and social philosophy. Second, toward that end, the editor of each part would, after receiving articles from former students and colleagues of Dr. Blau, assume the responsibility for reading and editing them and preparing them for final publication. In addition, each editor would then contribute a brief introduction to his part, describing the nature of its content and its relation to the general theme of the *Festschrift*. Third, on completing his own assignment, each editor would then read and comment on the other sections. In that way, the co-editors would, in part, share in the general editing of the entire volume, thus ensuring that, whenever possible, each section would in some way be connected to every other.

That these assignments were, for the most part, executed as

planned is due, in no small part, to the diligence, determination and dedication of the co-editors. They labored long to co-operate with each other and with me to maintain a sort of unity in our diversity. Since all but one resides away from New York City, the group had to travel considerable distances to attend editorial meetings, helping, thereby, to deal with some of the myriad details that usually accompany the publication of such *Festschriften*. This work, then, is in many ways the coordinate result of their sterling efforts.

It will not, of course, escape the attention of the reader that what links, interestingly, the work of the co-editors and their respective participants is not only the occasion of this celebration but also the dream that pervaded all of Dr. Blau's life: the uniting of people of totally different training and temperaments to work harmoniously toward a specific goal. The fruitful joining together of this disparate group of widely representative writers and thinkers—a humanist, a Catholic priest, a Presbyterian deacon, an orthodox rabbi, an ethical culturist to name but a few—is, therefore, as much a celebration of Blau the cultural ecumenist as Blau the man. And this may be, ultimately, the greatest tribute to his work in, among other areas, the philosophy of religion.

As editor-in-chief, I assumed, at the very outset, the responsibility for planning the entire volume, for coordinating the efforts of the co-editors, for writing the general introduction, a brief study of Blau's major intellectual interests, and, finally, for seeing the entire work through the various stages of editing, production, and publication. Though this editorship demanded interminable hours and an unending preoccupation with nettlesome minutiae, I was fortunate in being able to lean, when necessary, on my co-editors, whose active support and, above all, warm friendship made of this at times seemingly impossible project a genuine labor of love. And were it not, also, for the meticulous attention given to the final copy editing of the completed manuscript by Sam DeKay, Secretary of our Editorial

Committee, this volume might never have been submitted on schedule, a schedule demanding possible publication in Fall 1979, to coincide appropriately with the celebrant's seventieth birthday.

The editing of this book has placed me under many happy obligations. I am particularly grateful to *all* the contributors who answered our requests for their essays, comments and reflections with avidity and alacrity. Professor and Mrs. Salo W. Baron were especially helpful in many ways during every stage of the book's progress.

Further, I am indebted to Eliseo Vivas, Professor of Philosophy, Emeritus, Northwestern University; Frederick M. Keener, Professor of English, Hofstra University; and to my colleagues at Baruch College, City University of New York, Emile Capouya, Robert McDermott, Edward M. Potoker, Grace Schulman and Michael Schwartzman, who carefully read my introduction amid their own pressing work, giving me the advantage of their criticism and encouragement. I offer warmest thanks to Louis Levy, former Acting Dean of the School of Liberal Arts and Sciences, whose concern and assistance have always been a source of inspiration to me. To my trusted friend Andrew Lavender, Chairman, Department of English, for giving every draft of everything I write detailed and affectionate readings—he is, in fact, my unnamed co-author—and for his abiding concern for my welfare, I owe him more than I can every hope to express.

For encouragement and other aid, I am very grateful to ·a number of colleagues and friends—William F. Bernhardt, Leslie Bialler, Laiying Chong, John Dore, Jane Galloway, Matthew Goldstein, Gerald Green, Martin Stevens, Elie Wiesel and Michael Wyschogrod. My greatest inspiration remains, as always, my revered teacher and spiritual guide, Rav Joseph B. Soloveitchik. I am also very mindful of the generous help and counsel granted to me by my friend and colleague Rabbi Joseph H. Lookstein.

To my wife, Esther, and to our children, Debra, Elli, and

Beth, I am forever indebted for their love, abiding faith, and for their prayerful hopes for the future.

Eleanor Blau, for reasons too numerous to mention, most certainly deserves to share in this celebration.

The final sentence of this brief Preface, however, is reserved for Joseph L. Blau himself, to whom this book is dedicated with love, a love meant to echo that recorded at the close of his own preface to *Judaism in America:* "In a sense, then, my students are my unnamed co-authors. To all of them, past and present, I dedicate this work with love."

M.W.

Baruch College
   of the
City University of New York
February 1, 1979

Acknowledgments

The Editors wish to extend their deepest thanks to the following who, through their heartwarming generosity, have made the publication of this volume possible:

Dr. and Mrs. Salo W. Baron
Mr. and Mrs. Simon Cohen
Mr. and Mrs. Morris Dulberg
Dr. Morris Gellis
Mr. and Mrs. William Gellis
Mr. Bernard Goldstein
Mr. and Mrs. Ezra Goodman
Dr. and Mrs. Jacob Haberman
Mr. and Mrs. Norman Kaye
Dr. Corliss Lamont
Mr. and Mrs. David Levy
Mrs. Mary Millard

Mr. and Mrs. Hersh Neuman
Mr. and Mrs. Arthur Reiss
Mr. and Mrs. Samuel Roman
Mr. and Mrs. Barry Schreiber
Mr. and Mrs. Irwin Shapiro
Mr. and Mrs. William R. Shapiro
Mr. H. R. Shepherd
Dr. and Mrs. Auri Spigelman
Mr. and Mrs. Al Warren
Ms. Corinne Weslock
Dr. Viola D. Weslock

Wurzweiller Foundation:
Rabbi Joseph H. Lookstein, Chairman
Mr. Fred Grubel, Executive Secretary

Joseph L. Blau: In Appreciation

The editors have extended a special invitation to Salo W. Baron, James Gutmann, and Herbert Schneider—all former teachers of Joseph L. Blau—and to Justus Buchler and Paul O. Kristeller, former colleagues, to participate with brief statements in this jubilee volume. What follows is, perforce, only the shortest of tributes to their distinguished former student and colleague.

I HAVE HAD many opportunities to observe Joseph Blau in action. Ever since the early 1930s, when he joined one of my classes at Columbia University, I had the opportunity to see his creative mind at work, to admire his articulateness, both orally and in writing, and to be impressed by his perseverance in searching for the truth. I read his doctoral dissertation, "The Christian Interpretation of the Cabala in the Renaissance," with great interest. Although dealing with a subject important to Renaissance and Jewish scholarship for a long time, he was able to contribute both significant data and valuable insights to its understanding.

When Blau joined the Columbia faculty in 1944 and, at first, concentrated on American intellectual history, he collaborated with the then recently established interdepartmental Committee on Religious Studies which led to the establishment of the Department of Religion, in which he played a major role.

Ultimately, in 1967–76, he served as its chairman. As members of that Committee we frequently exchanged ideas, especially with respect to the work supervised by the subcommittee on the relations between religion and society, successively chaired by the late Reinhold Niebuhr, myself, and Blau. The ramified socioreligious relationships were, indeed, one of Blau's major preoccupations throughout his teaching and writing career. It was no surprise to anybody, therefore, that the two of us could collaborate on such diverse projects as the preparation of a selection of texts for *Judaism: Postbiblical and Talmudic Period,* which appeared in the Library of Religion series and the three-volume work *The Jews of the United States 1790–1840: A Documentary History.* This work was planned as a part of a comprehensive history of American Jewish life in ten sections in connection with the American Jewish Tercentenary celebrations of 1954. Regrettably, lack of funds prevented the completion of this project.

Another area of our collaboration was our work on the Conference on Jewish Relations, subsequently renamed the Conference on Jewish Social Studies. This organization, pursuing scholarly investigation and publication relating to the main trends of Jewish life in the more recent past and present, was served by Blau in various capacities. For a short time he acted as its executive secretary. At the same time he contributed some significant reviews to its quarterly, *Jewish Social Studies.* Since 1970 he has served with distinction as vice president of the Conference and as one of the editors of the quarterly.

Blau has approached all his works with complete open-mindedness. While perseverant in his own attitudes to life, he has always been ready to change his mind in the light of cogent contrary evidence. This was not an easy task, particularly in the study of religion. He realized very clearly, as he pointed out particularly in an essay on "Tradition and Innovation," the basic dichotomy between religious beliefs, which assume the permanence and immutability of revealed doctrines and commandments, and the need for their revaluation in the light of changing social needs or newly emerging historical evidence.

This problem of the contrast between *Glaube* and *Geschichte,* like the earlier discussions about conflicts between faith and reason, has long preoccupied the minds of students of religion of all faiths and is far from resolved among the scholars today. I still remember a personal experience which made a lasting impression upon me: The aftermath of a lecture on the problems of "Liberty" I delivered before an interdenominational scholarly audience. In that address I expatiated on various aspects of the liberty of conscience threatened by *outside* pressures as well as on those of liberty *within* each religious denomination. During the question period, a member of the audience, a monsignor, asked: "Dr. Baron, you have spoken extensively about liberty, but how about certainty?" To Blau no amount of religious certainty was to prove an insurmountable obstacle to the quest for truth. In the *Story of Jewish Philosophy,* a subject in which the problem of faith versus reason had played a preeminent role, he made it clear that "a philosopher is obligated by his profession to a far greater sensitivity to unexamined ideas than is any nonphilosopher. He is obligated to a perpetual questioning, a perpetual probing, a perpetual sifting and analyzing." The independent reexamination of the evidence which led him to frequent original conclusions manifested itself particularly in his studies of Reform Judaism, with its set of teachings and practices with which he had grown up in the household of his father, an eminent liberal rabbi in England. This approach has characterized his noteworthy study of *Modern Varieties of Judaism* and his more recent *Reform Judaism: An Historical Perspective,* just as much as his earlier analysis of *Cornerstones of Religious Freedom in America.*

In his studies of the history of Judaism and the Jewish people Blau has also always endeavored to penetrate behind the specifically Jewish aspects of each phase of that evolution into the environmental influences which helped to shape it from the outside. In a characteristic passage about the American Jews he emphatically stated: "The history of the Jews of the United States is part of the history of the United States as well as part of the history of the Jews. In the preparation of the introductory materials and notes for these volumes, the editors have made the effort consciously to demonstrate the interrelations of these two histories."

To be sure, the extent of these interrelations has differed from time to time and from area to area. Even in the United States a Jewish population consisting for the most part of first-generation immigrants is likely to adhere to much of its pre-American way of life and to cherish its earlier religious or, for that matter, anti-religious attitudes. A second generation, on the other hand, in its attempt to obtain full integration into American society, may consciously repudiate the old mores and beliefs, or else seek to modify them so as to make them almost unrecognizable as specifically Jewish. The third or fourth generation finally may look for some reconciliation between the two worlds and a new method of living simultaneously as full-fledged Americans and full-fledged Jews. To all these perplexing problems Joseph Blau has suggested that some answers may be obtained by reinterpreting the old tradition through the application of some of the ancient techniques of allegory and hermeneutics, adapted to the needs of the modern age.

All these approaches are no mere theory for Blau. From the outset he has been convinced that while an historian, including an historian of philosophy or religion, must accept the validity of logical deductions, "their truth and their consequent acceptability rests on the historian's understanding of what people are, how people live, and think and love. . . . His greatness as an historian and his greatness as a man cannot be separated." This characteristic, attributed by Blau to someone else, fully applies to himself. In his entire life and work, he has proved himself to be an outstanding humanist. It is indeed from this conviction that springs my profoundly affectionate wish for Blau to continue for many, many years to bring his brilliant creativity and its rich application to his own life and to that of society at large.

SALO WITTMAYER BARON

THERE WAS a long period at Columbia University—after the departure of Herbert W. Schneider—when only Joseph Blau taught the history of American philosophy. I prefer to say that he held the fort alone. If this suggests a defensive commitment, a militant determination, it is with good reason. The academic world has been friendlier to American philosophers individually than to the historic framework in which they arose and functioned. I am not in a position to document Blau's contribution in this regard, but I have always thought of it as valuable. The scholarship of his students has helped to perpetuate his way of perceiving a fertile tradition—a tradition not definable by the work of any single philosopher whom we might by tempted to select as Grand Exemplar.

As Blau sees them, the trends of American civilization have fed and have been fed by the trends of American philosophy. At the same time he espouses no scheme whereby these trends are to be neatly integrated. In *American Philosophic Addresses* the emphasis is on the cultural side. In *Men and Movements in American Philosophy* the emphasis is on what Blau calls "the more formal side of our philosophic history." Both books are modestly said by him to provide background for further investigation. We should nevertheless take this particular point seriously, for the books are (*inter alia*) scholarly achievements. *Men and Movements* relies for its effectiveness not on the production of unexceptionable conclusions, but on a method of exposition which avoids seductive extremes. One is the extreme of endless hemming and hawing; of qualifying without managing to affirm; of inculcating respect for accuracy by means of intimidation. The other extreme is the shaping of a merely untaxing narrative pleasantly free of interpretative uncertainties.

If some of the issues and thinkers featured in Blau's account are not visible in the philosophic climate of a given present, we should remind ourselves how ephemeral our criteria of importance can be. For example, in the twenty-five or so years since *Men and Movements* was published, a whole style and euphoric strain of positivism has petered out. Similarly, during that time the "ordinary language" phase of philosophic analysis has gained and lost its main influence. Among historical studies recently in fashion (say those centering on Descartes) the issues taken most seriously would have been derided as obsolete a generation ago. But whatever the abiding forces of American philosophy may turn out to be, it is a fair guess that the trends chosen and defined by Blau will continue to make sense.

JUSTUS BUCHLER

IT IS GOOD to know that Joe Blau is to receive the accolade of a *Festschrift* by his colleagues and former students. As one who witnessed the dignity with which he faced past obstacles and adversities and also the way in which he accepted the many rewards which came to him for his achievements, I gladly join his friends in congratulating him and Eleanor, at this time of wider recognition and celebration.

JAMES GUTMANN

MY ASSOCIATION and friendship with Joseph Blau spans almost the entire period of my long career at Columbia. Shortly after I had joined the Department of Philosophy, I was asked to serve as one of the readers of the doctoral dissertation on which Blau had been working. The thesis, which was published as a book in 1944, deals with the Christian interpretation of the

Cabala in the Renaissance, an interesting and previously neglected subject, and it has held its place ever since as a substantial contribution to Renaissance studies.

About the same time, Joseph Blau joined the Columbia Faculty, first in the Department of Philosophy, and later in the
Department of Religion. He has been for many years an influential teacher on our campus, and a productive scholar, especially
in American philosophy and history, and in the history of Judaism.

As a member of the same faculty, I have had many dealings
with Joseph Blau over the years, all of them pleasant. We were
repeatedly involved in the work and dissertations of the same
students, attended together the same department and faculty
meetings, and have had numerous informal conversations at the
luncheon table in the Faculty Club where we discussed rather
openly many university affairs as well as our own scholarly
problems and interests. We have seen eye to eye on a number of
significant occasions, and my respect for Joseph Blau as a
scholar and person has steadily grown. In recent years, when the
university and the scholarly life have been exposed to many at-
tacks from the outside and from the inside, Joseph Blau could
be counted upon as a firm defender of common sense and of academic integrity, and I retain a grateful memory of his support
and understanding in many delicate situations.

In joining the ranks of the congratulants on Blau's retirement
and on his seventieth birthday that is to follow soon, I wish to
express to him my warmest wishes for his health and continued
productive work.

PAUL OSKAR KRISTELLER

THOUGH Joseph L. Blau's academic career is coming to its
close, I believe that this retirement to the rank of Professor
Emeritus will promote his productivity by emancipating him

from burdensome responsibilities and permitting him to continue more freely to share with us his wide knowledge and wise judgment. The wider public whom he has instructed and delighted by his many published works will profit by his emancipation.

His intellectual insights remain unflagging, and all of us who have had the pleasure and privilege of working and thinking with him hope that his physical energy may be spared for him and for us during the coming years of greater peace and freedom. The wide range of his scholarly interest and productions as historian, philosopher, and emancipator of religion has not prevented him from being a constructive leader in contemporary religious life and thought. There is no pedantry in him and no mere love of erudition. His learning is highly relevant to the events and issues of the present.

We hope earnestly that he will be available to us and to our problems for the years to come. But whatever the future may bring for him and us, we are now deeply grateful to Joseph Blau for what he has already achieved.

HERBERT W. SCHNEIDER

Introduction
Joseph Leon Blau:
Four Ways of Religion and Philosophy

MAURICE WOHLGELERNTER

I

WRITING OF ONE of his former teachers of philosophy, Irwin Edman once observed that he was impressed by a "mind whose maturity had not dulled its enthusiasms, and an understanding uncorrupted by technical controversies of the academy, by the routine of the classroom, by the burden of administration of an elder statesman." True of that teacher, it is no less true of Joseph L. Blau, a teacher, administrator and friend of seven generations of students of philosophy and religion at Columbia University—a college generation being four years—who taught them, among many other things, "to keep their eye on the object, to see a thinker in his own terms, to cease to raise foolish and irrelevant questions, and, above all, to raise the central relevant ones about a man's teaching." And despite Blau's retirement from formal teaching at Columbia in June 1977, he remains their teacher still, primarily because what he helped them—and us—understand is the never ending endeavor which, like all great teachers, he called the "enterprise of learning."

To celebrate Blau's lifetime enterprise as teacher, a group of his enterprising students and colleagues have joined together to publish this Jubilee volume. If that, however, would seem to be in some ways an ending, what we are seeking in this Introduction is to know some of his beginnings, as teacher, writer, thinker, and enterprising spirit.

It all began in Brooklyn, where Joseph was born, the middle son of Joel and Anna Blau, in 1909. The household, dominated by the father, a Reform rabbi, stressed spiritual values over all other standards of life and living. An immigrant from Hungary who had studied at the illustrious and orthodox Yeshiva of Pressburg, as befits a descendant of a line of illustrious rabbis, Joel Blau nevertheless broke early with his tradition. Soon after his arrival in America, he was ordained in 1908 at Hebrew Union College, the seat of the Reform movement in America, while he was studying for his baccalaureate at the University of Cincinnati. After occupying pulpits in Brooklyn and Rochester, New York, and Trenton, New Jersey, in 1925 Joseph Blau's father was called to the position of Senior Minister of the West London Synagogue of British Jews, a bastion of English Reform Judaism, where three years later he died suddenly, ending a most promising, albeit itinerant career.

If we are to understand, in part, some of the reasons for the son's ultimate choice of career and its orientation, it might serve us well to catch a glimpse of some of the father's ideas. For it was these ideas that not only set the spiritual mood of the household but also helped shape and direct some of the son's thinking. When, in dedicating *The Christian Interpretation of the Cabala in the Renaissance,* his first published work, the son records his debts—in this case to his past, present, and future— he lists his parents first, apparently as his most singular debt to his past. Let us now look briefly at that past.

A gifted orator, Joel Blau was equally well known, especially in America, as a publicist, essayist, and critic. He wrote a regular column, for example, in *The American Hebrew* and *The Jewish*

Standard, both weeklies of great influence in the American Jewish community of the early decades of this century. What he possessed, apparently, was a deep feeling for language which made him, as one of his contemporaries remarked, "a great preacher, one of the greatest, because one of the most original and inspiring preachers [he had] ever heard." In fact, so involved was Rabbi Blau with this oral tradition that he would read regularly to his children from his weekly columns so that they too might be imbued with his philological instinct, his pure style, his "intoxication with Midrash and Aggadah."

And with this intense preoccupation with words, their nuances of meaning and expression, Joel Blau was—as his frequent changes of pulpit would indicate—a restless spirit. His intense restlessness, his often "irritating impatience," his intolerance of hypocrisy and sham, a close friend once recalled, "were symptoms of a haste, a feeling that his time was limited. He frequently estranged even some of his best friends. It would be idle to deny that there were those who disliked him as well as those who learned to love him." Such restlessness might also explain why, after studying at the Yeshiva of Pressburg, Hungary, the citadel of piety in that part of Eastern Europe, he switched his allegiance to the Reform movement, the extreme opposite of orthodoxy, and why, though basically conservative, he embraced a "progressive Judaism" whose Pittsburgh Platform of 1885 rejected some of the essential tenets of traditional Judaism; and, finally, why "roaming through the ages, he took up all the best the world had to offer in any part or time, transmitting the aspirations of one age or of one people into the terms of another, journeying in his thought far and wide."

It was such a "noble rage," then, that pushed him during the carnage of World War I, to formulate his own idea of God in a small, privately printed pamphlet, "The Problem of Modern Faith: Creedless Creed." His major point of departure was that "religion is a very personal thing, that religion is a matter of experience that carries its own assurance; better: God is the immediate revelation of the heart." Man, in his highest mood, is filled with a dissatisfaction with things as they are, a dissatisfaction "which stirs in him the longing for ideal circumstances in which life would bear the stamp of God-likeness." Religion for him, therefore, became primarily "individual," that is, "a man's most passionate longing should be to find himself in God here and now."

What becomes obvious is that, in accordance with his opinions, Joel Blau ruled out a number of expressed views about religion and, specifically, modern Judaism: first, that religion is ethics and nothing else, that religion and ethics are interchangeable terms, is ruled out because "nothing is so mischievous from the viewpoint of modern faith than this uninspired identification of ethics with religion."

Second, he found noxious the identification of religion with social service, for if one is in personal touch with God, all social actions will follow. Without one's personal communion with God, without this "aliveness," this "antemortem immortality," social service becomes "a mere fidgetiness of idle fingers." For not "action but God comes first: God in the human heart, God softening the passions of man."

Finally, what Blau's father opposed most passionately, in his fiery mood, was the substitution of "*r*eligion" for "*R*eligion," or, *r*eligion with "its elaborate ritual, religion with its vain structure of cathedral and creed—both equally stony and hard . . . religion degenerating into theology . . . theology, that madness gone systematic which tied God's fulness into a formula and a system!" That fulness Rabbi Blau found in a God shrouded in uncertainty, a God who cannot be defined but definitely *is,* a God who one must seek and find for oneself in the boldest venture of man.

In fact, in Joel Blau's scheme of things, one cannot depend on history to validate the existence of God. For, he argues, "if the 'God of the Fathers' helps me find *my* God—well and good; but if I accept the 'Fathers God' mechanically, without trying to find 'my God,' I have but found another idol—I have substituted History for Religion." What he is criticizing is not so much tradition—although that, too, has, he believed, many customs and rituals hindering the search for a personal God—but the "soulless, uninspired substitution of mere tradition for the living, breathing spirit of personal companionship with God." What he was after was a return to the original source of inspiration—to God, without, however, the laws that constitute what is generally accepted as the true essence of Judaism. Joel Blau's is the religion of personal communion, of individual realization which, for him, is the basis of modern faith. The heart becomes the Bible, the emotions his prayer, and breath his worship —these alone, he claims, will help man find his way to God.

Seeking his way to God, Joel Blau found that this worldly life is filled as well with joy. With an uncanny blend of mysticism and poetic expression, he records that joy in a short volume of sermonettes, based on various Biblical verses, which he appropriately titled *The Wonder of Life.* In it, he posits the belief that even as the "years glide silently by, let there ring forth, out of the stress of our days, the deathless refrain: Life is Wonderful." This paean to life clearly echoes, in more romantic terms, what he had stated earlier in "The Problem of Modern Faith"— namely, that there is "a reality beyond sense perception, beyond the grasp of the mind even, which presses into all things with incredible stress wherever it can find a precarious opening, like water rushing from the heights into every available opening." In other words, life is one with nature. Man and universe are one, "one with the earth and all that there is therein; one with the sky and its flaming desire." Man need only entrust himself to the "Infinite Stream" which, carrying him everywhere, "will unite him with everything."

Such faith leads not only to the wonders of life but also to its joy. For faith and joy are "twin flowers blowing under the same benevolent skies: in casting a blight upon one we cause the other to wither." With both faith and joy one never withers;

one is, instead, forever joyful, since joy is not something added to life but is, when wedded to faith, the quality of life itself. And throughout his rather turbulent life, Joel Blau, though not seeking the Promised Land, preached the faith in, and the joy and wonder of life that helped him find, first in America and then in England, a land of promise.

If, for the father, America was only a land of promise, it became the promised land indeed for the son, Joseph. A promising middle son, Joseph moved constantly forward in his career with a great deal of élan, striving for superiority under the usual familial and environmental pressures. For a second child sometimes works continually to surpass and, certainly, to differ from the other members of the family in the race of life, especially in a promised land. So this Joseph, too, in many ways differed from his brothers, and even his father, though resembling them in some.

Unlike his father, for example, Joseph did not seek an extensive formal Jewish education. After attending the traditional *cheder* for a brief period in his early youth, he studied Hebrew simply as a spoken language with Ittamar-Ben-Avi, the linguist, lexicographer, and editor. His formal study of religion actually began during his undergraduate years at Columbia, 1928–1932. The sole major in religion at the college at that time, he read extensively in the field for his teachers Herbert W. Schneider, Horace Freiss, Irwin Edman, Ruth Benedict, and Gardner Murphy, while pursuing courses in Jewish history with Salo W. Baron.

Upon graduating from the college in 1932, he planned a career in English, earning his Masters in the Graduate Department of English at Columbia in 1933. While Masters essays generally are not, we know, certain guides to the eventual academic interests of their authors, they do often indicate the writer's intellectual orientation and may even reveal some of his personality traits. As this, apparently, is true in Blau's case, it is illuminating to glance at his unpublished Master's essay for the interesting sidelights it reveals about its author.

Blau's short Master's essay, "John Biddle: Father of English Unitarianism," introduces the reader to that seventeenth-century figure, who, profoundly versed in the Bible, became convinced that the common doctrine of the Trinity accords with neither scripture nor reason. For proposing that view in his major work, *Twelve Arguments Drawn out of Scripture,* Biddle sat in prison and was banished to the Scilly Islands for two years, before he was rescued by friends through their intercession with Cromwell. Yet Biddle persisted in his long struggle against a narrow and bigoted orthodoxy.

What Blau's study reveals, if only generally, is that his early interest in that polemical unitarian may have actually given some direction to certain interests in his own future thought, his writing, and his personal conduct in academe. We need only recall that, throughout his entire career Blau never adhered to an "orthodox" position in most matters and that, like Biddle or his own father, he took an even more extreme position as regards what he would call the "narrow and bigoted." And Blau further implies that what he admired in Biddle was, first, his belief that "faith cannot believe anything contrary to or above reason." Second, that to the very end of his career, much as at the beginning, Biddle was a skeptic, "a doubting soul, who called all things to a serious examination, holding fast to that which was good." Finally, getting to the very source of Biddle's approach to all the tractarian polemics and religious feuding of seventeenth-century England, Blau, with a prescience that foretells his own future approach to the controversy which forever pervades academe, cogently observes: "The more animated and savage grew the conflict between Anglican and Puritan, the more both parties lost control of their tempers and dignities, and began to search for the more scathing, not the more convincing, word, the more did calm and reflective minds, pacific and gentle hearts, feel the need for discovering, beyond and above all parties, some mutual ground, where they could reunite on a basis of reason and piety. This is the source of the . . . Unitarianism of Biddle." Truly, then, it is this latter trait, as we shall see, that so decidedly marked the measure of the man Blau.

For reasons not entirely dissimilar to those recorded by Ludwig Lewisohn in *Upstream,* who found some of the people unsympathetic, to say the least, to his personal background, Blau decided not to take his doctorate in the English department. Instead, he pursued his degree in the department of Philosophy, writing his dissertation in 1944 on a much-neglected subject, *The Christian Interpretation of the Cabala in the Renaissance.* Of that work, published in the same year, Paul O. Kristeller comments above that "it has held its place ever since as a substantial contribution to Renaissance studies."

Of all his teachers at Columbia, Blau was most strongly influenced in his studies in philosophy by Herbert W. Schneider. What impressed Blau most strongly in Schneider's philosophic character was, first, that he saw philosophy "as a disciplined and systematic reflection upon all the problems of human life, not merely upon all the problems of reflection themselves." Second, in setting forth his philosophy of the philosophy of history, Schneider stated that "the perspectives of history are ever shifting, for human experience, being itself continually subject to change, affords no fixed point of reference for the mind. . . . Neither the mental world nor the physical has a center and a circumference. The motion of bodies must be measured from points themselves in motion, and the meanings of events are themselves events in a constantly shifting scene."

And yet, Blau points out, despite such "perspectival relativism" of seeing the ever-changing present and not the past that gives form to history, Schneider contends further that *this* present, similarly, has no meaning save in terms of that past. For "past and present are in themselves alike mysterious, but they mysteriously illuminate each other; and though things are never intelligible in themselves, they nevertheless make each other intelligible." There is, for Schneider, therefore, no fixed meaning for either past or present.

Third, what also impressed Blau was that after some twenty years of preparation for his *A History of American Philosophy,* Schneider refused to draw any moral from his portrait of America's ancestral soul and the basic dialectic of its existence. That fact, as Blau stresses, is itself a moral. What Schneider rejects is the view that there is "any one lesson to be learned from the multitude of events and experiences that make up American history or any one meaning to be derived from the many ideas and intellectual adventurings that make up American philosophy." The course of philosophical speculation in America is for Schneider, as for Blau, the "story of the many attempts to 'naturalize' imported philosophies—chiefly of European origin—even as the course of American history is in so many ways the story of the naturalization of many immigrants—chiefly of European origin."

Finally, Blau finds Schneider's use of the phrase "desperate naturalism" most illuminating because it "characterizes a mode of thought that was widely prevalent in a whole generation of Americans who were swept out of a supernaturalism absorbed at their mother's knee and who were impelled to seek in a Darwinian naturalism a substitute for their earlier certitudes." True of many Americans, it is no less true of Blau himself, in whose thought and writings "Darwinian naturalism," as we shall see, plays so heavy a role.

No less a role in Blau's immediate intellectual development was played by Salo W. Baron, the eminent Jewish historian. From Baron, Blau learned, among many other things, that to be an historian—of any discipline—requires a deep and sympathetic understanding of men. To gain that understanding, "one must be a full human being." Greatness in academe, for example, should not, ideally, be separated from one's greatness as a human being.

What further impressed Blau in Baron's teaching was his "pluralistic approach to Jewish history . . . that Jewish life in modern times cannot be explained solely on the basis of an internal revolution, that is, there has been, at all times, a process of interaction between Jews and their neighbors; that just as Jews have influenced the world, the world has influenced the Jewish people." It is precisely his concern with this interaction and influence which has shaped Blau's own understanding of Judaism.

In addition, in the writing and teaching of Jewish history, Blau admired Baron's uncanny ability to take into account a vast array of alternatives of which religion, economics, social patterns, and demography are but some examples. That Baron is as many-sided as the vast material that makes up his monumental *Social and Religious History of the Jews* is what most deeply impressed Blau.

Where Blau differs with Baron is on the latter's "conservatism," his "traditionalism," or, specifically, Baron's interpretation of Jewish Emancipation from the French Revolution to the present. Baron maintains that from the "internal viewpoint of the Jewish people, their solidarity and the development of their culture, emancipation was a tragic and possibly a fatal mistake." Blau, on the other hand, tends to disagree, finding emancipation "the force which enabled Jews, especially in America, to release themselves from any bondage to authority, to be loyal participants in the political, social and economic life of all countries, to welcome the secularization of modern man, a secularization in which traditional religious motivations are no longer central to his life."

Whatever the differences, Blau used both Schneider and Baron as guides when, a few years after receiving his doctorate, he began, first in the department of Philosophy and then in the department of Religion at Columbia, his long, effective and distinguished career as teacher, author, critic, and editor. The flowering of that career was accomplished through his deep concern, his involvement, his devotion, his total dedication to men *and* to learning, to men *of* learning. Baron and Schneider, among others, had shown him the way.

But, that way was not always easy. The notion that academe is tranquil is grossly misleading. Academe can be a more terrifying place than the jungle, where, at least, predators kill out of a natural need for food. One member of academe, who came late to its dangers after a highly successful career in the mass media has observed terrifyingly: "Academic people on the make have an instinct for the jugular that is driven by a deadly combination of ruthless ambition and sheer, malevolent, sadistic pleasure. The demolition of a colleague's paper or reputation consumes an extraordinary amount of time and energy that might best be used by minding one's own affairs or (horrible thought!) serving the students." For a short while along his way, Blau was subjected to such malevolence. Refusing, however, to compromise his dignity or his decency, he was able, by resolutely transcending human weaknesses, to persevere and survive.

To persevere in academe also demanded a number of important decisions. First, he decided to remain in New York, where, because of its size and impersonality, a Jew could more easily adjust as an historian of philosophy and religion. Second, he decided to devote much of his time to writing. Even a cursory glance at his bibliography at the close of this volume will immediately reveal the range of his prodigious productivity. Perhaps because most of his writing was done in the city, he was able to find the detachment, and possibly the solace, to offset some of his personal disappointments. His many publications, however, were most assuredly not the result of the relentless pressure of academe to publish or perish but rather of the natural pleasure of sharing with others matters to which he had given much thought. It was somewhat akin to the scientist's driving need to reveal his discoveries of the unknown.

Finally, and most significantly, Blau became deeply involved in the intellectual lives of his students. For the true teacher, even though he be a writer as well, inevitably reaches the conclusion—after all the books, after all the articles, after all the reviews—that in the end what is truly significant is teaching one's students. Books and articles—however important, however highly acclaimed—can never be for him a substitute for the intense dialogic relationship between teacher and student. To share with a student a body of knowledge, to see his face suddenly illuminated by an idea or a text, is no less significant than the accumulation of an extensive bibliography, however impressive, however enviable.

And Blau was a superb teacher. In fact, teaching, as Gilbert Highet was forever reminding us, is an art, an art that Blau wondrously mastered. That mastery may have derived from those sessions in his youth when his father—himself a fine teacher and orator—read aloud to young Joseph and his brothers from his weekly column. Or it may have grown out of a native talent, or simply his love of students and his subject. Whatever its origins, it is certain that he attempted, as nearly as humanly possible, to achieve during his three decades or so in the classroom what is best expressed by Santayana in *Character and Opinion in the United States:* "Teaching is a delightful paternal art, and especially teaching intelligent and warm-hearted youngsters, as most American collegians are; but it is an art like acting, where the performance, often rehearsed, must be adapted to an audience hearing it only once. The speaker must make concessions to their impatience, their taste, their capacity, their prejudices, their ultimate good; he must neither bore nor perplex nor demoralize them. His thoughts must be such as can flow daily, and be set down in notes; they must come when the bell rings and stop appropriately when the bell rings a second time. The best that is in him, as Mephistopheles says in *Faust,* he dare not tell them; and as the substance of this possession is spiritual, to withhold is often to lose it."

What Blau never withheld in all his classroom artistry is yet another quality: that of being able to recognize views other than his own with a calmness, a fairness, a firmness not vouchsafed to many others. The same quality is reflected, incidentally, in his publications. Witness, for example, *Modern Varieties of Judaism,* in which he gives an outstandingly fair-minded presentation of attitudes which were diametrically opposed to his own. It is this judiciously receptive temper—of deliberately, of steadfastly, showing the other side of every issue—that is central to Blau's success as a teacher. In fact, Peter Hare, a former student, recalled that very trait as Blau's claim to lasting influence: "All my philosophy teachers as an undergraduate at Yale and as a graduate student at Columbia had seemed to me to be fiercely partisan. My temperament is such that I was profoundly disturbed by such constant philosophical warfare between systems. My powerful ironic impulse led me to seek some way of doing justice both to the idealism I had been taught at Yale and to the naturalism in which I had been indoctrinated at Columbia. . . . But until I had Blau as a teacher in 1961, I had no contact with a distinguished philosopher who was not bent on showing that philosophers of other persuasions were fools and/or knaves. When I found that Blau, though a committed naturalist, was able to treat fairly the full range of recent philosophical schools, I was inspired to follow his example in working in the history of American philosophy. I had to do justice to the many dimensions of American philosophy as he had in *Men and Movements* and other writings. That hope modeled on Blau is still with me."

"That hope modeled on Blau" may be, finally, the occasion for this *Festschrift*. For that hope inspired some of his former students, colleagues and teachers—of various "schools" and of still more varied interests, backgrounds and dispositions—to join in sharing their various views in the many areas of Blau's lifetime interests. What has moved all of them is the desire to honor Blau, the teacher, who, with obvious distinction, was able during his long career in academe to discover, like John Biddle, "beyond and above all parties, some mutual ground, where they could reunite on a basis of reason and piety." Reunited, his students now declare that such a teacher surely deserves a festival of his own.

II

What motivated the participants in this celebration, however, was not only Blau the man and teacher, but also Blau the
student of the history of ideas. For in his role as historian of
philosophy and religion, his entire life has indeed been devoted
to the study of ideas, past and present. To discuss all of them
would naturally be impossible in so general an Introduction.
Hence, only some of his major concerns as reflected in his writings, particularly in the four areas of his abiding interest—the
philosophy of religion, the history and philosophy of Judaism,
American philosophy, and social philosophy—shall be considered here, and then only fleetingly.

It would seem that no consideration of Blau's concerns in the
philosophy of religion is possible without a reading of his essay
"The Influence of Darwin on American Philosophy," which first
appeared some twenty years ago in the *Bucknell Review*. For just
prior to his discussion there of Darwin's influence on American
philosophy, Blau reviews the Darwinian effect on religion,
something to which he refers repeatedly thereafter in his writings. Among other things, Blau asserts that, having established
organic evolution on a firm biological base, Darwin "came directly into conflict with the doctrine of special creation expressed in the first chapters of the Book of Genesis"; that by setting forth an explanation of differentiation in terms of natural
law Darwin "tended to minimize the scope of the miraculous
Divine intervention in the governing of the world"; that Darwin's theory of evolution reduced the "omnipotent, omniscient,
omnipresent God of theological tradition to a remote first cause,
who set the universe in motion and then left it severely alone,
in the grip of a multitude of second causes"; and, finally, that
Darwin, affirming the evolutionary argument, "cast serious
doubt on the Scriptural accounts of creation and of miracles, on
Biblical chronology, and on the position of man in the world."

All of which leads Blau to conclude that, henceforth, "Becoming would no longer be inferior to Being." Because every organic creature is in a state of perpetual change, "it could no longer be assumed that the permanent was superior to the changing; indeed, there was considerable warrant for arguing that since the changing was in the process of changing toward some state better adapted for life in the universe, change was, in fact superior to permanence." At the very least, biological evolutionism demanded an orientation toward "the study of change, growth, process and function, and away from permanence, static reality and structure."

Whether Blau subscribed fully to Darwinian evolutionism or whether it confirmed his declared agnosticism—an assertion he makes at least twice in his writings—one is not certain. What is, however, certain to the reader is that Darwinian evolution had a strong influence on Blau's thought. For, in much of his writing on religion, we find a steady preoccupation with "change, growth, process and function and away from permanence." Religion has apparently always been for him but one aspect of a cultural pattern which is "always changing as a result of the interaction between the various elements and as a result of the contacts with external culture."

Small wonder, therefore, that when invited to contribute an essay to a collection on *The Idea of God,* he offered what he considers to be one of his major contributions to the philosophy of religion: "God and the Philosophers." This is not meant as a discussion of the existence of God, since, Blau argues, God is "either to be believed or disbelieved, to be confronted or not to be confronted"; it is, instead, meant to be a discussion of men's conceptions of God, be they those of theologians, metaphysicians, poets, politicians, philosophers or pedestrians, all suitable material for analysis. What he wishes, here, is to restate the God-concept in such a way as to "permit its use in philosophical discussion and provide a basis on which believers and non-believers can collaborate in the humane enterprise of making this world a better world for all human beings."

Blau then proceeds to discuss some of these conceptions of God under three headings—"Infinite Regress and the Doctrine of Residues," "Intelligibility, Contingency and Necessity," "Of Permanence and Change"—refuting each of these conceptions presented in the past. In the fourth and final section, "God of Hope and Indeterminacy," he develops his novel idea of God as hope. Proposing some sort of linguistic reformation, Blau would retain the word "God" but give it an "adverbial" meaning, so that the use of the word no longer involves any recognition of the entity it names. For, to Blau, God is no longer determinate, no longer the noncognitive *mysterium tremendum,* no longer the permanent Being. God becomes, instead, the equivalent of our hope:

> If we are to argue (against the Deistic view of a single creative act) that the creative activity of God is continuous, then we must allow for a certain indeterminancy of God. At the very least we must say that the nature of God is permissive of novelty. If this is so, then the central religious virtue is not faith but hope. It is not an affirmation of a tradition concerning what has happened in the past, but an assertion of hope for what may happen in the future. To the theist, the future about which one hopes may be transcendent while to the naturalist it is immanent. . . . Here the important distinction lies . . . in the shift of our attention and concern from the past to the future, from faith to hope, from determinacy to indeterminacy. We have tended always to express ourselves historically in terms of the unity of the common pasts. If the experience of man in the Twentieth Century points to any meaning, it is that this way of thinking will no longer serve. It has become evident that we must learn to think in terms of the unity of a common human future. Of this common human future, the indeterminate God can be a symbol. We know *that* it must be; we cannot know *what* it must be, for it will be shaped by events that have not yet occurred.

God, in this scheme of things, becomes "God."

Even if we were to assume the validity of this conception of God's "adverbial" role, it need not necessarily follow, as Blau argues, that, in every religion based on revelation, the "ideal of a particular time, place, and situation becomes institutionalized in such a way that change and development are blocked." In fact, a close reading of the first two chapters of Genesis, as the Talmud, Midrash, and some medieval commentators have long ago observed, will reveal that not only is a determinate God vitally creative but also that man, granted immeasurable resources, most notably his intelligence, is instructed to be involved unceasingly in that creative process. Mandated "to fill the earth and subdue it," man, "transcending the limits of the reasonable and probable, ventures into the open spaces of a boundless universe." Man, imitating God, may also aspire to shape events that have and have not yet occurred. The Deistic view taken literally would make of creation a single act; but understood more fully it is, rather, the continuous activity of God.

Of course, one might venture to say, As Raymond Bulman does, that "while some Humanists undoubtedly intend their reconstruction of 'God' with utmost seriousness . . . other contributions, including Blau's, are presented somewhat 'tongue-in-cheek.' " For what was once called the "ecclesiastical method of theology" might, at times, require some Horatian satire, lest its religious authoritarianism be reduced to another of man's foibles. Yet, however, much such satire goads us to rethink the God-idea, one may find it difficult, if not impossible, to replace the traditional conceptions of God.

Besides, Blau is too serious a student of religion ever to approach the idea of God with tongue-in-cheek. What is, therefore, more disturbing in his theory of "God" as hope is not only that the Deity will constantly be subject to man and nature's "change, growth, process and function," and also that God will, thereby, lack a "permanence," a "permanence" Blau himself considers essential to any philosophy of religion. One need only recall his essay "Religion and the Newer Forms of Consciousness," in which he addresses himself to the "central phenomenon of the spirit in the modern world"—man's uprootedness. Referring specifically to the mass of young people who, in the 1960s and early 1970s, found religion—as perpetuated in traditional institutions—less than satisfying. Blau laments their flocking to the churches of a more fundamental cast, "the ones that make as little concession as possible to the modern world and demand as much commitment as possible from their adherents." This, he considers only an "affair of the moment." For, when they awaken—as many of them already have—from their "flirtation with fundamentalism," they will find "the way of the fundamentalists and of the orthodox valuable for teaching what we have failed to teach—the nature of commitment and of obligation, but they will also find it too crippling, too restrictive, too limiting; and they will turn back."

To what will they turn back? Blau presents a two-paragraph answer. He would offer the uprooted "a dynamic, centrifugal, prophetic spirit housed and made welcome within a conservative, centripetal, priestly institution [which] can survive because it can move with the times without breaking into fragments." Note carefully that, however much he advocates a prophetic spirit, surely not unlike his view of "God," now sacralized as hope, Blau insists that this prophetic spirit should be part of a conservative "priestly" institution. Such an institution cannot be other than one which houses a determinate God of tradition.

In fact, Blau says as much—ironically for his position—when he concludes: "The turn to the religious Right should reveal to us the need of a priestly sense of responsibility to the institution, the group, the past. The continuing ferment of new ideas and emotions should reveal to us the need of a prophetic sense of responsibility to the ideal, the individual, the future." But that future or hope is, by Blau's own admission, surely impossible of realization without, obviously, the element of tradition lodged clearly in a determinate God, in a God whose creative activity centers upon man's destiny.

This latter view of God is of special significance in our day when "depersonalization has insinuated itself into the individual's most intimate relations." At such times, man's specific need is for what will give meaning "to that most stubborn of all

particulars—the individual human person." Such meaning cannot frequently be found in indeterminate adverbial universals such
as "hope" for some, or "Deistic First Cause" or "Divine Cosmic
Process," for others, but may most often be found in the virtue
of a faith in the determinate, particularistic God of tradition.

What is also somewhat difficult to comprehend in Blau's definition of "God" is his conviction that it would serve as a viable
doctrine for man in the twentieth century when "we must think
in terms of a common human future." That we must think in
these terms is certain. But can this "common human future" really be achieved without, for instance, confronting, among these
other questions, *the* ineffable question of our century, or, for
that matter, of all time: the Holocaust? A philosophy of religion,
and, more specifically, of man, cannot escape the question of that
horror without a human response, however difficult it may be to
arrive at one that is adequate.

And here one must, if only pragmatically, wonder whether
an indeterminate "God" can possibly serve as the catalytic agent
to effect a "common human future." Perhaps, before seeking
that unity, one ought to contemplate differences, the differences
that resulted in the silence of man facing a world that went mad
in the smoke of blazing furnaces. What went wrong? Where
was man? Where *is* man? What future is possible without prior
scrutiny of the immediate past?

Perhaps modern man, in all his inhumanity, his failures, his
uprootedness, his degrading silence in the face of a common
evil, must open the channels of communication between himself
and the God of his past in order to refashion the present. And
only then, aware of the particularities of his past, may man find
his way to a "common human future."

III

It is certain that in the philosophy of religion, especially of
Judaism, Blau is far less preoccupied with intellectual system-
building, or theology, than with its development in various cul-

tures. Consider, for example, his brief talk at the Columbia University dinner in honor of the eightieth birthday of Herbert W. Schneider. Recalling Schneider's most significant contributions to the study of religion during his forty years at Columbia, Blau relates approvingly: "Herbert led at that time in the recognition that no one religious tradition could be used as a standard by which to judge the height or lowness of any other. He saw clearly that every religion is the spiritual expression of a particular culture at a specific time. He argued, then, for the examination of each religion in its own terms, and in terms of its cultural matrix." And it is precisely in that way that Blau follows his teacher not only in his study of all religions but also, specifically, of Judaism, his major concern during his own long tenure at Columbia.

A perusal of Blau's three major works on Judaism—*The Story of Jewish Philosophy, Modern Varieties of Judaism,* and *Judaism in America*—will indicate almost immediately that his concern everywhere is to see Judaism in its "cultural matrix." Hence, in *The Story of Jewish Philosophy*—a sympathetic, analytical, readable narrative of the major contributions to the Jewish intellectual heritage—Blau describes at every opportunity the environmental forces that shaped it.

Consider, for example, his treatment of Philo. Before discussing Philo's use of the allegorical method in his running commentary on the Bible and his fourfold argument for the proof of the existence of God, Blau first describes what in Alexandria made Philo's interpretations necessary, even mandatory: "Greek philosophic thought had early reached out to a much purer and more abstract conception of the unity of God, and it was to this higher form of Greek thought that the Jews turned when they tried to interpret their religion to the Greek speaking world. The need to provide such an interpretation was particularly acute in the city of Alexandria, the intellectual and cultural capital of the Hellenistic world. Here in Alexandria . . . [the Jews] had to defend Judaism both on its own terms and in terms of the very best that the Greek world had produced."

Further, after presenting a synopsis of the ideas of the major figures in Jewish philosophy during the Middle Ages, Blau devotes, naturally, a chapter to the two preeminent figures of that period: Halevi and Maimonides. He rightfully designates them as the "Peaks of Spanish-Jewish Philosophy." But their ideas, worthy of close study in our day, did not arise, Blau claims, out of an interest in pure speculation. Instead, the work of these two philosophers, like that of their predecessors, was the result of a need to respond to the immediate challenges of their times. A hostile world—intellectual and physical—demanded their replies. And they more than met that demand, each in his way: Halevi, as "romantic"; Maimonides, as "rationalist." "Temperamental differences among philosophers," Blau writes, "may have been the chief factor in determining what form the response would take. There may indeed be, as William James suggested, tender-minded or tough-minded temperaments, inclining philosophers to one form or other of philosophic activity. Behind these differences, however, lies the common incentive of the defense of Judaism in a hostile world."

The same need for a sound and effective defense of Judaism in a hostile world holds true in Blau's examination of Jewish philosophy during the Emancipation, when the walls of exclusion suddenly began to crumble at the end of the Middle Ages until at the end of the eighteenth century only little more than the wall that separated Jews from citizenship and participation in the countries in which they dwelt remained standing. That wall, too, crumbled, in Blau's view, "as in several countries in Western Europe there occurred a gradual transition from a more or less unified Christian community to a number of independent and competing national states." This change from a "status" oriented society of the Middle Ages to a "contract" organization of these modern European national states enabled the Jew "to make contacts with other individuals whether these others were

Jews or not." For in a "contract" organization, theological differences among groups do not—at least, should not—significantly affect the personal characteristics of individual men.

To the extent that this is true of politics, it is no less true of
philosophy, which contributed, in no small measure, to the
movement toward the emancipation of the Jews. Blau states it
best:

> Enlightened philosophy was contractual in its political theory, individ-
> ualistic in its moral theory. Its practitioners were advocates of humani-
> tarianism and of toleration. Most importantly, they viewed religion as
> an individual rather than a corporate matter, something between man
> and his God. Society had no rights to meddle with an individual's
> religious convictions, nor to impose any restrictions upon the individual
> because of his unwillingness to conform to the beliefs of the majority.
> The question of common concern was whether a man was a good man,
> not whether he was a good Christian. The philosophers of the Enlight-
> enment were spokesmen of a free secular society. In the society they en-
> visioned, a Jew might be as good a citizen as any other man.

Accepting the reality of his newly won political freedom, the
Jew examined once more his religious and cultural heritage. For
some, a "measure" of "reform" was the necessary response to
that freedom. A man like, say, Moses Mendelssohn would have
the Jews of his time govern themselves by three laws: "The law
of reason should govern their thoughts; the laws of the state
should rule over their political and social life; and the Biblical
and Talmudic codes should hold sway over their moral and
religious life."

For others—David Friedlander, Abraham Geiger and Solomon Steinheim, for example—the admission to full citizenship,
despite religious differences, made them call for a reform of
belief "to make the 'creed' of Judaism conform to the principles
of reason, for a reform of ritual to make the worship of the synagogue take on some of the dignity and decorum of the Christian
churches." They disparaged the patterns of belief and ceremo-
nial in order to find the essence of religion "in a universally felt,

inward sentiment." Their sense of nationality, apparently, yielded entire to the sense of universality.

Still others—Zechariah Frankel and Samson Raphael Hirsch—refused, each in his own particular way, to yield to any changes in the traditional practices or laws. Frankel argued for a "positive-historical" Judaism "which allowed for full freedom for scholarship and scientific investigation, of religion as well as of other subjects, but required conformity to traditional laws and practices." Hirsch, on the other hand, attempted to support traditional Judaism by means of "national argument." "Judaism," for Hirsch, "is to be understood as a historical phenomenon. It cannot be judged, therefore, nor can its success be measured by criteria that are imposed from outside its own tradition. Judaism must be conceived in accordance with its own sources, the Bible and the rabbinic tradition, and must be judged by its internal point of view . . . the world is seen as centered in the idea of service to God. . . . Israel's special mission requires spiritual separation from the rest of the world. . . . Israel accepts the necessity of being different, not for its own sake, but for the sake of all men."

If Hirsch, adapting to his new environment of freedom, indicated a willingness to abandon the idea of a Jewish nationality by offering "a nonpolitical interpretation of the Jewish state and Jewish territory of olden times as the means by which the Hebrew people could fulfill its spiritual calling," others—Moses Hess, Zvi Hirsch Kalischer, Theodor Herzl, Max Nordau—insisted on reestablishing Palestine as a national homeland. The "universalism" preached by those who emerged from the ghetto would not solve the immediate problem of those Jews, especially in Eastern Europe, whose future was paled by the confining circumstances of their settlement. "And it was uncommonly unjust for other nations, striving to establish themselves among the family of nations, to deny nationhood to one of the oldest nations on the face of the earth." Hence, the growth of the Zionist movement—quasi-religious in many of its aspects—culminating ultimately in the creation of the State of Israel, a nation among nations, in our time.

To elucidate further these latter movements in Judaism, which were, to one degree or another, gradual responses to the modern world, particularly after the Emancipation, Blau delivered, under the auspices of the Committee on the History of Religions of the American Council of Learned Societies, a series of six lectures at various American universities during the academic year of 1964–1965. These lectures were subsequently published as *Modern Varieties of Judaism,* an expanded version, actually, of the final two chapters—"Enlightened Ideas and Jewish Emancipation" and "Philosophies of Judaism in a Secular Age" of Blau's *The Story of Jewish Philosophy.* In these lectures, Blau examines some of the major attempts within Judaism, both on the theoretical and institutional level, "to come to grips with the novelties amid which Jewish life has been lived during the past two centuries."

Confronted with the basically secular nature of modern life— for Emancipation was, in part, a significant result of the secularization of modern life—Judaism attempted to bring about radical changes in religious thought and practice without destroying the sense of continuity with an age-old past. In other words, modern Judaism had to cope with the problem "of retaining the benefits of Emancipation without being swept under by its disadvantages while, at the same time, reformulating its theology and adapting its practices to the secular character of the modern world." Blau concluded that the one characteristic of modern Judaism in all its varieties is the "constancy to which the ancestral faith has been more of a problem than has adaptation to the surrounding world." Despite his own predilection for change, however, Blau readily concedes that none of the adaptations made by the movements discussed in his *Modern Varieties of Judaism* may ever prove, ultimately, to be successful in making their adjustment between Judaism and modernity:

neither Reform, neo-Orthodoxy, Conservatism, Reconstructionism, nor Secular or Religious Zionism.

In any event, what becomes abundantly clear from Blau's discussion of these two works is the relentless search in the long history of Judaism for the element of constancy. And what is constant, as Blau sums up in a short piece, "What Is Jewish about Jewish Philosophy?" is that there is "no chasm, no concealed opposition or antagonism, no 'great divide' between God's world and man's. The two worlds are the same. Body as well as spirit is of God; the spirit as well as the body is of man. God and man seek the same end, the ever-increasing perfection of the one world that God made and rules, but that man inhabits." There exists a condition of eternal reciprocity between God and man.

Whether this conclusion that the worlds of God and man are the same is historically correct may be subject to question. One might, rather, conclude that, though a divide does indeed exist between these worlds, it is man's function, nay, obligation, to advance his world closer to that of the divine. And, conversely, if God, in His world, is transcendent, distant, removed, a *mysterium tremendum* completely other than and entirely independent of all aspects and manifestations of nature and being, He is also immanent, in the sense that there is "no element or phase of existence that does not reflect His presence and activity. These two concepts of transcendence and immanence, although tending in opposite directions, never really existed separately in classic Jewish thought, but always intermingled so as to form a unitive Jewish doctrine of God."

Whatever the formulation of the worlds of God and man, one thing is clear: Jewish thought has never lost its sense of relevance to human life or its contact with the immediate present. And if theology, as Blau correctly defines it, is the "rational structuring and defense of beliefs about God, man, the universe and their interrelations," Jewish philosophy goes further in insisting that there is "an actual living-in-relationship, which tries to understand more fully, not so much for the sake of resolving intellectual doubts as in order to fulfill the partnership purposes more adequately." In short, God and man are inextricably bound to each other.

If God and man are inseparable, then, inferentially, so too are God, man, and society, since man shares with God a responsibility for perfecting this world, and, specifically, his immediate social and political world. And, of all countries in the modern world, and of all the nations of the world, the United States has served—and still serves—as the most propitious place where the Jews could attempt a creative adjustment with modernity. As a result, during some three hundred years of unhampered adaptability and mobility, Judaism could, as we shall see, move gradually on the American scene from "curiosity to third faith."

Of all his studies in the history and philosophy of Judaism, Blau considers *Judaism in America,* published in 1976, his most significant work. A volume in the Chicago History of American Religion series, it attempts, and in great measure succeeds, in describing "what has happened to Judaism in the United States" and, more significantly, "the impact of the American experience on Judaism." To be sure, some of the material appeared originally in *Modern Varieties of Judaism;* nevertheless, the concise and precise presentation of the internal dynamics of this complex subject marks a significant contribution to our understanding of what has happened to Judaism as it interacted with American society and culture during these past three centuries.

According to Blau, the outstanding recurring trait in American culture is its "dislike for intellectual systems." The most accurate symbol of American thought may very well be, then, the "hollow tube open at both ends," symbolizing an openness to beginnings and conclusions. The assumptions from which implications are drawn are, therefore, "unlimited, various in origin, widely regarded as of equal validity and often mutually incompatible." American thinkers are, apparently, open to the past as well as the future.

This native American distrust of intellectual systems has had, Blau argues, "a characteristic religious expression," thereby unifying the disparate trends and events in the history of religion in the new world. All of which leads Blau to analyze these trends—his major achievement in this work—relating them carefully to the history of religion and, specifically, Judaism in America. First is "protestantism," which he defines as the "denial of the values of consistency, or system, with respect to conclusions." Applied to religion, this term does not refer to the Protestant churches but rather to religions which are openended, where no authority can force them all to a single conclusion—religions, in short, which allow for a multiplicity of conclusions.

The second is "pluralism." This motif, born out of the legal parity assured to all in the American system, manifests itself in religion in that "all starting points are equally valid," and that all religions have "an openness to beginnings." Such "pluralism" seems to be the basis for much of the interfaith or multifaith activity in the United States, moving religionists "to be loyal to their own religion while recognizing the positive discernments of other approaches to the sacred." This Blau considers the most characteristically American of all American religious phenomena.

"Moralism," the third phenomenon in American life, Blau defines as the "tendency in religious life to evaluate individual conduct in terms of the relations of man to man alone without regard to ulterior considerations of the relations of man to God." Religions are called upon to define themselves less in terms of ritual and more in terms of morals. In effect, therefore, the "distinction between morality and religion is today unimportant and virtually nonexistent."

Finally, there is "voluntaryism," or the belief that the rights of the individual should always take precedence over the rights of society, that "an individual's duty to himself should always come before his duties to society." Instead of tradition or heritage, the individual will (or *voluntas*) becomes the basis of association. All association is voluntary. In the American scene, this can mean two things: "freedom *of* religion and freedom *from* religion," both integral parts of "voluntaryism."

Taken together, these four motifs make up, for Blau, the main features of American religious life. In Blau's summation: "It is my conviction that the combination of these principles— voluntaryism, pluralism, protestantism, and moralism—is what makes it perfectly possible for an American to shift his affiliation from church to church with every shift in his economic or social status or with every move from neighborhood to neighborhood or town to town, and still to be regarded as a religious person if he leads a reasonable moral life."

These principles, then, form for Blau the basis of his analysis of American Judaism. And since all four are reflected in Jewish life in America, Blau asserts, first, that what has shaped the spiritual life of the Jews is the constellation of two elements: the "aggregate of external forces working on the Jews from the host culture" and the "aggregate of the internal forces of the varieties of Judaism brought by the Jewish group from its previous places of residence." Because of these elements, these four principles—the heart of American life—have had a major impact on Judaism.

The influence of "moralism," for example, is made all the simpler, Blau stresses, because Judaism has "characteristically inclined to moralism rather than to ecclesiasticism." Jewry's stress could remain comfortably fixed on its program for living the good life, with institutional arrangements being regarded as entirely of secondary importance to this purpose. The prophetic rather than the priestly tradition has, apparently, flourished in America.

Furthermore, since pluralistic multiplicity has been a regular feature of Jewish life, there has never been an overarching unity in American Jewry. Hence, Blau contends, "there has occurred a 'protestation' of American Jewry into congregational bodies, each of which is to all intents and purposes completely independent of every other congregation, a law unto itself." American Jewry has, in most instances, refused to see its religion in monolithic terms.

The key to the understanding of American Jewry as an emergent variety of American life, Blau argues, is really, after all is said, "voluntaryism," or the principle that "man's religious affiliations are his own concern and not the business of the community." And "voluntaryism" is a novel experience for Jews, since they had in, say, Europe, only one of two choices: either to conform to the orthodox religious norms or cease to be Jews. In America, on the other hand, "a Jew could be very religious or non-religious, or any place in between; he could choose the most congenial point on that spectrum, no matter where it was, and still be considered a Jew." Small wonder, therefore, that "voluntaryism," according to Blau, "has proved to be the capstone of Jewish emancipation, for it has emancipated the Jews of America from any necessary connection with Jewry." To support or not support Judaism in America is, in the final analysis, totally determined by one's will which, in turn, is his law.

Having set forth these principles which form his thesis, Blau engages in a brief historical sketch of how, after their coming to America, Jews witnessed the "protestantization" of their faith into five major groupings: Reform, Orthodox, Conservative, Reconstructionist, and Zionist, already discussed, at far greater length, in *Modern Varieties of Judaism*. He then confronts one of the problems—basically sociological—that appears in almost every discussion of American Judiasm: Why are Jews, though a decided minority, considered on a par with the enormous Protestant and Catholic groups in matters of public policy? And why, too, after rising from abject poverty to middle- and upper-class status, have Jews, more than any other minority group, become acculturated so rapidly with American middle-class values? Resorting to sociohistorical reasoning, Blau posits three answers: First, the immigrant Jews—especially those arriving at the end of the nineteenth and the beginning of the twentieth centuries—brought with them those middle-class attitudes which, in America, at least, are the result of the Calvinist tradition: "an ethos consisting of hard work, thrift, readiness to defer satisfaction in the present for the sake of goals to be achieved in the future, temperance in personal habits, even an intense feeling for social respectability."

Second, the solidarity of family kinship produced strong mutual assistance. Because philanthropy and mutual aid stood at the center of the family unit, "any Jew who moved ahead saw to it that he carried others with him, as far as it was possible for him to do so."

Third, for generations—in fact, from their very beginnings—Jews have regarded the vocation of study as the most proper, even the sole, concern of man. To be a scholar was life's ideal, an ideal to which one dedicated all his time and talents. This tradition accompanied the immigrants to this country, where, because of the pressures of America's ethos of success, they shifted direction from Torah to secular study. Hence, Blau concludes, "scholastic achievement in the public elementary schools, distinction in the work of the high schools, admission to college, the winning of scholarships, prizes and awards, admission to a professional school, all leading to a secure and respectable place in society as a doctor, a dentist, a lawyer, an accountant, a teacher—this was the kind of vision each family had for its young male hopefuls." Hence, when a young member of the family showed exceptional promise, all other members would sacrifice to ensure the fulfillment of that potential.

Potentially, then, America became the idea place where, after centuries of exile, Jews were able to feel comfortable in their suurroundings. In fact, many Jews once considered America a giant "melting pot" in which Judaism might well become so Americanized that many of its tenets and practices could be neglected and even totally discarded. Hence, "voluntaryism" became, for most, the principle of their religious existence—if indeed it was a matter of principle—for Blau recognizes the potential dangers inherent in "voluntaryism" for the survival of this "third faith." However much he affirms these four principles in the context of pluralism in American culture, Blau wishes, nevertheless, to maintain the differences which distinguish religions and cultures from each other: "It is good, too, for Judaism that in other than religious matters there should be a recognizable difference between Jews and non-Jews. There must, after all, be Jews if Judaism is to be America's 'third faith,' as there must be Jews if the four-thousand-year-old Jewish culture is to continue as an organically sound, developing ingredient in the American pluriculture." Unfortunately, neither here nor elsewhere does Blau indicate how that venerable culture is to be preserved, especially when, if he is correct, his four principles are forever at work changing that four-thousand-year-old tradition.

In any event, what Blau sees as perhaps one of the most positive signs in the "acculturation" of Judaism as a "third faith" is the increased quest for interfaith understanding. The purpose of these "dialogues" is not, as in former times, conversion but rather, the need for each participant to recognize that the other faiths, too, have a "fractional" insight into the truth. "Our religions," Blau argues, "to the extent that they have genuinely entered into modern ways of thinking, must inevitably achieve the paradoxical position of accepting religious doctrines both totally and tentatively, for without total acceptance there can be no commitment and without tentativeness there can be no true modernity."

Of course, just how one could comfortably maintain this "paradoxical position" may in itself be paradoxical. For the nature of commitment is inherently such that it seems unequivocal and, at least in matters of faith, uncompromising. Tentativeness can only with great difficulty enter into the domain of commitment. To be committed and to be tentative are very close to being mutually exclusive and, even at the risk of not being "modern," these are to be avoided. For, on a practical level, maintaining the contradiction of being committed and being tentative has indeed helped promote interfaith dialogue in America, even on doctrinal matters. But these dialogues for "them which say they are Jews" have merely increased not their "commitment" but their "tentativeness." This has not, as history has proved so often in the past, secured their solid standing as a "third faith" in America, or even as citizens. For Jewish history has long ago taught the supreme lesson of the diaspora, a lesson which Blau wisely recalls: "The wise guest, however much he is made to feel at home, may unpack his bags but should always keep them close at hand for instant repacking." The interaction of faiths may enhance the principle of "pluralism" in America, but it adds little to preserving the "recognizable difference between Jews and non-Jews" which Blau himself has found necessary for the survival of Judaism.

Among the newer forms of "religious creativity," which Blau considers germane to the survival of Judaism in America, are the new groups—the "ignostic" humanist Jews of Birmingham, Michigan, on the one hand, and the *havurot* or religious communes on the other—which have recently been engaged "in experimenting with new ritual forms as well as with a new social organization of the 'congregation.' " These fringe groups, Blau believes, represent "the creative force in Judaism. Their creativity is so novel and so vital that, says Blau, it can be maintained only outside the traditional structures. New ideas, new inspiration, new aesthetic forms do not develop in calcified institutions, but rather in flexible, supple communities." Apparently, for Blau, their "voluntaryism" adds to the survival of Judaism in America.

All of which leads one to question not only Blau's assertion

about these newer forms of religious consciousness but also some
of his other assumptions both here as well as in some of his
other writings on Judaism. When, for example, Blau speaks, in
historical terms, of the "religious creativity" in America, he
nowhere accounts for the ever-increasing group of young people
who, committed absolutely to "Halachic" Judaism, are creating
large communities of learning based entirely on tradition. Yet
they are no less "novel" or "vital" on the American scene than
Blau's "fringe groups," and are, in their particular way, as far
removed from our formally structured society, or, to use a current term, the "establishment" as Blau's "ignostics" and *havurot.* That they refuse to be "tentative" in their irrevocable
commitment to their faith, exercising their "voluntaryism" to
further solidify tradition in their daily life, is no less creative, to
be sure, than the newly formed "extreme groups."

And this turn to the "religious right" need not be an "affair
of the moment," nor is it necessarily "crippling" or "restrictive," especially since many of those who have made their commitment to "Halachic" Judaism have done so after experiencing
intimate contact with American secular culture. This does not
necessarily make Judaism of the "right" "seclusive, anachronis-
tic, and irrelevant." On the contrary, this commitment to the
Shulhan 'Aruk, or code of Jewish law, attests readily to the
resiliency and buoyancy of the "Halachic" tradition in Judaism.
For "Halachah " itself is, as any serious student of its system
can readily affirm, "a tense, vibrant, dialectical system which
regularly insists upon normativeness in action and inwardness in
feeling and thought. It undertook to give concrete and continuous expression to theological ideals, ethical norms, ecstatic
moods, and historical concepts but never superseded or eliminated these ideals and concepts. 'Halachah' itself, is, therefore, a
coincidence of opposites: prophecy and law, charisma and institution, mood and medium, image and reality, the thought of
eternity and the life of temporality." The life of "Halachah" led
by these young people may, in time, very well prove to be one

of the "third faith's" most vital contributions to American religious life.

To be sure, Blau's refusal to recognize, much less herald, the
vibrancy of this commitment to Halachic Judaism may be the
result of his fundamental view, expressed in one form or another
in many of his writings, that "with no important exception,
every creative period in the history of Judaism has come at a
time when, and in a place where, the Jews have been in intimate contact with other cultures." And since, in its millennial
history, Judaism has never been in so close contact with other cultures as in America, the creative possibilities for Judaism should
be, Blau believes, greatest in the United States.

But even this thesis is open to question. Consider, for example, the post-Emancipation period and, particularly, the
period in Poland just before World War II. Here the student of
modern Jewish history relies on Salo Baron, "preeminent among
Jewish historians" and Blau's own teacher, who, in a brilliant
essay, "The Modern Age" (all too frequently left unheralded by
some cultural historians) offers an entirely different view of the
creative possibilities of Judaism in the modern world. Baron
remarks, first, that both in medieval and modern times, the
"most creative and most widely honored contributions . . . of
Jewish thinkers consisted precisely in reformulating established
systems in such a fashion as to meet new intellectual and social
changes. The same thing holds true for rabbinic learning
throughout the ages. Bound by tradition it developed through a
process of interpretation and reinterpretation that constantly
brought learning up to date and whetted the speculative appe-
tites of student and masters."

Baron then turns, by way of example, to a consideration of
pre-war Polish Jewry just before the Holocaust—a "faith community" which, by all accounts, was not nurtured in a climate
of cultural pluralism, but in a place where "intimate contact"
with other cultures, except for fringe groups and sundry others,
was decidedly not the norm. Surveying that period of darkening

clouds, Baron observes sharply: "The productivity of rabbinic scholars remained extremely high down to the end of East European Jewry during the Hitler era. In the years 1938 and 1939, on the very eve of its greatest tragedy, Polish Jewry produced a formidable number of books in such traditional fields as Law, Aggadah, Kabbalah, and Hasidism, together with traditional commentaries on the Bible. The impressive thing is that Polish Jewry, harassed politically and economically, and divided linguistically into Hebrew, Yiddish, and Polish reading groups, was yet able to produce in those two years more works of the kind just mentioned than were produced in any two decades of the seventeenth century, when rabbinic learning was in its heyday all over the world. Apart from quantity, moreover, many of these works were distinguished for their quality. If they had been written a thousand years earlier they would now be counted among the revered classics of Jewish literature. And the same may be said of some of the numerous rabbinic works which have appeared in the United States during the last decade." Clearly, then, creativity in Judaism does not necessarily demand contact with other cultures in order for it to be "novel," "vital," "inspirational," "supple" or "flexible."

Moreover, Blau has hardly ever used "Halachah" as a vehicle for his historical interpretations of Judaism, even though "Halachah" not only formulates laws, regulations and legal precedents but also "speaks history." Hence, when Blau, reviewing the post-Emancipation period in *The Story of Jewish Philosophy* and other writings, notes the growing opposition of Judaism to the newly acquired religious, political and social freedom, he refers mainly to Samson Raphael Hirsch. He does not—even in a work not necessarily written for scholars—refer to the writings of, say, Hatam Sofer, Akiba Eiger or Maharam Schick, all giants of "Halachah," who categorically opposed the Emancipation and its tendency to reform, seeing as they did in the secularization of religion an avenue to assimilation and the destruction of a faith community. What they were anxious to achieve was the preservation of Judaism by a conscious enhancement of tradition. Hatam Sofer, as Jacob Katz observes, "conceived the idea of a culturally self-contained Jewish community at the price of voluntary limitation of its contact with the surrounding world and of the exclusion of members who were not prepared to live up to the strict demands of religious discipline. And his ardent discples even went further, carrying the idea of cultural asceticism and organizational separation to extremes scarcely contemplated by the master." Obviously, Rabbinic Judaism had something to add to the "philosophies of Judaism in a secular age" and, most certainly, in our age of denial and despair.

Similarly, what seems somewhat puzzling is the scanty discussion given by Blau—except toward the very end of *The Story of Jewish Philosophy,* and there only tangentially—of the significance of the Holocaust to Jewish philosophy and religion. That this cataclysmic event has sorely tested the thinking of historians, philosophers, and writers of all faiths is clearly evident from any adequate reading of post-Holocaust literature. For, to be a Jew—especially a thinking Jew—after Auschwitz is to "confront the demons of Auschwitz and to bear witness against them in all their guises." One begins to wonder seriously whether, in our time, we dare still allow ourselves the luxury of being arrested in some sort of nineteenth- or early-twentieth-century euphoria, "claiming that man was still infinitely perfectible, God still an inspiring idea, and Judaism still no more than an admirable idea for progress, democracy and mental health." There is a need, now more than ever before, for a shaking of the socio-political-historical superstructures and a return to the foundations.

To all this, of course, Blau could—and does—simply reply that "agnostics must be allowed to cope with these questions in their own terms, and to be protected from theologians who ascribe to them a faith or a despair of which they are not aware." What Blau is aware of is the need to analyze, objectively, the long history of Jewish thought, culminating for him

in the free interplay of ideas in the "voluntaryism" of American
life. His interest lies not in "intellectual system building" but,
rather, in a general analysis of the development of Jewish
thought through the ages to our day. To see Judaism, like all
religion, in its cultural matrix, as "one elment of a cultural pattern which is always changing as a result of interaction between
various elements and as a result of contacts with external cultures" has been—and is—his philosophical posture. From that
position he has never moved in his thinking and writing on
Judaism.

IV

The principle of adaptation, central to Blau's understanding
of "tradition" in Judaism, is no less central to his analysis of
"tradition" in American philosophy. For, just as Jewish thought
"has never stopped growing and changing to meet the needs of
people," so too has American thought adapted the wisdom of
the ancients to the service of man and society. To support that
view, Blau quotes, approvingly, the words of Max Lerner, the
social scientist and journalist: "The best thing about a tradition
is that it is continuity as well as heritage. It is, as Francis Bacon
saw long ago, a way of transmission: what a civilization takes
from its past and reshapes and hands on to its future, and so it
is a link with that future. There are resources in the tradition of
each of the great civilizations which, when rightly laid hold of,
can help to heal and make whole its future. A tradition can be
an instrument as well as an inheritance."

It is that tradition which Blau surveys exhaustively in his
Men and Movements in American Philosophy—even now, after almost three decades, one of the best surveys in the field. In this
study of the ten major "movements" or "schools" of American
thought, he gives the reader an account of the philosophical inheritance bequeathed by thinkers in all walks of life, within and
without academic circles.

Beginning with a description of the Puritan God-centered

universe, a universe in which "every event was regarded as involving God . . . unusual, extraordinary and noteworthy events were thought to have special meanings for those who could discover them," Blau traces the movements that followed that God-centered world to our man-centered one. And our own universe, to use Herbert W. Schneider's felicitous phrase, is pervaded by "desperate naturalism," a phrase that characterizes, as previously indicated, "a mode of thought that was widely prevalent in a whole generation of Americans who were swept out of a supernaturalism absorbed at their mothers' knees and who were impelled to seek in a Darwinian naturalism a substitute for their earlier certitudes." *Men and Movements,* then, traces the changes that occurred in American philosophy as men left their certitudes of theological tradition, of immutable first principles, for a series of evolutionary changes in mind and society.

And it is to those evolutionary changes that Blau, after surveying dispassionately and judiciously the whole range of men and movements constituting American philosophy, addresses himself centrally. In the final chapter, called the "Emergence of Naturalism," Blau describes the naturalistic temper that pervades much of his own philosophical thinking. For "naturalism," he informs us, is "neither a doctrine nor a system, but only an attitude, a temper, a program, a mood." That temper rejects, first, "all philosophies which maintain that a supernatural realm of superior reality dominates and is the directive force, superimposed upon nature and human life. Terms like 'God' refer, in a totally untraditional way, to something natural, or at least something within the area of human experience," and it does not refer to "any transcendent source of knowledge of a reality which is by definition beyond the scope of human experience."

For the system of nature is argued to be "self-contained, self-sufficient and self-explanatory." Naturalism would insist not only that there is no aspect of man which is outside of nature but, also, that there is "no realm to which the methods of science which have been so successful in achieving control of nature cannot be applied. Only knowledge arrived at by methods resembling those of the scientist is acceptable to the naturalist." And what is acceptable to the naturalist is all that can be experienced by human beings.

That is not to say, of course, that naturalism would necessarily deny things of the spirit. Things of the spirit, however, can be spoken of only "as some aspect of man's natural behavior; but you may not describe that 'soul' of man as immortal, for to do so would be to remove it from nature." The naturalist would gladly give just consideration to "spiritual" values, provided they are not offered on the "basis of faith or authority." They must, like all things "physical," be objectively verifiable and open to public inspection. Otherwise, these values become private, subjective, intuitive, matters to which "nature," as seen by the naturalist, is indifferent. And, if the naturalist, not indifferent to matters other than matter, should consider these value judgments concerning the spirit, he does not give them preferential status. And all because he cannot disregard the centrality of human experience in his naturalistic philosophy.

Underpinning this naturalistic philosophy is, of course, the influence of Darwin. And as one reads Blau, especially *Men and Movements* and his many articles and reviews in American philosophy, it becomes increasingly evident that he places much emphasis on how Darwinism had an influence in altering the patterns of philosophic thought. That pervasive influence can be traced, Blau argues, in the three traditional areas of philosophic concern: the problems of Being, the problems of Knowing, and the problems of Doing.

Citing John Dewey, whose starting point is always Darwin, as well as other American philosophers, Blau shows how the definition of permanence was formulated in terms of change: "There is no Being, no anterior or persistent structure of reality, to serve as the criterion of meaning and truth. This does not necessarily imply that there is no standard of meaning and truth. It means, rather, that our standard, the ideal toward which we aspire, is ahead of us; it is prospective, not retrospective. Our standards, like our experience, are ever in process, growing and changing. Meaning and truth refer always to something that is yet to be, rather than something that has been."

Similarly, we note the influence of Darwinism on the problems of Knowing. The human mind, Blau points out, was no longer regarded as something given, resulting in a basic distinction between mind and matter. "Mind was not something outside of the natural order but, rather, was regarded as an organ of adaptation, naturally developed according to principles of natural selection and, therefore, something within natural order. . . . Mind was adjectival rather than substantive." Mind was not a substance but an effective agent of adaptation.

All of which leads to Dewey's conception of mind as an "instrument" of survival. Thought becomes more than explication of what is already there; it is a form of creation. "When in any doubtful situation," Blau explains, "intelligence is called into play, its function is to create from the elements present in the situation a hypothetical resolution of the doubt, a prediction that can be verified in subsequent experience by its success in dealing with the problematic situation." Since such situations are analogous to those deliberately created by the experimental scientist, "it is the method of the scientific laboratory that should be applied in all fields of thought." Ideas are, in effect, "instruments" of control and adjustment in the interaction of an individual and his environment.

The effects of these ideas can be seen in the problems of Doing. Codes of moral behavior, for example, "can no longer be regarded as having been established by divine decree; they have to be thought of as evolutionary products, developed over a long period of time out of some animal instinct which was transformed in the process." The moral laws of any community were not absolute beyond the borders of that community and had no sanction beyond the combined weight and prestige of the ancestors and present leaders of the community. Morals are, then, a form of cultural relativism. And even law is not fixed or immutable. "Law had evolved, and was still evolving, in the light of evolutionary changes that were going on within society."

In addition to elucidating these three basic concerns of philosophy, Blau added the dimension of "ethical" or "religious" humanism. At the center of his liberal faith is the belief that "mankind's obligation to itself is to achieve the maximum potential of humanity; that man is encouraged to realize his potential human stature." Deprecating any reliance on revelation and on supernatural intervention in the processes of nature, Blau finds the Divine in our moral career and in man's dutiful self-dedication to infinite perfection. "Man is to substitute the centrality of ethics for the centrality of theistic belief as the foundation of a religious system that could serve as the inspiration of human effort to improve the human condition."

What is curiously interesting, and at times somewhat surprising, is that, though following Dewey and Schneider in glorifying the intellect in the transformation of reality, and in proposing that ideas are, or ought to be, instrumentalities in improving the human condition, Blau seems intent on abandoning all interest in the idea and mystery of the universe at large. He manifests no sense of the universe's dark and unfathomable seas of being, the world of myths and illusions, the world of feelings and emotions of which human consciousness occupies but an infinitesimal portion.

Equally disturbing in this brave new world, where the method of the scientific laboratory has been applied to all fields of thought, is the fact that the myths and illusions which supported man in the past are no longer valid. The scientific reading of the modern world has not only robbed man of many of his cherished beliefs and opinions but has also been responsible for a sharp division between his feeling and his thought. This condition was recognized long ago and in his pessimistic mood lamented by Joseph Wood Krutch in *The Modern Temper*. This led him to observe cogently that, "try as man may, the two halves of his soul can hardly be made to coalesce, and he cannot either feel as his intelligence tells him that he should feel or think as his emotions should have him think, and thus he is reduced to mocking his torn and divided soul." For, however much man is capable of an apparently endless extension of his intelligence, he is not really happy in that knowledge. Man, incapable of belief in anything that his intelligence is forced to reject, is not left, obviously, with the best of all possible worlds.

Moreover, even if one were to agree that the structure of our ideas can be understood only in the light of the transformation of our environment which they effect, it is no less true that "philosophic knowledge arises from man's natural wonder and curiosity, from his desire to know just for the sake of knowing." For without that sense of wonder, without that idle and unfettered curiosity about the world, few might have reached some of the momentous findings recorded in the sciences and in the history of ideas. A tendency solely on behalf of the practical leaves "little room for purely theoretic studies, for contemplation," which can be, and has been, as intense a kind of action as the one that directs philosophy to the improvement of the human condition.

To be sure, since nature includes "both the changeless and the changing . . . permanent patterns and changing forms," Blau would readily reply that he too finds room in his philosophic thought for ideal values in, say, morals, art, and religion. Nevertheless, he would insist that, since "any denial of natural contingency leaves the philosopher with no hint of the real character of the universe about which he is reflecting," there can hardly be any aspect of man which is outside of nature. And what guides man, therefore, in his desire to improve the human condition, is, according to Blau, naturalism.

V

Of all Blau's many interests in the methodology of improving the human condition, it is American democracy and its social order that looms largest. Quite early in his career—the fall of 1950 to be exact—he was invited to deliver a series of four lectures at the University of Arkansas under the general title "The Influence of America on the Mind," in which he defines the meaning of the democratic social order as well as what, in his opinion, should be the social goals of America. And he is quite emphatic when, assessing the climate of a free culture, he states: "I believe that the essential meaning of America, both historically and prophetically is freedom. American history is an act asserting independence. . . . The Declaration of Independence asserts self-determination as a right, consequent on the abuse of authority by the British government. Of necessity, or of right, self-determination has been the nexus of our culture. In general, freedom, independence, self-determination has been a large part of what we have meant by our use of the word 'democracy.' " Both as value and fact, democracy as social order based on freedom is, for Blau, the ultimate ideal of man.

Lest the term "freedom" be misunderstood as mere license or *laissez-faire* or even a sort of anarchism, Blau is at pains to define it otherwise—and very carefully. Blau reviews first the ideas of some of the philosophical anarchists of the nineteenth century— Josiah Warren, Stephen Pearl Andrews, and Lysander Spooner—who, together, believed that the essence of human freedom lies in complete autonomy in the expression of individuality and that without the individualization of needs and desires freedom cannot exist, that all governmental authority is subject to question, and that the only valid form of group life is one in which the individual can maintain his needs irrespective of the needs of society. Blau finds them seriously wanting. Despite their apparent intensification of a mood and a belief

that had been part of an American theory of liberty, he finds
them, under close scrutiny, in fact, trailing in their conception of
liberty and democracy. This leads him most reasonably not only
to criticize philosophical anarchism but to clarify his own view
of freedom, his social philosophy and, in a sense, the meaning
of spiritual democracy.

Conceding that "Americans generally resent the authority of
political, economic, social, religious, ethical, educational
hierarchies," Blau asks, "What next?" and Blau answers this
crucial question with another, sharper even than the first: "In
the aphoristic treatise, *Ethics of the Fathers,* of the Jewish tradition, the anarchistic question, 'If I am not for myself, who is for
me?' is asked, but this question is followed immediately by the
far more probing question, 'If I am for myself alone, what am
I?' This is the more searching question that the nineteenth-century philosophical anarchists failed to answer adequately. It
faces all who are dissatisfied with the negative impact of anar-
chist ideas, but who cannot find the resolution of their dissatisfaction in the usual twentieth-century prescription of a return to
authoritarianism, to some form of *archism.*"

Clearly, Blau does not accept a social philosophy based on either the "anarchism" of former times or the "archism" of modern
times. He proposes instead that, recognizing the implication of
"If I am for myself alone, what am I?" every individual in a free
society must be concerned with life other than one's own. And
he found, interestingly, a kindred spirit in Emerson—another
nineteenth-century figure, although one far removed from the
"philosophical anarchists" of his time—whose social philosophy
was developed "for a society, like our own, hopelessly committed to an extreme individualism."

What Blau proceeds to demonstrate in his remarkable essay
"Emerson's Individualism as a Social Philosophy" is that, contrary to common intepretation, "Self-reliance" does not mean
that "rugged individualism" which inspired the "robber barons"
of the late nineteenth century. It is, rather, the "very pivot on

which Emerson's individualism transforms itself into a social philosophy of altruism." Furthermore, "self-reliance" is not a doctrine of limited self-centeredness; instead, "in striving to reach his innermost self or soul, the individual transcends himself." Hence, Emerson's "individualism was transcendentalist; it found the universal within the individual, and in that discovery it forced the individual beyond individuality to universality." It is, therefore, the duty of man, especially representative man, to open his eyes to more than self, more than individuality, to a world in which, serving as a co-equal partner in society, he can achieve greatness. That greatness will result from man's contribution "to what mankind could ideally become rather than what mankind now is."

The greatest people are, to Emerson, those whose unique qualities enable their influence and effect to spread most widely, while not losing their essential private selves. "Emerson's kind of individualism," Blau argues, "did not issue in any sort of egotism, whether of the spiritual or the material economy. He recognized that the human being is a social being. Indeed, he considered that without a rooting in society any person is lost. People are nothing except in relation to other people. And yet, in his sense, the essential human being is the private self. What seems paradoxical in the opposition of these two ideas is resolved, in Emerson's thought, by the belief that the private self does not exist for itself, but for the contribution that it can make to the human race." Man is forever fluctuating between his sense of individuality and his sense of common humanity.

That Blau would, in some sense, adopt as a basis of his social philosophy the doctrine of self-reliance as meaning being oneself while, at the same time, making of oneself society, seems clear from his final observation on Emerson's individualism: "Emersonian individualism can appear, even in our day, as an admirable and defensible social philosophy. Emersonian individualism is not self-centeredness, despite the apparent turning inward of the principle of self-reliance. It is a way to find within ourselves that which is universal for the sake of betterment of the social order."

To find an additional basis for his social philosophy, Blau turned, once again, to Dewey who, arguing that "selfhood is itself a social product," went further even than Emerson. For democracy to Dewey is an ongoing experiment in social order, a social order whose primary concern is the liberation of whatever potentialities an individual might have. He insisted that "government, business, art, religion and social institutions have a meaning, and purpose. That purpose is to set free and to develop the capacities of human individuals without respect to race, sex, class or economic status." And all because there exists a reciprocal adaptation of men to their social environment and of the environment to the needs of men.

To fulfill these needs best, the democratic community, like the community of laboratory scientists, Blau agrees, should give "every individual the opportunity to contribute in his own way to the solution of the questions of living together that are the common concern of all." Hence, democracy, like intelligence, is not a gift but an achievement "which cannot be imposed from without nor can it be forced upon men, whether by old fashioned dynastic despotism or by new fashioned dictatorships." It can only be achieved by individuals who, finding within themselves something universal, join together to win it.

The ideal of democracy, Blau hastens to note, is also predicated on morality. For Emerson and, later, Dewey, had already added the principle of morality to the views of the political liberals of the late eighteenth century. Emphasizing the moral element in his political thought, Emerson wrote: "The end of all political struggle is to establish morality as the basis of all legislation. It is not free institutions, it is not a republic, it is not a democracy that is the end—no, but only the means. Morality is the object of government . . . the government of the world is moral." Institutional arrangements, of whatever kind, are therefore only a means to the ultimate end of every democratic form of government: the moral well being of its constituents. These constituents are "of self-reliant individuals who, because they have common goals, can often agree on the means to those ends"—the ends achieved when men go beyond egotism toward the moral life.

Small wonder, therefore, that when Blau earlier traced the "emergence of naturalism" in American philosophy, he stressed, among other things, the role that "faith" played in that movement, especially as regards Dewey's faith in the universal possibilities of shared experience. It was Dewey's belief, Blau pointed out, that "by extending the method of the community of scientists to the solution of all the problems of men, advances in human relations comparable to our advances in the control of nature can take place. The principle of 'cooperative association' or 'shared experience' is the heart of Dewey's religious attitude." And Dewey's own words in this regard are most significant: "Faith in the continued disclosing of truth through directed cooperative human endeavor is more religious in quality than is any faith in a completed revelation." That faith rests, of course, in the capacities of human nature and human intelligence, and in the conviction "that men thinking and working together, sharing and pooling their experience like laboratory scientists, could build a better world."

Not only did Blau find such faith in the works of avowed secularists of the nineteenth century—men like, say, Henry Demarest Lloyd, Laurence Gronlund, and Henry George, who shared an apocalyptic vision of the secular state—but also found more pointed views among religious humanists of our time, notably Mordecai M. Kaplan. In his extended essay on this religious philosopher, Blau points out that democracy for Kaplan "is itself a religious faith," a faith resting on the belief that democracy should function in the spirit of community, it being defined as "that form of social organization in which the welfare of each is the concern of all, and the life of the whole is the concern of each." Hence, democracy must get away from the shal-

low and superficial individualism with which it has too often
been identified, for the essence of democracy, in all its political
and economic problems, is the nation or state and not the individual.

Freedom in democracy, then, is conceived, in all this, as a
condition of society; as previously mentioned, it is not anarchic,
nor an appeal to license, nor to *laissez faire*. It is instead, "an
aspect of self-realization," a realization that the crucial problem
of freedom is "how to guard our own individuality and the capacity to think for ourselves, and yet cooperate with those
whose background, upbringing and whole outlook are different
from our own." Because this is, indeed, an art which human
beings are slow to learn, Blau adds that "if the goals of democratic society are ever to be achieved, the defenders of democratic freedom must have not only a fearless will to live, but
also a resolute will to live together."

All of which inevitably leads Blau most reasonably to a probing of the nature of equality. Equality, as Blau reads Kaplan, is
not a natural endowment but is, instead, an ideal end-product
of society, a social objective. It is "neither natural nor, in a narrow sense, social. It is ethical and religious." An individual is
an end in himself, not merely as a means to another. And that
becomes, therefore, the "only adequate rationale for democratic
equality." Equality is "fraternity as cooperation."

Given this ethical and religious sanction to democratic values, one can more readily resolve the paradox in democracy concerning the freedom of the individual and the proclamation of
the equality of all individuals. For, in an ideal democracy, society, recognizing the "spiritual value of human personality," will
also "feel responsible for enabling the individual to realize his
vital values. Simultaneously, society must realize the spiritual
value of human brotherhood in such a way as to have all human
beings benefit from its vital values. And only in a society in
which cosmic values are realized will individuals be inspired to
sacrifice purely individualistic values for the achievement of
social values as expressive of what life means to them."

Because democracy becomes, in light of these values, "a doctrine of national salvation" to promulgate social solidarity, it rests on faith: "Its validity is not scientifically demonstrable. It demands *a priori* acceptance of ideals which can be proved valid only by our committing ourselves to their realization."

What is, however, somewhat difficult to comprehend in this value system of "spiritual democracy"—aside from the need to base it on "non-demonstrable" facts, the essential basis for naturalists who demand facts fit for the laboratory in order to be acceptable—is that hardly anywhere are we offered an answer as to what is good. What, in trying to improve the human condition, is to be the test as to which of two alternatives *is* better? All naturalists and most social philosophers seem to fall back on a relatively simplistic atomism: every situation has its own good. But does that not dodge the problem since, in every ethical question, there is inherently the conflict of rival situations? What are they?

Moreover, these naturalists tend to be misleading with their phrase, "making the world a better place to live in," which suggests a mastery of the environment rather than of our own desires. But, as a philosophical critic once remarked, "As long as human desire outruns human capacity, as the range of man's vision exceeds the field of our reach, the way of happiness must include not only the mastery of nature but also the mastery of our own selves." And it is first in the mastery of our selves that we can really achieve the *summum bonum,* for ourselves as well as others. Unless man controls those desires which outrun his capacities, unless man's grasp does not, indeed, exceed his reach, the vision of a "spiritual democracy" can never become an abiding reality.

Furthermore, an equally probing question, and one that John W. Gardner posed some years ago, is, "Can we be," in a democracy, "equal and excellent too?" Blau is equally aware of this problem; in fact, this awareness is the point of departure for David L. Norton's essay. For, in a talk entitled "Ethics, Equality and Excellence," still unpublished, Blau tells us clearly and emphatically that he considers this "perhaps the most serious question about democracy that we can raise." As Blau formulates the problem: "There is certainly a sense in which any striving to excel—to be better than others in whatever doings one shares with them—is on the face of it destructive of equality leading, perhaps, to the Orwellian *Animal Farm,* where all animals are equal, but some animals are more equal than others. On the other hand, where no one strives to excel, so that all animals are *equally* equal, we shall surely witness that apotheosis of mediocrity, leading to a static and unprogressive and moribund society." And this problem has become terribly acute ever since the 1960s and its shaking of America's foundation, when the element of "meritocracy" began to fade from our societal scene.

To the drop-outs, of whatever kind, of that time and ours, Blau would most constructively redefine or reemphasize the meaning of success and excellence: "How can each be made to realize that excellence consists in doing well whatever one is able to do, reaching out for the maximum expression of one's own talents, rather than trying to do what one is not fit for and, of course, doing it poorly? Perhaps the way is to be found by a stress on the equivalence—the equal value—of all occupations as opportunities for serving human needs. Perhaps we need to reemphasize a factor in our definition of success that has always been there but that we have given less stress than it deserves— that success includes being satisfied that we are doing whatever we can do as well as we can do it." Every talent must flourish without comparison of talents, "for every talent fully realized is excellence in its own way."

To sustain "excellence, equality and freedom" requires a deep personal involvement not only with one's own talents but also with the society where these ideals could flourish. In fact, it is a moral imperative for one to become so involved, since, Blau claims, these three qualities cannot be sustained unless they are conceived morally. Moreover, as Dewey and his followers assert, if philosophy must serve the human condition, one might have expected that Blau himself would have participated actively in one or another movement, helping to prepare the way for "excellence, equality and freedom" to flourish in our society. Except for one very brief period in the 1930s, Blau remained personally uninvolved in the often smearing, blearing toils of man. "As a young man back in the nineteen-thirties," he tells us, "I had a tiny role in the fusion movement that elected Fiorello La Guardia mayor of New York City. One of our major concerns was to break down the discriminatory housing patterns that were leading to the emergence in our city of some of the worst slums in the modern world." After that, we do not find him playing any active social role in the pursuit of these three ideals of democracy.

But then, again, one might conceivably argue that "activism," or the "fidgetiness of idle fingers," may not be the function of the philosopher, even the social philosopher. For philosophy is vision, imagination, reflection, and the free play of ideas, which may be superior to the skill of accumulating external products. The obligation of the philosopher is to take nothing for granted, to question perpetually, to sift and analyze continually. And that, obviously, Blau has executed superbly.

Besides, being a *social* philosopher in New York City is, Irwin Edman once commented, no simple task. "If to be a citizen means to be a conscious member of a community conscious of one's existence, one is a member of no city at all in New York, of no neighborhood, of no group. One is alone spiritually as if one were in an Arabian wilderness, and sometimes the sense is that of a desperate anonymity." But, if New York is a bad place to be a *social* philosopher, Edman continues, "it is not a bad place in which to cultivate the detachment of the metaphysician. Here where one fits no frame of reference, one can imagine all possible worlds. Here, committed to no group and to no localism, one can contemplate all time and all existence."

Committed always to the contemplative life, Blau was able,

as well, to commit himself most effectively to his students. Over thirty years of uninterrupted teaching, counselling, directing students—many of whom now occupy important positions and distinguished chairs in departments of religion and philosophy in major universities across the country—is a commitment equal to the constant rushing to and from the barricades. Moreover, not everyone is temperamentally suited to race to public meetings and marches and political matches; there are some better suited actively to contemplate the best of all possible worlds. And then to share, freely, happily and wisely, those thoughts with their eager students, who, marvelling at that inexhaustible miracle, the human mind, rethink those thoughts and then create new thoughts in still other minds. Then, as these students read and think, they conclude "that the lowest misery is slavery, not of the body, but of thought; and that even when our life is harsh and inexplicable, we may still make it in a worthy and heroic destiny, provided we maintain the invincibility of the mind."

Because Joseph L. Blau, in the midst of our harsh and inexplicable lives, so very often helped students marvel at the powers of man's inexhaustible, unconquerable mind, he deserves, preeminently, to share, and perhaps to delight in, the thoughts of some of his own students in this—his commemorative, his Jubilee volume.

ONE

Naturalism and Supernaturalism Revisited

Introduction

Joseph Blau's multiple interests and achievements are celebrated in each section of this volume. Many of them come to a unique focus in his work in the philosophy of religion. The nature and status of that discipline, like the nature and status of the discipline of philosophy as such, are matters of considerable discussion and debate at the present time. There are those who think of philosophy in terms of its classical concerns for synoptic vision and critical reflection on the problems of humanity. Others direct attention to more limited methodological and analytical issues. Classical philosophers of religion, also, articulate concern with the warrants for and broadest implications of religious belief, within the parameters of critical and constructive philosophical systems. More recently the entire enterprise of philosophy of religion so conceived has been called into question by thinkers who would focus on limited issues of logical analysis within the canons of fixed epistemological positions. Unfortunately, some scholars of both persuasions seem to have insufficient knowledge of basic data from the history of religions to sustain responsible philosophical reflection on religion.

Blau has both a general knowledge of the history of philosophy and of religions and specialized knowledge of Judaism as a religious tradition. As a student of social philosophy he has also been aware of the social significance and implications of religious movements. As a student of, and spokesman for, the American tradition of humanistic naturalism, he has written and spoken persuasively of the resources of that tradition for the philosophy of religion.

It is appropriate, therefore, that the first essay in this section is a thoughtful study of the evolution of the religious philosophy of John Dewey. Rockefeller's paper not only adds depth to our understanding of Dewey's development; it also recounts a story of development from a form of traditional religious faith to a form of philosophically grounded belief and practice which is typical of the experience of many thoughtful people in the past century. Bulman's essay, in turn, places humanistic belief in a broader context, while it offers at the same time a critical appraisal of it from a different perspective—thereby reminding us that many who have learned much from Joseph Blau have not felt pressured or constrained to adopt all aspects of his personal philosophy; he has taught them not simply a philosophy, but respect for the philosophical enterprise. Shea's contribution continues the work of appreciative assimilation combined with a striking reminder of a position in the supernaturalist tradition which might provide a basis for constructive dialogue between naturalistic and nonnaturalistic humanists. The concluding essay in the section suggests that closer attention to the relation of the esthetic to the religious in naturalistic and other positions may provide important insights for philosophy of religion and a fruitful theory for the understanding of religion.

J.A.M. JR.

John Dewey: The Evolution of a Faith

STEVEN C. ROCKEFELLER

1

THE EVOLUTION of the religious outlook of the American philosopher and educator John Dewey (1859–1952) is a classic example of what in the past hundred years has been a common phenomenon in American religious life. More specifically, many Americans are led to acquire during their childhood a traditional and fairly conservative form of religious faith, which is usually characterized by supernaturalism, theism, an element of other-worldliness and a strict moral code. Then, at some point during adolescence—when the drive for individual self-realization becomes stronger, the powers of critical reason are developed, and modern secular society exercises its influence—the original childhood faith is radically modified in the direction of some form of religious liberalism. Religious liberalism, however, is often found to be an unstable and unsatisfactory halfway house between a dogmatic supernaturalism and a thorough-going naturalistic humanism. In time, it, too, is abandoned, and the naturalistic and humanistic perspective is adopted. Nonetheless, this may not involve the complete rejection of everything religious. There may be some attempt to redefine the meaning of the term "religious," and then to harmonize the religious with the natural and the secular. Further, something of the old faith may linger on in the moral consciousness and in the heart.

A full account of the evolution of Dewey's religious thinking would require an extensive inquiry into his psychological and social as well as intellectual growth. In this brief essay, however, attention will focus on one central aspect of it: the development of his idea of religious faith and its object. In ways that have not been fully appreciated, the religious outlook Dewey, as a naturalistic humanist, adopted during the latter part of his career is a reconstruction of ideas he originally adopted in the nineteenth century, first as a Vermont Transcendentalist and later as a Neo-Hegelian ethical idealist. This is especially true of Dewey's ideas of religious faith and its object, and this essay is, therefore, particularly concerned with noting the connection between Dewey's early and later thought on this subject.

For the purposes of this analysis, five important phases in the evolution of Dewey's religious thinking may be distinguished. First, during his childhood, Dewey was under the strong influence of his mother's evangelical pietism. Second, during his college years (1875–1879) Dewey adopted a more liberal religious outlook. It may be best described as a form of Vermont Transcendentalism (which had its roots in the thought of Kant, Samuel Taylor Coleridge, and James Marsh) and it was closely associated with a liberal brand of Congregationalism. Third, at Johns Hopkins University, where Dewey attended graduate school from 1882 to 1884, and during his early years as a young philosophy teacher at the University of Michigan in Ann Arbor, the liberal tendencies in his thought led him to embrace the Neo-Hegelian metaphysics and psychology of T. H. Green and John and Edward Caird. While teaching at the University of Michigan, Dewey continued to identify himself as a liberal Congregationalist. Fourth, in the course of the ten years Dewey spent in Ann Arbor he was radicalized politically, and as a result he tried to integrate thoroughly the religious and the secments above that "it has held its place ever since as a subular. This led Dewey to develop his ethical idealism into a justification for American democracy and to develop a radical version of the Social Gospel, in which Christianity in the contemporary world is identified with commitment to democracy and to the scientific method of inquiry. Finally, in 1894 Dewey moved to the University of Chicago. Soon after, he severed his connections with idealism, traditional theology, and the church, and began working out a new American brand of naturalistic humanism which articulated faith in democracy, science, and education, while trying to formulate a naturalistic theory of the religious value of such a faith.

II

Dewey was born in Burlington, Vermont, just before the Civil War. Early in the war his father, Archibald Dewey, joined the Union army. As a result, young Dewey saw very little of his father during the first eight years of his life, and it was his mother, Lucina Dewey, who gave him his early religious education. Having been converted in a revival meeting as a young woman, Lucina came to identify religious faith with three things: first, belief that Jesus is a supernatural savior who will redeem some, but not all, men and women from sin and damnation; second, the possession of strong feelings of love for, and dependence upon, God and Jesus; third, obedience to Puritan moral values.[1] She made a persistent effort to instill in John and his two brothers a religious outlook of this nature, placing special emphasis on the cultivation of religious feelings, especially those of sin and guilt, desire for forgiveness, and devotion to Christ. When John was eleven, Lucina helped him write a

[1] Jane Dewey, ed., "Biography of John Dewey," in *The Philosophy of John Dewey*, Vol. 1 of *The Library of Living Philosophers*, ed. Paul Arthur Schilpp (LaSalle, Ill.: Open Court Publishing Co., 1970), p. 7; Sidney Hook, "Some Memories of John Dewey, 1859–1952," *Commentary*, 14 (1952): 246.

confession of faith which he brought to the local Congregational Church seeking membership. It began: "I think I love Christ and want to obey him."[2]

Dewey was never entirely at ease with the type of sentimental evangelical faith taught by his mother. He resented the way she would regularly examine his conscience and feelings, and he began early to rebel against the pressure she put on him to confess belief in various theological doctrines he did not understand.

In the Congregational Church, which Dewey regularly attended throughout his youth, and at the University of Vermont, which Dewey entered at age fifteen, he found a less sentimental and more liberal religious atmosphere than the one that prevailed in his home. Both these institutions continued to emphasize faith in Jesus Christ as a supernatural savior and commitment to Puritan moral values, but they also introduced Dewey to the larger world of theology and philosophy where he began to find what he felt were liberating religious ideas. This was especially true at the University of Vermont, and it was there that he discovered the thought of Coleridge and Marsh.

James Marsh was a Congregational minister and a professor of philosophy at the University of Vermont in the 1820s and 1830s, and he helped to launch the American Transcendentalist movement by publishing, in 1829, a widely read and influential first American edition of Coleridge's *Aids to Reflection*. He introduced readers to the book with a forty-five-page essay written in support of Coleridge's synthesis of seventeenth-century Cambridge Platonism, Kant, and German idealism. It was principally Marsh's edition of *Aids to Reflection* that provided Dewey with a religious outlook in which he was able to find meaning and hope as a young man. Towards the end of his career, he said of *Aids to Reflection:* "Yes, I remember very well that this was our spiritual emancipation in Vermont. Co-

[2] George Dykhuizen, *The Life and Mind of John Dewey,* ed. Jo Ann Boydston (Carbondale: Southern Illinois University Press, 1973), pp. 6–7.

leridge's idea of the spirit came to us as a real relief, because we could be both liberal and pious; and this *Aids to Reflection* book, especially Marsh's edition, was my first Bible."[3]

In order to appreciate the appeal of the ideas of Coleridge and Marsh and the later attraction of Hegel, it is necessary to note several details concerning Dewey's emotional and intellectual development at this time of his life. First of all, during his college years and for several years thereafter, Dewey underwent a fairly severe adolescent emotional crisis. His mother and Vermont Congregationalism generally had instilled in him an unhealthy sense of sin and guilt. He became very self-conscious and had an especially difficult time in relating to girls.[4] He also found himself intellectually disoriented as regards his basic beliefs. During his late teens and early twenties, his tendency was to withdraw into himself and the world of books. Years later he summarized his adolescent difficulties as follows: "The sense of divisions and separations that were, I suppose, borne in upon me as a consequence of a heritage of New England culture, divisions by way of isolation of self from world, of soul from body, of nature from God, brought a painful oppression—or rather, they were an inward laceration."[5]

As Dewey's first book, *Psychology* (1887), makes clear, there were three major problems that then troubled him: the gulf between God and the world; the estrangement of the actual self from its true or ideal self; the separation of the self from real community with others. Confronted with these divisions and the sense of isolation and estrangement they involved, Dewey found himself filled with "an intense emotional craving" for "unification."[6] In psychological and social terms, Dewey's crav-

[3] John Dewey as quoted by Herbert Schneider in *Dialogue on John Dewey* ed. Corliss Lamont (New York: Horizon Press, 1959), p. 15.

[4] Max Eastman, *Great Companions* (New York: Farrar, Strauss and Cudahy, 1959), p. 254.

[5] John Dewey, "From Absolutism to Experimentalism," in *On Experience, Nature and Freedom*, ed. Richard J. Bernstein (Indianapolis: Bobbs-Merrill, 1960), p. 10.

[6] *Ibid.*

ing for unification was a search for integration of personality and for achievement of a satisfying social adjustment. In religious terms, it was a quest for God—for unification of the self and its world with the absolute good. Despite his feelings of estrangement and confusion, Dewey did not seriously doubt the existence of God. In the depths of his heart he seems to have trusted that life somehow makes sense and is essentially good. He seems to have been confident that union with God, the absolute good, could be found, and that if he could realize this union he could find personal wholeness, community with others, and peace.

In the midst of this emotional crisis, Dewey's powerful intellect was beginning to awaken, and his passionate craving for unification was channeled into the intellectual quest for a great philosophical vision of unity involving God, the world, and humanity. Dewey found a perfect metaphor for all that his young heart and mind craved in the idea of organic unity, which he first encountered in a physiology textbook by Aldous Huxley.[7] The concept of organic unity attracted Dewey because it involved the idea of harmony in the midst of diversity. In an organic unity there are distinct parts with unique functions, but the activities of all the parts are interrelated and harmonized by the presence of an organizing purpose that pervades and governs the life of the whole. Oppressed by divisions and separations, Dewey craved organic unity in his own life, in society, and in the world. He turned to philosophy because he wanted intellectual certainty that the deeper metaphysical truth of the universe is organic unity; and he trusted that, if he could understand the organic unity of all things, he could overcome his disorientation, and realize this organic unity in his own life experience. In this way Dewey was drawn to philosophy, and especially to metaphysics and psychology, from which emerged a faith in reason or intelligence that rivaled his childhood faith in Jesus Christ as the source of liberation.

[7] *Ibid.* p. 4.

Dewey received his introduction to philosophy at the University of Vermont in the classroom of Professor H. A. P. Torrey. Torrey was influenced in his thinking and teaching to some degree by Scottish common sense realism, but his own philosophical outlook seems to have been basically a kind of transcendentalist revision of Kant along the lines suggested by Coleridge and Marsh. What he taught Dewey, then, was a variation on the main themes of the "Burlington philosophy" of Vermont Transcendentalism, with an especially heavy emphasis on Kant.[8] Some of Marsh's writings were read in Torrey's courses, but not Marsh's edition of *Aids to Reflection*. However, like Emerson's essays in New England generally, *Aids to Reflection* at the University of Vermont was something most people read for their edification. Dewey read it, and even though his reaction to the Burlington philosophy as a whole was very mixed, he did find in this book certain ideas that led to his "spiritual emancipation in Vermont."

First, what Dewey found liberating in the thought of Coleridge and Marsh is the conviction that there is no necessary conflict between faith and reason, religion and philosophy. More than that, they taught that Christians have an obligation to think and to act rationally. Quoting a seventeenth-century Cambridge Platonist, Coleridge saw that "No man serves God with a good conscience, who serves him against reason," and Marsh affirms that "what is not rational in theology . . . cannot be of the household of faith."[9] Coleridge and Marsh found no contradiction between reason and Christianity. They argued that the philosophical search for truth is perfected in the Christian faith. This is just what Dewey wanted to hear. It suggested to him that the truth is a coherent system in which there are no radical divisions and separation, and that he could harmonize science, philosophy, and religion into one intellectual system.

[8] H. A. P. Torrey to Kant Centennial Committee, *Journal of Speculative Philosophy*, 15 (July 1881): 300; Dykhuizen, *The Life and Mind of John Dewey*, pp. 15–16.

[9] Samuel Taylor Coleridge, *Aids to Reflection*, in *The Complete Works of Samuel Taylor Coleridge* (New York: Harper & Brothers, 1853), 1: 321; James Marsh, Preliminary Essay to *The Complete Works of Coleridge*, 1: p. 78.

In this way, Coleridge showed Dewey how he could be both "pious and liberal."

Second, Coleridge's interrelated concepts of Spirit and faith had great appeal to young Dewey, and they led him to an understanding of religious experience and faith that had an enduring influence. The essence of human nature, Coleridge taught, is Spirit, and he defines Spirit as rational will. When Coleridge identifies Spirit with "reason" he does not mean the Kantian "understanding" (*Verstand*), which is the discursive intellect, but rather he has in mind Kant's Pure Reason and, especially, what Kant called Practical Reason. However, Coleridge's idea of Pure Reason involves an idealist revision of the Kantian concept. He attributes to the Pure Reason a power of real knowledge of ultimate reality that Kant never allowed. The Spirit is understood to be capable of a direct knowledge of God, free will, and immortality. Further, and of most importance, it has the power to apprehend the universal moral law, which is identical with the will of God, and is the true end of every person understood as a rational will.

Religious faith for Coleridge is an apprehension of moral and religious truth by the Spirit, that is, by Pure Reason. However, whereas Kant had conceived the Pure Reason as basically something intellectual, Coleridge expands the concept of it so that it involves the heart, the conscience, and the will as well as the intelligence. Spiritual truth is apprehended in an act that involves the whole person. In other words, faith in God or a supreme moral ideal involves being grasped in the depths of one's personal being by the truth. Further, Coleridge taught that in order really to know spiritual truth one has to do it, to live it.[10]

Dewey's study of Coleridge and Marsh left him convinced that there is a distinctively religious dimension of experience.

[10] Coleridge, *Aids to Reflection,* pp. 134, 215, 241–42, 367; John Dewey, "James Marsh and American Philosophy," in John Dewey, *Problems of Men* (New York: Greenwood Press, 1968), p. 360, W. J. Bate, *Coleridge* (New York: Macmillan Company, 1968), pp. 221–22.

True religion, however, is neither a form of pious sentimentalism nor simply a matter of intellectual belief in unintelligible doctrines accepted out of obedience to revered authority. Authentic religion involves concrete personal experience of spiritual truth, faith, and moral action. Further, Dewey learned from Coleridge to conceive of faith as an act that involves the whole personality—heart, mind, and will—in a commitment to some supreme ideal value. For Coleridge and the young Dewey such faith means believing that the ideal is both supremely real and worthy of guiding conduct. Further, despite whatever doubts Dewey may have had in the early 1880s about Jesus as a supernatural savior, he does not seem to have doubted that, in Jesus' life and teachings, the supreme moral ideal was made manifest. For example, in 1884 he could still speak of "the perfect and matchless character of Christ."[11]

Dewey, however, was never entirely satisfied with what he learned from Coleridge, Marsh, and Torrey, because in the final analysis none of these men believed that the deeper truth about God and the world is organic unity. Unlike the Emersonian Transcendentalists, Coleridge and the Burlington Transcendentalists retained a belief in the doctrine of original sin and divine redemption through Christ. In their view, a real gulf separates humanity and God. When Dewey departed Vermont to pursue graduate study in philosophy he had worked out for himself the general outlines of a liberal religious faith, but the content of it was yet to be clearly defined.

III

It was at Johns Hopkins University, in the classroom of Professor George Sylvester Morris, that Dewey found what he was looking for. Morris, whose early religious and intellectual

[11] John Dewey, "The Place of Religious Emotion," in *The Early Works of John Dewey, 1882–1898*, ed. Jo Ann Boydston, (Carbondale: Southern Illinois University Press, 1969), 1: 92.

experience had been remarkably similar to Dewey's, had studied theology but, unsatisfied, he went off to Germany to study philosophy. There he discovered Hegel and, inspired especially by the British Neo-Hegelians like T. H. Green and John and Edward Caird, he became a convinced Hegelian. Morris' enthusiasm for Hegelian thought was typical of many religious liberals in late-nineteenth-century America. Hegel's great philosophical system which views the universe as a dynamic, evolutionary process governed by mind, and his rationalized version of Christianity seemed to provide the best way of reconciling the Christian faith with the revolutionary discoveries of the new science, and with the widespread faith in progress that animated American secular society. It was the synthesizing power of Hegel's ideas that drew Dewey. In short, he found in Hegel the vision of the world as an organic unity that he was seeking, and he described his discovery of Hegel "as an immense release, a liberation."[12] Upon completing his doctoral studies, Dewey joined the Philosophy Department at the University of Michigan, where he focused his primary attention on the way the Neo-Hegelian philosophy of Morris, T. H. Green, and the Cairds could be used to work out a solution to his threefold problem of unification involving the relation of God and the world, the integration of the self, and the realization of authentic community. In the philosophy of ethical idealism he developed, the act of religious faith occupies a position of central importance.

As a Neo-Hegelian, Dewey conceptualized the problem of unification in all three of its basic aspects as that of the unification of the ideal with the actual. Throughout his life, he regarded the relation between the ideal and the actual to be the most fundamental and significant of all human problems. It is the problem of "idealizing the world," as Dewey often puts it or, more simply, of realizing the identity of what *is* with what

---

[12] John Dewey, "From Absolutism to Experimentalism," p. 10.

ought to be, of uniting the real and the good. In his early philosophy, Dewey struggled with this issue in metaphysics, psychology, and social theory, endeavoring to discover the nature of the relationship of God and the world, the ideal self and the actual self, and the moral ideal and actual community life. In brief, the solution he worked out in his early essays and first two books, *Psychology* (1887) and *Leibniz's New Essays Concerning the Human Understanding* (1888), is as follows:

First, in his early metaphysics Dewey adopted a form of absolute idealism in which the universe is conceived at once as an organic unity and a unity of the ideal and the real. In this view, ultimate reality is Mind, Reason. Hence, the universe is conceived to be a spiritual whole, an organic unity, in which each part has a unique function, but in which each and every part is animated by one and the same spiritual principle which harmonizes the activities of all. In short, young Dewey's most basic solution to the problem of idealizing the world, of uniting what is and what ought to be, was a purely intellectual or theoretical solution as opposed to a practical one. The point is that the ideal and the real have always been, are now, and always will be one.

God, in this scheme, is precisely the principle of organic unity, that is, the principle of the unity of the ideal and the actual.[13] Here it is important to note that, for young Dewey, God is not just the ideal. If God were no more than the ideal, there still would be a gulf between God and the world, and this young Dewey would not accept. Dewey's Neo-Hegelian doctrine of God is not a set of ideas about a divine being named God who exists apart from the world; rather it is, first and foremost, a set of ideas about the nature of the world, centering around the notion that the world is an organic whole governed by an immanent divine reason or mind. In this way did the

---

[13] John Dewey, *Psychology*, in *The Early Works*, 2: 212; John Dewey, *Leibniz's New Essays Concerning the Human Understanding* in *The Early Works*, 1: 420–22.

Neo-Hegelians lead Dewey beyond classical Christian theism to a form of panentheism. This doctrine is, of course, a very appealing and comforting teaching if one can believe it, but it leaves one with the seemingly insoluble problem of why, if God and the world are one, the world is so full of suffering and moral evil. Dewey had no ready answer to this problem and it troubled him.

Dewey also states in his idealist writings that God is the perfect personality or the ideal personality.[14] By this he does not mean that God is a particular person among other persons. Rather, he means that the organizing purpose of the world and the supreme moral ideal is the realization of personality. Personality emerges as the supreme value in Dewey's Neo-Hegelian philosophy.[15] When he calls God the ideal personality, he means that God is in some sense the ground of personality. The universe is, then, conceived to be a great dynamic process, the final end of which is the realization of the one thing that is really divine—personality. Did Dewey believe that God is in any sense a conscious personality apart from the realization of personality in individual human beings? About this he was never very clear, and, by closely identifying God with the realization of personality in individual men and women, his panentheism had in it a strong humanistic emphasis, which could easily be developed in the direction of a naturalistic humanism that abandoned talk about God altogether.

Let us now turn to Dewey's psychology. Dewey's first book was a psychology that tried to fuse the latest findings of the new psychology with Neo-Hegelian philosophical categories. The result was an elaborate theory of self-realization, integration, and perfection of personality. Dewey defines the self as will, as an active process of self-determination, and he argues that the chief end of the will is the realization of itself. In other words, the task of the actual self is to realize the ideal self. The ideal

[14] John Dewey, *Psychology,* pp. 245, 361–63.
[15] John Dewey, *The Ethics of Democracy* in *The Early Works,* 1: p. 244.

self is, in Aristotelian terminology, the formal and final cause of the self. Dewey goes further and identifies the ideal self of each individual with God, who is the perfect personality. In short, the process of individual self-realization is a process through which the divine is reproduced in the human. Self-realization means identification of the individual and the universal, the ideal and the actual.

Dewey's *Psychology* contains an elaborate explanation of how the actual self finds its true or ideal self, that is, reproduces the perfect personality of God. The ideal personality combines absolute truth, beauty, goodness, and being, and it is reproduced in the self in, and through, science, philosophy, art, moral action, and religion. The process culminates in moral and religious faith.

In moral experience, a person becomes conscious that he or she has an obligation to realize the ideal self. The feeling of obligation is rooted in the fact that the ideal self is the true self. The moral law is not an arbitrary code imposed by an external divine power, but rather the law of realization of personality. Dewey puts special emphasis on moral autonomy, free personal determination of right and wrong. Only in, and through, a knowledge of alternative ends of action and a free choice of the good can the individual realize personality and actualize the universal will of God. The moral life culminates in the choice of some one ideal as the supreme ideal governing all conduct, and this act is of major importance for the integration of personality.

Dewey, however, argues that the self is never perfected in the moral life. The gulf between the ideal self and actual self is not completely overcome. The problem is not some bondage of the will to sin. The difficulty is that the moral life only establishes that the ideal ought to be real and not that it is real. Further, moral effort can never by itself guarantee the perfection of the

[16] John Dewey, *Psychology,* p. 360.

will in the future; and hence the union of the ideal and the real in moral experience is partial and incomplete.

The perfect identification of the ideal and the actual comes only in and through religious experience. Religious experience involves various emotional and intellectual factors, but it is primarily volitional: "It is religious will which performs the act of identification once for all. The will, as religious, declares that the perfect will is the only reality; it declares that it is the only reality of the universe, and that it is the only reality in the individual life." [16]

Religious will affirms the ultimate identity of God and the world, and of God and the essential nature of each and every person. This act of what he calls "religious will" is what he also terms religious faith. The section in Dewey's *Psychology* indicating it is only by an act of faith that the identity of the ideal and the real is finally established states that, just as moral experience by itself cannot prove that what ought to be in fact is, so metaphysical speculation by itself cannot conclusively demonstrate the unity of the ideal and the real, of God and the world, and of God and the self. [17] Dewey's position on this matter is close to that set forth in John Caird's *Introduction to the Philosophy of Religion,* which appeared in 1880. [18] However, in the background of Dewey's idea of faith lies Coleridge's reinterpretation of Kant's idea of Pure Reason and Practical Reason and Coleridge's idea of faith as an act of the whole feeling, thinking, willing person.

For Dewey, then, faith involves a whole-hearted commitment of the self to some supreme ideal as worthy of guiding action. For young Dewey this meant more than just believing that the ideal ought to be real. It meant believing that this ideal is identical with God, ultimate reality, and therefore is the final meaning of human life and the universe. During his early career Dewey believed that the chief defense against pessimism, de-

[17]*Ibid.,* p. 361.
[18] Reprint, Glasgow: James Maclehose and Sons, 1901, pp. 280–84.

spair, and a sense of meaninglessness is just such an act of religious faith in the ultimate reality of the ideal.[19] Further, when one has made the movement of faith, the moral will is strengthened and more profoundly identified with the universal will. Moral action carried on in the light of religious faith Dewey calls "religious action."[20] The whole process of harmonizing and perfecting personality is brought to fulfillment in and through religious faith and religious action. It is noteworthy that even though the young Dewey tried to idealize the world principally in and through metaphysical speculation and faith, he also, from the beginning, put considerable emphasis on moral action, which was, of course, in keeping with Vermont Transcendentalism. During the late 1880s this strand of his thought emerged as the dominant theme.

IV

Beginning with an essay entitled *The Ethics of Democracy* (1887), Dewey's writings begin to focus attention on social theory and the specific content of the moral ideal. Consequently, he put increasing emphasis on the moral and social meaning of religious faith. Further, he began to teach clearly that a person finds God principally in and through the moral life. There is no dualism of the religious and the secular, argues Dewey, and he takes the position that Christianity and the Kingdom of God in the contemporary world should be identified with democratic life.

In order to appreciate how and why Dewey arrived at this viewpoint it is necessary to understand that, during his years in Ann Arbor, the sensitive moral conscience that had been developed in him by his mother and Vermont Congregationalism was transformed into the conscience of a liberal social reformer. There were many factors at work in this process. The last three

[19] John Dewey, "The Lesson of French Literature," in *The Early Works,* 3: 41–42.
[20] John Dewey, *Psychology,* p. 361.

decades of the nineteenth century in the United States were a
time of great industrial and technological progress. As a result,
it was a time of great hope for the future. However, for many
Americans the progress was accompanied by the growth of
serious social ills, and these problems produced great unrest in
many quarters. The unrest led to the emergence of a number of
reform movements, including the American labor movement,
the Populist Party, the Social Gospel, and inner city settlement
houses, leading eventually to the formation of the Progressive
movement. All of these reform efforts had their influence on
Dewey, and he was deeply affected especially by what he learned
about the plight of the industrial workers and the urban poor.
By the late 1880s, he had become convinced that T. H. Green
was right: "the problem of social deliverance" should be the
central concern of philosophy and Christianity.[21]

In line with this argument, Dewey's Christian theology developed into a radical version of the Social Gospel; this is illus-
trated by an address entitled "The Value of Historical Christianity," which he delivered, on a Sunday morning in 1889,
before the Student's Christian Association at the University of
Michigan. The Social Gospel movement emerged in America
during the mid-1880s and included many Congregationalists
among its leaders, such as Washington Gladden and Josiah
Strong. Its central doctrine was that the individual is a part of
society and cannot be saved apart from a reformation of the
social order. Many of its adherents believed that the effort to
reform society would culminate in the realization of the Kingdom of God on earth. Dewey's radical brand of Social Gospel
Christianity emphasized that God is immanent in the social
world and that a person finds unity with God in and through
relations. As he put it:

> God is neither a far-away being, nor a mere philosophical conception by
> which to explain the world. He is the reality of our ordinary relations

[21]John Dewey, "The Philosophy of Thomas Hill Green," in *The Early Works*, 3:
16, 31.

with one another in life. He is the bond of the family, the bond of society. He is love, the source of all growth, all sacrifice and all unity. He has touched history, not from without, but has made Himself subject to all the limitations and sufferings of history; identified Himself absolutely with humanity, so that the life of humanity is hence-forward not for some term of years, but forever, the life of God.[22]

This statement shows the influence of the Hegelian doctrine of the immanence of God in human history, but it also contains a criticism of Hegel. For Hegel, the most perfect communion with God occurs in and through philosophical knowledge. For Dewey, the most perfect communion with God is realized in and through concrete interpersonal relations and moral action. This truth for Dewey is the heart of the meaning of the Christian doctrine of the incarnation. In Dewey's view, the point of this doctrine is not that God is incarnate in Jesus alone. Jesus' distinction is that he was the first to become conscious of the unity of the ideal and the actual, of God and the world, of God and the essence of human nature. God, however, is not incarnate in the individual as an isolated self but in the individual as a member of the social organism. The heart of the Christian Gospel is the proclamation of the unity of God and each and every person understood as a social being, that is, the unity of God and society. When Dewey asserts that God is "the life of humanity" he means that God is the shared life of real human community. Faith means believing this wholeheartedly and committing oneself to the common good, the moral ideals that make community function well and grow. Through faith and ethical action, the unity of God and humanity is realized, the social order is idealized, and the personality of the individual is harmonized.

Dewey explains that the individual does not need to wrestle with the problem of sin and guilt as an isolated individual alone before God. If Dewey had read Kierkegaard, he would have had no use for his theology and psychology. Dewey contends that a

[22] John Dewey, "The Value of Historical Christianity," in *The Monthly Bulletin,* 11 (November 1889): 33–34.

person "does not have to deal with God face to face, but through the mediator of that corporate humanity of which he is a member, and Jesus the head. . . . The individual has but to surrender himself to the common interests of humanity in order to be freed from the claim upon him as an individual. He stands no longer isolated, but a member of that humanity whose very spirit is God himself."[23]

For Dewey, then, humanity, not the historical Jesus, is the Mediator; and the Body of Christ is the human community at large. All of this leads Dewey to conclude "The Value of Historical Christianity" with a complete identification of the sacred and the secular: "The healthy religious life knows no separation of the religious from the secular, which has no Sunday or week-day divisions in it, which finds in every daily duty, whether in study or business, or recreation an approach to God as surely and truly as in the retirement of the closet."[24]

As Dewey moved in this direction, he became increasingly impatient with the idea of the church as a special, uniquely sacred institution. All human relations and institutions, and not just the church, should be understood to possess religious meaning and value. Had Dewey as a young man been introduced to Martin Buber's philosophy of "I and Thou," he would probably have been very enthusiastic about it.

Dewey, like many of his optimistic contemporaries, actually believed during the late 1880s and 1890s that the Kingdom of God could be established on earth in America, which Hegel had called "the land of the future," the place where the next great evolution of the World Spirit is to occur.[25] Further, Dewey believed that democracy is the very essence of life in the Kingdom. He had often heard Christianity and American democratic institutions linked in the Congregational church in Vermont. In

[23]*Ibid.*, p. 35.

[24]*Ibid.*, p. 36.

[25]G. W. F. Hegel, "America Is Therefore the Land of the Future," in *The American Hegelians: An Intellectual Episode in the History of Western America,* ed. William H. Goetzmann (New York: Alfred A. Knopf, 1973), pp. 19–20.

addition, a tradition of idealist, democratic social theory had grown up in America under the influence of Hegel. It had its origins in the work of the St. Louis Hegelians and it included the widely read theologian Elijah Mulford and the poet Walt Whitman. Dewey's thinking was much influenced by this tradition, and he tried to base his democratic social ethics on his Neo-Hegelian metaphysics. For example, he argues that a universe in which there is unity in the midst of real diversity is an ideal democratic order. He further reasons that, since God, the principle of organic unity in the universe, is the ideal personality, the supreme purpose of the universe is realization of personality; this, he contends, requires democracy—that is, the ideals of freedom, equality, and shared community life.[26] The ethical ideal of equality recognizes that every human being is a person and, as such, deserves the opportunity to realize his or her full potential as a person. The ideal of shared community life is essential to the realization of personality because persons fully realize the ideal self only by identifying their wills with the common will or common good. The ideal of freedom recognizes that the essence of personality is self-determining will and that personality can be perfected only by voluntary choice. Dewey was optimistic that freedom would not lead to moral chaos and, following Emerson and Whitman, he put his trust in the intelligence and good judgment of the common man and woman.

"Democracy and the one ultimate, ethical ideal of humanity are to my mind synonymous," wrote Dewey in 1887.[27] Hence, he identifies Christian ethics and democratic ethics and arrives at the position that faith in God involves faith in the ultimate spiritual meaning and value of democracy. Here it is important to recognize that for Dewey democracy is not just a system of government. It is a supreme moral ideal which should govern all human relations—in the family, in the school, in industry, in commerce, and in government. As Dewey put it toward the

[26] John Dewey, *The Ethics of Democracy*, pp. 243–48.
[27] *Ibid.*, p. 248.

end of his life, in 1939: "Democracy is a *personal* way of individual life; . . . it signifies the possession and continual use of certain attitudes, forming personal character and determining desire and purpose in all the relations of life." [28]

In "Christianity and Democracy" (1892) and "Reconstruction" (1894), Dewey introduces the idea that the scientific method of inquiry is intimately related in a positive way to both Christianity and democracy. In the 1890s, Dewey followed a number of German and British philosophers like Lotze, Bradley, and Bosanquet in accepting the scientific method as the sole authority in matters of intellectual belief. It became Dewey's position that the scientific method has proven itself to be THE method for establishing the truth of concrete fact, and hence it also is entitled to be called THE method of truth.

Dewey believed that there is no limit to the knowledge and power that the social as well as physical sciences can deliver into the hands of humanity. Furthermore, he followed thinkers like the early Ernst Renan and adopted the view that scientific method may be used as a method of knowledge in the search for an understanding of moral ideals—of what ought to be, as well as of what is. Dewey writes in his *Outlines of a Critical Theory of Ethics* (1891): "The intelligence that is capable of declaring truth, or what is, is capable also of making known obligation. For obligation is only *practical* truth, the 'is' of doing." [29] By developing such thoughts, Dewey became the prophet of a new social science which would be able to make objective moral valuations and would operate as a major, unifying force in contemporary society. He devoted much time and effort during his career to explaining and defending the idea of a scientific theory of moral valuation. It is, of course, a highly controversial idea, and considerations of it here must be limited to noting that it is

[28] John Dewey, "Creative Democracy—the Task Before Us," in *The Philosopher of the Common Man; Essays in Honor of John Dewey to Celebrate His Eightieth Birthday* (New York: Greenwood Press, 1968), p. 222.

[29] John Dewey, *Outlines of a Critical Theory of Ethics*, in *The Early Works*, 3: 361.

fundamental to Dewey's belief that the scientific method of inquiry is itself an ideal value in which modern men and women should put moral faith. Since Dewey, as an idealist, identified God with the absolute truth and science with the best method of discovering truth—including practical truth—he was able to argue that science in the contemporary world is an instrument of revelation possessing high religious as well as moral influence.

Dewey's faith in science is intimately related to his faith in democracy. The democratic ideal of freedom involves a faith in the intelligence of men and women generally, and science provides intelligence with the critical intellectual tools it needs to function well. In addition, democracy creates a social system in which a cooperative, scientific search for truth can be carried on without restrictions, and in which new truth can be freely distributed and institutionalized for the benefit of all. In brief, Christian faith in the contemporary world should mean, according to Dewey in his last years at Ann Arbor, a faith in the liberating power of the ideals of democracy and cooperative scientific inquiry.

During these years at the University of Michigan, Dewey's general concern was to work out a solution to his threefold problem of unification with God, integration of personality, and realization of community. He found the key to this solution in an act of religious and moral faith in God, understood as the principle of the unity of the ideal and the real, and as the embodiment of the interrelated ideals of personality, democracy, and scientific truth. To a significant degree, Dewey practiced what he preached. He put his faith in the immanent God of his Neo-Hegelian, democratic philosophy; guided by the ideals he associated with this God, he found—in his secular life as a family man, teacher, scholar, and increasingly active social reformer—the sense of identity, the social adjustment, and the inner peace that he had craved as a young man. Dewey had managed to work all of this out for himself fairly well by 1894, when, at the age of thirty-five, he departed Ann Arbor for the University of Chicago. It is not surprising that this date marks the end of the formative period in his religious development, because, from the beginning, his religious quest had been intimately related to a search for self and community.

V

The final chapter in the story of the evolution of Dewey's religious faith concerns the way he reconstructed the religious ideas he developed while under the influence of Coleridge, Marsh, and the Neo-Hegelians, so as to adjust these ideas to the philosophy of naturalistic humanism with which he came to identify himself during the early decades of the twentieth century as he worked out his own version of American pragmatism and progressive education theory at the University of Chicago and Columbia University.

From the religious point of view, the most significant difference between Dewey's early and mature thought is that the latter involves rejection of the idea of God as the unity of the ideal and the real. This idea had been a source of consolation to young Dewey, and it had given his moral ideals a form of cosmic justification he felt they needed in order to be worthy of moral faith. However, by the early 1900s Dewey came to believe that the need for such consolation and cosmic justification is childish.[30] Increasingly, he seems to have found that the democratic life and the scientific search for truth are inherently meaningful and need no supranatural or transcendental justification. Dewey also concluded that belief in the unity of the ideal and the real creates an insoluble problem as to why the world appears to be so unideal, and that it encourages men and women to rely irresponsibly upon God for the solution to social problems which they could overcome if they applied themselves

[30] John Dewey, "Nature and Its Good: A Conversation," in *The Influences of Darwin on Philosophy* (Bloomington: Indiana University Press, 1910), pp. 23–25.

to the task. Furthermore, employing the scientific method of inquiry, Dewey could find little evidence that supported belief in the reality of the Hegelian Absolute. For all these reasons he abandoned belief in God as the unity of the ideal and the real. The idea seemed neither emotionally nor intellectually necessary or defensible.

Rejection of his Neo-Hegelian theology was accompanied by a permanent breach with the church and traditional Christianity. This was not easy for Dewey in the light of his upbringing in a New England culture which identified Christianity with all that is most sacred in life. Indeed, he was able to do it only after he had, in a sense, extracted the blessing of the tradition upon his new venture by demonstrating that Christianity in the contemporary world means democracy and science.

Following his rejection of Neo-Hegelian idealism, Dewey reconstructed his idea of the universe or nature. Even as an idealist, Dewey had rejected any idea of a radical dualism between the transcendental and the natural; as a naturalist, he emphasized that there is only one world, the world of nature, and all that exists, including the human race, is a part of nature. In this world nothing is absolutely fixed or permanent. Change is the only thing that is absolutely universal. Whatever is, is a process, and nature is a complex of processes. The universe is infinite in space and time and in complexity. No absolute mind or divine intelligence coordinates all things. Dewey abandoned monism for pluralism. There are interrelations between events and organic unities amidst the plurality of events, but there is no overruling cosmic purpose or preestablished harmony. The processes that constitute nature are proceeding in an undetermined direction.

Nature, as Dewey envisions it, is a hazardous place for human beings and human values. However, even though there is no ultimate unity of the ideal and the real in the universe, he argues that "nature . . . is idealizable. . . . Nature gives, not always freely but in response to search, means and material by which the values we judge to have supreme quality may be embodied in existence."[31] Genuine ideals are to be thought of as possibilities of natural events rather than as actualities, but since they are possibilities they may be actualized in and through intelligent effort. Hence the kind of philosophical idealism that tries to develop intellectual certainty of the ideal and the real as already united in some realm of absolute being should be replaced with an idealism of practical action.

It is with these ideas that Dewey, over a period of four decades, gradually reconstructed his concept of religious faith and its object. The most complete statement of his views is contained in A Common Faith (1934), a small volume, in which he argues that contemporary men and women can embrace Naturalism, humanism, and secularism and still find in their lives religious value through faith. Dewey's interpretation of the nature and function of religious faith is prefaced by a discussion of what he calls the religious dimension or quality of experience.

He argues that the distinctively religious quality of experience has no necessary connection with any religion, by which he means "a special body of beliefs and practices having some kind of institutional organization." He explains that certain experiences which people undergo have what he variously calls a religious "force," "function," or "value." When this occurs a person's life acquires a "religious quality," and such a person develops a distinctively "religious attitude." An experience with a religious force is described by Dewey as one which effects "a better, deeper and enduring adjustment in life" involving "a sense of security and peace." Dewey is here concerned with deep-seated and lasting changes in the self as a whole in its relation to the world as a whole. He asserts that human experience acquires a religious quality when "there is a composing and harmonizing of the various elements of our being such that, in spite of changes in the special conditions that surround us, these

[31] John Dewey, The Quest for Certainty (New York: G. P. Putnam's Sons, 1929), p. 302.

conditions are also arranged, settled, in relation to us." The kind of lasting integration of personality and accommodation with the world that Dewey has in mind is, in a sense, a voluntary act of will, but it is not the result of a particular volition. It follows from "a change of will conceived as the organic plenitude of our being, rather than any special change *in* will." In other words, the whole feeling, thinking, willing self is involved and, as Dewey explains, "an adjustment" possesses the will rather than is "its express product." Further, while an enduring accommodation with the world involves an element of submission or acceptance of conditions in life that are unalterable, a truly religious attitude is more affirmative, "more outgoing, more ready and glad" and "more active" than Stoic resignation. This is so, explains Dewey, because it includes a "sense of values which carry one through periods of darkness and despair to such an extent that they lose their usual depressive character." It involves a sense of the meaning and worth of existence along with a sense of peace.[32]

Dewey notes that religions claim to effect this kind of change in attitude and adjustment, but he argues that it can occur quite apart from any religion and that it is not necessary to appeal to supernatural causes to explain it. Furthermore, since the idea of the supernatural and the practices of the religions have been discredited in the minds of large numbers of contemporary people, it is desirable to free the religious values in experience, which are vitally important, from any necessary connection with the supernatural and institutional religion. In making these assertions, Dewey is much influenced by his own experience. As a young man his religious quest had been intimately tied up with a search for his own identity and social adjustment. Once he realized, in his own experience, what he had been searching for, it seemed that institutional religious beliefs and practices and supernaturalism had nothing essential to do with it.

[32] John Dewey, *A Common Faith* (New Haven: Yale University Press, 1934), pp. 9–19.

Explaining, further, how people find and achieve an enduring adjustment and a religious attitude, Dewey notes that it may come about in "a multitude of ways"; however, he finds an act of religious faith at the heart of an experience with a religious function. He writes: "I should describe this faith as the unification of the self through allegiance to inclusive ideal ends, which imagination presents to us and to which the human will responds as worthy of controlling our desires and choices." First of all, then, a religious faith is a moral or practical faith. A moral faith is to be distinguished from an intellectual belief. "Conviction in the moral sense signifies being conquered, vanquished, in our active nature by an ideal and. . . . Such acknowledgement is practical, not primarily intellectual. It goes beyond evidence that can be presented to *any* possible observer." Second, a moral faith is religious in nature only when the ends of moral conviction are so inclusive in relation to the self and its world that these ideals are capable of inspiring the emotional commitment necessary to unify the self.[33]

The roots of Dewey's naturalistic idea of a moral faith that is religious in value may be traced back both to Coleridge's idea of faith, which is a reconstructed version of Kant's Practical Reason, and to the Neo-Hegelian idea of faith as an act of religious will. In both cases an act of religious faith involves a unifying commitment of the whole self to some supreme practical ideal governing the world of human relations. Sometime after publication of A *Common Faith,* Dewey commented to Professor Herbert Schneider: "All I can do on religion is to say again what I learned from Coleridge way back in my childhood."[34]

That aspect of Dewey's naturalistic philosophy of religion which provoked the most debate in the 1930s was his idea of God. His new concept of God is a naturalized version of his

---

[33] *Ibid.,* pp. 14, 20–23, 33.

[34] John Dewey as quoted by Herbert Schneider in Oral History Interview, Center for Dewey Studies, Southern Illinois University, Carbondale, Illinois, Summer, 1966.

Neo-Hegelian idea of God as the unity of the ideal and the real. In *A Common Faith*, God is defined as the *"active* relation between the ideal and the actual."[35] God, explains Dewey, may be identified with the unification of all positive human values or ideal ends, which unification is a product of the human imagination. However, God is more than an imaginative unification of ideal possibilities. The idea of the divine encompasses all those natural conditions and human activities which are involved in the active process in and through which the world is idealized, that is, through which the ideal and the real are being united. In other words, the idea of God or the divine comprehends for Dewey all that from a human point of view is most important and valuable in nature and society. God is, then, a finite, natural reality identified with only a limited portion of the universe as a whole. God is not a being or a center of conscious intelligence and will.

Dewey uses the term "God" to designate that complex of natural processes involved in the uniting of the ideal and the real because the term still conveys for him the idea of all that is most significant and valuable in life. In 1934, it still retained for him a certain power to stir deep emotion, to focus attention, and to direct action. However, there is more to it than that. Dewey had no use for a despairing kind of atheism which envisions the human race as utterly isolated in a hostile and indifferent universe. Nature does often frustrate human efforts to realize the ideal, but human beings are part of nature, nature is idealizable, and all ideal possibilities have their origin in nature and all attained human goods have their abode in nature. Dewey hoped that reference to God and the divine would foster an attitude of piety toward nature as well as moral faith and help guard against the extremes of despair. Dewey viewed piety toward nature as an important ingredient of a religious attitude.

In the 1880s and the 1890s, Dewey had tried to integrate the

---

[35] John Dewey, *A Common Faith*, p. 51.

religious and the world of human relations, and he had closely identified God with the values involved in realization of personality, democratic ways of living together, and the continuous revelation of practical truth in and through cooperative scientific inquiry. As a naturalistic humanist, the general content of Dewey's religious faith remains closely related to these ideals even though he continued to refine his understanding of their meaning. During the first two decades of the twentieth century, when Dewey was heavily involved in the progressive education movement, he put special emphasis on the religious meaning of a faith in education; for Dewey, however, a faith in education is only a correlate of his democratic faith in human nature and intelligence.[36] The heart of Dewey's faith in democracy and science is a confidence in the power of human intelligence to criticize and reconstruct the moral beliefs and social values that govern human relations so that human experience over the years and centuries grows in richness of meaning and value. Historically, the object of religious concern in all the higher religions has been a set of essentially human ideals, argues Dewey, and people have struggled to transmit, rectify, and expand the heritage of values they have received so that it is more "widely and generously shared" in succeeding generations. It is his contention that "such a faith has always been implicitly the common faith of mankind. It remains to make it explicit and militant."[37] Dewey's idea of faith in democracy and cooperative scientific inquiry is his attempt to achieve this end.

Throughout his philosophical career, Dewey persistently sought to discover continuity and interrelations where others could see only radical oppositions and separations. The most significant contribution of his philosophy of religion is the way it endeavors to reconcile democratic humanism, naturalism, secularism, and science with religious values. He does this by trying to naturalize Vermont Transcendentalism and his own

---

[36] John Dewey, "Creative Democracy—the Task Before Us," p. 224.
[37] John Dewey, *A Common Faith*, p. 87.

American version of Neo-Hegelian idealism, and by reinterpreting the meaning of the term "religious." The result is an ingenious philosophy of religion which is appealing because it seems so balanced, sensible, and morally constructive.

Dewey would have had little trouble in getting his American intellectual forefathers—like Marsh, Emerson, Torrey, and Morris—to accept his general theory that the social values of a democratic humanism have inherent religious significance. But, could Dewey have convinced them that he had successfully reconciled naturalism and religious faith? It is very doubtful that he could, even though his insights into the dynamics of faith are close to those of Coleridge and are very perceptive. Their fundamental objection would center on Dewey's idea that a person can have a faith with a religious quality in a universe in which there is no eternal and absolutely good reality that transcends time, change, and death. Does not a religious faith involve a basic trust that life is somehow good and meaningful in spite of all that is evil and meaningless? Dewey would not deny this. A religious attitude, in his view, involves such a trust. In *Experience and Nature* he argues that his idealism of action, coupled with natural piety, can foster such trust: "When we have used our thought to its utmost and have thrown into the moving unbalanced balance of things our puny strength, we know that though the universe slay us still we may trust, for our lot is one with whatever is good in existence." [38] How can a person trust that life, in the final analysis, is good and meaningful unless there is some *ultimate* meaning and value in life; and does not the latter necessarily involve the idea of an eternal ground of meaning and value that is transcendent of all that comes to be and passes away? Dewey, as a naturalist, carefully avoids speaking about *ultimate* meaning, but there is a question as to what he really means when he paraphrases the King James Version of Job 13:15 and asserts that "though the universe slay us still we may trust."

[38] John Dewey, *Experience and Nature* (New York: W. W. Norton, 1925), p. 420.

Transcendentalists like Marsh, Torrey, or Morris would argue that Dewey's naturalistic metaphysics fails to make intelligible how such peace and trust which, he asserts, accompanies a practical faith with a religious quality, is possible. They would find an element of Vermont Transcendentalism in his naturalism despite his disclaimers, and would point out that when he insists that enduring trust in the goodness of life is possible, his heart is wiser than his metaphysics. This is the most problematical issue raised by Dewey's attempt at a naturalist theory of religious faith.

TWO

"The God of Our Children":
The Humanist Reconstruction of God

RAYMOND F. BULMAN

THIS ESSAY deals with ideas that are close to Blau, both as a Humanist and as a philosopher. As a major intellectual spokesman for the American Humanist movement and as a professional philosopher of religion, Blau has made some important contributions over the years toward a clarification and appreciation of the religious dimension of human experience. He clearly belongs to that branch of the Humanist movement which has maintained a vital and serious interest in religious questions. Philosophically, Blau continues in his own creative way a rich tradition of American thought which combines the naturalism of Frederick J. E. Woodbridge, Irwin Edman, George Santayana, and John Dewey with the radical empiricism and pragmatism of Charles S. Peirce and William James. These movements in indigenous American philosophy have—in contrast to such imported movements as positivistic analytical philosophy—persistently recognized the important place of religious issues in philosophical investigation. While the Naturalists, for example, are careful to limit their understanding of religion to what Dewey called the "human abode," they are equally insistent that any philosophy which neglects man's religious concerns can produce only a seriously "truncated"[1] vision of human existence.

The Humanist movement in America has close ties with developments in American philosophy. From the point of view of religious outlook it can be divided into two clearly distinguishable strands. The first abhors any use of religious language, avoiding as far as possible any direct reference to religious questions. This part of the movement can suitably be called "Secular" Humanism, in the strictest, and perhaps narrowest, sense of the term. The second, on the contrary, is not only open to explore religious issues, but also sees them as quite central to the Humanist thrust. In fact, it proudly describes its own world outlook as "Religious Humanism." It is this latter category of humanists that will constitute the focus of our attention in this essay.

Religious Humanism has a long and hallowed ancestry in America, descending in uneven and intersecting lines from such diverse sources as the nonconformist colonial churches, New England Transcendentalism, the Unitarian and the Universalist Church movements, culminating, in recent times, in two historic "Humanist Manifestoes"—the first published in 1933 and the second, an updated version, in 1973. The varied religious developments that constitute the Religious Humanist movement have had an impact on American philosophy from its inception through the influence of religious liberal intellectuals, such as Ralph Waldo Emerson, Theodore Parker, and Francis Ellingwood Abbot. By the same token the successors of these early religious liberals were able to draw intellectual support and sustenance from the developing American philosophical tradition. To cite one example: Curtis Reese, a Unitarian minister and leading force in the American Humanist movement of the 1920s and 1930s, was able to appeal to the philosophical

---

[1] John H. Randall, Jr., "Towards a Functional Naturalism," *Contemporary American Philosophy*, ed. John E. Smith (Muirhead Library of Philosophy, 2nd series; London: George Allen & Unwin, 1970), p. 54.

authority of both Felix Adler and John Dewey in support of his humanistic interpretation of religion.[2]

Characteristically, the Religious Humanist places central importance on man's religious concerns, while molding them to the requirements of what appears best in modern thought and humanistic ideals. From this vantage point, religion becomes "the repository of all that a culture holds sacred."[3] It is identified with what is "humanly significant,"[4] and with "the best that man does or thinks or dreams."[5] Enthusiasm for democratic ideals, commitment to freedom of thought and conscience, confidence in our scientific future, and the inclination to transform religious symbols by assigning to them purely secular values are all characteristic features of American culture. In the Religious Humanist movement, these attitudes have been organized and made explicit policy.

Blau, as I suggested earlier, is unmistakably a Humanist of the religious stamp—certainly not in the sense of allegiance to traditional doctrines or institutional religious authority, but in the sense of humanistic concern for man's religious needs and aspirations. His naturalism in philosophy provides support and structure for his humanistic-religious attitude in a way that typically exemplifies the whole movement. In a controversial 1968 article on the meaning of the term "God," Blau gives us a succinct picture of the naturalistic and humanist elements in his own religious thought:

> As a naturalist and a humanist, I cannot accept this relegation of "God" to irrelevancy. "God" is too important a concept to be left to the mys-

[2] Curtis W. Reese, Preface, *Humanist Sermons,* ed. Reese (Chicago: The Open Court Publishing Co., 1927), p. viii.

[3] Joseph L. Blau, *Modern Varieties of Judaism* (New York: Columbia University Press, 1966) p. 168.

[4] "A Humanist Manifesto," first published in *The New Humanist,* 6 no. 3 (1933), reprinted in Corliss Lamont, *The Philosophy of Humanism* (Frederick Ungar Publishing Co., 1949), p. 387, n. 7. Henceforth to be referred to as "Humanist Manifesto I."

[5] Curtis W. Reese, *Humanism* (Chicago: The Open Court Publishing Co., 1926), p. 13.

tical theologians. As a naturalist, I must insist that there is empirical
evidence for the belief in God, and that this belief is therefore a proper
theme for investigation. As a humanist, I must point to the world-
shaking importance that this belief has had in human affairs, in the
shaping of human destinies, and therefore attempt to rescue its value
for humanity.[6]

The idea of "rescuing the term 'God' " or other religious values from the distorting power of the religious institutions (or
the "mystical theologians") is clearly reminiscent of Dewey's
philosophy of religion, which was a major influence on Blau,
and, in general, on Religious Humanists. This basic Deweyan
framework should put us on guard against confusing the religion of the Humanists with any of the traditional biblical
faiths. The Humanists reject biblical theism, supernatural revelation, and religious authority in the name of autonomy and
human dignity. Religion is seen rather as a natural, human
quality, grounded in experience and empirical observation.
While the secularity of Religious Humanism is apparent, its
religious character is no less evident in the zeal and ardor with
which it pursues "a full and comprehensive vision of human
destiny."[7] The First Humanist Manifesto called for a new, dynamic, humanistic religion shaped and suited "for the needs of
this age."[8]

But while the Manifesto looks to the future of human culture
and religion, it also gives honest recognition to the "vast debt"
modern man owes to the traditional faiths. This tribute does
not prevent the same document from declaring the inadequacy
of "the religious forms and ideas of our fathers,"[9] but it is indicative of Humanism's openness to abiding moral and human
values that are often hidden and implicit in the beliefs, myths,
and ritual of the ancient supernatural religions.

[6] Joseph L. Blau, "God and the Philosophers," *The Idea of God,* ed. Edward Madden, et al. (Springfield, Illinois: Charles C. Thomas, 1968), p. 157.

[7] Julian Huxley, "The Humanist Frame," in *The Humanist Frame: the Modern Humanist Vision of Life* (New York: Harper, 1961), p. 40.

[8] "Humanist Manifesto I," p. 286.

[9] *Ibid.,* p. 288.

The difficult task of preserving the religious aspects of culture in a strictly anthropocentric and moral context becomes the courage and determination to engage in an endless process of modernizing and reinterpreting even the most central of traditional religious symbols. Without doubt the most powerful and significant of all Western religious symbols is the image or concept of God. This essay explores the Religious Humanist efforts to redefine the meaning of "God," with a view toward throwing some light on the nature and implications of this religious reconstruction. Blau, in my judgment, has supplied one of the most interesting and impressive Humanist reconstructions of the term "God." In one place, he describes his effort as a quest for "The God of Our Children"—a poetic phrasing of a redefinition which, I believe, will serve as a good paradigmatic case.

Humanism as a Religion

Almost from its inception, the Religious Humanist movement has struggled to make religion more human and humanism more religious. Emerson, for example, lamented the way the early Church distorted the true image of the man, Jesus, petrifying his humanity with official titles, and thus transforming him from "the friend of man" into the "injurer of man."[10] Theodore Parker was more concerned with the autonomy and dignity of human intelligence, in defense of which he persistently argued against the divine authority of the Scriptures and the binding force of the minister's interpretation. A much better criterion of truth, he insisted in 1858, was "the Facts of the Universe, as the human mind interprets them."[11] Fundamentally, Religious Humanism works on the principle that "the

---

[10] Ralph Waldo Emerson, "The Divinity School Address," in *Three Prophets of Religious Liberalism: Channing, Emerson, Parker,* ed. Conrad Wright (Boston: Beacon Press, 1961), p. 98.

[11] Theodore Parker, "The Philosophical Idea of God and Its Relation to the Scientific and Religious Wants of Mankind Now," in *American Philosophic Addresses, 1700–1900,* ed. Joseph L. Blau (New York: Columbia University Press, 1946), p. 669.

distinction between the sacred and the secular can no longer be maintained."[12] From the point of view of psychology, we can only applaud Humanism's dedication to the unity of the sacred and the secular, for it is obviously unhealthy for human concerns to be divided into such rigid compartments. Modern scripture scholarship has also persuasively shown that a sharp division between the religious and the secular realms cannot be defended on biblical grounds. The Christian theologian Paul Tillich strongly defended "the principle of the consecration of the secular" on theological grounds and even declared that the separation of the secular and the sacred in our culture is the clearest sign of sin and estrangement.[13] The Humanists, of course, try to effect this principle by their secular transformation of religious symbols.

For the religious believer, this transformation process might well appear blasphemous, while to the nonbeliever it might seem the work of doubletalk or intellectual deception. But despite these objections, a look at Religious Humanism from within should make it clear that the intention is neither to undermine or to mislead, but rather to update and put new life into our venerable but time-worn religious traditions. Two specific and essential aspects of Humanism as a religion support my contention, and in fact illustrate that the *aim* of transforming symbols in this context is really constructive, or perhaps we might even say salvific and redemptive.

In the first place, it is crucial to understand that Religious Humanism sees itself as "an *imaginative* interpretation of human living" . . . whose true function becomes evident only "after mythology and superstition have been quietly and firmly put to one side as no longer a thoroughfare for an adult humanity."[14]

---

[12] "Humanist Manifesto I," p. 287.

[13] Paul Tillich, *Systematic Theology* (3 vols., Chicago: Harper & Row, 1967), 3: 247.

[14] Roy Wood Sellars, "Humanism as a Religion," *The Humanist,* Spring 1941, p. 8.

In support of this view, Humanists frequently appeal to the work of George Santayana, who made a strong philosophical case that the real essence of religion is *poetry*, "in the sense in which poetry includes all imaginative moral life."[15] Santayana's appeal to the central role of imagination in religion was accompanied by his rejection of dogmas and religious authority as superstition and intellectual repression. This combined view had a strong attraction for the Humanists.

The primacy of imagination for Santayana did not imply that religion entailed an escape from truth or flight into fancy. The naturalist philosopher Irwin Edman gives us a faithful rendition of Santayana's meaning in his description of the current task facing the creative religious person. The vital role of religious imagination, Edman argues, especially in our modern situation, is that of establishing goals and ideals for human living, insofar as "the formulas of the engineer, the chemist, and the medical technician leave something unexpressed, and the techniques of all of them make no adequate statements of the ends that give point to our ever more ingenious means."[16] Elsewhere, Edman defines religion as the "poetry of the race objectified into dogma," under whose magical power "the serene and winning forms of life became the gods of the Pantheon."[17] Modern man's rejection of religion is due to his forgetting its poetic origin, which over the centuries has been distorted and frozen into dogmas.

Man's religions, in this view, are institutionalized expressions of his devotion to the highest and noblest ideals which are symbolized through religious myths, symbols, and stories. If religion were generally understood in this way there would be an immediate end to the wasteful disputes, conflicts, and wars

[15] Cited by John H. Randall, Jr., *Philosophy: an Introduction*, ed. John H. Randall, Jr., and Justus Buchler (New York: Harper & Row, 1942), p. 300.

[16] Irwin Edman, *Four Ways of Philosophy* (New York: Henry Holt & Co., 1937), p. 180.

[17] Edman, "Religion and the Philosophical Imagination," *The Journal of Philosophy*, 25 (December 1928): 681.

that so often arise from theological and religious differences. Religions should conflict with each other no more than do poems. If there must be rivalry between religions, it should take the form of challenging each religion to explore to what extent "its symbolism and poetry are richer and morally more elevating."[18] However one appraises the naturalistic explanation of religion, it seems clear that its intent in viewing religion as poetry is not to undermine but to restore religious symbols to their original power.

From our discussion of religion as the work of imagination emerge hints of the second essential feature of Religious Humanism. The poetry that religion is has much to do with *moral* life—it establishes ideals; it is morally elevating. In short, the true essence of religion necessarily includes what Emerson called the "moral sentiment." While today's Humanists would hardly describe this sentiment in Emerson's terms, i.e., as "an insight of the perfection of the laws of the soul,"[19] they would certainly share his conviction as to the central place of morality in religion. In a recent article in the *Religious Humanist,* W. S. Fisk, a regular spokesman for the movement, makes the typical comment: "respect, love, equality, faith, honor, wisdom; all of these are the children of religion."[20] In a similar vein, Humanist Manifesto II, written forty years after the first declaration of Humanist ideals, reaffirmed "the need to preserve the best ethical teachings in the religious traditions of humankind," and restated its conviction that the chief function of religion is to "inspire dedication to the highest ideals."[21] This second aspect of Humanism as a religion makes its ambivalence toward the religious traditions more understandable. For while the Humanists will reject the doctrinal and theological elements in the

[18] Randall, *Philosophy: an Introduction,* p. 300.
[19] Emerson, "The Divinity School Address," p. 92.
[20] W. S. Fisk, "God is Dead—Long Live Religion," *The Religious Humanist,* 1, no 1 (Winter 1967): 14.
[21] Humanist Manifesto II," *The Humanist* 33, no. 5 (September–October 1973): 5.

traditions, they view the ancient faiths as carriers of profound human values. The old symbols and practices, they insist, provide us with a rich patrimony of images which can help organize and give vitality to our ultimate hopes and noblest ideals. In explaining his formidable program of *reconstructing* the ancient beliefs and symbols of Judaism, Mordecai Kaplan gives us a succinct statement of the procedure. It is a question of singling out "those implications which can help us meet our own moral and spiritual needs: the rest may be relegated to archeology."[22]

The American Religious Humanists consciously trace their spiritual heritage back to Emerson, who spoke of the "poetic truth" which is concealed in prayers, sermons, and dogmas, and identified the role of religion as the "exploration of the moral nature of man, where the sublime is, where are the resources of astonishment and power."[23]

The essence of religion is poetry and morality. We can expect that any Humanist reconstruction of "God" will reflect these two fundamental concerns of the Religious Humanist world view.

The Humanist Reconstruction of "God"

The promise of a new and better age through radical scientific and technological discoveries, accompanied by educational advances geared to conquer human ignorance, created an atmosphere of optimism annd enthusiasm in turn-of-the-century America. John Dewey reflected this spirit and articulated these hopes in his prodigious array of philosophical writings. We have already seen that it was to Dewey's thought that many

---

[22] Mordecai M. Kaplan, *The Meaning of God in Modern Jewish Religion* (New York: Behrman's Jewish Book House, 1937), p. 6. While Kaplan was engaged in a project analogous to that of the Religious Humanists, he was tied in his own special way to the Torah and the Jewish tradition, and felt that the Humanist approach was inadequate to the task of reconstruction (See *ibid.*, pp. 320ff).

[23] Emerson, "The Divinity School Address," pp. 104–5.

Religious Humanists appealed for the intellectual grounding of
their ideals. The direct influence of Dewey's optimistic view is
reflected throughout the various articles of Humanist Manifesto
I. The final statement of the document, for example, has an unmistakably Deweyan ring: "Man is at last becoming aware that
he alone is responsible for the realization of his dreams, that he
has within himself the power for its achievement. He must set
intelligence and will to the task."[24]

In attempting to meet the new and challenging opportunities
of our era, Dewey was convinced that the philosophy of the past
is now totally inadequate. A complete "reconstruction" in philosophy is necessary. In order to speak intelligibly to the cultural issues of our day and of the future, philosophy will have to
incorporate the principles of scientific method into its system. It
will have to become more empirical and view its theories as hypotheses to be tested. Once philosophy learns to accommodate
the methods that have proven so successful in the physical
sciences to the vital realm of human and moral subjects, we will
honestly be able to speak of a real reconstruction in philosophy.[25] While many Religious Humanists are staunchly committed to these fundamental Deweyan goals and methods, some
are temperamentally more akin to Santayana, who maintained,
at the same time, a genuine, though perhaps nostalgic, respect
for the rich symbolic forms of historical religion. Like Santayana, they feel urged to reinterpret these forms in new and
meaningful ways.

In order to meet the task, nothing less than a reconstruction
in religion comparable to Dewey's in philosophy will be
required. Understandably, then, Humanists will talk about redefining, transforming, or reformulating the poetic imagery
that constitutes the stuff of religion. Mordecai Kaplan, a disciple of Dewey, found the term "reconstruction" appropriate to

---

[24] "Humanist Manifesto I," p. 288.
[25] See Dewey's "New Introduction" (1948) to his classic work, *Reconstruction in
Philosophy* (Boston: Beacon Press, 1920), p. iv.

designate his own special project of modernizing and reinterpreting the Jewish faith,[26] and I believe that it accurately
describes the Religious Humanist program as well.

Santayana used his own poetic naturalism to *reconstruct* the
God-idea so as to symbolize man's highest, noblest, and total
ideal. Religious imagination attributes substance to the term
'God" as it does to other religious fictions. In reality, the term
"God" does not designate substance, but refers rather to "the
sphere of momentous events and ultimate destiny."[27] God really stands for nothing other than "that desired perfection, that
eternal beauty, which lies sealed in the heart of each living
thing."[28]

The reason for our insistence on thinking of God as substance
is our inherent tendency to objectify and literalize the essentially poetic nature of religion. Blau, updating the form of Santayana's argument, attributes our confusion to "a disease of
thought . . . that has long been observed whereby we tend to
confuse syntax with ontology, and to assume that whenever we
use a noun, there must be an actual entity that corresponds to
that noun."[29] Humanists, following Santayana and Dewey, will
argue that Divinity is to be understood *adjectively* or, better yet,
adverbially rather than substantively, for the term is really intended to describe a certain quality or function of human experiences and transactions. In a recent statement of the humanistic
meaning of "God," Gardner Williams, appealing to Santayana's
Reason in Religion, distinguishes two clearly different meanings

[26] See, for example, Kaplan, *The Future of the American Jew* (New York: The Reconstructionist Press, 1967), pp. 34–57. Professor Blau is no doubt indebted to the
ideals and methods of Kaplan's Reconstructionist project, the goal of which is "to
discover what meanings are holy in a secular world and then to celebrate these holy
meanings in the old forms." Blau, *Modern Varieties of Judaism* (New York: Columbia
University Press, 1966), p. 169.
See "God and the Philosophers," p. 159 for his own treatment of "desacralization"
and "sacralization."
[27] George Santayana, *Obiter Scripta,* eds. Justus Buchler and Benjamin Schwartz
(New York: Charles Scribner's Sons, 1936), p. 185.
[28] *Ibid.,* p. 297.
[29] Blau, "God and the Philosophers," pp. 158–59.

of the term "God" in Western religious tradition. The first
refers to a "basic physical cosmic substance," while the second is
the *"summum bonum,"* the goal of man's ultimate rational devotion, aspiration, striving and commitment.[30] The first concept,
according to Williams, must be rejected as incompatible with
scientific knowledge and the naturalistic scheme of things. The
second, on the contrary, makes perfect sense and corresponds to
the fact that many people regularly recognize and strive for
ideals which continue to defy their achievement. "God," then,
comes to stand for the "real, factual nonexistent potential"[31] of
humankind toward which we ever strive and which we never
quite achieve.

Blau's work in philosophy of religion continues the tradition
established by James, Santayana, and Dewey, with all its intricate ties to the Religious Humanist movement. Like Dewey,
who had once offered a definition of "God" in terms of ideals
and values,[32] Blau also gives us his own version which, he
suggests, might be incorporated into the theist's conception of
God and, at the same time, provide the nontheist with an acceptable understanding of the term. The following statements
should suffice to provide the reader with the essential picture of
this reinterpretation of "God":

> God is the name for the continuous activity of creating imaginative
> visions of the good life that spur men on to the betterment of the
> present life.
>
> Our ideals are many and divergent. They arise out of the many and
> divergent situations of our lives. Yet for each of us there is an imagina-
> tive and creative synthesis that shapes these ideals into a unity that
> gives unity to our character.
>
> The unified ideal moves men to seek change, the change itself moves
> men to a revision of the ideal. Thus the ideal is not an "unmoved

[30] Gardner Williams, "Humanistic Theism," *The Humanist Alternative: Some Definitions of Humanism,* ed. Paul Kurtz (Buffalo, New York: Prometheus Books, 1975), p.
68.

[31] *Ibid.*

[32] See John Dewey, *A Common Faith* (New Haven: Yale University Press, 1934), p.
42.

mover" but a "moving mover." Ideals that are realized are, by that token, desacralized; but this very process suggests new ideals for sacralization.

Except as in each cultural tradition, in each generation, we human beings sacralize certain ideals by including them in our description of God, the term *God* is void of any content.[33]

As if anticipating a flood of objections, especially from the side of the theistic believers, Blau informs his readers that a religious belief can be hallowed by "aspiration" as well as by tradition. He concludes his argument with a *fervorino* worthy of the best Sunday homily: "Too long we have deplored our inability to search out the 'God of our Fathers.' Let us, rather, turn to exploring the possibility of discovering the 'God of our children.' Let us pin our hopes to the God who is hope."[34]

What is particularly useful about Blau's attempt to redefine "God" is that it incoporates all the major features of Religious Humanism's understanding of the God-idea. It is not difficult at this point to identify these characteristic qualities as:

PROJECTIONISTIC: The poetic imagination which organizes and unifies our experienced values into abstract ideals, projects them onto an unchanging, empty symbol or "screen" men call God.

ANTHROPOCENTRIC: The Humanist understanding of "God" is purely human-centered and exclusively immanent. It does not attempt to offer an explanation of the world, its meaning, or direction. The world and human consciousness are simply *given.* The "God Within" of the Humanists is strictly bounded by the world of human concerns. While Humanists use the substantive language of religious discourse, they really intend to describe a function or process whereby their values and ideals project onto the imaginative image of a supernatural entity.

NATURALISTIC: It assumes that the scientific world view and the requirements of empirical thought render the "super-

---

[33] Blau, "God and the Philosophers," pp. 161–62.
[34] *Ibid.,* p. 163.

naturalistic" outlook unacceptable to the modern mind. The confidence in human intelligence and the trust in human resources naturalism implies make it particularly appealing to the modern heirs of Emerson, the apostle of "self-reliance," and to the disciples of William James, the proponent of "radical empiricism."

DYNAMIC: Religious Humanism is closely tied to the evolutionary view of man. Human ideals, like consciousness and experience, are constantly changing. This dynamism is so central to the Humanist outlook that the very content of the God-concept is totally dependent on the changes, the new sacralizations, that occur "in each cultural tradition, in each generation."

CONCILIATORY: The Humanist "God-Within" is intended as a compromise proposal, for it is based on a decision and desire to retain all that is worthwhile in the traditional faith. What is worthwhile, of course, is that which is morally and spiritually elevating—"The rest may be relegated to archeology."[35] The Humanist sees the importance of continuity with the past, and this insight urges him to assign new, naturalistic meanings to central religious symbols such as "God."

A suitable and adequate critique of Religious Humanism and its reconstruction of "God" would certainly require a full-scale assessment of its sources and presuppositions. Since this is far beyond the scope of this essay, I wish to conclude by drawing attention to what I believe are some significant strengths and weaknesses of the Humanist project.

Comments

There is no doubt that the projectionist interpretation of God offers a serious challenge to biblical faith in reminding us that our historical images of God "have often been the all-too-human projections of our own imperfect aspirations."[36] But to admit

[35] See above.
[36] John Macquarrie, *Thinking About God* (New York: Harper & Row, 1975), p. 89.

that projection is part of the picture does not justify *reducing* God to a product of human projection. Any projection theory of God simply fails to explain the tenacity of the God-concept. If everything else changes in human consciousness-awareness, ideals, hopes, then why has the human habit of projecting our ideals onto a supernatural screen remained so constant since the dawn of human history?

The anthropocentrism of the Humanist reconstruction, on the other hand, does appear to have certain advantages. It certainly helps us to avoid any image of Divinity which is demeaning to human dignity or conducive to unworthy behavior. The Humanist "God Within" is undoubtedly a Protector and Supporter of our moral interests, precisely because these same interests constitute the very substance of the God-concept. But a purely subjective notion of Divinity, a "God" created by man, is inadequate to the basic human quest for a meaningful universe. While the Humanist view of Divinity is unquestionably geared to foster that inspiring and contagious enthusiasm for the moral life that is the legacy of Emerson, it fails to provide an objective foundation for the credibility of the hopes it inspires. In his critique of Humanism, Mordecai Kaplan made precisely this point when he reminded his readers that "all ideals rest on the assumption that there exists in reality that which, if we can discover it, assures their realization."[37]

I believe that the Humanists are correct in recognizing that the modern world view is naturalistic. The triumph of technological reason in our time tends to make scientific empiricism the model for all legitimate knowledge. I also believe that they are completely justified in rejecting the childish and unworthy images of God which accompany a naive kind of supernaturalism derived from an outmoded world view. But the biblical and classical formulations of God, correctly understood, do not present the image of a "Super-Entity" who speaks to us from a

[37] Kaplan, *The Meaning of God*, p. 325.

transcendence that has been "reified as a second story to the observable world."[38] While naturalism proves very helpful in purifying the God-concept of superstitious and anthropomorphic projections, there is no reason why it should serve as the ultimate criterion for our thinking about God. Naturalism is too tightly bound by the limits of the world picture we ourselves create to provide a serious objection to an idea of God, conceived not as part of the world, as, say, Gardner Williams' "cosmic substance," but as its transcendent presupposition.[39]

In terms of the dynamic or evolutionary nature of our God-concepts, Humanism seems to be on sound historical and anthropological grounds. But while it is true that our religious rhetoric and conceptual formulations continually change, there is no good reason to suppose that the objective referent of these descriptions is as ephemeral and impermanent as our mental constructs. Only the bias of projectionism and naturalism would justify that conclusion. While theology today is seriously challenged to update the notion of God, I would be inclined to agree with the Oxford theologian John Macquarrie that the task before us is not one of radical reconstruction but rather of *rehabilitation,* by which he means a reexploration of the ancient sources behind our traditional God-idea.[40] Reconstruction would assign to the term "God" meanings that are quite foreign to the biblical world view. The Humanist redefinition of "God" belongs to a totally different paradigmatic structure than that from which the term derives.

Granted the genuiness of the conciliatory intent behind the Humanist reconstruction of "God," religious believers are unlikely to accept a notion of God so incongruous with the substance of their faith. For them it is not just a matter of theoreti-

[38] Michael Novak, *Belief and Unbelief: A Philosophy of Self-Knowledge* (New York: New American Library, 1965), p. 37.

[39] Karl Rahner, *Do You Believe in God?* trans. Richard Strachan (New York: Paulist Press, 1969), p. 67.

[40] Macquarrie, *Thinking About God,* p. 97.

cal difference; the Humanist understanding of God, if accepted, will inevitably create a radical change of world view and self-understanding. Not a few Humanists have also strongly protested this technique of retaining the term "God" while completely transforming its meaning. Corliss Lamont, a well-known proponent of Humanist philosophy, warns us that the "semantic game of redefining God" can only produce greater philosophical and religious confusion.[41] Such evidence clearly does not appear to support the prediction that the Humanist conception of God will create a basis for harmonious discussion between believers and Humanists.

Finally, while some Humanists undoubtedly intend their reconstruction of "God" with utmost seriousness, I believe that other contributions, including Blau's, are presented somewhat tongue-in-cheek.[42] From its very beginnings Religious Humanism has been a protest against doctrinaire, pretentious, and humanly demeaning theology. I have no doubt that redefinitions of God, such as the one proffered by Blau, serve to deflate the hubris of what Theodore Parker called the "ecclesiastical method of theology."[43] I am convinced that the Humanists render a genuine service to society, as well as to the Church, whenever they stand up to defend human dignity against the destructive power of religious authoritarianism. Indeed, in this prophetic defense of human values lies the principal merit of Humanism and its reconstruction of "God." Parody and ridicule can serve as powerful instruments of protest.

Hence, the Humanist revision of the God-idea has justly dramatized the urgent need for rethinking our notion of God. At its very best, however, it represents a parody and protest,

---

[41] Corliss Lamont, "Commentary on Joseph Blau's Paper: Professor Blau and the Redefinition of 'God,' " *The Idea of God,* pp. 170–71.

[42] See Lamont, "Commentary," p. 169. Lamont is obviously aware of the subtle roguery behind Blau's redefinition when he refers to it as a "witty essay." Cf. John T. Kearns' commentary, p. 164ff for a respondent who takes the suggestion on face value and, I propose, misses an important aspect of the essay.

[43] Parker, "The Philosophical Idea of God," p. 666.

and as such should not be expected to replace the traditional conceptions of God. Perhaps the Humanists, having come so far, would be willing to cooperate with theologians in the difficult task of "rehabilitation." Theology would certainly have much to gain from such a joint effort.

For their part, I would only ask the Humanists to try to break the bonds of their own self-imposed anthropocentrism and address themselves once more to those big issues which transcend our subjective concerns. Questions about the existence, structure, and meaning of the universe are even more significant in our scientific space age than they have ever been through man's long history. The urgent need for universal ethical principles and the crucial struggle for world unity demand a serious response to the classical question about the ultimate structure of reality. We must know whether the world is so constituted as to make for the realization of our ideals.[44]

In my judgment, the spiritual hopes of both Humanists and "believers" are closely tied to our success in restoring and rehabilitating our conception of God. If we should fail in this important project, I fear that there simply might not be any "God of our children."

[44] See Kaplan, *The Meaning of God,* p. 306 and Morris Cohen, *American Thought: A Critical Sketch,* ed. Felix S. Cohen (Glencoe, Illinois: The Free Press, 1954), p. 297. Cohen, a Naturalist, criticizes the anthropocentrism of Deweyan philosophy, insisting that: "no philosophy which lacks a cosmic outlook can hope to do full justice to the specifically human problem."

THREE

The Supernatural in the Naturalists

WILLIAM M. SHEA

I OFFER HERE a brief study of what the term "supernatural" means to the American naturalists and why they judge it as they do. I shall make special reference to the positions of John Dewey, Frederick J. E. Woodbridge, and John Herman Randall, Jr. I shall distinguish three senses of the term, outline the naturalists' usage, indicate the grounds and limits of their understanding, and suggest the necessity for and direction of further research and dialogue on the issues involved.

1. The Senses of Supernatural

"Supernatural" is used in contemporary liberal, radical, and revisionist theological discourse with invariably pejorative connotations. The term designates what no reasonable, contemporary person would affirm. Paul Tillich changes the spelling to "supranatural" (the change sharpens the issue for him, apparently) and uses it in several contexts with these meanings: revealed truths alien to actual human existence; a rationalistic theory of miracles which interprets them as interruptions of the natural law; the Roman Catholic ontology of grace wherein

I am grateful to the Ludwig Vogelstein Foundation for its support and the Harvard Divinity School for its hospitality during a year of study of the naturalists.

grace becomes a substance; a theory opposed by naturalism, which involves a divine world alongside the natural world; and the attribution of individual substance to the divine.[1] Supernaturalistic theory involves a literalist understanding of Jesus of Nazareth as a divine individual with 'supranatural' powers, and a theological method which takes mythical images literally.[2] The term refers, then, to a realm of being and the action of that realm on a second and lower realm, and a theory which attempts to justify these conceptions as literal descriptions.

Schubert Ogden, a highly regarded contemporary Protestant philosophical theologian, uses the adjective "supernaturalistic" to qualify the theism of the classical Christian theological tradition. That tradition he finds rooted in a Greek metaphysical reading of the religious insights of Scripture. "The supernatural" refers to an order of being unrelated to common human experience, to the superhuman, to the miraculous, to mythological thinking in Rudolf Bultmann's sense.[3]

David Tracy, a Catholic theologian, in a widely read book in fundamental theology, *A Blessed Rage for Order* employs the term as equivalent to fundamentalism.[4] Supernaturalism designates a belief "in a realm of ultimate significance or in a supernatural God who seems, in the end, indifferent to the ultimate significance of our action."[5] The term means classical theism and dogmatism. It can be placed as a dialectical opposite to nontheistic, anti-Christian secularism and to the liberal theological reduction of religion to ethics, esthetics, and pseudo-scientific meaning.[6] For these theologians the term refers to a conception of

[1] Paul Tillich, *Systematic Theology* (Chicago: University of Chicago Press, 3 vols., 1951–1963), 1: 64, 115–17, 258–59, 267; 2: 5–10.

[2] *Ibid.,* 3: 15.

[3] *The Reality of God and Other Essays* (New York: Harper & Row, 1963), pp. 17–25, 46–56; *Christ Without Myth* (New York: Harper & Row, 1961), pp. 26–31.

[4] *A Blessed Rage for Order* (New York: Seabury Press, 1975), p. 145 *n*93.

[5] *Ibid.,* p. 8.

[6] *Ibid.,* p. 33. He is careful to except "the more restricted medieval sense where it is a strictly theoretical concept for thematizing the Christian religion." See 19, *n*40.

God other than their own, to belief in dated theological interpretations of God and the doctrines of Christianity, and to a naive way of reading traditional religious texts.

The Oxford English Dictionary distinguishes adjectival and substantive forms of the word in ordinary discourse. As an adjective, supernatural modifies that which transcends the ordinary course of nature, a realm or system higher than nature, and that which is unnatural, abnormal, or extraordinary ("conseringe the supernaturall teeth, it is sometimes dangerous to drawe them" 1579). As a substantive, it denotes a realm or system of things or being above nature. The first meaning, according to the Random House Dictionary, is what is beyond nature and cannot be explained by natural laws: variously, the characteristics of deity, the preternatural, the unearthly, beings whose origin is considered outside the natural order (God or goblins), and behavior or occurrences caused by the intervention of a god.

There are, then, two distinct and related basic meanings of the term and its cognates in ordinary English, both of which are consistent with the Greek *hypophyseis:* what is beyond the senses, experimental observation, and the sciences; and the miraculous, prodigious, and unnatural. It means, in effect, superior substances and peculiar effects. The meanings are framed in relation to nature and natural, so that one's understanding of one set is dialectically controlled by one's understanding of the other. These popular uses appear to be the ordinary usage of the Christian religious tradition. They are the two senses commented upon by the American naturalists. A third sense will claim our attention below: the technical meaning developed between the eleventh and thirteenth centuries in relation to an equally technical meaning of the terms nature and natural.[7]

[7] J. P. Kenny, "Supernatural," in *The New Catholic Encyclopedia* (New York: McGraw-Hill Publishing Co., 1967) 13: 812–17; Ronald Hepburn, "Nature," in *The Encyclopedia of Philosophy* (New York: McMillan Co., 1967) 5: 454–57.

II. The Two Senses:
Divine Action and Existence

The naturalists speak of the supernatural in two senses: actions and means attributed to divine agency and causality, and the existence of the Divine as an order of being. Actions we may break down into miracles in Locke's sense (a direct intervention in violation of the laws of nature), and religious means or states or contents which can be explained only by reference to the Divine. For the naturalists miracles are not an issue.[8] Hume, it is thought, finished them off. While there is little or no arguing against the "old, old inference to the supernatural from the basis of ignorance" in the case of miracles, the term is applied by them to divine actions which in the Christian tradition might ordinarily be termed mysteries.

Hence, Randall regards the conversion described by Paul and the Augustinian tradition "supernatural and magical," "literally a deification" transforming the Christian into a "supernatural being."[9] Hence, too, Christianity became a "supernatural religion."[10] Such a peculiar view is not, in his opinion, confined to the ancients. It struck the modern world hard in the years after the Great War with the advent of Protestant neo-orthodoxy.[11] Again, the sacraments, especially in the Augustinian and Catholic view of them, "work *ex opere operato,* not *ex opere operantis . . .* by magic, or supernaturally."[12] One is reminded of Tillich's interpretation of Catholic sacramental theology.[13]

---

[8] The same must be said of many theologians these days. On the subject of miracles, there is, from the center to the left wing of contemporary theology, either a reticence bordering on embarrassment or demythologization of texts and claims.

[9] *Hellenistic Ways of Deliverance and the Making of the Christian Synthesis* (New York: Columbia University Press, 1970), pp. 152, 154.

[10] *Ibid.,* p. 156.

[11] *Ibid.,* p. 196.

[12] *Ibid.,* p. 226.

[13] "The theory of *ex opere operato* (by its very performance) makes the sacrament an objective event of a quasi-magical character." Tillich, *A History of Christian Thought* (New York: Harper & Row, 1968), p. 157; also pp. 215–18. This is an inaccurate, if

Dewey uses the term to modify the celebration of the sacraments, persons and literatures, "influences and powers"; the creation of the universe and the special creation of man; the view
that the soul is distinct from and set over against the natural
world; and more generally, any theory accepting such acts and
results.[14]

I regard my father's story, told me as a child, of why the
Banshee will never sing her doom song at the death of a Shea,
to be quaint. It seems that my great-grandfather managed to
snatch away her ghostly comb one night and practiced a bit of
Irish extortion. Supernatural actions and effects are for the naturalists more than quaint; they raise a serious methodological
question. The naturalists, no less than the theistic theologians
who interest themselves in validating such occurrences, are interested in intelligibility. Both are convinced that events are intelligible, and ought not and need not be left unexplained. The
naturalists raise the charge of obscurantism against the supernaturalist, for the supernaturalist offers a nonscientific explanation of the occurrences. Scientific method, for the naturalist, is
the one road to a grounded explanation of events. The objection
is not that unusual events do not take place but that they are in-
adequately explained. We shall find, in our consideration of the
third sense of supernatural, that the naturalists take the occurrence of conversion seriously, while rejecting an explanation of
it by appeal to anything beyond nature.

Supernatural in the second sense, meaning an order of being,
is logically presupposed by the first. The miracle or special
means or truth can be qualified by the adjective or adverb "su-

popular, understanding of the intention of the doctrine. It was meant to express the
constancy of divine love represented in the sacraments and not any "magical" power
of the minister apart from that love. As such, the doctrine is part of what is called
below the third sense of the supernatural.

[14] *A Common Faith* (New Haven, Conn.: Yale University Press, 1934), pp. 1, 2,
12, 14, 30, 54, 69–70; see also John Dewey, "Anti-Naturalism in Extremis," in
Naturalism and the Human Spirit, ed. Y. Krikorian (New York: Columbia University
Press, 1944), p. 12.

pernatural" only on the condition that its cause or origin exists.
The noun form is paramount both for the religious tradition and
for the naturalists. The naturalists' rejection of the existence of
an order of being above or beyond what can reasonably be designated nature is unequivocal and unqualified. As Randall writes,
"naturalism finds itself in thoroughgoing opposition to all forms
of thought which assert the existence of a supernatural or transcendental Realm of Being and which make knowledge of that
realm of fundamental importance to human living." [15] There are
reasons for the rejection.

First, claims for the existence of the transcendent order are
methodologically unfounded. There is no area or realm of existence to which scientific method cannot be extended. [16] The
basic naturalist position is a rejection of all dualisms on the
principle of the inclusive character of scientific method, or
what, in *Naturalism and the Human Spirit* is called the continuity
of analysis. [17] Once cognitional operation is identified with the
methods of the sciences, the affirmation of an ontological dualism of any sort is methodologically impermissible. There are,
in other words, no special truths or peculiar avenues to truth. [18]
If one is tempted to respond—a familiar ploy with theists—that
religious discourse is symbolic and that symbols, while they
may give no literal knowledge of the transcendent, yet point
beyond themselves to the transcendent, the answer is firm and
direct: the referent of symbols must be verifiable in general and
public experience. [19] The transcendent is not in fact or by definition so verifiable. Occasionally the philosophical arguments
for the existence of the transcendent are examined and found

[15] "Epilogue: The Nature of Naturalism," in Krikorian, *Naturalism*, p. 358; see
also Sidney Hook, "Naturalism and Democracy," in *ibid.*, p. 45; and Arthur Danto,
"Naturalism," *Encyclopedia of Philosophy* V pp. 448–450.
[16] Randall, "Epilogue" p. 358.
[17] T. Z. Lavine, "Naturalism and the Sociological Analysis of Knowledge," in
ibid., pp. 184–185, 206–7; and Randall, "Epilogue," *ibid.*, pp. 357–58.
[18] *A Common Faith*, pp. 32–33.
[19] *Ibid.*, p. 41.

logically inept and inadequate to experience.[20] But the issue is fundamentally methodological.

Second, belief in the supernatural is regarded as a violation of the possibilities of an authentic *praxis*. In terms of the text space it takes up and the rhetorical power it delivers, this argument is more important to the naturalists than explicit argument against the existence of the transcendent order of being. Belief in the supernatural is not only nonscientific on this count, but antiscientific as well; not only undemocratic but antidemocratic. Such belief breeds a dogmatic attitude of mind opposed to disinterested inquiry, rejects the procedures central to scientific method, and distracts from the necessary interest in control of the conditions of life by appeal to unverifiable powers.[21] It is a form of obscurantism innately suspicious of the intelligence and cooperative endeavor necessary to the scientific enterprise.[22] In Dewey's words,

> Men have never used the powers they possess to advance the good in life, because they have waited upon some power external to themselves and to nature to do the work they are responsible for doing. Dependence upon an external power is the counterpart of surrender of human endeavor.
>
> The objection to supernaturalism is that it stands in the way of an effective realization of the sweep and depth of the implications of natural human relations. It stands in the way of using the means that are in our power to make radical changes in these relations.[23]

Scientific method, "broadly and generously conceived," provides "the means." The charge here is that belief in the supernatural

[20] Ernest Nagel. "A Defense of Atheism," in *A Modern Introduction to Philosophy*, eds. P. Edwards and A. Pap, 2d ed. (New York: Free Press, 1965), pp. 460–72; and Joseph L. Blau, "God and the Philosophers," in *The Idea of God: Philosophical Perspectives*, eds. E. H. Madden and R. Handy (Springfield, Ill.: C. C. Thomas, 1968), pp. 139–63, 173–78.

[21] *A Common Faith*, pp. 77–78; "Anti-Naturalism," in Krikorian, *Naturalism*, pp. 3, 4, 11.

[22] *A Common Faith*, p. 26.

[23] *Ibid.*, pp. 46, 80.

is inimical to responsible inquiry as well as intellectually unfounded.

Nor can there be any ease in a democracy with traditional
belief. The very meaning of a democracy is responsible public
communication built upon common and natural relations, for it
is the relations extended and improved by public criteria for discussion, which form the basis of democracy. Religious beliefs in
the supernatural stand apart from relations and public criteria,
insofar as they are founded not on public but on secret, and so
undemocratic, procedures, and insofar as they concern the salvation of the individual rather than the advancement of the common good.[24] Occasionally there is reference to the historical
oppressions practiced by religions.[25] Such antidemocratic action
is no accident, for, in Dewey's view, "dependence upon the
absolutist and totalitarian factor . . . is involved in every form
of anti-naturalism."[26] Belief in the supernatural can be explained and is even understandable on psychological grounds
when the means to adjust the often terrifying conditions of existence are not at hand. Human beings project, hypostatize some
value or other, and turn that ideal into an antecedent existence.
Nonetheless, such belief, in the final analysis, represents an
"easy way out" of responsibility and leaves existence exactly as it
was.[27] Democracy and scientific method are at once the means
for improvement of the human condition and ideals worthy of
faith. Supernaturalism is a violation of both. Nor is compromise
possible:

> one has to choose between alternatives. One alternative is dependence
> upon the supernatural; the other, the use of natural agencies. . . . one
> must choose between a continued and ever more systematic *laissez faire*

[24] On the contrast of secret and public and so democratic methods, see *A Common
Faith*, pp. 27, 31–33, 39–40; or an earlier statement of Dewey's, "Religion and Our
Schools," in *Characters and Events* (New York: Holt, Rinehart, & Winston, 1929),
11, p. 512. On individualism, *A Common Faith*, p. 53.

[25] Dewey, "Anti-Naturalism," pp. 6–7.

[26] *Ibid.*, p. 13. Randall softens the judgment considerably in *The Meaning of
Religion for Man* (New York: Harper Torchbooks, 1968), pp. 21, 46.

[27] *A Common Faith*, pp. 21–22, 42–43, 73.

depreciation of intelligence and the resources of natural knowledge and understanding, and the conscious and organized effort to turn the use of these means . . . to larger human purposes.[28]

Belief in the transcendent is intellectually irresponsible and socially corruptive.

Although the reality of the transcendent is consistently denied, the naturalists often attempt to reformulate the problem of devotion and either replace or reinterpret the religious tradition. The hypostatization is reversed: the transcendent real is idealized.[29] The basis for both rejection and reformulation is the empirical principle itself. That principle can be stated in several ways: in terms of experience, whatever is encountered in whatever way is real; and in terms of method, scientific method provides the one access to truth. The latter grows out of the former when one distinguishes between unreflective and reflective experience. The principle excludes an affirmation of what is beyond experience or the reach of scientific method. Thus the transcendent real cannot be reasonably affirmed. But the principle includes an exigence for analysis of all human experience and language. Hence, religious experience, behavior, and language is in need of corrective analysis, and beliefs are in need of reformulation. Naturalism, "scientific method critically aware of its assumptions and implications," does not intend to deny the meaning and value of any human experience or achievement.[30] It may deny the existence of the religious object, but it will attempt a constructive theory of religion. There may be no room for any supernatural entity in naturalism, but "there is room for religion, to be sure, since that is an encountered fact of human experience."[31]

The matter is not settled simply by inquiry into the question

[28]*Ibid.*, pp. 81–82.
[29]The procedure provides at once an exploration of historical religions and a presentation of the possibility of religious devotion without adherence to religions. For a contemporary example of the latter, see Humanist Manifestoes I & II (Buffalo, New York: Prometheus Books, 1973).
[30]*Ibid.*, p. 358.
[31]Randall, "Epilogue," p. 358.

An deus sit? The inquiry can be engrossing, but acceptance and rejection of the existence of the transcendent is settled elsewhere, on nonphilosophical or deeper philosophical grounds.[32] The way in which I have been able best to understand the issues involved is not in terms of the logic of specific arguments but in terms of what the naturalists call the empirical principle. What gives philosophical force to arguments for and against the supernatural is the underlying position on method and on the limits of experience and understanding. This problem has been with us since Hume and Kant, and has not moved considerably since they demolished theological and philosophical rationalism.

The naturalists have formulated their basic position with clarity and without falling into the more egregious blunders of either Hume or Kant. The position marks off a basic philosophical horizon within which a question either does or does not make sense. They have done this through their explication of what knowing is. Their version of what knowing is, most adequately and consistently thematized by Dewey in his pragmatic theory of knowing, excludes not only a positive answer to the question of the supernatural order of being, but makes the question nonsensical in the light of the position on the limits of knowing. While they have profoundly reshaped the cognitional theories of Hume and Kant, they have accepted their strictures on arguments that press "beyond experience." If the naturalists are to be challenged in this matter, one must also challenge the major set of assumptions and explicit theories of Western philosophy of knowledge of the past two hundred years. No mean task, this.

    [32] This is not to say that the argument over arguments is not philosophically instructive, but only that attention to it is a starting point for a more searching analysis of the cognitional theories underlying them. For valuable contemporary Catholic formulations of the problem see William Hill, *Knowing the Unknown God* (New York: Philosophical Library, 1971); Bernard Lonergan, "Natural Knowledge of God," in his *A Second Collection* (Philadelphia: Westminster Press, 1974); and Karl Rahner, *Hearers of the Word* (New York: Herder and Herder, 1969). I regard the arguments on both sides more valuable for what they reveal of the thinkers' world of discourse than for "proof."

Thus for the naturalists existence is a brute fact, a given, needing no explanation. They are consistent and direct on this. Their various systems of metaphysics do not permit the question of an explanation for finite existence. The controlling factor in their metaphysics and natural theologies is their cognitional theory. The metaphysical position that existence calls for no explanation is founded on the cognitional position that human experience and understanding never encounter "existence itself"; that while experience and understanding are intensively unlimited (that is, any question may and indeed should be raised about the existences encountered) they are extensively limited to questions and answers regarding what in fact is encountered. The metaphysical horizon set by pragmatist or instrumentalist or empiricist cognitional theory disallows any question about "existence itself." Regardless of the philosophical fun of examining arguments for and against, one is quickly driven beneath them to a far more basic issue, one put by Bernard Lonergan in the form of three questions: what does one do when one knows, what is meant by knowing, and what does and can one know when one does that? It is here, on the level of basic philosophical horizon, that the discussion must be conducted.

Although the issues are plain enough, the past two hundred years have taught us not to be sanguine about the possibilities of agreement, for agreement means a radical philosophical conversion from one set of assumptions about knowing to another. The unlikelihood of such a conversion, and a consequent end to the dialectic of philosophical horizons, should not forestall a significant advance in another aspect of the disagreement, that is, a sympathetic attempt on each side to enter the horizon of the other, at least in imagination, to "see" what may be there. With this homiletic injunction, I turn to the third sense of "supernatural" to see what supernaturalists and naturalists have seen of it.

III. The Third Sense

I do not intend to engage in a shell game when I introduce a third and arcane meaning of the supernatural. I want to provide a context for discussion with naturalists rather than avoid their closure on debate on the first two meanings. While the naturalists think that reflection on human experience is a reflection on nature and the natural, and that talk of the supernatural is an unwarranted abstraction, a major strand of the Catholic theological tradition, medieval and contemporary, understands reflection on human experience to be reflection on the supernatural. and holds that nature and the natural in the context of such reflection are abstractions. To put it baldly, when the naturalists reflect on human existence in the concrete, they are in fact reflecting on the supernatural. I wish to suggest that this curious overlap may provide a bridge of sorts between quite distinct philosophical and linguistic positions.

We have seen two senses of "supernatural." The first contrasts it as unnatural, or an occurrence beyond the laws of nature, with the expected, the ordinary, or events in accord with the laws of nature. The second intends a distinction between orders of beings, supernatural and natural. The first sense is basically Greek. The second usage of the term entered the Christian tradition in the fifth century with Proclus of Constantinople and Pseudo-Dionysius.[33] The two are the inherited and popular meanings. The third was developed in the medieval debate, in the eleventh to the thirteenth centuries, on the relation between grace and free will.[34] The third sense embodies

---

[33] Kenny, "Supernatural."

[34] For a technical systematic interpretation of the issues and an extensive bibliography of modern work on the question see Bernard Lonergan, *Grace and Freedom* (New York: Herder and Herder, 1971). The major historical studies are: A. M. Landgraf, "Studien zur Erkenntnis des Uebernatürlichen in der Frühscholastik," *Scholastik* 4 (1929): 1–37, 189–220, 352–89; and O. Lottin, "Les définitions du libre arbitre au douzième siècle," *Revue Thomiste* 10 (1927): 104–20, 214–30; "La théorie du libre arbitre pendant le premier tiers du XIIIe siècle," *ibid.*, pp. 350–82; and "Le traité du libre arbitre depuis le chancelier Philippe jusqu'à saint Thomas d'Aquin," *ibid.*, pp. 446–72 and 12 (1929): 234–96.

a strictly theoretical attempt to solve a nest of problems left un-
solved by the Augustinian tradition, such as prevenient grace,
freedom, virtue, merit, sin, initial conversion, and continued
religious *praxis*. I shall try to provide a brief and admittedly un-
technical report of the meaning of the "theorum of the supernatural."[35]

The third sense designates a "new" relationship between the
Creator and creature in addition to the relation "creation." The
latter is a natural relationship. Supernatural in this context
means a new or, better, a different relationship, the self-gift of
the Divine to the creature and what that gift has in fact "done"
to human existence. The theologians called the self-gift and its
effect *gratia Increata* and *gratia creata*. Most often, and technically
in the writings of the Medievals as the debate reached clarity,
"supernatural" refers to the relation between God and Jesus
Christ; to the final union of God and the creature in the *visio
beatifica;* and to the graced life of the Christian in God's love, or
gratia operans et cooperans. It was used as a technical term especially with reference to the last. Moreover, in its theological
meaning "supernatural order" designates not an order of beings
above the natural order but the means by which the Christian
life is lived and its end attained.

In the later post-medieval Scholastic period, Catholic and
Protestant, "supernatural" was often used in what we have
called its popular senses, to mean miracle or an entitative superstructure beyond experience, an external which can only be
known through positive verbal revelation accepted in faith, and
which nowhere appears in human experience. The later Scholastics agree with the naturalists: reflection on human experience
will discover only the natural when it prescinds from revelation.
Theology becomes a deductive reflection on the truths of revelation and in no way includes or is founded on an analysis of ac-

---

[35] Henri de Lubac outlines the medieval development and traces the decline to Car-
dinal Cajetan's sixteenth-century commentary on Aquinas. See De Lubac, *The Mystery
of the Supernatural* (New York: Herder and Herder, 1967).

tual human experience. The medievals, and the theologians who in our time have attempted a retrieval of the medieval world of theory, see it quite differently. For them "supernatural" does not mean "beyond experience" but "unowed," "unexacted." It intends concrete historical existence precisely as it is graced by God; not "supra-natural," where "natural" means ordinary experience, but "supernatural," where natural means what belongs to human experience by right, is owed, exacted, demanded. Since in this view human beings are in fact, always and everywhere, called beyond their right to faith and to the vision of God, ordinary human experience is already supernatural.

"Nature," then, becomes an equally technical concept. It is not the Aristotelian concept of nature, but a remainder-concept, an abstraction for use in dialectical analyses of experience, a *Restbegriff*. It means not the green grass, the earth, the city and all that in them are, but what human life would be did God not give himself in love. The naturalists, then, when they deal with human existence apart from God's entry into it, are dealing in abstraction. For the naturalists, as for the later Scholastic tradition,[36] "nature" and "natural" become designations of the concrete, and "supernatural" becomes the extraordinary, the unnatural, or that which is "beyhond experience." So the vagaries of language.

Many modern commentators and theologians use the term "supernatural" to mean the historical destiny of human beings to the vision of God and the transcendental condition of its possibility in human nature (the latter often called the "supernatural existential" when the concrete order is described). The point they mean to make in their discussion of what is natural and what is supernatural is that God's call and grace are not demanded by the fact of human existence but always remain God's free gift. This transcendental possibility of the vision of God (the *desiderium naturale* of Aquinas) is thoroughly natural.

---

[36]*Ibid.*, pp. 8–11, 18ff, and Karl Rahner, "Nature and Grace," *Theological Investigations* (Baltimore: Helicon Press, 1966) 4: 165–88.

"Transcendental" here means always and everywhere the case in this historical order. Again, the call and grace, the properly supernatural, are neither beyond nature concretely taken nor beyond experience, but unowed, unexacted, unexpected, a gift.

And so, for the classical Christian theological usage, in distinction from some Reformation formulae and from the neoorthodoxy of our own century, natural or ordinary human existence is not fallen and corrupt, since God's gift permeates and is active in all human experience. Fallen and corrupt nature as existence alienated from God is either another abstraction or a justifiable Augustinian rhetorical comment on actual human sin. The duality implied by the supernatural is between two radically concrete possibilities of human existence, and not an alien God over against ordinary experience. The naturalists are rhetorically involved in a struggle with later Scholastic usage and neo-orthodox pessimism. The language of the natural and the supernatural is about gifts: the first, the gift of creation; the second, the gift of grace. The second is a gift which might not have been given but in fact is given in concrete human existence and experience. The point of the language is to make available a systematic expression which protects the utter independence of God, the utter gratuitousness of his love, the fact of human freedom, and a way of interpreting historical existence and its possibilities.

Contemporary theologians, especially those who have engaged in retrieval of the medieval world of theory, have attempted analyses of human experience in the light of the assumption that the supernatural does appear there.[37] Their efforts need not occupy us here. For our purposes we ask two questions: first, is the character of experience which the tradition designates "supernatural" actually natural in the sense that it is the ordinary and common experience of human beings? Sec-

[37] See, for example, Rahne, *Hearers of the Word* and *Theological Investigations* 3: 86–90; 4: 183–84. For a statement in the American context, see Tracy, *Blessed Rage*, pp. 91–131 on religion as a limit-language for limit-experience.

ond, do the naturalists in fact give clues that they recognize
that character and have found ways of expressing it? My answer
to the first is tentatively affirmative. On the second, a reading
of several naturalist texts convinces me that they recognize and
express the supernatural in their own philosophical context.
Among the many texts available I choose a few from Dewey,
Woodbridge, and Randall.

IV. The Supernatural and the Naturalists

The naturalists justifiably pride themselves on attention to
experience. Several of their analyses should, then, prove to be illuminating for theologians interested in a description of the
gifted character of human experience. In their efforts, the naturalists give evidence that they recognize what some theologians
meant and mean by the supernatural. The naturalists, of course,
do not use the term technically; their vocabulary is neither medieval nor theological. But the naturalists and the theologians
sometimes deal with the same experiences and qualities of experience, even though they use quite different vocabularies in
explicating their meaning and structure. Let us begin with John
Dewey.

> A work of art elicits and accentuates the quality of being a whole and
> belonging to the larger, all-inclusive, whole which is the universe in
> which we live. This fact, I think, is the explanation of that feeling of
> exquisite intelligibility and clarity we have in the presence of an object
> that is experienced with esthetic intensity. It explains also the religious
> feeling that accompanies intense esthetic perception. We are, as it
> were, introduced into a world beyond this world which is nevertheless
> the deeper reality of the world in which we live our ordinary experi-
> ences. We are carried out beyond ourselves to find ourselves . . . the
> work of art operates to deepen and to raise to great clarity that sense of
> an enveloping undefined whole that accompanies every normal experi-
> ence. This whole is then felt as an expansion of ourselves. . . . When
> egoism is not made the measure of reality and value, we are citizens of
> this vast world beyond ourselves, and any intense realization of its pres-
> ence with us and in us brings a peculiarly satisfying sense of unity in it-
> self and with ourselves.

Yet every act may carry within itself a consoling and supporting consciousness of the whole to which it belongs and which in some sense belongs to it. With the responsibility for the intelligent determination of particular acts may go a joyful emancipation from the burden for responsibility for the whole which maintains them, giving them their final outcome and quality. . . . Within the flickering inconsequential acts of separate selves dwells a sense of the whole which claims and dignifies them. In its presence we put off our mortality and live in the universal.[38]

These texts and their meaning are not unique in Dewey's work. They need the background of his metaphysics and esthetics if they are to be adequately interpreted. We are interested here in the suggestiveness of his position on experience, quality, and the whole. There is in ordinary experience, in esthetic experience, and in what he calls the religious aspect of experience, a sense of the whole, a sense so important that without it we should be insane.[39] The sense is a discoverable psychological fact and a constant, for we are never free of the experience that "something lies beyond" the "bounding horizon," something he names "an indefinite total setting." It would be difficult to see how such a sense can exist since there is no ontological whole, no whole experienced. But wholeness is a quality rather than a thing in Dewey's view. While it is the content of no single experience or an aggregate of experiences, this indefinite total setting nevertheless qualifies every experience. Dewey's descriptions of unification in esthetic experience are carried over into his work on the religious aspect of experience where they are stripped of their esthetic and take on psychological and moral overtones.[40]

The supernatural emerges in Dewey's language about the qualitative wholeness and unity of human experience, and it

---

[38] Dewey, *Art as Experience* (New York: Capricorn Books, 1958), p. 195; *Human Nature and Conduct* (New York: Modern Library, 1930), p. 302.

[39] *Art as Experience,* p. 194.

[40] The stripping is unfortunate in my view. In wrestling with organized religion and its inherited language Dewey blinked. Had he not, we might have had as superb a book on religion as those he produced during the same decade on metaphysics, theory and practice, esthetics, and logic.

strains his postulated empiricism.[41] It is not primarily in his transformation of the transcendent real into the ideal, nor in his substitutes for religious language (Democracy, Science, Method of Intelligence) that we find the chief point of contact with the theologians. What the theologians have called the supernatural is met, for Dewey, in every human experience and is mediated with particular clarity and power in art and religion. Surely Dewey is not talking about God and the supernatural when he speaks of the whole and the sense of the whole. But the language of the transcendent is in good part about the very quality of experience. Dewey's "undefined totality," the "world beyond," and the whole are his objectification of the transcendent mystery in human experience so variously thematized by the religions. His analysis of the sense of the whole permeating every human experience is perilously close to what theologians call the *Vorgriff,* the natural desire to know God, and the "supernatural existential." A theologian might take him, in his deft descriptions of "adjustment," to be talking about *gratia operans* or saving grace.[42]

Frederick J. E. Woodbridge makes bold to use the term supernatural itself: "Nature as the field where knowledge is pursued presents no problem of her own being or status. As the field where happiness is pursued, her being and status become equivocal. Then a dualism of the natural and the supernatural arises."[43]

There are many points at which Woodbridge's *Essay on Nature* is disconcerting. The style is often cryptic, and borders occasionally on poetry. One can easily dig out formulations of the empirical principle and the metaphysics controlled by it. There

---

[41] For a comment on Dewey's empiricist and romanticist strains, see Virgil Aldrich, "John Dewey's Use of Language," *Journal of Philosophy* 41 (1944): 261–71. Aldrich's point is that Dewey not only analyzes but attempts to induce experience. Aldrich seems to regret the second. I do not.

[42] *A Common Faith,* pp. 14–16.

[43] Frederick J. E. Woodbridge, *An Essay on Nature* (New York: Columbia University Press, 1940), pp. 332–33.

is no naturalistic heresy. Then suddenly one is brought face to face with a nonnaturalist use of the term "supernatural." As he uses it in the fifth chapter and concluding remarks of the *Essay* he means an order of being. It has been transformed in accordance with a naturalist metaphysics, but he insists that the term ought to be used. It emphasizes better than "ideal" the inclusive character of the imaginative projection involved in religious experience.[44]

There are two points to be noted. First, nature itself allows and in a sense calls for an affirmation of the transcendent in the second sense explained above. With its "unfinished look," nature "hints" at it in the pursuit of knowledge; thus, faith in the supernatural order is natural.[45] Second, and closer to our point, while the relation between the *knower* and nature excludes any affirmation of a supernatural order of being, the relation between the *person* and nature reveals a need for that order. The pursuit of happiness, the moral quest, breeds a dualism. We need security, "justification," "kinship with the Divine," and we find them in One who judges and in worship.[46] We are not only knowers whose disinterested inquiry is met in the knowledge nature provides; we are persons who find nature superseded and subordinated, "incidental to a wholly different scheme of things,"[47] where the meaning and value of the pursuit of happiness is supported and justified; we seek a "supernatural knowledge."

The sense of the supernatural for Woodbridge arises because the human quest for meaning and value, and the question of the worthwhileness of the quest, will not be stilled by any answer nature can deliver. It is precisely this kind of "question" and its "answer" in faith in what is beyond nature that the theologians

---

[44] He excludes the supernatural in the first sense entirely in a brief section on "superstition"; *ibid.*, pp. 326–30.

[45] *Ibid.*, pp. 282–85.

[46] *Ibid.*, pp. 279–80, 306.

[47] *Ibid.*, pp. 289, 332–33, 336–37.

term supernatural, or an experience of spirit and grace. As regards an analysis of the experience, the theologians are in agreement with Woodbridge: not only does nature wear an unfinished look, but our quest cannot be stilled and can find no answer in what we cognitively conquer but only in what conquers us.

John Herman Randall, Jr.'s works on religion evidence a solid grasp of the history of Christian thought and theology. He, like Santayana, shows deep interest in understanding a religious tradition and grappling in a sympathetic and detailed way with the functioning of religious language and its peculiar symbols. He holds to the empirical principle in the cognitive order, but makes out a case that, after all, religious vision is a kind of knowledge:

> We have now come somewhat closer to a statement, not of all the many things religion does for man, but of what the essential religious function is. On the one hand, religion is a practical commitment to certain values. Religious symbols serve to strengthen that kind of religious commitment, to strengthen men's 'faith,' to intensify and enhance and clarify a practical commitment to one's ultimate concern. On the other hand, religion is the vision of the Divine; awareness of the religious dimension of experience and of the world, the awareness of the 'order of splendor,' and the fostering and clarification of that awareness. . . . But men are in the end saved, I am convinced, by vision rather than by works.[48]

Randall succeeded in bringing Dewey's concepts of unification and his position on the esthetic character of experience to bear on the problem of religious conversion and practice. While insisting with Dewey on the natural conditions of both conversion and practice, he states the character of the ideal as transcendent in more than moral and social terms. And he corrects Dewey's individualistic understanding of the religious aspect of experience, transferring it to a communal context. With Wood-

[48] Randall, *The Role of Knowledge in Western Religion* (Boston: Starr King Press, 1958), p. 121.

bridge he attempts to formulate and use a "religious language," another set of symbols to clarify what inherited symbols intend. With Woodbridge he accepts the necessity of personal language in prayer.[49] He situates religious conversion in a concrete context, connecting it with the problem of evil and sin, and is able to render religion intelligible in terms of this context. What religion offers, he claims, is a solution to the problem of evil in its devotion to the transcendent, and he knows that for the religious person this is only possible in the "presence" of a gracious God: "How, then, can a man live with the evils nature forces on him? How can he live with the evil he has allowed to grow up in the hearts of his fellow man? How can a man live with himself? It is to these tragic problems that the most profound religious insight has attempted to discover the answer."[50] In fact, he formulates with clarity the very Augustinian position which led to the medieval development of the theorem of the supernatural: "Grace is, for Augustine, first a 'free gift' to those on whom God chooses to bestow it. God's choice is based on no human condition or effort on man's part; it is entirely undeserved. It is not given as the reward for any merit of righteousness in man, but is, on the contrary, the cause and necessary condition of all human merit. Second, grace is 'prevenient': the beginning of the process must come from God, not from man himself, even the desire to pray for God's grace."[51] The points at which Randall's analyses are of particular interest to the theologian are his extension of Dewey's theory of unification to the interpretation of historical religious practice; his extension of Dewey's esthetics to the interpretation of religion as an art; his contextualization of religious conversion in the experience of evil and sin; and his recognition of a new linguistic horizon created by religious conversion (his "order of

---

[49]*Ibid.*, pp. 116–21, 128–29; and *The Meaning of Religion for Man*, pp. 86–87.

[50]*The Meaning of Religion for Man*, p. 52. On the problem of evil, see as well pp. 47–48, 82–83, 99–102.

[51]*Hellenistic Ways of Deliverance*, p. 219.

splendor"). Dewey's moralism is corrected. Randall is serious when he maintains that salvation comes by vision rather than by works, even though, once one has seen, works must follow. One could hardly hope for a defter statement of the working of *gratia operans et cooperans.*

V. Conclusion

The naturalists analyze, each in his own way, what the theologians term the supernatural as a character or quality of life lived. They also correct and reinterpret the order of being called the supernatural. Joseph Blau, for example, understands God to be the noun form of the "adverbial concept of acting continuously in a creative manner."[52] Dewey, in what some thought a Homeresque nod, used the term to designate the active relation between the actual and the ideal. Woodbridge was happy to speak of God and the supernatural in a plausible, if "irrational," dualism. And Randall proposes a symbolic reconstruction in terms of an "order of splendor" manifesting itself through nature and human action. The question may be asked, Why bother? What is at stake here? Surely these men cannot be accused of sentimental attachment to traditional modes of speaking. What are they up to?

My conviction is that their efforts in the area of reformulation or reinterpretation, as halting and inadequate as they are from the theological perspective, rest on their common conviction that the supernatural in the third and experiential sense of the term is a fact of experience and must be spoken of. The third sense is basic not only to the theological tradition but to a naturalistic theory of human life. It does, of course, make a great deal of difference how grace is explicated theoretically, and the how depends on the philosophical horizon of the thinker and the resources of his or her linguistic tradition. There is the clash

[52] *The Idea of God,* p. 159.

of horizons, and so a clash of interpretations, but the clash does not eliminate the possibility and need for philosophical and theological analysis of the fact in common human experience.

The naturalists represent only one among several methodological possibilities for the correction and restatement of the tradition and of contemporary religious language. Religious communities and their languages continue, so far as I can see, on their merry way, with their symbols, rites, creeds, and structures, and with their ever-developing and ever-shifting theologies offering to make intelligible what they do. The naturalists have not succeeded, if such was ever their hope, in educating religiously committed persons out of their communities or out of their many nonnaturalistic theological interpretations of their religious language and practice. Symbols continue to function, interpretations continue to be formulated which negate the naturalists' negations and strictures. There is no need to plead for a reopening of the question of the supernatural. The question is there because the experience is there and insistently demands commentary. Grace and the Divine are facts of experience. On this the theologians and the naturalists can agree. On interpretations they do not. That each learn the language and "world of discourse" of the other is a necessity. That there be a common exploration of the facts and texts is also necessary; and here there is no easy division into philosophy and theology, or "the study of religion" and theology. The clash of horizons of interpretations will go on, but here something of the "temper of humility" so often mentioned by Randall would be helpful, along with a recognition in this context of the significance of Professor Blau's words: "Unfortunately, most of us have horizons that are in one way or another limited; our vision can be no more inclusive than our horizon. The more limited that is, by our circumstances, the less inclusive will be our vision."[53]

[53] *Ibid.*, p. 174.

FOUR

The Esthetic, the Religious, and the Natural

JAMES A. MARTIN, JR.

Jonathan Edwards

JONATHAN EDWARDS was the first major spokesman in America for the tradition which relates religion to the arts. Edwards, of course, was not a naturalist, and many would not think of him as an empiricist. Perry Miller is correct, however, when he says that "Although he is customarily represented as an archreactionary Calvinist, Edwards is properly to be described as the first American empiricist; yet from the beginning he . . . recognized that empiricism meant a living relation between man and the world, not the dead schematic rationalism from which William James was later to attempt to rescue it."[1] William Clebsch also has correctly placed Edwards in a spiritual tradition which runs from Emerson to William James and John Dewey, which he characterizes as basically esthetic.[2] Certainly it is the case that for Edwards the concepts of beauty and sensibility provide media of translation between the experiences of history, nature, and God.[3]

---

[1] Perry Miller, ed., *Images or Shadows of Divine Things,* by Jonathan Edwards (New Haven: Yale University Press, 1948), p. 20.

[2] William Clebsch, *American Religious Thought* (Chicago: University of Chicago Press, 1973).

[3] See Roland Delattre, *Beauty and Sensibility in the Thought of Jonathan Edwards* (New Haven: Yale University Press, 1968).

Edwards was heir to the tradition of Cambridge Platonism, which had informed much Puritan reflection in philosophical theology, and especially to the logic of Peter Ramus, which had emphasized *techne* in the logical operations of dialectic and judgment over the more structured and hierarchical logic and metaphysics of the Scholastics. He was, however, also captivated by Newtonian science and its implications as philosophically expressed by Locke and other British empiricists. His task as Christian theologian was to work through the implications of the new worldview for a consistent and persuasive statement of Christian belief. In this task he was aided by the rhetorical tradition employed by Puritan divines, in which the notions of types and tropes were used to articulate virtually literal identifications of divine patterns and actions with historical and natural events on the one hand, or fanciful aids to allegorical understanding of divine transactions on the other.

His employment of this tradition was, however, as radically innovative as the intellectual situation in which he found himself was radically new. "To Edwards," says Miller, "we may go so far as to suggest, his 'Images of Divine Things' was what the *Preludes* was to Wordsworth, a secret and sustained effort to work out a new sense of the divinity of nature and the naturalness of divinity. He was obliged by the logic of his situation to undertake an investigation of the visible world as though no man had seen it before him." [4] The result, with respect to mode of articulation, was *Images or Shadows of Divine Things.* In it he conceives of "naked ideas" as meaning much the same thing as Coleridge would later mean by "imagination," though he relegated what he called "imagination" to the role of what Coleridge and others would call "fancy." The point was to provide a base and medium for knowlege of the divine which was at least as sensory as the sense-data or "impressions" of natural science, and which would provide apprehension of the divine as

[4] Miller, *Images,* p. 18.

the ultimate context of nature and society—of what another essayist in this volume might call "the supernatural in the natural."[5] This mode of apprehension he called "sensibility," and
the paradigmatic form of its object and expression he called
"Beauty."

Within beauty he distinguished "primary" and "secondary"
types. Primary beauty he defined as "Being's cordial consent to
being," and this is theologically identified as God. Special notice must be taken of the adverbial/verbal character of the definition. Primary beauty is neither static nor substantial, in the
classic sense of the latter term. It is beautifying—essentially the
activity of pouring out into the natural and human realms that
creative ordering which may result in beatitude. Theologically
speaking, its work is the work of grace. Furthermore, it is essentially social: internally it is the loving sociality of the Trinity; externally it is the work of that grace which may lead
human society into that perfect (perfectly beautiful) community
which has traditionally been called "the City of God." The transcendence and sovereignty of God, so powerfully celebrated by
Edwards, is the transcendent power of His love understood as
beauty. His transcendence consists in "His having His beauty in
Himself," and in His being "the sum and comprehension of all
excellence."[6] His immanence, in turn, consists of His "presence" as "immediately related to everything that has being."

His immanence is reflected in what Edwards called "secondary Beauty," which consists of all harmonious forms to be discovered in nature and cherished in society. These are discerned
through "natural sensibility." Sensibility contains elements of
speculative cognition and of practical engagements, but its co-
hering agent is affection. We are affected, says Edwards,
through our desires and aversions, our loves and hates. So motivated and disposed, we "naturally" adhere to that which is our

---

[5] William Shea, "The Supernatural in the Naturalists," chapter 3 above.
[6] Jonathan Edwards, *The Nature of True Virtue* (Ann Arbor: University of Michigan
Press, 1960), no. 15, Quoted in Delattre, *Beauty and Sensibility*, p. 164.

apparent good. As natural sensibility is educated toward more intelligent discernments, the range and richness of our apparent good are broadened and deepened. Esthetically we may move from ill-formed taste for the merely agreeable to deeper perception of more complex forms. Morally we may move from blind self-love to perception of the "amiableness" of mutuality in social relationships. Natural sensibility, however, is incapable of providing that consummatory experience which enables the self to perceive and participate in the Primary Beauty which is God. For this a transformed and transforming "spiritual sensibility" is required, and this is the religious experience which provided Edwards with his basic confidence and the motivation for his evangelical activities. If man's chief end is to glorify God (interpreted in esthetic terms by Edwards) and to *enjoy* Him forever, he must have that transforming experience which renders acquiescence in the divine will delightful and enjoyment of the divine beauty salvific.

Edwards, then, espoused an empiricism which was both experiential and experimental. Experience, for him, includes affective and volitional elements as genuinely and fundamentally as it includes cognitive elements. Consummatory experience would be an appropriate blending of these through the agency of the affective. The "religious affections" are those which add to apprehension of the divine in the secondary beauty of natural and social harmonies the culminating and transforming experience of "Being's cordial consent to being," which is primary Beauty. We see in Edwards some basic themes, theologically expressed, which appear later in some forms of naturalistic humanism: an insistence on the unity of the real in its broadest reaches; an insistence on the dynamic character of the natural and the social, or the social-in-the-natural; and an employment of basically esthetic idioms and concepts for the expression of those forms of experience which are fundamentally orienting, idealizing, and transforming—in other words, those experiences which are religious.

George Santayana

Not all thinkers who would call themselves naturalists or humanists, however, would exhibit in their thought the specific functioning of the religious as esthetic which had been adumbrated in the supernaturalism of Edwards. George Santayana brought to his reflection on religion and philosophy a background from a different religious tradition, and a metaphysics which was derived from a much different reading of the implication of scientific inquiry for the understanding of nature. Materialism, he felt, is the only metaphysical view which is warranted by fidelity to scientific inquiry for knowledge of what is the case. The materialism, in turn, is atomistic in the tradition of Lucretius and Democritus, and mechanistic in the tradition of many empiricist interpretations of Newton. That which is ontologically ultimate, and therefore ultimate in power, is nonsentient and nonteleological—a "great engine of mud and fire." In its arbitrary ways it has, for a time, come into conditions which produce and sustain the human. But it did not have the human in mind, and it will go its own ways when the human has disappeared. Any appraisal of and prescription for human good must, therefore, keep this fundamental metaphysical fact in mind.

The human, nevertheless, must be understood and cherished for what it is, in its own terms. Nature is such that, for a time at least, the human has appeared as that which is endowed with imagination and is capable of the "Life of Reason." Not only can men know something—though not much—of the character and power of nature which produces and sustains them; they can also envision ideas and ideals which are of timeless value precisely because they have no ultimate ontological power. The capacity to envision and to live in the presence of the ideal is spirituality. Like Edwards, Santayana could say that spirituality requires spiritual sensibility—the capacity to discern and to celebrate the ideal factors in experience and nature. Like Edwards, too, he could say that man's chief end is to enjoy the unified ideals to which spiritual vision provides access.

Unlike Edwards, however, he would maintain that man's espousal and enjoyment of things of the spirit can effect no enduring change in either nature or society. The appearance of spiritual beings in nature is fortuitous, and is not indicative of the basic character of nature. Societies which provide harmonious relations of what is known to what is hoped for are those which are most stable and satisfying. But there are and have been many forms of such societies, and there is no reason to believe that human effort can bring about a culminating superior and enduring form.

This is no reason, however, for man not to enjoy that which is spiritual. And religions and the arts provide the major media for that enjoyment. Religion is rooted in natural piety, and it expresses itself in charity and spirituality. Piety is reverent attachment to the sources of our being, and the steadying of life by that attachment. What are the sources of our being? Family, obviously—so filial piety is a natural ingredient of natural piety; ancestors; country; humanity at large and the whole natural cosmos. The farther piety is removed from the immediate sources of our being, however, the less intense and less warranted it is. Patriotism is noble, and political loyalties, like religious loyalties, need specifics of time and place for rootedness which can be nourishing. There is an extended sense in which humanity at large is an appropriate object of piety—not, however, humanity as it actually is. Piety to mankind as it is "must be three-fourths pity." One can respect specific human virtues, but the ennobling factors among men are *aspirations,* not achievements. The aspirations, in turn, are related to that spiritual world which is ideal, and ontologically ineffective. Consideration of piety to the cosmos underscores the latter point. There is a sense in which respect for that which has produced us is appropriate. But we should not imagine that such respect is recognition of a cosmic purpose, or that the cosmos is either mindful or needful of our respect.

As fellow spiritual creatures, however, we can recognize fellow creaturehood and can learn to respect the aspirations of others along with our own. To practice such respect is to embody the virtue of charity. The universe, however, is no more supportive of charitable relations, in the long run, than it is supportive of other relations which may occur in its nonsentient ways. Santayana could not agree with Edwards that nature as well as society could conspire in movement toward a City of God characterized by the "consent" which is a reflection of "Being's cordial consent to being." It is therefore primarily in the life of spirituality itself that piety and religion find their most authentic, and authenticating, expression.

To be spiritual is to live in view of the ideal—so to live that whether one live or die it is unto the ideal. Religions provide visions of the ideal world; their function is to "provide another world" in which to live. Their power and their importance derives from their other-worldliness. And the chief expressions of religions' ideal worlds are poetic and mythological. Through the medium of myth ordinary folk may perceive the ideal in moving vividness and may order their lives accordingly. Unfortunately, however, for many people acceptance of the power of the ideal entails a belief that the matters narrated in the basic stories of religion are literally true—that they are faithful accounts of that which has ultimate ontological power. Indeed, Santayana at times seems to say that only if the stories of religion are taken as literally true can they have religious power. Men need such stories, yet taking them in the way which makes them most powerful all too easily results in superstition and fanaticism.[7] It is only when the Christian story is understood as "the Christian epic," and when the power of Christ is seen to reside in "The *Idea* of Christ in the Gospels," that men and women may live within the Christian story without illusion, superstition, or fanaticism.

This is as much as to say that it is only when religious articulations of the ideal are understood as esthetic that religion can

[7] George Santayana, "Reason in Religion," in *The Philosophy of Santayana,* ed. Erwin Edman (New York: The Modern Library, 1942), pp. 179ff.

find its appropriate place within "The Life of Reason." The arts are the other principal forms of spiritual expression, and it may be that it is only when religion is seen as an art, as regards both mode of apprehension and mode of expression of the ideal, that it can play its appropriate role in human affairs. Santayana never quite says this, though, as we shall see, some who have been influenced by him do. Santayana himself seems to leave religion in an ambiguous position, as regards both its character and its role. In one of his most quoted statements on the subject he says that "Poetry is called religion when it intervenes in life, and religion, when it merely supervenes upon life, is seen to be nothing but poetry."[8] Religion is poetry which is believed—but the belief is too often corrupted by literalness and by the assumption that its intervention in life may alter the basic character of things enduringly. Poetry, on the other hand, may straightforwardly provide "another world to live in," without the illusion that there is some other world which is more important because it is more powerful. This is not to suggest that Santayana's view of the role of the arts results in a "mere estheticism." He would counsel men to do what they can through the art of science to know, and perhaps, for a while, to change existing arrangements of nature. He would also counsel them to live in charity with their fellows, and to respect and mutually to encourage aspirations toward the spiritual realm. He is also aware that the materials and the forms of art are felicitous, but temporary, expressions of nature. Yet if the chief end of man is—and it should be—happiness, then it must also be acknowledged that:

> If happiness is the ultimate sanction of art, art in turn is the best instrument of happiness. In art more directly than in other activities man's self-expression is cumulative and finds an immediate reward: for it alters the material conditions of sentience so that sentience becomes at once more delightful and more significant. In industry man is still

[8] George Santayana, *Interpretations of Poetry and Religion* (New York: Scribner's, 1900), p. v.

servile, preparing the materials he is to use in action. In action itself, though he is free, he exerts his influence on a living and treacherous medium and sees the issues at each moment drift farther and farther from his intent. In science he is an observer, preparing himself for action in another way, by studying its results and conditions. But in art he is at once competent and free: he is creative. He is not troubled by his materials, because he has assimilated them and may take them for granted; nor is he concerned with the chance complexion of things in the actual world, because he is making the world over, not merely considering how it grew or may consent to grow in the future. Nothing, accordingly, could be more delightful than genuine art, nor more free from remorse and the sting of vanity. Art springs so completely from the heart of man that it speaks to him in his own language; it reaches, nevertheless, so truly into the heart of nature that it co-operates with her, becomes a parcel of her creative material energy, and builds by her instinctive hand. If the various formative impulses afoot in the world never opposed stress to stress and made no havoc with one another, nature might be called an unconscious artist. In fact, just where such a formative impulse finds support from the environment, a consciousness supervenes. If that consciousness is adequate enough to be prophetic, an art arises. Thus the emergence of arts out of instincts is the token and exact measure of nature's success and of mortal happiness.[9]

Santayana was both a philosopher and a poet. Both his poetry—and his other literary work—and his philosophy focus the religious in close proximity to the esthetic. At times he seems virtually to identify them; at other times he seems to distinguish them, to the advantage of the one or the other, but usually to the advantage of the esthetic. There are passages in which he seems to say that both the religious and the esthetic may make a difference in social affairs through exemplification of ideals which have social consequences. Frequently, however, there is a note of irony in his celebration of the esthetic, and of resignation in his appreciation of religion. Seldom does he speak of that esthetic category which may be closest to the distinctively religious category, the holy—namely, the sublime. In this connection we may be reminded of the comment of James C. Meredith in his edition of Kant's *Critique of Aesthetic Judg-*

[9] Santayana, "Reason in Art," in Edman, *Philosophy of Santayana,* pp. 255–59.

ment: "the sublime may be said to be the point of divergence of art and philosophy. Hence it may mark the point at which philosophy is in danger of becoming mere poetry, and poetry in danger of becoming mere philosophy."[10]

John Dewey

From the beginning of his philosophical career, Dewey abjured dichotomies such as that between nature—or matter—and spirit, which informed the thinking of Santayana. Yet he, like Santayana, saw the religious in experience as closely related, in form and import, to the esthetic. In his earlier days it was a form of Hegelianism which, as he put it, liberated him from intellectual, moral, and religious dichotomies which had troubled him in his youth. In Hegelian philosophy he found both a point of settledness and wholeness and a dynamic view of the processes of nature and history. For a time he could translate his New England Protestant religious concerns into the idiom of Hegelian idealism. Indeed, a convincing case has been made for a continuing impact of this philosophy on his ethical thought, which has been described as a form of ethical idealism.[11] But it was the impact of James's "radical empiricism," a fuller appropriation of the significance of evolution, especially in its biological forms, and the social philosophy of Mead and others which moved him away from his earlier Hegelianism into his own distinctive form of naturalistic humanism, or humanistic naturalism.

He always insisted that both terms, "nature" and "man," should be used in any summary characterization of his philosophical position. He felt that many forms of humanism are

[10] James C. Meredith, ed., *Kant's Critique of Aesthetic Judgment* (New York: Oxford University Press, 1911), p. xcviii. For a judicious exposition and appraisal of Santayana's views on art and religion see Willard E. Arnett, *Religion and Judgment* (New York: Appleton-Century-Crofts, 1966), pp. 161ff.

[11] See Steven C. Rockefeller, "John Dewey: The Evolution of a Faith," chapter 1 above.

truncated, in that they fail to recognize the rootedness of man in nature and his dependence on natural processes. He also felt that some forms of naturalism are too narrow or reductionistic, in that they fail to recognize the distinctively human as being as truly revelatory of nature as are nature's nonhuman manifestations. Like Jonathan Edwards, and unlike Santayana, he saw the human and the natural as bound together in an ongoing process which may sustain indefinite progress toward ideal goals. Like Edwards, also, he described consummatory experience of the ideal in nature in esthetic terms. And, like Edwards, he sought to articulate a responsible view of the nature of the divine in terms of the divine in nature. As he understood the supernaturalist tradition represented by Edwards, however, he believed that that tradition impoverished and enervated the full possibilities of a common faith in carefully discriminated ideals translated into social action and realization—through God as the active relation of the ideal to the actual, if one chose to speak theistically.

Like Edwards, Dewey understood experience to be the ongoing process of all of man's doings and undergoings. It is not preeminently cognitive or volitional or affective, but it is all of these to the extent that it exhibits itself to be so. The character of its ongoingness is frequently described by Dewey in biological idiom, as a process of movement from stability to problematic situation to resolution. The process is inherently social, entailing interaction between organism and environment, including both other organisms and nature in its inorganic aspects. Experience is in and of nature; whatever is experienced is natural, and nature is all that experience discloses nature to be. Cognition occurs when human organisms, encountering problematic situations, imagine ways out and experiment with their implementation. Scientific method is paradigmatic for the cognitive process, in that it operates with clearly defined hypotheses to be tested by carefully chosen instrumentalities. The movement is from the problematic to a resolution, which in turn becomes the basis for further inquiry. The moment of resolution, however, may engender what Moritz Schlick has called "the joy of cognition," which has esthetic overtones.[12]

Moral reflection, also, moves from the problematic conflict of desires toward undiscriminated ends, through intelligent discrimination between ends-in-view and ends desired as endings, as related to the means inextricably involved in the achievement of those ends, to the resolution of moral judgment. In general, those ends are to be chosen which best facilitate the indefinite enrichment of the experience of the largest number of moral agents, in carefully discriminated situations. Like scientific inquiry, moral inquiry and action cannot rest in any achieved truth or good. Yet the good may be enjoyed as an integral configuration of nature as experienced.

The esthetic in experience is that in experience which makes any experience *an* experience. In experience as esthetic means and ends, material and form, are experienced as discriminable wholes, whose apprehension is intrinsically enjoyable. Experience as esthetic is both consummatory and paradigmatic. Therefore, Dewey could affirm that the idea of art is "the greatest intellectual achievement in the history of humanity"[13] and that "art—the mode of activity which is charged with meanings capable of immediately enjoyed possession—is the complete culmination of nature."[14]

Like Edwards, Dewey could affirm that apprehension of the esthetic is a matter of sensibility—though he preferred the unadorned term "sense," because "sense, as meaning so directly embodied in experience as to be its own illuminated meaning, is the only signification that expresses the function of sense organs when they are carried to full realization."[15] But does Dewey see sensibility as the mode of apprehension of the divine?

[12] Moritz Schlick, "The Foundation of Knowledge," in *Logical Positivism,* ed. A. J. Ayer (Glencoe, Ill.: The Free Press, 1959), p. 223.

[13] John Dewey, "The Live Creature and Ethereal Things," in *Art as Experience* (New York: Capricorn Books, 1958), p. 25.

[14] John Dewey, *Experience and Nature* (New York: W. W. Norton Co., 1929), p. 358.

[15] Dewey, "The Live Creature and Etherial Things," in *Art As Experience,* p. 22.

I believe that he does, though when he does so he places sensibility in the biological idiom of adaptation and accommodation. This occurs in *A Common Faith,* at the point where he attempts to characterize the distinctively religious in experience. There are, he has said, transactions of man in nature which result in the adaptation of natural means and conditions to human ends. There are also transactions which involve the accommodation of man to natural conditions which cannot be adapted to his ends. The broadest and deepest accommodation relates to the principal exigencies of life. In this act (of sensibility?) there occurs a fundamental orientation, in relation to which the major imponderables and their consequences are perceived as "settled." This is not mere Stoic resignation. It is, says Dewey, "outgoing and glad."

Edwards might have described it as delight in Being's cordial consent to being. It is voluntary, "but that does not mean that it depends on a particular resolve or volition. It is a change *of* will conceived as the organic plenitude of our being, rather than any special change *in* will." Edwards had said that will is a matter of the *inclination* of the self toward its apparent good. This basic orientation effected through religious sensibility may, in turn, become the foundation for ongoing adaptation of those matters which can be changed, in nature as social, in the service of those ideals whose actualization would result in a more generous and harmonious social order—Edwards might have called it "The City of God."

Dewey describes the distinctively religious in experience in these words: "there is a composing and harmonizing of the various elements of our being such that, in spite of the changes in the special conditions that surround us, these conditions are also arranged, settled, for us." [16] Composing . . . harmonizing . . . settling . . . consummatory . . . inclusive . . . lasting . . . providing perspective and meaning for ongoing venture.

[16] John Dewey, *A Common Faith* (New Haven: Yale University Press, 1960, [1934]), p. 12.

These are terms which are appropriate for description of both the esthetic and the religious in experience.

Unlike Santayana, Dewey believes that the religious, esthetically described, may provide the basis for valuable and enduring changes in the human condition. The faith which it engenders is faith in intelligence as the medium of "active relation of ideal and actual." The ideals which are envisioned are as real as all things natural, because they are rooted in imagination, which is a function of the natural as human. Their actualization requires intelligent appraisal of means and ends in relation to carefully discriminated situations. The possibility of realizations, in turn, entails a sense of grace in the form of the unmerited favor of those who have aspired and labored before us, and of those whose current aspirations and labors enable and sustain our own. The sense of grace is also a sense of humility engendered by the realization that nature sustains and implements all ideals, and all actions in their behalf, and that nature is more than we can imagine. Nature is neither Santayana's "great engine of mud and fire" nor Edwards' locus of a beauty which is only secondary to that primary beauty which is supernatural. In nature itself, those with eyes to see may discern the operations of being's cordial consent to being.

John Herman Randall, Jr.

John Herman Randall, Jr. has been informed in his religious sensibility both by the natural piety of Santayana and by the common faith espoused by John Dewey. Like Santayana, he has prized a sense of spirituality which he describes as discernment of "the order of splendor in things." Like Dewey, he abjures a dichotomy between the realm of spirit and the realms of nature, and sees the fruit of religious devotion in intelligent social action. Perhaps more than Dewey, however, he cherishes religious *vision* as religion's fundamental gift to the human spirit. And not only does Randall identify the esthetic as the category closest to the holy; he understands religion itself to be an art.[17] The emphasis, as in Peter Ramus whose work formed part of the context for the work of Jonathan Edwards, is on *techne,* and on the arts as *technai.* As regards cognition, this means that "religious truth" is not so much a matter of "knowing that" as it is a matter of "knowing how." It is knowing how to discern the order of splendor in things, just as the work of other arts is knowing how to discern and enhance the significance of things as apprehended in line and color, sound and form. Neither painting, poetry, music, religion, nor any of the arts teach us *that* anything is so. "They do not explain the world in the sense of accounting for it; rather they 'explain' it in the sense of making plain its features. But they certainly teach us *how to do* something better. . . . The work of the painter, the musician, the poet, teaches us how to use our eyes, our minds, and our feelings with greater power and skill. It teaches us how to become more aware both of what is and of what might be, in the world that offers itself to our sensitivity. It shows us how to discern unsuspected qualities with which that world, in cooperation with man, can clothe itself. . . . Is it otherwise with the prophet and saint? They too can do something to us, they too can effect changes in ourselves and in our world. They teach us how to see what man's life in the world is, and what it might be. . . . They enable us to see and feel the religious dimension of our world better, the 'order of splendor,' and of man's experience in and with it. They teach us how to find the Divine; they show us visions of God."[18]

This means that the appropriate language of religion is the language of myth and symbol, and that the appropriate nonlinguistic expressions of the religious are those expressions of the nonverbal arts which articulate basic orientation and vision. This does not mean that there is no place in religion for respon-

[17]John Herman Randall, Jr., *The Role of Knowledge in Western Religion* (Boston: Starr King Press, 1958), pp. 124ff.
[18]*Ibid.,* p. 129.

sible attempts to relate the "know-how" of ritual expression of myth to the "know-that" of scientific inquiry interpreted in a comprehensive metaphysical scheme. Indeed, Randall offers an impassioned *Apologia pro Theologia Rationali* as a sorely needed defense against intellectual obscurantism, esthetic sentimentalism, and moral fanaticism.[19] It may be suggested, however, that theology thus conceived is better understood as an art than as a science, if the meaning of science is derived from natural science.[20]

In any event, the relation of the esthetic to the religious discerned and celebrated in a philosophical tradition which is represented on the American scene by figures as diverse and as similar as Edwards, Santayana, Dewey, and Randall is a relation whose further investigation and discrimination, as regards the history of religions, may lead to a theory of religion more adequate for the interpretation of phenomena in a variety of traditions, cultures, and historical epochs than any theory currently in use.

[19]*Ibid.*, pp. 135ff.
[20]See J. A. Martin, Jr., "Theology: Science or Art?" *The Journal of Religion*, 32, no. 1 (January 1952): 8–17.

TWO
Perspectives on the History of Judaism

Introduction

In the beginning, Judaic Studies was not a part of the university curriculum. Old Testament, Biblical Hebrew, and Semitic languages were taught, but not Judaic Studies. In the beginning, too, it was historical method that became the battleground between modern and traditional Jewish culture. It was historical method, and not the innovations of modern science, that challenged and shaped the nature of Jewish identity in the modern world. As historical method developed, it generated three modes of study: a disembodied contextualism which sought to identify the roots and sources of texts and events without any interpretation of their wider meaning, a tendentious historicism which sought to justify changes in modern Jewish culture by studying the development of doctrines and institutions, and a tendentious culturalism that sought to define Jewish identity in terms of the Jewish people and its historic national culture. Because these modes of study were not part of the university curriculum, they were left largely in communal hands. As a result, while the work often showed great competence, it was almost always institutionally related and hence the tendentious trends grew in strength. With the establishment of the great theological seminaries of the West and the university system of the modern Jewish state, these modes of study have become, with some exceptions, deeply ensconced in modern Jewish culture.

In time, however, Judaic Studies came to be regarded as a vital part of the university curriculum. At first, they fit into the language and literature disciplines and later into history. In very recent times, these modes of study have been seen to fit easily into the "interdisciplinary" structure.

But after all, Judaism had been a religion for the first three-and-one-half millennia of its existence. What was now to happen to Judaism as a religion? Was there no approach to the data of the Jewish tradition from within the discipline of religion? Herein, lies the importance of Professor

Blau. Nearly alone, he insisted that Judaism had to be considered as a religion in the university setting and that it was properly the congery of disciplines that form the field of religious studies that was best suited to the study of that data. Dr. Blau published books and articles dealing with the history-of-religions analysis of Judaism, and he encouraged generations of students in these disciplines. His analysis ranged over the entire sweep of Jewish cultural history, but his approach was always from within his discipline.

It is appropriate, therefore, that each of the contributors to this section has chosen a different aspect of Jewish culture and has applied his or her own methods to that data. We demonstrate the variety of that culture and of the methods used within the field to analyze that culture. In the first article, Jacob Neusner has challenged, on logical and literary-redactional grounds, the view of Louis Ginzberg that the tractate Tamid is one of the earliest Mishnah-tractates. He has also set forth the evidence for his own conclusion, based on extended textual study, that the tractate is actually Ushan. In the second article, I have presented a computerized solution to a puzzling text in the Sefer Yesira, a solution which recovers a meaning that was lost through the centuries. Significantly, the solution was the effort of teacher and student together. And, in the third article, Edith Wyschogrod has presented a comparison of the concept of self and non-self in Buber, Buddhism, and Nietzsche.

D. R. B.

FIVE

Dating a Mishnah-Tractate: The Case of Tamid

JACOB NEUSNER

ROM THE PRIMITIVE beginnings of the modern historical study of Talmudic literature in the nineteenth century to our own days a fundamental difficulty has been the failure of scholars to articulate their methodological (or even programmatic) presuppositions and to criticize them. As a result it is taken for granted that we all know what we are doing and why, that we have in hand a reliable corpus of methodological principles in accord with which we define and effect our substantive work, and that, as a result, our results are available as foundations for still further work along established lines.[1] The "we-all-know"-school of Talmudic history continues to flourish. Scholarly and methodological hypotheses, not subjected to sustained and vigorous testing and criticism in the nineteenth century, are repeated as dogma in the twentieth. We all know, it is generally assumed, what the facts are, what questions we must ask, and how we must answer them. And we all know precisely what we must now do in the continuum of scholarly progress.

[1] "The Mishnah Tamid," *Journal of Jewish Lore and Philosophy* 1:33–44, 197–209, 265–95.

One of the assured results of this scholarship is that Mishnah-tractate Tamid is the earliest, or one of the earliest, Mishnah-tractates, and that it is to be dated in the very first generation following the destruction of the Second Temple in A.D. 70. The reason we all know about the origins of Tamid is that Louis Ginzberg discovered and announced them, and, with astonishingly few allusions to Ginzberg's article, Y. N. Epstein accepted and repeated Ginzberg's data and conclusions, restating them with no important additions.[2] To be sure, we are not told what it is that we know about Tamid. Is it the accuracy (and antiquity) of its factual allegations, or merely the point at which they are believed? Is it the verbatim formation of its language as we now have it, or merely the gist of its principal conceptions, that we assign to the period shortly after 70? One could assemble a long list of questions awaiting sustained inquiry. In the case of Tamid, we shall limit our analysis to the statements and suppositions of Ginzberg's article.

Dating Mishnah-tractates depends upon four facts. First, the document as a whole is conventionally assigned to Rabbi Judah the Patriarch, and for the moment we shall assume that the document, in pretty much its present state,[3] came into being about A.D. 200. So the document as a whole provides the outside limits of its several tractates.

Second, many sayings in the document are assigned to particular authorities, who lived in two fairly neatly delineated periods, one before, the other after, the war of Bar Kokhba. For

[2] *Mebo'ot lesifrut hattana' im* (Tel Aviv, 1957), pp. 27–31. Epstein did not write this book, which merely assembles class notes taken by some of his students. We therefore cannot condemn him for, among many other blatant inadequacies of the book, the amazing indifference to the work of other scholars.

[3] By this I mean its present contents as a whole, mode of organization, and redaction. One of the two greatest achievements of modern Talmudic scholarship (the other being Lieberman's *Tosefta Kipshutah*) is Y. N. Epstein, *Mabo lenusah hammishnah* (Tel Aviv, 1954), which shows that the readings of immense numbers of pericopae were fluid for centuries after 200. For a sound exposition of Epstein's thesis and methods, see Baruch M. Bokser, in *The Modern Study of the Mishnah*, ed. J. Neusner (Leiden, 1973), pp. 13–55.

convenience's sake, we shall refer to the former as the period of Yavneh, to the latter as the period of Usha, after the names of the two towns generally assumed to have served as important centers of Rabbinical activity in their respective periods.

Third, attributions of these sayings to specific authorities are subject, in many instances, to a test of falsification, therefore of verification.[4] If a saying assigned to an authority of Yavneh in fact is prior in conception to another saying on the same theme or principle assigned to an authority of Usha, then it is likely that the former really does precede the other. For there is a correlation of chronology and logic. If what is attributed to a later authority, on the other hand, clearly is taken for granted in a conception assigned to an earlier authority, then the attribution to the later authority is on the face of it dubious. Moreover, since the Ushans stand only a generation removed from the redaction of Mishnah—(ca. 140 to 170 with the work of redaction hypothetically in the period from 170 to 200), we have no reason to take a position of extreme skepticism on the allegation that named authorities among the teachers of the generation of the redaction did hold the positions assigned to them. The real problem of dating tractates and their contents is in finding solid grounds to suppose that anything in them goes back to the period before Bar Kokhba.

Fourth, Mishnah-tractates generally take shape around a clearcut didactic-philosophical purpose. They rarely intend merely to supply facts pertinent to a given topic. They ordinarily propose to investigate some aspect of a topic and to say

[4] I first worked this matter out in acute detail in my *History of the Mishnaic Law of Purities* (Leiden, 1974–1977), vols. 1–22. It is spelled out in brief in "The History of Earlier Rabbinic Judaism, Some New Approaches," *History of Religions* 16 (1977): 216–36. However, through the unfolding of *Purities,* the methods underwent substantial modifications and refinements, as concrete problems of analysis of data had to be confronted and taken into account. In any case a mere statement of the basic principle, divorced from the encounter with concrete texts, gives neither satisfactory conception of what is alleged, nor, self-evidently, access to the substantive consequences, for the history of ideas and of religions, of what I have worked out. For the present purpose, it suffices to state matters in a rather general way.

something important about it. That is to say, Mishnah-tractates tend to develop around the interplay between a topic and a generative problematic, and propose to say something specific about a given subject. Mishnah is not an encyclopedia of legal facts, but a highly purposive and didactic document; in many of its tractates it expresses viewpoints on profound and controverted philosophico-legal issues. It follows that, when we claim to state the point at which a tractate begins its journey through the history of Judaism, it should be that moment at which we are able to uncover the most primitive and fundamental expression of the tractate's particular interest in its given topic or theme: its generative problematic. Before that point, we may have a collection of facts, or allegations, about a topic. Afterward, we have a fully structured tractate, proceeding along its own, now inexorable, line of development, articulation, amplification, and, especially (and this, commonly, in the Ushan stratum), acute refinement and instantiation of said generative problematic.

Let us proceed to consider the kinds of data Mishnah-tractate Tamid presents and to consider how these relate to the four facts just specified.

Data of Mishnah-Tractate Tamid

The literary character of Tamid (and its two successors, Middot and Qinnim) makes it impossible to proceed along the lines of laying out the tractates' propositions in the names of Yavneans and determining their logical relationship to other propositions in the names of Ushans. Tamid and Middot are descriptive narratives bearing few attributions. But we do have attributions and, while not subject to falsification or verification, these have to be taken into account. Our examination will suggest, though hardly conclusively demonstrate, that Tamid takes up issues on points moot at Usha or gives other evidence of having been put together after 140. We shall rapidly con-

sider the relevant attributions, stressing throughout the work
that these are beyond testing. In the case of Tamid, that is not
of much consequence, since, in any event, the attributions
always lead us back to Usha.

The remarkably smooth and coherent narrative of Tamid
bears the following attributed pericopae:

1. M. 3:2B–C: If it had come, the one who sees it says, "It is day-
   light." Matya b. Samuel says: [He says,] "The whole eastern
   horizon is light." "Up to Hebron?" "Yes."
   Matya provides an alternative discourse to saying, "It is day-
   light."
2. [M. 3:8K: Said Eleazar b. Diglai: My father's house had goats on
   the mountain of Mikhwar. And they sneezed from the smell of
   the compounding of the incense. This is a gloss for M. 3:8J,
   which is external to the primary narrative and part of its own,
   independent unit.]
3. M. 5:2A–E: The superintendent said, "Those who are new to the
   preparation of the incense come and cast lots. Those who are
   new with those who have had a chance, come and cast lots on
   who will bring up the limbs from the ramp to the altar.
   Eliezer b. Jacob says: He who brings up the limbs to the
   ramp [without a lottery] is the one who brings them up onto
   the altar.
   The anonymous statement takes up a position contrary to
   Eliezer b. Jacob's and inserts it whole into the flow of narrative.
4. [M. 7:2H–I: Except for the high priest, who does not raise his
   hands higher than the frontlet. Judah: Even the high priest
   raises his hands above the frontlet. This dispute is external to
   the narrative.].

Clearly at Nos. 1 and 3, the narrator shapes his story along lines
different from those of named authorities, one of them certainly
Ushan. At Nos. 2 and 4 we have materials external to the
primary narrative, bearing the names of Ushans.

As I have stressed, we have no way of finding out whether the
attributions are sound. There is no independent corpus of sayings, for example, of Eliezer b. Jacob or Judah, a collection
well-attested as deriving from those Ushan authorities. It follows that we cannot know whether or not Judah or Eliezer b.

Jacob has really said what the tractate claims. We also cannot test the allegation that these are opinions held, in particular, in Ushan *times*, because they do not relate to sayings, in the names of Yavneans on the same topics but of a more fundamental character. The probability is that what is assigned to Usha belongs there, on the grounds that the ultimate voices of Mishnah are those of the disciples of the Ushans. But this is merely a statement of what seems reasonable, not of what we are able to demonstrate.

Ginzberg's Thesis

Louis Ginzberg has approached the problem of analyzing Tamid not from the perspective of its literary context (what do we find in Mishnah-Tosefta of a given tractate and Order?) but from the perspective of its legal theme, inclusive of sayings on the issues of Tamid located throughout the ancient rabbinic literature. He therefore assembles much more evidence[5] that the tractate takes up a position on issues moot at Usha. This (considerably less probative) evidence powerfully supports the thesis that the tractate originates after 140. He states:

> Now it can easily be shown that many Halakot sanctioned in our tractate were contradicted not only by many other Tannaim, but even by the compiler of our Mishnah himself, who, in other parts of his work, decided against them.
> The Halakah I, 1, with reference to the priests who became defiled at night, is contradicted by R. Eliezer ben Jacob, *Middot* I, end. The statement concerning the Two Wickets, I, 3, is at variance with that given in *Middot* I, 7. The view of our tractate II, 4–5, that the priests build only two fires on the altar, is in agreement with that of R. Judah, but against that of R. Meir and R. Yosé, *Yoma* IV, 6. The "Chamber of the Lambs" was according to our tractate III, 3, on the northwest corner, but according to *Middot* I, 6, on the southwest. The solution of this contradiction in *Yoma* 17a is far from being acceptable. The distribution of the parts of the sacrifice among the officiating priests is different in our tractate III, 1, from that in *Yoma*, III, 3. According to

[5] *Tamid*, pp. 42–44.

Yoma, I, 2, the incense was first offered and then the candlestick put in order, in *Tamid* IV, 1–2, the order is reversed. The coal pan used in the offering of incense measured according to our tractate V, 5, *five kab* in contradiction to the view held by R. Josse, *Yoma* IV, 4, according to which it only measured *four kab.* In *Tamid* VII, 3, it is supposed that the high priest ascended the altar in the same way as the ordinary priest, which, according to R. Judah, *Yoma* IV, 5, was by no means the case. If we turn from the Mishnah to the other Tannaitic sources and compare them with our tractate we find many more Halakot in it which do not agree with the views laid down in these collections. A few instances may serve as an illustration. What *Tamid* IV, 1, has to say about the "sprinkling of the blood" is in opposition to the view held by many Tannaim in *Tosefta Zebahim* VI, 12–13, and *Yoma,* 14b–15a. The Halakah *Tamid* (IV, 1), with regard to the rest of the blood, is contradicted by *Tosefta Zebahim* VI, 4. That all kinds of wood with the exception of two may be used for the altar (III, 3) is contradicted by R. Eliezer Tosefta, *Menahot* IX, 14, and *Targum Yer.* Genesis XXII, 6. Compare the further discussion of this Halakah later on. The Halakah (III, 1) concerning the use of the water of the Laver at the morning service in the Temple is not accepted by Rabbi; comp. *Zebahim* 20a–20b.

The result of our investigation of the Halakah in *Tamid* is that a good deal of it is controverted, and that further the compiler of our Mishnah has, in different parts of his work, expressed opinions which contradict those given in our tractate.

The names cited in the evidence assembled by Ginzberg are entirely Ushan or later: Judah, Meir, Yosé, or Rabbi. We certainly have to conclude, therefore, that, taking up a position on issues moot at that time, the tractate must originate in the period after 140.

We cannot ignore Ginzberg's conclusion, based upon the facts just now cited as well as an extensive account of unusual philological usages in the tractate, which does not require summary, that Tamid originates much earlier, shortly after A.D. 70. Let us consider his entire argument exactly as he states it: [6]

> *After eliminating additions, explanations and glosses found in the present text of Tamid, we have in this tractate the oldest Tannaitic work, which though in Mishnic form is distinguished from the Mishnah of Rabbi by method and language.*

[6] *Tamid,* pp. 284–93, *passim.* Italics are his throughout.

Two Halakas of our tractate (III, 1 and the last part of IV, 1) are given in the Tosefta (*Yoma* I, 13; *Zebachim* VI, 13) as statements of R. Simon of Mizpah. The formula used by Tosefta Zeb. I, c. in introducing one of the statements reads: "The version of *Tamid* according to R. Simon of Mizpah maintains etc." A Tanna by this name is mentioned in one other passage only, in *Peah* II, 6. A thorough examination of this Mishnah will enable us to fix approximately the time of this Tanna and the date of the composition of *Tamid*. We are told in *Peah* I, c. that R. Simon of Mizpah and R. Gamaliel, not being able to decide a certain question of law betook themselves to the "Chamber of Gazith" and "asked." There they received the authoritative answer from the scribe Nahum who was in the possession of an old tradition bearing upon the question. Nahum said, "I have received this tradition from Miyyasha who had received it from Abba, who had received it from the *Zugot*, who had received it from the Prophets, etc." The "Chamber of Gazit" was located in one of the temple-buildings, hence the incident referred to in *Peah* must have occurred before 70 C.E., and the Rabban Gamaliel who accompanied R. Simon to the "Chamber" is the elder one, the head of the Pharasean School c. 25–50 C.E. If we accept as historical the Talmudic tradition that the Sanhedrin left the "Chamber" in 30 C.E., we have to assume that *Tamid* was composed before the destruction of the Temple. It is certainly not likely that a septuagenarian, as R. Simon of Mizpah must have been in 70 C.E., should have taken up the study of a work of contemporary composition. There are, however, many reasons against fixing the time of R. Simon as early as to make him a contemporary of Rabban Gamaliel I. The title of "Rabbi" as attached to this R. Simeon was not borne by scholars prior to the time of Rabban Johannan ben Zakkai's disciples. The Tannaitic sources mention several contemporaries of R. Gamaliel I, but none of them has the title of Rabbi. The Mishnah *Peah* speaks further of R. Gamaliel as appearing before the Sanhedrin assembled at the "Chamber" to receive instruction on a point of law. But according to Rabbinic tradition this R. Gamaliel was the President of the Sanhedrin, and it is surely very strange to see him appearing before a body of which he was the President. The words of Nahum show quite distinctly that he belonged to a generation far removed from that of Shammai and Hillel, the last *Zug*. The tradition which Nahum communicated to R. Gamaliel, had been received by him from "Miyyasha who had received it from Abba, who had received it from Shammai and Hillel, the last *Zug*." But Rabban Gamaliel I was the grandson, perhaps the son, of Hillel, whom he had succeeded immediately, or after a short interval, as the head of the Pharisees. It should also be mentioned that the Munich manuscript reads Nahum the Median, instead of Nahum the scribe, of the editions, and we know that Nahum the Median belongs to the generation of

Rabban Gamaliel II, and not to that of the Elder Gamaliel. And one more reason against the assumption that R. Gamaliel I is referred to in *Peah,* I, c. The Mishnah *Peah* II, 4, mentions R. Gamaliel and as the contents shows the young bearer of this name is meant. It would therefore be very strange if in *Peah* II, 6, Rabban Gamaliel I, should be referred to without the addition of "the elder" to his name to distinguish him from his grandson mentioned shortly before. One is therefore safe in assuming that the incident related in *Peah* II, 6, occurred shortly before 70 C.E. and that it was R. Gamaliel II, who accompanied R. Simon to the "Chamber." At that time R. Gamaliel II was not yet the head of the Sanhedrin, his father R. Simon then being still alive, and there is nothing strange in the story told of him that he appeared before the Sanhedrin assembled in the "Chamber." His contemporary, Nahum, gave the required information based upon a tradition which he could trace back to Shammai and Hillel the last *Zug.* The statement of this Mishnah which supposes that shortly before 70 C.E. the Sanhedrin met in the "Chamber," does not contradict the Talmudic tradition according to which the Sanhedrin were exiled from the "Chamber" forty years before the destruction of the Temple. We have to assume—and this independently from our Mishnah—that during the Revolution in 66–70 C.E., the Sanhedrin had returned to its old meeting place.

We have approximately fixed the time of R. Simon of Mizpah, and we will now proceed to ascertain the exact relation of this Tanna to the tractate of Tamid. The Tosefta, Zeb. I. c., proves only the existence of a compilation containing a description of the daily Temple service, known as *Tamid,* but not the identity of our tractate by this name with that made use of by R. Simon. We first find this view expressed by the Palestinian Amora R. Johannan (Babli, *Yoma* 14b and Yerushalmi, II, 39d), who may have inferred it and, perhaps, wrongly so, from the Tosefta I. c. The statement of the Tosefta and the inference drawn from it by R. Johannan appear, however, in an entirely different light, if we take them in combination with the conclusion we have reached after our critical study of *Tamid. We have seen that this tractate is of a very archaic character; that it does not form a part of Rabbi's Mishnah, that it did not go through the hands of a redactor; and, finally, that, abstratis abstrahendis, it came down to us in its original form.* There is, therefore, no reason whatsoever to doubt R. Johannan's statement *that our tractate of Tamid is the same as made use of by R. Simon of Mizpah, the contemporary of R. Gamaliel, II.*

We have thus gained a *terminus ad quem* for the date of the compilation of *Tamid,* but not yet a *terminus a quo.* To argue *a priori* that a compilation like *Tamid* could not have been composed at the time when the Temple was still in existence would be fallacious. One might even argue in favor of fixing an early date for such a compilation as the prac-

tical need of giving the priest a guide for the daily Temple service did
exist before the destruction of the Temple, but not after it. If, however,
we turn to our tractate and find that the Temple-officers mentioned in
it are Mattahias ben Samuel (III, 2) and Ben Arza (VIII, 3) who, as we
know, occupied their positions in the very last days of the Temple, the
probability is very great that *Tamid* was composed after the destruction
of the Temple. To this conclusion we are urged by all that we have
found about the peculiar character of *Tamid* which distinguishes it from
the rest of the Mishnah. The question: why did not Rabbi who was
thoroughly acquainted with the contents of *Tamid,* as the quotations
from it in his work show, incorporate this old Tannaitic tractate of
Tamid in his Mishnah, can only be satifactorily answered, if we assume
that *Tamid* was composed after 70 C.E. The foundation for the Mishnah
was laid by the schools of Shammai and Hillel, and though later generations added one stratum after another, they never attempted to alter
the foundation. The division of the Mishnah into fifty-eight tractates is
a part of the ground work laid by the two schools mentioned at the
time when the Temple was still in existence. The Halakoth which have
the Temple service for their object were dealt with by these first com-
pilers of the Mishnah in the tractates of the Order of Kodashim according to the nature of the different parts of the Temple service. After the
destruction of the Temple, however, it was felt advisable to have a continuous description of the daily service, not so much in the interest of
the study of the Temple Halakah, the material was too vast to be con-
densed into a small compilation—but rather to enable the student to
get a vivid picture of what had been going on daily in the Temple. One
must further not forget that the generation living immediately after the
destruction of the Temple expected its restoration in their own day, and
a knowledge of the routine of the Temple was considered to be of practical use. To these expectations and desires we owe the compilation of
Tamid, the object of which was to give a coherent description of the service, rather than to systematize the Halakoth dealing with it. The Tannaim from the time of Rabbi Simon of Mizpah to that of Rabbi studied
Tamid with great care, but none of them thought of incorporating it
into their Mishnah collections. The Mishnah is a code of law, *Tamid* an
archeological study, and hence neither the Mishnah of Rabbi nor the
Tosefta contains a tractate of *Tamid.* The fact that there is no Tosefta
Middot points to the peculiar character of this tractate, and I hope to
deal with this problem on some other occasion.

Ginzberg's dating of Tamid rests upon two pillars. First, it is
different from "the rest of Rabbi's Mishnah" and therefore
derives from some other source. Second, two statements given

anonymously in *Tamid* appear in Tosefta elsewhere in the name
of Simeon of Mispeh. He is explicit that when we may "fix approximately" the time of Simon, we establish also "the date of
the composition of Tamid." The connection between the one
fact and the other is not made explicit, because everyone is assumed to concur in the proposition that one or two anonymous
statements, elsewhere given to a named authority, are ample evidence that the entire chapter or even the whole tractate belongs
to said authority. This massive generalization rests on the basis
of an insignificant sample of evidence and hardly reflects serious
and systematic research. The conception that a tractate has an
individual "author," furthermore, has never been demonstrated
or even carefully defined.[7] Let us now turn to the two chief
arguments in Ginzberg's statement, since everything else—the
dating of Simeon, the reasons for the creation of *Tamid,* let
alone the absence of Tosefta—is of no weight whatever in the
demonstration of Ginzberg's stated thesis but, where it is relevant, merely flows from it.

The Alleged Singularity of Tamid

What makes *Tamid* peculiar—principally its descriptive-narrative style and exclusion of explicit disputes, but also, let us
readily concede, its occasionally odd word-choices—characterizes other sizable descriptive-narrative aggregations of Mishnah, for example, M. Bikkurim 3:2–6, M. Sheqalim 5:1–6,
6:1–6, M. Yoma chapters 1 through 7, M. Sotah 3:1–3, M.
Negaim chapter 14, and M. Parah chapter 3. Ginzberg himself
is well aware (p. 38) that there are "most archaic forms" in
these descriptions of the Temple rites or of other public ceremo-
nies. Certainly these passages are different from others, reveal-
ing stylistic peculiarities. But there are surely yet other types
(*Gattungen*) of Mishnaic materials. Without analysis of

---

[7] The literary evidence in *Purities* 21, *The Redaction and Formulation of the Order of
Purities in Mishnah and Tosefta,* hardly supports that proposition.

Gattungen and their attributions, it hardly serves to jump to the conclusion that Rabbi stands behind the whole of Mishnah, excluding only Tamid and, possibly, pericopae or chapters similar in style to Tamid. (Ginzberg should, but does not, make such a claim.)

In any event the parallel passages, part of the same *Gattung,* in Parah and Negaim are laden with Ushan attestations and take up positions on issues moot after the Bar Kokhba War, just as Tamid does. It follows that both attestations and even sayings integral to the narrative which bear names point toward Usha as the setting in which this particular mode of formulating materials proves important. More interesting: apart from allusions to ancient days, the relevant passages of Negaim and Parah omit all reference to authorities of Yavneh. It follows that the stylistic or formal distinctiveness of our tractate is attested, where it bears useful attestations at all, not to Yavneh as Ginzberg claims, but to Usha. That by itself does not mean Tamid also is Ushan. But it calls into question the certainty that, for "stylistic" reasons, we must assign the tractate to the time of Gamaliel II.

Two Anonymous Statements of Tamid
Belong to Simeon of Mispeh

As we shall see in a moment, Ginzberg's exact language on this matter is difficult to interpret. Let us first consider the relevant passages of M. Tamid and T. Yoma, and T. Zebahim, then pursue the issue as phrased by Ginzberg.

M. Tam. 3:1	*T. Yoma 1:13* (Zuckermandel, p. 181, ls. 25–27, p. 182, ls. 1ff.)
The superintendent said to them: Come and cast lots [to determine] who executes the act of slaughter	The superintendent said to them: Come and cast lots [to determine] who executes the act of slaughter

who tosses the blood
who removes the ashes of the
  inner altar
who removes the ashes of the
  candlestick
who carries out the limbs to the
  ramp:
the head,
the [right] hind-leg
the two fore-legs
the rump
(and) the [left] hind-leg
the breast
the neck
the two flanks
the innards
the fine flour
the cakes
the wine
[They drew lots to see who won.]

who tosses the blood
who removes the ashes of the
  inner altar
who removes the ashes of the
  candlestick
who carries out the limbs to the
  ramp:
the head,
the [right] hind-leg
the two fore-legs
the breast
the [left] hind-leg
the rump
the neck
the two flanks
the innards
the fine flour
the cakes
the wine
—*these are the words of Simeon of
  Mispeh.*
*R. Yosé says, The head, the hind-
  leg, the two fore-legs, the breast,
  the neck and the two flanks, the
  rump, and the hind-leg.*
Said Ben Azzai before R. Aqiba
in the name of R. Joshua,
"When it goes in, the head,
the foot, the breast, the neck
and the two flanks, the rump,
and the hind-leg are offered up."
(And thirteen are appointed for
that purpose, sometimes four-
teen, sometimes fifteen, etc.)

When we view this in its entirety, we discover that there is a
dispute, between Simeon of Mispeh and Yosé about the order in
which these selections are made. It is true, then, that our pericope expresses the opinion assigned by T. to Simeon of Mispeh
vis a vis Yosé. But to give to Simeon the *whole* of the tractate (!)
because one anonymous passage is elsewhere attributed to him is

simply not very likely.[8] And in any case it surely would appear that, here, Yosé and Simeon are presented as contemporaries—therefore Ushans, since Yosé without further identification is Yose B. R. Halafta, the authority who flourished after 140.

M. Tam. 4:1J–M	*T. Zeb. 6:13* (Zuckermandel, p. 488, Is. 25–37, p. 489, I. 1)
	R. Simeon of Mispeh did repeat concerning the Tamid:
The one who receives the blood received the blood.	
He came to the northeastern corner.	He came to the northeastern corner.
He tosses the blood in a north-easterly direction.	He tosses the blood in a north-easterly direction
[Then he came] to the south-western corner.	[Then he came] to the [south] western corner
He tosses the blood in a south-westerly direction.	He tosses the blood *westward,* [then] he tosses the blood *southward.*
	(If he put it on the horn on either side [and not on both sides], it is valid. But if he put it on the horn and inward, it is invalid.)

[8] The supposition that if we can find what is in an anonymous saying also stated in the name of a particular authority, we shall then demonstrate that said authority stands not only behind the anonymous version but also behind all else which is anonymous in the same literary unit, is difficult to grasp. For, to begin with, no one has spelled out a theory of the literature and its formation which will explain why it *must* follow that if a saying is given both anonymously and in someone's name, then the latter stands behind (not merely concurs with) said saying and also all the other sayings in the same context.

But I do not know who has shown that it is so, nor can I even imagine the kind of tests of falsification and verification which are possible in the corpus of literature available at present. Still, as we notice, a commonplace of discourse in Talmudic history is to allege that Judah the Patriarch has given us all the material he received and that he changed nothing and revised nothing. These allegations by definition cannot be tested. For we only have what Rabbi has given us. And we have it only in the form which Rabbi imposed upon it. So we can never know what he did not give us nor how he has revised, or refrained from revising, what we now have. That is, we have only the documents which we have, not those that we do not have. And that is precisely the sort of tautological argumentation called for in this curious realm of discourse formed by scholars of Talmud history.

Clearly, Simeon's version is *not* that of M. Tam. 4:1. This fact
forms the basis of the discussion of B. Yoma 14b, at which
Huna wishes to assign Tamid to Simeon. Yohanan, however,
rejects Huna's view and gives to Simeon Yoma (!) instead. Certainly what is given in Simeon's name in T. Zeb. 6:13 and what
is said at M. Tam. 4:1 are not the same, as we see spelled out in
the following:

> R. Huna said, "Who is the Tanna of Tamid? R. Simeon of Mispeh."
> But surely we have learned the opposite [that Simeon of Mispeh rejects
> the teachings of Tamid].
> For we have learned:
> [When] he came to the northeastern corner of the altar, he sprinkled
> east and north; then he came to the southwestern corner and sprin-
> kled west and south.
> And with reference to this statement it was taught:
> R. Simeon of Mispeh repeats the following tradition in regard to Tamid
> [*in regard to the daily whole offering* (MSNH BTMYD)]:
> As he came to the northeastern corner he sprinkled it to the east and to
> the north; then he came to the southwestern corner and sprinkled it
> to the west and then to the south [in two separate applications, west,
> then south, *not* as in M. Tamid].
> Said R. Yohanan: "Who is the authority for the order in Yoma? Simeon
> of Mispeh."

Yohanan thus rejects the view of Huna and holds that Simeon of
Mispeh does not stand behind Tamid.

Ginzberg's exact claim here, in fact, is rather difficult to interpret. He concedes that the cited passage "proves only the existence of a compilation containing a description of the daily
Temple service, known as Tamid, but not the identity of our
tractate by this name *with that made use of by R. Simeon.*" The
italicized words suggest that Ginzberg will not claim in any
event that Simeon "wrote" or "is the Tanna of" or "stands
behind" Tamid as we know it, merely that the cited passage
shows that Simeon "made use of" said tractate. (Epstein, ever
less careful in his formulations, will claim precisely that Simeon
produced Tamid.) It follows that Simeon is meant to supply an
attestation to the tractate. But T. Yoma gets Simeon into a

dispute with Yosé, which should move the attestation of Simeon of Mispeh forward by seventy-five years or so, on to Ushan times.

If all we ask of Simeon, in any case, is that he attest to the *existence* of the tractate Tamid as we now know it (and not one or two of its pericopae, in a document which in any event is hardly unitary and surely cannot be seen to emerge from a single hand or circle!), then what difference does it make whether Yohanan or Huna is right? Both Yohanan and Huna can concede that Tamid drives from the *time* of Simeon. Only Huna wants Tamid to have been made up by Simeon, and Huna's name is curiously absent from Ginzberg's account.

Of greater importance: Ginzberg would have to show us that Tamid is a unitary tractate, wholly the work of a single hand—in both its formal and its conceptual character—for the evidence herein adduced to prove what he wants it to demonstrate. Otherwise, all he has shown (if he has shown it) relates to two pericopae among a diverse collection of units. If Tamid exhibited that remarkably coherent character we see in Qinnim, then the evidence he presents at the very least would be suggestive, if not entirely probative. But as matters now stand, Ginzberg's claim is wildly out of phase with the problem.

In any case Ginzberg jumps to the following: "The statement of the Tosefta and the inference drawn from it by R. Johannan appear . . . in an entirely different light, if we take them in combination with the conclusions we have reached after our critical study of Tamid. . . . There is . . . no reason whatsoever to doubt R. Johannan's statement that our tractate of Tamid is the same as made use of by R. Simeon of Mizpah." But that is not what Yohannan has claimed. It is Huna who has made that claim, and Yohanan has said Simeon stands behind a pericope—*one pericope!*—in Yoma.

Conclusion

We need not differ from Ginzberg's judgment that Yohanan attests to the existence of the saying in T. Zeb. assigning to Simeon of Mispeh a saying different from one in our tractate. But that fact simply leads nowhere. The tractate in some ways is different from other tractates. But other tractates, too, exhibit their own distinctive traits, choice of words, formal preferences, and so on. Until we have a survey of all the tractates of Mishnah, statements such as these can only beg the question. Tamid, after all, does fall into a literary style familiar in important tractates not singled out by Ginzberg as "archaic" at all.

What Ginzberg means about the tractate's "not going through the hands of a redactor" is not known to me. It seems to me that redaction is part of the literary history of anything which comes down to us in a document such as Mishnah. It also is hard to know how Ginzberg knows that the tractate is "in its original form." If our tractate comes down from the time of Gamaliel II, as Ginzberg concludes, then we have to ask ourselves why it is that the tractate takes up its clearcut positions on mooted questions of Ushan times. It would seem that (following Ginzberg's way of thinking) Ushans are remarkably indifferent to the opinions of their predecessors, who presumably also were their masters. For he shows how they take positions contrary to those held by the authorities of Yavneh and wholly ignore opinions in "so ancient" a document as Tamid. In all, Ginzberg's thesis on *Tamid* rests upon false assumptions, an astonishing misreading of the Talmudic text he cites, and, above all, faulty reasoning.[9]

---

[9] Epstein, *Tan.*, pp. 27–31, covers the same ground in the same dubious way. The choice of words and style are distinctive, inclusive of the use of rhetorical questions. Simeon of Mispeh is the author: "Tamid is the Mishnah of Simeon of Mispeh" (*Tan.*, p. 28). As proof are adduced the cited pericopae of Talmud. But the tractate has been reworked by later authorities (*Tan.*, p. 29). Following Ginzberg, Epstein further observes that the tractate contains later additions of materials originally occurring as Talmudic *baraitot* (p. 30).

SIX

The Creator and the Computer

DAVID R. BLUMENTHAL

IN HIS WORK on the Christian cabala,[1] Professor Blau has argued that the study and use of cabala by Christian scholars was but a momentary occupation. Yet, while it lasted, it was an intense and literate enterprise, for "each scholar thought he had found in the cabala what he was seeking. . . . Each man could derive the aid he sought from its philosophical system, its canons of interpretations, its techniques, or its hermeneutical rules." In the end however, Christian cabala was destined to die, for "like astrology, alchemy, and other pseudo-sciences, cabala fell a legitimate victim to the development of scientific thinking." It is therefore wistfully appropriate that this article, which also deals with a brief but intense moment in Jewish gnostic-mysticism and with a pseudo-science which was also destined to die out, be dedicated to him.

The Problem

According to the Bible, God created the world through speech. He spoke and the world came into being. But just ex-

[1] Joseph Blau, *The Christian Interpretation of the Cabala in the Renaissance* (New York: Columbia University Press, 1944; rpt., Port Washington, N.Y.: Kennikat Press, 1965) 113–14, vii.

actly how did He do that? How does speech, which is immaterial, create the world, which is material? And what is "speech" to a God who is utterly transcendent? It cannot be the same as human speech for it takes place in a nonmaterial realm and, furthermore, it is creative. The *Sefer Yesira,* which dates from the early centuries of this era and is actually a group of texts which has been edited into one whole,[2] sought to provide some answers to these questions. According to *Sefer Yesira,* God's "speech" was not talking in the sense of someone speaking, but rather a manipulation of the letters of the Hebrew alphabet. These letters, *Sefer Yesira* teaches, are not merely linguistic symbols. They are real, having existence outside the human mind. They are made of a special spiritual substance and, hence, could be formed, weighed, shaped, etc. by God. Creation, then, was the process of shaping the letters so as to form reality. There are several accounts of this process in *Sefer Yesira.* One such account found in chapter 2, tells us:[3]

> Mishna 4: He set the fundamental twenty-two letters in a wheel, as a wall, in two-hundred-and-thirty-one gates. The wheel moves forward and backward. And the sign of the matter is: "There is nothing in

[2] For the literature on *Sefer Yesira,* see G. Scholem, *Major Trends in Jewish Mysticism* (Schocken, N.Y.: 1941; hereinafter *Trends*), 75–78, and *idem.,* "Kabbala," *Encyclopedia Judaica* (Keter, Jerusalem: 1971) 10:507. See also G. Vajda in *Introduction à la pensée juive du moyen âge* (Paris: Vrin, 1947) and his studies in *Revue des études juives,* vols. 7, 10, 12, 13, and 16. (The reference in 10:87, n32, to Haberman's article in *Sinai* should be to vol. 20 thereof and not to vol. 10). There is a translation of the *Sefer Yesira* in German and several into English (see *Trends,* 427). See now my own translation and explicatory commentary in *Understanding Jewish Mysticism* (N.Y.: Ktav, 1978).

[3] The manuscript tradition of *Sefer Yesira* is very irregular. See I. Grunewald, "A Preliminary Critical Edition of *Sefer Yesira,*" *Israel Oriental Studies,* 1 (1971): 132–77 for an attempt at a critical text. However, N. Sed, "Le *Sefer Yesira,*" *Revue des études juives,* 132 (1973): 513–28 contains a strong critique of Grunewald's theory and a coherent summary of the various manuscript traditions. The "best" manuscript appears to be Vatican, Hebrew, 299ff. 66a–71b. To allow easy access to the Hebrew original, I have chosen to translate the text ostensibly used by the Vilna Gaon which appears in *Sefer Yesira* (Heb.), ed. unknown (Jerusalem: Lewin-Epstein, 1964–65), part 3, pp. 25–26 (hereafter *SY*). The Mantua edition (reprinted, *ibid.,* at the end) has slightly different readings.

goodness above pleasure and nothing in misfortune below a [leprous] lesion."[4]

Mishna 5: How did He combine, weigh, and permute them? Aleph with all of them and all of them with Aleph. Bet with all of them and all of them with Bet. They turn round and round, and there are two-hundred-and-thirty-one gates. It results, then, that all creation and all speech go forth from one term.[5]

The problem of this essay then, is: according to this text, just exactly how did God arrange the letters of the Hebrew alphabet, and how did He manipulate them so as to create the world?

The Solution:
The Sequence and Arrangement of the Letters

Beginning with Mishna 5, the basic sequence of the letters can be reconstructed. According to it, each letter is to be combined with all the other letters but not with itself. That would yield 462 pairs of letters (22 letters x 21 other letters). By deleting the mirror-images (e.g., AB, BA), one arrives at 231 basic pairs. Since, however, the text says that these pairs are to be made two ways—forward ("Aleph with all of them") and reverse ("all of them with Aleph")—there are actually two sets of the 231 basic pairs. The basic sequence, then, consists of two sets of the 231 basic pairs.[6]

[4] Some manuscripts, including the Vatican Heb. 299, and Grunewald, *Critical Edition,* 148, omit the reference to the wall. Others include it (L. Goldschmidt, *Das Buch der Schöpfung* [Frankfurt: Kaufmann, 1894], 55). Some read 221, and not 231, gates (see below). The wording of the quotation also varies: Some read "if in goodness there is nothing" and some read "above" twice (see below).

[5] Some manuscripts and edition Mantua add: "And He created with them the bodies [or souls] of all the creatures and of all that He would yet create."

[6] Using the English alphabet, the following sequences are generated: forward AB, AC, AD . . . BC, BD, BE . . . CD, CE, CF . . . YZ; reverse: ZA, YA, XA . . . ZB, YB, XB . . . ZC, YC, XC . . . ZX. Figure 6.1 charts the sequences according to the Hebrew alphabet.

The nature of this sequence was already clearly seen by Saadia Gaon (10th century) in his *Commentary to the Sefer Yesira* (edited and translated into French by M. Lambert, *Commentaire sur Sefer Yesirah* [Paris: E. Bouillon, 1891]; edited and translated into Hebrew by Y. Qafih, *Sefer Yesira, Kitab al-Mabadi, im Perush R. Saadia* [Jerusalem:

Given this basic sequence, how does one put it into its two forms, the wall and the wheel, as specified in Mishna 4? The word "wall," though apparently not well-attested in the early manuscripts, suggests a chart or a table and it is possible to display the basic sequence in the form of a chart. This has been done in figure 6.1 where the lower line of each row represents the 231 basic pairs moving forward ("Aleph with all of them") while the upper line of each row represents the 231 basic pairs moving in reverse ("all of them with Aleph").[7] The word "wheel," in some texts rendered in the plural, suggests a wheel with spokes, or a star, and it is possible to display the basic sequence in the form of two such stars. This has been done in

Deror, 1972]). In the *Commentary,* Saadia notes that his manuscripts read "221 gates," but he argues against that reading on mathematical grounds. He then explains the basic sequence, calling each pair a two-lettered "word" (see Qafih, 118–19, n42, where all this is clearly set forth). It seems to have been envisioned by Isaac the Blind, too. See G. Scholem, *Hakabbalah be-Provence* (Jerusalem: Akadman, 1953) p. 10 of the Appendix.

Eleazar of Worms (12th–13th century) in his *Commentary to Sefer Yesira* (Przemysl: M. Spiro, 1888) also knew of two readings. His calculation for the 231 pairs is, however, different (5a–b and, in more detail, 17a–20a): each letter is combined with the one immediately following it; then, with the letter which is two letters from it; then with the letter which is three letters from it; until only the first and last letters can combine. Using the English alphabet, this generates the sequence: AB, BC, CD, DE . . . AC, BD, CE . . . AD, BE, CF . . . AZ. Eleazar's calculation for the 221 pairs follows a similar principle (4b–5a and, in more detail, 15b–17a): each letter is listed; every other letter is listed; every third letter is listed; every fourth . . . every eleventh, every twelfth. . . . For the purpose of this sequence, the alphabet is viewed as a continuous, repeating ribbon. Using the English alphabet, the sequence is: ABCD . . . ACEG . . . ADGJ . . . AM . . . ANOB. . . .

[7] This method of transliteration is as follows:

Hewbrew letter	transliteration	Hebrew letter	transliteration
aleph	A	lamed	L
bet	B	mem	M
gimel	G	nun	N
dalet	D	samekh	S
hey	H	ayin	O
vav	V	peh	P
zayin	Z	tsade	C/Σ
het	X	qof	Q
tet	T	resh	R
yod	I	shin	$\$/\psi$
kaf	K	taf	$\&/\theta$

ROTATION = 1   ADVANCE = 1

reverse: forward

	1	2	3	4	5	6	7	8	9	10	11	12	13	14	15	16	17	18	19	20	21
1:	&A / AB	$A / AG	RA / AD	QA / AH	CA / AV	PA / AZ	OA / AX	SA / AT	NA / AI	MA / AK	LA / AL	KA / AM	IA / AN	TA / AS	XA / AO	ZA / AP	VA / AC	HA / AQ	DA / AR	GA / A$	BA / A&
2:	&B / BG	$B / BD	RB / BH	QB / BV	CB / BZ	PB / BX	OB / BT	SB / BI	NB / BK	MB / BL	LB / BM	KB / BN	IB / BS	TB / BO	XB / BP	ZB / BC	VB / BQ	HB / BR	DB / B$	GB / B&	&G / GD
3:	$G / GH	RG / GV	QG / GZ	CG / GX	PG / GT	OG / GI	SG / GK	NG / GL	MG / GM	LG / GN	KG / GS	IG / GO	TG / GP	XG / GC	ZG / GQ	VG / GR	HG / G$	DG / G&	&D / DH	$D / DV	RD / DZ
4:	QD / DX	CD / DT	PD / DI	OD / DK	SD / DL	ND / DM	MD / DN	LD / DS	KD / DO	ID / DP	TD / DC	XD / DQ	ZD / DR	VD / D$	HD / D&	&H / HV	$H / HZ	RH / HX	QH / HT	CH / HI	PH / HK
5:	OH / HL	SH / HM	NH / HN	MH / HS	LH / HO	KH / HP	IH / HC	TH / HQ	XH / HR	ZH / H$	VH / H&	&V / VZ	$V / VX	RV / VT	QV / VI	CV / VK	PV / VL	OV / VM	SV / VN	NV / VS	MV / VO
6:	LV / VP	KV / VC	IV / VQ	TV / VR	XV / V$	ZV / V&	&Z / ZX	$Z / ZT	RZ / ZI	QZ / ZK	CZ / ZL	PZ / ZM	OZ / ZN	SZ / ZS	NZ / ZO	MZ / ZP	LZ / ZC	KZ / ZQ	IZ / ZR	TZ / Z$	XZ / Z&
7:	&X / XT	$X / XI	RX / XK	QX / XL	CX / XM	PX / XN	OX / XS	SX / XO	NX / XP	MX / XC	LX / XQ	KX / XR	IX / X$	TX / X&	&T / TI	$T / TK	RT / TL	QT / TM	CT / TN	PT / TS	OT / TO
8:	ST / TP	NT / TC	MT / TQ	LT / TR	KT / T$	IT / T&	&I / IK	$I / IL	RI / IM	QI / IN	CI / IS	PI / IO	OI / IP	SI / IC	NI / IQ	MI / IR	LI / I$	KI / I&	&K / KL	$K / KM	RK / KN
9:	QK / KS	CK / KO	PK / KP	OK / KC	SK / KQ	NK / KP	MK / K$	LK / K&	&L / LM	$L / LN	RL / LS	QL / LO	CL / LP	PL / LC	OL / LQ	SL / LR	NL / L$	ML / L&	&M / MN	$M / MS	RM / MO
10:	QM / MP	CM / MC	PM / MQ	OM / MR	SM / M$	NM / M&	&N / NS	$N / NO	RN / NP	QN / NC	CN / NQ	PN / NR	ON / N$	SN / N&	&S / SO	$S / SP	RS / SC	QS / SQ	CS / SR	PS / S$	OS / S&
11:	&O / OP	$O / OC	RO / OQ	QO / OR	CO / O$	PO / O&	&P / PC	$P / PQ	RP / PR	QP / P$	CP / P&	&C / CQ	$C / CR	RC / C$	QC / C&	&Q / QR	Q / Q	RQ / Q&	&R / R$	$R / R&	&$ / $&

Figure 6.1. The lower line of each row represents the 231 basic pairs moving forward; the upper line, the pairs moving in reverse.

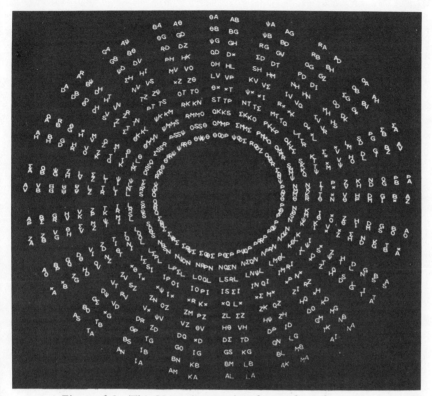

Figure 6.2. The 231 pairs moving forward, and reverse,
reading clockwise.

figure 6.2, which presents the 231 basic pairs moving forward,
and reverse, reading clockwise. All this would seem quite
straightforward were it not for the fact that Saadia, followed by
pseudo-Abraham ibn Daud and various epitomizers, understood
the Hebrew *galgal* ("wheel") as "sphere," i.e., as the celestial,
diurnal sphere. According to these thinkers, the 231 basic pairs
were set into the surface of the diurnal sphere which is in continuous rotation.[8] This mixture of Ptolmaic astronomy with

[8] For Saadia, see ed. Derenbourg, pp. 50–55 (Arabic), pp. 73–78 (French); ed.
Qafih, pp. 84–88. For pseudo-Rabad, see *SY* part 1, pp. 79–80 in great detail. An
example of a modern epitomizer would be I. Kalisch, *Sepher Yezirah* (New York:
Frank and Co., 1877), p. 49.

neopythagorean magic vastly confused the issue. The tradition of a wheel, circle, or star can be found, however, in Shabbatai Donolo, Judah Barceloni, and Eleazar of Worms.[9] It must be added though that, while charts of the basic sequence abound, I have found only one instance of a representation of it in the form of a circle or star.[10]

The Solution: The "Gates," The "Sign," and Their Function

Having deciphered the basic sequence (231 pairs of letters, forward and reverse) and the basic arrangement of the sequence (as a wall and as a wheel), the reader remains with the question: What exactly were the "gates" and how did they work? Saadia seems to have understood each pair of letters in the basic sequence to be a "gate." Eleazar of Worms seems to have understood the "gates" to be a series of letters, paired (or grouped) according to one of his magical alphabets. Thus, in his instructions on how to create a homunculus (Heb., *golem*), he seems to have required that these alphabetic series be recited in order.[11] Neither interpreter, however, sought to define the "gates" by superimposing one set of the basic sequence upon the other, i.e., the forward ("Aleph with all of them") upon the reverse ("all of them with Aleph"). Such a definition may have been the intent of Judah Barceloni, who gives instructions on how to cut

[9] For Shabbtai Donolo, see *SY* part 2, pp. 134–35. For Judah Barceloni, see *Commentar zum Sepher Jezira von R. Jehuda b. Barsilai*, ed. S. J. Halberstam (Berlin: M'kize Nirdamim, 1885), pp. 209–10 in great detail. He seems to have envisioned actually a sphere within a sphere. For Eleazar of Worms, see *Commentary*, ed. Przemysl, 4b, 15b.

[10] Knut Stenring, *The Book of Formation* (London: 1923), facing p. 24 (reprt, New York: Ktav, 1970) p. 21. I do not know how this diagram is to be read.

[11] See his *Commentary*, ed. Przemysl, 15b–22a. To destroy the homunculus, the various alphabets must be recited backwards. See the excellent essay by G. Scholem, "The Idea of the Golem," *On the Kabbalah and its Symbolism* (Schocken, N.Y.: 1965) 158–204 with special attention to 165–73, 184–95. For Saadia, see Footnote 8, above.

leather to make such a device.[12] None of the interpreters claim to have a long tradition behind them and their efforts may, therefore, represent nothing more than individual medieval attempts to reconstruct the possible meaning of this very early text.

The solution I propose to the problem of the "gates" is to set the 231 basic pairs of the reverse sequence above the 231 pairs of the forward sequence such that the second letter of the upper line of pairs coincides with the first letter of the lower line. This has been done in figure 6.1. Each such grouping of two pairs forms, then, a "gate," there being 231 "gates" in the chart as is required by both Mishnayot. This suggestion has some basis in Barceloni's *Commentary* and in that of Isaac the Blind. It also conforms to the solution I propose to the problem of the "sign."

The next problem to be addressed is, which grouping of "gates" constituted the table of magical letters with which God created the universe?[13] The solution is hidden in Mishna 4:[14] "And the sign of the matter is: 'There is nothing in goodness

[12] Barceloni, *Commentar zum Sepher,* p. 210. An interesting parallel may be the text in "Hilkhot ha-Kisse," *Merkabah Sheleymah,* ed. S. Mussajoff (Jerusalem: 1922; reprt, Jerusalem: Makor, 1972), 21b: "All the letters were called before God in pairs, except Lamed [*sic*]."

[13] There can be no doubt that Scholem is correct in asserting that *Sefer Yesira* is a magical as well as a speculative text (cf., e.g., ch. 1, Mishna 4, and the last Mishna of the text together with my commentary in *Understanding Jewish Mysticism*) and in connecting it with the magical traditions in talmudic literature. *Sefer Yesira* most certainly was viewed as a magical text by Eleazar of Worms and his medieval followers (Scholem, *Trends,* ch. 2, "The Idea of the Golem," etc.). Scholem, however, appears to have misinterpreted these pericopae as linguistic lessons (*Ursprung und Anfänge der Kabbala* [Berlin: de Gruyter, 1962], p. 29 and "The Name of God," *Diogenes,* 79 [1972]: 75).

[14] Heb.: *ain be-tovah le-maalah me-oneg, ve-eyn be-raah le-mattah mi-nega;* Alternate reading: *im be-tovah, le-maalah me-oneg; ve-im be-raah, le-mattah mi-nega.* Conflated reading: *im be-tovah, ain le-maalah me-oneg; ve-im be-raah, ain le-mattah mi-nega.* (Grunewald, *Critical Edition,* p. 148, shows the many variations.) The English here follows the first reading. The alternative reading yields: "If in goodness, it is above pleasure and, if in misfortune, [it is] below a [leprous] lesion." The conflated reading yields: "If in goodness, there is nothing above pleasure and, if in misfortune, there is nothing below a [leprous] lesion." As we shall see, it makes no difference which reading is used.

above pleasure and nothing in misfortune below a [leprous]
lesion.' "

The commentators, uniformly, construe this "sign" in a moralistic vein. Thus, Saadia, Donolo, Eleazar and the others interpret: [15] "If you put your mind to this Book for 'good,' [i.e.,]
to amplify the exaltedness of God, 'there is nothing greater than
pleasure.' But, [if you put your mind to this Book] for 'misfortune,' 'there is nothing below a [leprous] lesion.' " The commentators also, uniformly, notice that the letters of the word for
"pleasure"—ONG—yield the letters of the word for "[leprous]
lesion"—NGO—when the letter 'ayin—O—is put at the end,
and not at the beginning, of the word.[16] This venerable tradition of commentary, however, is unconvincing. First, it introduces a moralistic note into an otherwise clearly magical and
speculative text. Second, it fails to show how the quotation fulfilled the function for which the author-editor of Sefer Yesira
designed it—to act as a "sign" within the permutational scheme
of the whole system.

I propose that the quotation, moralistic though it may
sound, actually functions as a mechanical-magical "key," or
"sign," by which the "correct" grouping(s) of "gates" can be
identified. This can be shown as follows: [17] The quotation contains four key words: TVBH (pronounced tovah, meaning
"goodness"), ONG (pronounced 'oneg, meaning "pleasure"),
ROH (pronounced ra'ah, meaning "misfortune" or "evil"), and

---

[15] I have followed the Donolo text (SY, p. 135), but all the texts are parallel and
can be found in the various commentaries. To this, Eleazar of Worms adds: "If for
goodness"—[If] one comes to create some creature with them, he should recite them
according to their order. And, if one wants to return it to the dust, he should [recite
them in] the opposite order. . . . This is the meaning of "If in goodness." He thus
interprets "amplifying the exaltedness of God" as the performing of a magical, creative act using the same magical alphabets God used. (ed. Przemysl, 4b–5b.) See also
Scholem, Ursprung . . . p. 26.

[16] Saadia (ed. Qafih, p. 85) points to other such words in the Hebrew language,
e.g., $KR (a "lie") and KR$ (a "wooden beam"). He is followed by Barceloni and
others.

[17] I am deeply indebted to my student Harry Sparks for the mathematical theory
and the computer program which has enabled me to propose this solution.

NGO (pronounced *nega‘,* meaning "a [leprous] lesion"). Disregarding the meaning, note that three of these key words have three letters. The remaining key word ought, I think, to reflect the same structure. I propose, therefore, emending the text to read either TVB (pronounced *tuv,* meaning "goodness," this being the masculine form of the noun) or TBH (pronounced *tovah,* same meaning, but with "defective" spelling).[18] Now, set theory in mathematics provides that any four-unit set can be converted into a three-unit set when it reaches the form AB—BC, i.e., when the medial term of the two units is common. The key to the permutational system, therefore, lies in one or more of the following "gates:" TV—VB (or, TB—BH), ON—NG, RO—OH, NG—GO. It is necessary, then, to move the elements in the chart until one or more of these key "gates" appears. By keeping the lower line on figure 6.1 fixed, and moving the top line 17 spaces to the left, one of the two "correct" charts is generated. This can be seen in figure 6.3, where the "gate" NG—GO appears twice, at coordinates 3:12 and 3:10 (where it is upside-down). The other "correct" chart is generated from figure 6.1 by moving the upper line 12 spaces to the left. This can be seen in figure 6.4, where the "gate" TB—BH appears twice, at coordinates 2:3 and 2:7 (where it is upside-down).[19] The quotation, then, functions to arrest the

[18] On the relative merits of these two emendations, neither of which is drastic, see below.

[19] Each such movement of the upper line one unit to the left we called a "rotation," the pairs of letters going from position 1 to position 21 when they reached the edge of the chart. Since, however, there are 11 lines on the chart, it was necessary to move each of the upper lines simultaneously. After each move of one unit (i.e., after each "rotation"), the computer printed out a new chart. There are, thus, theoretically 21 charts, each of which contains 231 "gates." This yields 4,851 possible gates. Actually, since we did not know which chart would yield the key words, the computer performed an additional (and, it turned out, an unnecessary) operation: after printing out the first set of 21 charts, the computer moved each lower line up one rank on the chart. This we called an "advance." After each advance all 21 possible rotations of the upper line were performed, yielding 21 charts for each advance. Since there are 11 advance positions, and 21 rotation positions for each of the "advance" positions, the computer had to generate a total of 231 charts. Each chart has 231 gates and so we actually had to examine 53,361 gates. Had we, then, set the forward sequence above

reverse: forward

	1	2	3	4	5	6	7	8	9	10	11	12	13	14	15	16	17	18	19	20	21
1:	HA AB	DA AG	GA AD	BA AH	&A AV	$A AZ	RS AX	QA AT	CA AI	PA AK	OA AL	SA AM	NA AN	MA AS	LA AO	KA AP	IA AC	TA AQ	XA AR	ZA A$	VA A&
2:	HB BG	DB BD	GB BH	&G BV	&B BZ	$B BX	RB BT	QB BI	CB BK	PB BL	OB BM	SB BN	NB BS	MB BO	LB BP	KB BC	IB BQ	TB BR	XB B$	ZB B&	VB GD
3:	DG GH	&D GV	$D GZ	RD GX	$G GT	RG GI	QG GK	CG GL	PG GM	OG GN	SG GS	NG GO	MG GP	LG GC	KG GQ	IG GR	TG G$	XG G&	ZG DH	VG DV	HG DZ
4:	RH DX	QH DT	CH DI	PH DK	QD DL	CD DM	PD DN	OD DS	SD DO	ND DP	MD DC	LD DQ	KD DR	ID D$	TD D&	XD HV	ZD HZ	VD HX	HD HT	&H HI	$H HK
5:	OV HL	SV HM	NV HN	MV HS	OH HO	SH HP	NH HC	MH HQ	LH HR	KH H$	IH H&	TH VZ	XH VX	ZH VT	VH VI	&V VK	$V VL	RV VM	QV VN	CV VS	PV VO
6:	KZ VP	IZ VC	TZ VQ	XZ VR	LV V$	KV V&	IV ZX	TV ZT	XV ZI	ZV ZK	&Z ZL	$Z ZM	RZ ZN	QZ ZS	CZ ZO	PZ ZP	OZ ZC	SZ ZQ	NZ ZR	MZ Z&	LZ Z&
7:	QT XT	CT XI	PT XK	OT XL	&X XM	$X XN	RX XS	QX XO	CX XP	PX XC	OX XQ	SX XR	NX X$	MX X&	LX TI	KX TK	IX TL	TX TM	&T TN	$T TS	RT TO
8:	KI TP	&K TC	$K TQ	RK TR	ST T$	NT T&	MT IK	LT IL	KT IM	IT IN	&I IS	$I IO	RI IP	QI IC	CI IQ	PI IR	OI I$	SI I&	NI KL	MI KM	LI KN
9:	ML KS	&M KO	$M KP	RM KC	QK KQ	CK KR	PK K$	OK K&	SK LM	NK LN	MK LS	LK LO	&L LP	$L LC	RL LQ	QL LR	CL L$	PL L&	OL MN	SL MS	NL MO
10:	QS MP	CS MC	PS MQ	OS MR	QM M$	CM M&	PM NS	OM NO	SM NP	NM NC	&N NQ	$N NR	RN N$	QN N&	CN SO	PN SP	ON SC	SN SQ	&S SR	$S S$	RS S&
11:	RQ OP	&R OC	$R OQ	&$ OR	&O O$	$O O&	RO PC	QO PQ	CO PO	PO P$	&P P&	$P CQ	RP CR	QP C$	CP C&	&C QR	$C Q$	RC Q&	QC R$	&Q R&	$Q $&

Figure 6.3. The "gate" NG-GO appears at coordinates 3:12 and (upside-down) 3:10.

ROTATION = 12   ADVANCE = 1

reverse: forward	1	2	3	4	5	6	7	8	9	10	11	12	13	14	15	16	17	18	19	20	21
1:	KA/AB	IA/AG	TA/AD	XA/AH	ZA/AV	VA/AZ	HA/AX	DA/AT	GA/AI	BA/AK	&A/AL	$A/AM	RA/AN	QA/AS	CA/AO	PA/AP	OA/AC	SA/AQ	NA/AR	MA/A$	LA/A&
2:	KB/BG	IB/BD	TB/BH	XB/BV	ZB/BZ	VB/BX	HB/BT	DB/BI	GB/BK	&G/BL	&B/BM	$B/BN	RB/BS	QB/BO	CB/BP	PB/BC	OB/BQ	SB/BR	NB/B$	MB/B&	LB/GD
3:	IG/GH	TG/GV	XG/GZ	ZG/GX	VG/GT	HG/GI	DG/GK	&D/GL	$D/GM	RD/GN	$G/GS	RG/GO	QG/GP	CG/GC	PG/GQ	OG/GR	SG/G$	NG/G&	MG/DH	LG/DV	KG/DZ
4:	XD/DX	ZD/DT	VD/DI	HD/DK	&H/DL	$H/DM	RH/DN	QH/DS	CH/DO	PH/DP	QD/DC	CD/DQ	PD/DR	OD/D$	SD/D&	ND/HV	MD/HZ	LD/HX	KD/HT	ID/HI	TD/HK
5:	&V/HL	$V/HM	RV/HN	QV/HS	CV/HO	PV/HP	OV/HC	SV/HQ	NV/HR	MV/H$	OH/H&	SH/VZ	NH/VX	MH/VT	LH/VI	KH/VK	IH/VL	TH/VM	XH/VN	ZH/VS	VH/VO
6:	PZ/VP	OZ/VC	SZ/VQ	NZ/VR	MZ/V$	LZ/V&	KZ/ZX	IZ/ZT	TZ/ZI	XZ/ZK	LV/ZL	KV/ZM	IV/ZN	TV/ZS	XV/ZO	ZV/ZP	&Z/ZC	$Z/ZQ	RZ/ZR	QZ/Z$	CZ/Z&
7:	KX/XT	IX/XI	TX/XK	&T/XL	$T/XM	RT/XN	QT/XS	CT/XO	PT/XP	OT/XC	&X/XQ	$X/XR	RX/X$	QX/X&	CX/TI	PX/TK	OX/TL	SX/TM	NX/TN	MX/TS	LX/TO
8:	PI/TP	OI/TC	SI/TQ	NI/TR	MI/T$	LI/T&	KI/IK	&K/IL	$K/IM	RK/IN	ST/IS	NT/IO	MT/IP	LT/IC	KT/IQ	IT/IR	&I/I$	$I/I&	RI/KL	QI/KM	CI/KN
9:	QL/KS	CL/KO	PL/KP	OL/KC	SL/KQ	NL/KR	ML/K$	&M/K&	$M/LM	RM/LN	QK/LS	CK/LO	PK/LP	OK/LC	SK/LQ	NK/LR	MK/L$	LK/L&	&L/MN	$L/MS	RL/MO
10:	PN/MP	ON/MC	SN/MQ	&S/MR	S/M	RS/M&	QS/NS	CS/NO	PS/NC	OS/NC	QM/NQ	CM/NR	PM/N$	OM/N&	SM/SO	NM/SP	&N/SC	$N/SQ	RN/SR	QN/S$	CN/S&
11:	&C/OP	$C/OC	RC/OQ	QC/OR	&Q/O$	$Q/O&	RQ/PC	&R/PQ	$R/PR	&$/P$	&O/P&	$O/CQ	RO/N$	QO/C&	CO/C$	PO/QR	&P/Q$	$P/Q&	RP/R$	QP/R$	CP/$&

Figure 6.4. The "gate" TB-BH appears at coordinates 2:3 and (upside-down) 2:7.

movement of the pairs of letters against one another at a certain
point (or points). The "sign," thus, is not a moralistic preach-
ment but a device for identifying the correct "wall." For when
the proper key word has been reached, it acts like a tumbler in a
lock, falling from the upper line to the lower line and locking
the movement of the sets. (Actually, since the key words appear
rightside-up and upside-down, there is a "double-lock" effect in
both "correct" charts.) To be sure, there is also a "correct" setting (or settings) for the "wheel" or "star." This can be seen, for
the NG—GO "gate" only, in figure 6.5 (which is a birdseye
view) at the bottom and in figure 6.6 (which is an eye-level
view).[20]

The final question to be confronted is, how was this chart (or
charts) used? We do not know. The text of *Sefer Yesira* does not
tell us. None of the other early rabbinic gnostic-mystical texts
tell us, though some mention the use of the alphabet in Creation. I do not know of any Hellenistic parallels that might
explain such usages. And the attempt to adjucate the merits of
the two proposed emendations sheds no light on the subject.[21]

the reverse sequence and repeated the whole procedure, we would have had to examine 462 charts with 106,722 gates. It must be clearly stressed that the author-editor
of the *Sefer Yesira* had only to draw a maximum of 18 charts containing 4,158 gates
to reach his goal. This was not an overly burdensome task. Note, too, that the
number 18, when transmuted into Hebrew letters by *gematria* (10 = *yod*, 8 = *het*)
yields the word *hai*, which has the meaning "alive." The letters of this word are, to
this day, worn as a piece of jewelry (subconsciously, an amulet) by many Jews.

[20] I am deeply indebted to Mr. Russ Burns of the computer graphics program at
Brown University for his patience and skill in generating these programs, especially
on such short notice. My thanks, too, to Professor Sol Bodner, Visiting Professor of
Engineering, who photographed the graphic displays. The two stars displayed in figure 6.2 and 6.5 actually could be rotated and, with judicious handling, the medial
letters of NG-GO and OG-GN could be made to superimpose exactly. The two stars
displayed in figure 6.6 could also rotate and, in doing so, they slipped in and out of
perspectival infinity. See *Understanding Jewish Mysticism* for other diagrams from this
series.

[21] The emendation to TV-VB has one advantage and one disadvantage. The advantage is that all the key words except NG-GO then appear only in the upper line (figure 6.3 as follows: TV [6:8], VB [2:21]; ON [10:17], NG [3:12], and RO [11:7],
OH [5:5]). One can then read the "sign" as follows: "All the key words before the

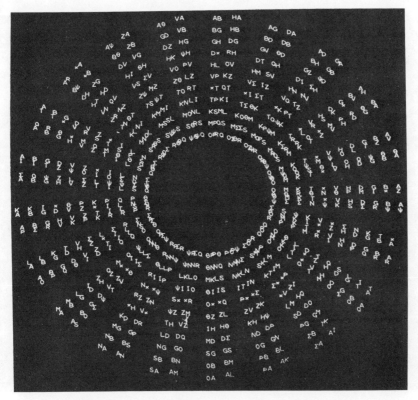

Figure 6.5. The "gate" NG-GO: Birdseye view.

It is even possible that both charts were meant to be used.[22] It does seem clear, though, that the author-editor of *Sefer Yesira*

word 'below' are 'above' (i.e., in the upper line) while the word that occurs after 'below' (i.e., NGO) is the sign (because it appears in the lower line)." The disadvantage to this emandation is that it destroys the stylistic unity of the quotation. The emendation to TB-BH also has one advantage and one disadvantage. The advantage is that it preserves the stylistic unity of the quotation: the two-syllable structure of the key words, the internal rhyme, and the alternating masculine-feminine form of the nouns. The disadvantage is that the words "above" and "below" lose their meaning, since NG-GO is not contained in the upper line only. In neither case is there support from the manuscripts. In both cases, it may be that we are dealing with a deliberately deceptive style which is a common element in magical texts.

[22] In this case, the "sign" may have to be read: "For good things, use the TB-BH chart, for bad things, use the NG-GO chart." Even in this interpretation, we still do not know how the charts were actually used.

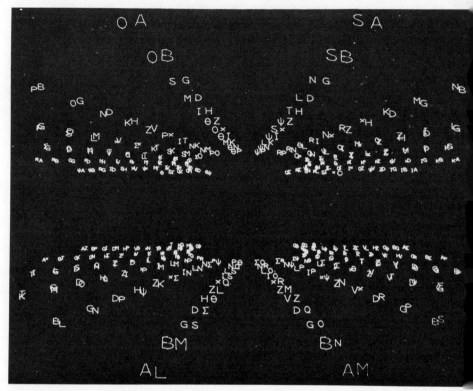

Figure 6.6. The "gate" NG-GO: Eye-level view.

intended this pericope[23] to be an account of the speech of God, possibly reflecting the magical practices of his day.

Even in the exciting world of magic and cosmogonic speculation, it is passing strange that the *Golem* of twentieth-century

[23] There appear to be two other magical alphabetic sequences in the *Sefer Yesira:* the sequence of "mothers," "doubles," and "simple letters," each of which "rules over" several aspects of existence (chapters 3, 4, 5), and the sequence of alphabetic permutations called "stones" and "houses" (at the end of chapter 4). They are discussed in *Understanding Jewish Mysticism.* See also N. Sed, "Le *Sefer ha-Razim* et la methode de 'Combinaison des Lettres,'" *Revue des études juives,* 130 (1971): 295–304. Scholem, too, has pointed out that the text of *Sefer Yesira* contains disconnected elements.

science should have come to the aid of the researcher to explain something of the mighty deeds of the Creator.[24]

[24] This name for the computer was coined by Scholem at the dedication of the computer in Rehovot, Israel. That speech is included at the end of his *The Messianic Idea in Judaism* (Schocken, N.Y.: 1971).

It may seem strange and even unwarranted to have utilized twentieth-century mathematical analytical tools on a second-century magical text. I must, therefore, stress again that, for the author-editor of *Sefer Yesira,* the formulation of the chart and the circles was conceptually and practically simple and rather straightforward. It is only we who had to utilize extended tools of analysis to arrive at his conclusions.

I wish to acknowledge with thanks the criticism and cautions of my teacher, Professor G. Vajda, and my colleague, N. Sed, in formulating these issues.

SEVEN

Martin Buber and the No-Self Perspective

EDITH WYSCHOGROD

MARTIN BUBER is widely regarded as a philosopher of the human person. His conception of the person stands in sharp contrast to that of the no-self doctrines of early Buddhism [1] and of Friedrich Neitzsche. I shall try to show that, despite the seeming incompatibility between the no-self position and that of Buber, a sense can be given to the former that would render it complementary rather than opposed to Buber's ethical personalism since the self that is disposed of by the no-self perspective is in fact the self Buber finds obstructive to the emergence of ethical existence. I shall also try to show

[1] I take the key difference between early and late Buddhism to be that in the former the permanence of the real is denied, and that permanence is the result of a subjective and erroneous intepretation we place upon what is actually transitory, whereas in the latter there is no becoming in the real. For late Buddhism the Absolute alone is real but it is identical with phenomena. The emphasis upon momentariness of early Buddhism forms the foundation of the no-self doctrine and is therefore important for any attempt at de-structuring the self. This distinction between early and later Buddhism is supported in T. R. V. Murti, *The Central Philosophy of Buddhism* (London: George, Allen and Unwin, 1960), esp. pp. 121f and 232f; Edward Conze, *Buddhist Thought in India* (London: George, Allen and Unwin, 1962), ch. 2. This distinction holds whether or not Conze's conception of an "archaic Buddhism" is accepted. Late Buddhism, however, which emphasizes the figure of the compassionate saint, the Boddhisattva, who forsakes his own enlightenment, is temperamentally more appealing to Buber. See Philip Wheelright, "Buber's Philosophical Anthropology," in *The Philosophy of Martin Buber*, eds. Paul Arthur Schlipp and Maurice Friedman (La Salle, Ill.: Open Court, 1967), p. 79ff.

that Buber fails to grasp the significance of the no-self perspective for the development of his own position because of the
divergence between his view of the higher self and that of both
early Buddhism and Nietzsche.

According to the no-self view, nothing substantive accounts
for the unity of experience. The existence of a subject behind
what we do, what we think or what we feel is denied. If we understand the factors that give rise to the idea of a self, the self
can be reduced to these factors and its illusory character exposed. The no-self position is opposed to at least one conception
of the person maintained in more or less unitary fashion in Rabbinic tradition and which persists in the work of Buber—that of
the person as moral agent. For Buber the person in the fullest
sense is the whole being, identifiable with his or her past, self-
determining, value-seeking, and capable of living in community with others.[2] This is the self of the primary word I-Thou.
Buber contrasts this full personal being with the solidary monadic existence of a self which neither turns toward nor receives
the address of other persons, the self of the primary word, I-It.
This self is less than human in the fullest sense since genuine
personality is constituted intersubjectively, in the relationship
between man and those who solicit his response. By taking the
It-self to constitute the exclusive meaning of the person and also
to be something substantive which "has" thoughts, percepts
and feelings, we mistakenly attribute the properties of things to
persons.

Higher Selves

Buber acknowledges that the It-self is necessary for the conduct of everyday affairs, but he does not hesitate to characterize

[2] Buber's view is in conformity with that of many professed personalists. The characteristics enumerated are also cited in E. S. Brightman, "Personalism (Including
Personal Idealism)," in *A History of Philosophical Systems*, ed. V. Ferm (New York,
1950), pp. 34–352.

it as an illusory form, an intellectual construct without ontological foundation. Lacking genuine being, it "remains a functional point, experiencing and using, no more."[3] Buber writes:

> Individuality [the It-self] revels in its special being or, rather mostly in
> the fiction of its special being which it has made up for itself. For to
> know itself means basically for it . . . to establish an authoritative ap-
> parent self, capable of deceiving it ever more and more fundamentally,
> and to procure for itself, in looking to and honoring this apparent self,
> the semblance of knowledge of its own being as it really is. *Real knowl-*
> *edge of its being would lead it to self-destruction—or to rebirth.*[4]

For Buber, the It-self is "of the unreality." In order to come to
grips with "real being" the It-self must give way so that the
higher self can emerge.

But how can the higher self come into being as long as the
It-self stands in the way? And, if the self of I-it is illusory, how
are we to dispel the illusion? Buber fails to provide an adequate
account of how the transformation of the It-self comes about. It
appears to be a mysterious event which arises spontaneously as a
response to the appeal of the other. But, I would argue, the dismantling of the It-self can be understood cognitively as a reduction to something more primary, and that this reduction consists of a revelatory insight into its nature that is sufficiently
radical to lead to the dissolution of its solidary being. This
dissolution creates a free space—the "between," or "the narrow
ridge" which, for Buber, is the space of dialogue. Without an
adequate understanding of the dismantling process, the
emergence of a higher self remains an unfounded assumption.
Buber's work lacks an account of this crucial intermediate phase
which, I believe, can be supplied by borrowing from the no-self
positions to which I have alluded.

Buber discusses both Buddhism and Nietzsche in consider-

---

[3] Martin Buber, *I and Thou*, trans. Ronald Gregor Smith (New York: Scribner's,
1958), p. 64.
[4] *Ibid.*

able detail although not, of course, in regard to the matter of the utility of the no-self doctrine for his own position. Rather, each, for quite different reasons, is seen to foreclose the possibility of dialogue: the Buddhist by failing to perceive the significance of the everyday as the sphere in which dialogue arises and Nietzsche for making man problematic only to attempt a transcending of man in a leap away from the human. I shall consider in detail Buber's actual remarks on each of these positions in due course. Suffice it to say at this point that the main thrust of Buber's criticism is directed at each of these positions for its view of a higher plane of existence, since what is higher in each case precludes the life of dialogue. For the Buddhist, the aim of life is to transcend life, to attain *Nirvana,* the "blowing out" of consciousness. Through the extinction of the self-sense, suffering is eliminated and the endless round of rebirths is overcome. The state of Nirvana is a state of being about which nothing can be said, since it lies beyond all distinction. For Nietzsche, higher existence also leaves human existence as we know it behind. While the features of this new being cannot be clearly discerned, the next stage will culminate in the triumph of the life forces against the reactive forces of traditional morality.

Neither the Buddhist position nor that of Nietzsche could be further removed from Buber's conception of the relational self which comes into existence when one stands over and against the being who addresses one, a relation in which the whole being of the respondent is involved. Buber's view can be seen as a contemporary gloss upon the traditional statement of this position in the *Ethics of the Fathers* with which it is in strict conformity: "R. Hanina b. Dosa said: He in whom the spirit of his fellow creatures takes delight, in him the spirit of the All-present takes delight; and he in whom the spirit of his fellow creatures takes not delight, in him the spirit of the All-present takes no delight."[5]

[5]*Aboth,* 3: 13.

While Buber's ultimate aim, deriving from classical Jewish sources, contrasts sharply with that of the Buddhists and of Nietzsche, some significant claims in regard to the self are nevertheless held in common by Buddhism and Nietzsche. Both share the view that there is no substratum underlying mental processes, that unity is conferred upon the fleeting stream of experience by hypothesizing a subject in order to control this otherwise chaotic content, and that the given is, in actuality, a disorderly flux, a river into which we never step twice. Furthermore, the putative self is merely part of this flux. To put the matter otherwise, we presume, falsely, that since there are mental processes (thinking for example) there must be something that thinks. In fact, all that can be said is: "There are thoughts (or for that matter images, affects or speech)."

It may seem that this interpretation flouts the most obvious assumptions of common sense, since the ordinary person ascribes unity to the flow of impressions as belonging to the same memory stream or as attributable to one and the same body.[6] But the force of this critique of the subject lies not in its conformity with common sense but rather in its eliciting of what is taken for granted by common sense—that is, that the self confers upon itself the same sort of being that it confers upon physical objects. Common sense interprets the self as a substance of sorts having a quasi-materiality; materiality, in this view, is understood as something that persists through time, despite the alterations of its properties. While thoughts, moods, percepts flicker into existence, then disappear, we may posit some mind or soul as lending them support since in our observations of physical objects we notice that objects retain their identity through noncatastrophic change. If we "eject the ghost from the machine"[7] we may hold that the unity of the

---

[6] The bodily criterion and the memory criterion have been central to the discussion of the criteria for reidentifying persons. See Terence Penulham's account in *Encyclopedia of Philosophy* (New York: Macmillan, 1967), *s.v.* "Personal Identity."

[7] The "ghost" is what Descartes means by mind, an entity having an existence of its own and somehow "hitched up" to bodies according to Gilbert Ryle, *The Concept of Mind* (London: Hutchinson and Co., 1949).

person depends upon the body, since the body can be interpreted in a straightforwardly mechanistic way as a physical object which subsists side by side with other physical objects. But, in either version of the common-sense view, a coherent account of the self's persistence is purchased at the price of the self's monadic isolation. The self of common sense criticized by the Buddhists and by Nietzsche is identical with the It-self as Buber describes it. Why then has it been so difficult to jettison the common-sense view? No-self thinkers argue that by positing a "within" and a "without," self and world, we retain an illusory but pleasurable sense of control over both.

The Perspective of Buddhism

For the Buddhist the denial of a self is the simple corollary of the transitoriness of things; the real is impermanent. Similarly, personality cannot be lasting since it, too, is nothing but the consequence of certain transitory psychological conformations. These are designated as the five groups of grasping: material shape, feeling, perception, impulse, and consciousness. It is particularly the last, consciousness, the awareness of ongoing experience as one's own, that gives rise to the illusion of a self. The error takes place at a metaphysical level but is seen to have important ethical consequences. The metaphysical error consists in attributing permanence to the world when flux and impermanence, coming-to-be and passing away, the rise and fall of momentary events (*dhammas*) are all that exist. If we allow ourselves to experience freely, if we stop "clinging," we can penetrate the flux and see into the "own-being" of these momentary events. Similarly, if we relinquish "clinging" we can recognize the self as an appearance which is no more than the functional unity of the five groups of grasping.[8]

Once the transitoriness of things is recognized, we can see the practical consequences entailed by this altered perspective. Since

[8] This is the account given to Majjhima Nikaya 1: 49–54, in *Buddhist Texts through the Ages*, eds. Edward Conze et al. (New York: Harper and Row, 1964), p. 67f.

no state endures, even those states which are pleasant must give way to those which are distonic. Hence, not only unpleasant experience, but pleasant experience as well, if properly understood, is seen as "ill" until, at last, we realize that all existence is ill. Similarly the notion of an enduring self must be dismissed: "If one does not behold any self or anything of the nature of the self in the five groups of grasping . . . . one is an Arhant, the outflows extinguished." [9]

This account of the rudiments of early Buddhism was certainly well-known to Buber. But while there are frequent and often lengthy allusions to Buddhism in his work, Buber's interest lies in assessing the extent to which Buddhism allows for the emergence of dialogue rather than in descriptions of Buddhist techniques for de-structuring the self. For Buber Buddhism represents a mid-point between a full merger with the Absolute as it is described in the Upanisadic tradition on the one hand and the genuine life of dialogue on the other. Unity with the Absolute is one of the most seductive ways of betraying the life of dialogue. The path of mysticism originates in the religious sphere and as such its derogation of the life of everyday experience in which dialogue must remain is particularly dangerous. In mysticism, as Buber describes it, the I sinks into the Absolute so that one of the terms in the I-Thou relation is sublated. When the terms of relation disappear, relation itself disintegrates and there is only undifferentiated oneness. But, Buber claims, Buddhism avoids this perilous course. The Buddha refuses to assert that unity exists or, for that matter, that it does not exist, that the person persists after death or does not persist. This is the "noble silence" of Buddhism. For Buber, the Buddha refuses to speak out on these questions because Enlightenment is beyond all the categories, beyond existence or nonexistence, and also because on practical grounds concern with such questions leads to idle disputation and distracts the novice from the life of sal-

[9] Samyutta Nikaya 3: 19, in *Buddhist Texts,* p. 75.

vation. All this, Buber claims, is commendable in the teaching of Buddhism: "Loyal truth of our meeting we can follow the Buddha as far as this but a step further would be disloyalty to the reality of our life." [10]

While the Buddha refuses to say anything about Nirvana, whether or not the I is absorbed into the Absolute, or even whether there is an Absolute, still Buber argues, the *goal* of Buddhism is "the cessation of pain, that is of becoming and passing away—release from the cycle of rebirth," and this, for Buber, is an anodyne which falsely masks the tragic dimension of human existence:

> [This] is the formula of the man who has freed himself from the appetite for living and thus from the necessity to become ever anew. . . . [We cannot know if there is rebirth] but if we did know . . . we would not seek to escape it, and we would long not indeed for gross being but for the power to speak in each existence in its own way and language, the eternal I that passes away and the eternal Thou that does not pass away. [11]

In contrast to Buddhism, Buber, like Nietzsche, asserts that one ought to act so that one would be willing to relive one's action of the moment eternally. Hence, for Buber, an interpretation of the world which reduces the sphere of concrete experience to "names and forms," an illusory realm of appearances, deprives our moral acts of seriousness. "Despite all the paradoxes connected with it in observation for us," Buber writes, this is the only world we have. This attitude toward the quotidian reflects deep roots in traditional Jewish sources which emphasize obedience to God in the concrete particular context of the individual's life and prohibit self-mortification in order to

[10] Buber, *I and Thou*, p. 91. Hugo Bergman, "Martin Buber and Mysticism," in *The Philosophy of Martin Buber*, eds. P. A. Schilpp and M. S. Friedman (La Salle, Ill.: Open Court, 1967), pp. 297–308. Bergman distinguishes Buber's early mysticism in which the world is the sphere of completion for man's realization and his later view of reciprocity.

[11] Buber, *I and Thou*, p. 91.

attain a higher plane of existence; it is forcefully expressed in a
text from the Jerusalem Talmud:

> R. Isaac said: are not the things prohibited in the Law enough for you
> that you want to prohibit yourself other things? A vow of abstinence is
> like an iron collar, such as is worn by prisoners, about a man's neck:
> one who imposes upon himself such a vow is like a man who meets a
> detachment of soldiers with such a collar, and puts his own head into
> it. Or he is like a man who drives a sword into his body.[12]

If, for Buber, Buddhism falls short of real relation because of
its world-rejecting view, still Buber's description of the It world
reflects a Buddhist understanding of fate and causality. The
world of It is the sphere in which mechanism (the view that all
existing things are produced by matter in motion) and determinism (the view that everything physical or psychological is
produced by prior conditions) prevail.[13] In the realm of It, the
laws of cause and effect are operative and freedom is excluded;
the sphere of It "rises up," and becomes "an oppressive and
stifling fate." Buber specifically associates the realm of fate and
causality with the rule of karma from which, in cultures where
the doctrine of karma is a religiously operative principle, man
cannot escape. While the karma doctrine is not exclusive to
Buddhism, it permeates the Buddhist understanding of human
life in its relation to the order of existing things. For Buber, the
It-self is similarly dominated by a chain of causes.

But, while there are resemblances between the realm of It
and karmic causality, the two conceptions cannot be equated
with one another in any simple fashion. The law of karma is ir-
reversible; once karmic taint has been acquired, it continues to
be operative until its causal efficacy is depleted. When karma is

---

[12]*Jerusalem Talmud,* Nedarim, 9: 1, 41b.

[13]For the relationship between freedom and determinism in Buber, see Paul Edwards, "Buber and Buberism—A Critical Evaluation," (The Lindley Lecture, University of Kansas, 1970). Edwards argues against the incompatibility of relational
openness and determinism claiming that another's actions may be caused and pre-
dicted even if *we* refrain from controlling or predicting them.

exhausted the realm of karma can be transcended but the course of karma, once acquired, is inexorable. For Buber the Jewish doctrine of sin and forgiveness does not posit the consequences of sin as inevitable; one is able to alter the order of the world of It. Sin is the failure to respond to the word of God, thus disturbing the fundamental relationship between God and man. But man may turn toward God and again be restored as God's creature: "Turning, provided the individual exerts his whole soul to accomplish it, is not prevented by anything, not even by the sin of the first men." [14] Thus, for Buber, the sin of Adam does not predetermine man to sin or to persist in sin nor does it prevent repentance. Original sin is absent from the Jewish perspective from which Buber derives his view, so that the force of causality, comparable to the rule of karma, cannot prevail.

While many texts that succeed *I and Thou* appear to diminish the differences between Buddhism and biblically derived religion, the shift is one of emphasis rather than a radical change in perspective. In his essay "Religion and Philosophy," [15] Buber stresses the dialogical possibilities of Buddhism, but his stress is in the interest of showing that affirmation of the existence of the gods alone does not distinguish religion from philosophy. Even a relation to a nonpersonal world ground when it is undertaken with the whole being "counts" as religion, while a distanced apprehension of the gods indifferent to man's fate belongs within the realm of philosophical theism. Thus Buber writes: " 'The Awakened One,' freed and freeing from the wheel of births . . . knows a genuinely divine, an Unborn, Unoriginated, Uncreated." [16] Although the Buddha knows it only negatively, refusing to make any assertions about it, "yet he stands related to it with his whole being." [17] The one the Buddha

[14] In Martin Buber, *Two Types of Faith,* trans. Norman P. Goldhawk (New York: Harper and Row, 1951), p. 158.

[15] Martin Buber, *Eclipse of God,* trans. Maurice S. Friedman, (New York: Harper and Row, 1952), pp. 27–62.

[16] *Ibid.,* p. 27f.

[17] *Ibid.,* p. 28.

addresses is not a person but what defines Buddhism as a religion is, for Buber, "still founded on the duality of I and Thou." [18] Still, Buddhism remains for Buber infradialogical in the crucial realm of the interhuman because of its disdain for the mundane. "The realer religion is, so much the more it means its own overcoming. It ceases to be the special domain 'religion' and wills to become life." [19]

Buber carefully avoids easy thematic comparisons which arise so frequently in the folkloric material of the history of religions. The individual motif must be considered in its wider context in order to assess its significance. There is a diffusion from the core doctrines of a religion to its periphery. Thus Buber interprets tales from Hassidic sources and Zen parables, both of which have mystical import and bear close resemblance to one another as, nevertheless, bearing divergent significations. In his essay dealing with Hasidic and late Buddhist spirituality, "The Place of Hasidism in the History of Religion," [20] Buber is at pains to establish the this-worldly emphasis of the Zen masters in contradistinction to earlier Buddhist traditions. Buber writes: "Not by turning away from reality, but only by surrendering himself to it, can man achieve salvation. In accordance with this Zen cloisters are not places of contemplation for individuals but fellowship settlements of landworkers; the work is the foundation of their life." [21]

Activity is emphasized in Zen tradition in accordance with the principle of Mahayanna Buddhism that *Nirvana* (Enlightenment) and *samsara* (the round of rebirths) are one. If this is so, then salvation lies in the here and now. The teacher no longer conveys doctrinal content but a doing. [22] At this point, however, the resemblance ends. Buber cites the Boddhidharma, the

[18] *Ibid.*, p. 31.
[19] *Ibid.*, p. 34.
[20] In Martin Buber, *Hasidism*, trans. Carlyle and Mary Witton-Davies, (New York: Philosophical Library, 1948), pp. 184–201.
[21] *Ibid.*, p. 189.
[22] *Ibid.*, p. 192.

first patriarch of Zen: " 'If you wish to seek the Buddha, look into your own nature; for this nature is the Buddha himself.' "[23] For Buber this position differs radically from that of Hasidism: "Even the most personal mysticism reposes here in the shade of historical revelation. Never in the eyes of the soul, has this God become to such an extent its God, the God of the soul, that he would cease to be the God of Sinai."[24]

Buber's critique of Zen rests on a foundation explicated in *I and Thou,* as we have seen, and thereby sublates the possibility of dialogue. The self sinks into the Absolute. In fact, there is little difference between Buber's general remarks on mysticism and his interpretation of Zen as a species of inwardly directed mysticism. Thus, on Buber's reading of Zen, distinctions within the phenomenal sphere disappear: When the character of phenomenality is penetrated it is seen as non-different from the Absolute. Since this position is incompatible with Buber's rejection of the mystical, it falls short as a model of reductive technique for the dissolution of the It-self whereas the emphasis of early Buddhism upon the five groups of grasping (*skandhas*) is better able to provide the foundations for the self's dismantling. The no-self doctrine holds consciousness to be the chief culprit among the skandhas for producing the illusion of a self. The illusion is dispelled once the character of the relationship between consciousness and self is apprehended. Part of the chain of dependent co-production, consciousness, like all existing things, is dependent upon causes outside itself. The condition which gives rise to a particular state of consciousness gives consciousness its character. "It is just like a fire which you call by the name of the fuel—a wood fire, a fire of sticks, a cow dung fire etc.,"[25] a text of early Buddhism comments. The It-self of

[23]*Ibid.,* p. 197.

[24] *Ibid.,* p. 199. Gershom Scholem in "Martin Buber's Conception of Judaism," in *Jews and Judaism in Crisis* (New York: Schocken, 1976), p. 169 sees Buber's polemic against gnosis as distorting his view of Hasidism's relation to the world.

[25]Majjhima Nikaya, 1: 256ff, in *The Buddhist Tradition,* ed. Wm. Theodore de Bary (New York: Random House, 1969), p. 18.

Buber, which does not recognize this dependency, necessarily tends to self-will. It is unable to pry itself loose from the habits of its preceding behavior. The Buddhist view provides clues to the nature of cognitive acts which suggest correlative therapeutic praxes that might provide both an intellectual and psychological basis for loosening the hold of the It-self while remaining well within the ambit of Buber's theoretical scheme.

Nietzsche and the Philosophy of Life

The rejection of the self as subject is central to Nietzsche's destructuring of metaphysics, the attempt to show that metaphysical categories are created out of human needs. For Nietzsche, the existence of a self founds the distinction between appearance and reality which runs through the history of Western metaphysics no matter how differently this distinction has been articulated. The distinction arises not from the nature of things but because of a human prejudice, the prejudice against corporeality: Whatever is bodily "becomes," changes, and is therefore designated as unreal. Reality is, instead, ascribed to the unchanging. But the unchanging is itself a psychologically derived notion founded upon our belief in a subject. Hence, "the concept of substance is a consequence of the concept of the subject, not the reverse."[26] We believe so firmly in the subject that all our notions of truth and reality are founded on it: "The subject is the fiction that many similar states in us are the effect of one substratum but it is *we* who first created the 'similarity' of these states: our adjusting and making them similar is the fact, not their similarity . . . . (which ought rather to be denied)."[27]

The distinction between appearance and reality is, for Nietzsche, (in contrast to the case of Buddhism) the result of a vested

[26] Friedrich Nietzsche, *The Will to Power*, trans. Walter Kaufmann and R. J. Hollingdale (New York: Random House, 1968), p. 268.
[27] *Ibid.*, p. 269.

interest, of a particular moral perspective. The reason for making the distinction is then to deploy it in the interest of the very moral perspective which accounts for its inception. This is one of the many circles which Nietzsche believes he has located in the history of Western moral philosophy. For Nietzsche all thinking done within the ambit of Western metaphysics is of this sort.[28] It can be compared to what psychoanalysts call "rationalization," an elaborate intellectual system constructed to save some protected or relatively secure view of reality while refusing to come to grips with the actual character of things. For Nietzsche, it is only by conceiving a true world that man has been able to *imagine* values.[29]

Could it not be argued that Nietzsche himself engages in the surreptitious use of the very standards of truth and validity he criticizes? Nietzsche tries to bring his thought into conformity with this act of rejection by developing a new method, that of going back to the origin of a phenomenon or concept, either to original linguistic usage or to an original psychological need. This works well for Nietzsche in his analysis of the origin of the self. Nietzsche writes:

> Through thought the ego is posited; but hitherto one believed as ordinary people do, that in the "I think" there was something of immediate cer-

[28]The interpretations of Nietzsche deriving from Martin Heidegger stress this point. But, for Heidegger, Nietzsche's man is a metaphysical being *par excellence,* the one who makes beings present to himself. Thus, in Heidegger's view, Nietzsche has not himself escaped this circle but instead represents its consummation. See esp. Martin Heidegger, *What is Called Thinking?* trans. Glenn Gray (New York: Harper and Row, 1968), pp. 57–99. Some French interpretations attempt to find in Nietzsche strategies for avoiding this pitfall. Michel Foucault sees Nietzsche's genealogical method as an attempt to overcome the pursuit of the origin, which, for Foucault, is the real interest of metaphysics. See Michel Foucault, *Language, Counter-Memory, Practise,* trans. Donald F. Bouchard and Sherry Simon (Ithaca: Cornell University Press, 1977), p. 142. Giles Deleuze in "Nomad Thought," in *The New Nietzsche,* ed. and trans. David Allison (New York: Dell, 1977), p. 142 sees Nietzsche as avoiding the "codification" system of Western metaphysics by attaining to a new conception of corporeality. For Deleuze Nietzsche transmits "something that does not and will not allow itself to be codified . . . to a new body" which Nietzsche himself invents.

[29]Nietzsche, *The Will to Power,* p. 297.

tainty and that this "I" was the given cause of thought from which, by analogy, we understood all other causal relationships. However indisputable this fiction may have become by now—that in itself proves nothing against its imaginary origin.[30]

The genealogical method, the tracing of origins, is best understood by reverting to the example of psychoanalytic strategy: the psychotherapist does not enter the arbitrary and fanciful system of the patient in order to expose its falsity, a method which would merely reinforce the system. Instead the level of discourse is altered and attention is turned to the unconscious needs and drives which gave rise to it. Attention is deflected to the psychological origin of these distorted beliefs. Similarly Nietzsche claims: "The inquiry into the origin of our evaluations and tables of the good is in no way identical with a critique of them."[31]

If cognitive standards are not to be trusted, how then is one to weigh moral evaluations? What interest do they serve? Nietzsche's answer is "life," and what he means by "life" is a form, a special case of the "will to power."[32] This conception is central to Nietzsche's thinking and serves as a heuristic device in an otherwise aphoristic nonsystematic "structure." It is also central in Buber's critique of Nietzsche and therefore merits a brief excursus.

---

[30]*Ibid.*, p. 267f.

[31]*Ibid.*, p. 148.

[32] See *Ibid.*, esp. pp. 341–47. The centrality of the will to power in Nietzsche's work has generated a large critical literature. Central to any understanding of the problem for the English-speaking reader are: Walter Kaufmann, *Nietzsche: Philosopher, Psychologist, Antichrist,* (Princeton: Princeton University Press, 1950), pp. 178–207; R. J. Hollingdale, *Nietzsche: The Man and his Philosophy* (Baton Rouge: Louisiana State University Press, 1965), pp. 170ff, pp. 218ff, pp. 264f. Heidegger's approach can be derived from his *What is Called Thinking,* 1968, pp. 57–110. Also of interest are Joan Stambough, *Nietzsche's Thought of Eternal Return* (Baltimore: Johns Hopkins University Press, 1972), pp. 94–102; Alphonso Lingis, "The Will to Power" in *The New Nietzsche,* pp. 37–63. Bernard Magnus, *Nietzsche's Existential Perspective* (Bloomington: Indiana University Press, 1978, p. 21ff and Rose Pfeffer, *Nietzsche, Disciple of Dionysus* (Lewisburg, Pa.: Bucknell University Press, 1972), pp. 145ff stress the will to power is a metaphysical rather than a psychological principle, a point that seems not always to have been grasped by Buber.

For Nietzsche, the will to power is the most basic form of affect from which all other affects are merely derivative. The will
to power strives to increase itself. When a quantum of desired
power has been attained pleasure ensues, but this pleasure is not
power itself. The will to power is not the source of anything.
Thus it cannot be viewed as the cause of change: it must be
identical with change itself. There is nothing other than increase or decrease of power; this alternation constitutes the flux
of becoming. Nietzsche's destructuring of the self uncovers flux,
the changing quanta of the will to power, the will to grow
stronger of every center of force.[33]

Buber and Nietzsche

The relationship between Buber, a thinker committed to
Jewish values, and Nietzsche is complex. It might be imagined
that the many anti-Semitic passages in Nietzsche would merit
comment in such contexts as Buber's extended analysis of
Nietzsche's philosophical anthropology in the essay "What is
Man?"[34] But this does not occur. For Buber the Nietzschean
critique of values leads inevitably to their replacement by ideology. Without inner restraint, no force prohibits the self-
proclamation of supermen. But an attempt to establish a direct
relationship between the genealogical de-structuring of value
and Nietzsche's problematic relationship to the prophetic writings and to Jews is not, for Buber, of central concern. Buber
sees in Nietzsche a forerunner of National Socialism, but adds
that "Nietzsche did not foresee that his idea of "becoming God"
would be taken possession of not by the type he called the
'higher man.' but by the lower man who is, to be sure, without
restraint, but . . . assailed by doubts in his innermost being
strives to be worshipped in order to believe in himself."[35]

[33] Nietzsche, *The Will to Power*, p. 349.

[34] Martin Buber, *Between Man and Man*, trans. Ronald Gregor Smith (Boston:
Beacon Press, 1955), pp. 118–205.

[35] Martin Buber, "People and Leader," in *Pointing the Way*, ed. and trans. Maurice
S. Friedman (New York: Harper & Row, 1957), p. 160. Walter Kaufmann, *Nietzs-*

The influence of Nietzsche's work on Buber is pervasive despite Nietzsche's problematic relationhip to Jewish values.[36] It can be discerned in two contexts: First in Buber's borrowing of Nietzschean vitalism as a response to what Buber saw as the unviable character of German idealism.[37] For German idealism an unmediated grasp of reality was no longer possible without taking into account the role played by the understanding. Thus man, world, and God remained forever out of reach. The second context in which the relationship between Buber and Nietzsche can be found is denser, more complex. Here the values of Nietzschean vitalism are retained but are now juxtaposed, against the emphasis of classical Judaism, upon ethical personalism. On the one hand, Nietzsche equates the ethical values of Jewish prophetism with slave morality and the overthrow of the instincts; on the other, Buber finds in the life-affirming aspects of Hasidism an emphasis quite compatible with Nietzschean vitalism and the philosophy of realization, characteristic of Buber's early period, without abandoning the morality of prophetism. In Buber's view, love, joy, and humility are the central virtues of Hasidism; joy is the form in which the other two are expressed.[38] And this stress upon joy is in conformity

che: *Philosopher, Psychologist, Antichrist* (Princeton: Princeton University Press, 1950), cites numerous anti-Semitic passages in Nietzsche. See esp. pp. 284–306. But Tracy Strong, *Friedrich Nietzsche and the Politics of Transfiguration* (Berkeley: University of California Press, 1975), p. 279, writes, "It simply won't do to pile up the quotations which say nice things about the Jews and nasty things about the Germans." And Karl Lowith, *From Hegel to Nietzsche,* trans. David E. Green (New York: Holt, Rinehart and Winston, 1964; German ed. 1941), p. 200, writes: "To see the abyss which separates Nietzsche from his latter day prophets, it suffices to read his writings against Wagner and his remarks on the Jewish question. But this does not contradict the obvious fact that Nietzsche became the catalyst of the [Nazi] "movement," and determined its ideology in a decisive way. The attempt to unburden Nietzsche of this intellectual guilt is as unfounded as the reverse effort."

[36] For an assessment of Nietzsche's influence on Buber's life, see "Autobiographical Fragments," in *The Philosophy of Martin Buber,* p. 12ff. Of Zarathustra, Buber writes: "It worked on me in the manner of an invasion . . . and it was a long time before I could liberate myself from it."

[37] For Buber's relation to German idealism see Maurice Friedman, *Martin Buber: The Life of Dialogue* (Chicago: The University of Chicago Press, 1955), pp. 34ff.

[38] *Ibid.,* p. 22.

with the vision of joy in Nietzsche's *Zarathustra, The Gay Science* and elsewhere.

Buber, in accord with Nietzsche, argues for the inseparability of religious and ethical values. But the ethical and the religious can be differentiated. In Buber's view, the former concerns the affirmation or rejection of a particular line of conduct in relation to an intrinsic sense of value or disvalue, while the latter concerns "the relation of the person to the Absolute."[39] But the ethical cannot originate values independently of the religious; it can only serve as the sphere of their actualization. "Living religion wishes to bring forth living ethos," Buber writes.

The relationship between values and their ground in Buber's thinking makes it impossible for him to treat the ethical as a separate problematic in Nietzsche's work. Since this view is also in conformity with Nietzsche's own stand, it is not surprising to find in Buber's analysis of Nietzsche's treatment of moral question an emphasis upon Nietzsche's view that God is dead. In "Religion and Reality," Buber finds in Nietzsche's saying a summing up of the post-Hegelian philosophical situation.[40] In "Religion and Modern Thinking," Heidegger and Sartre are read as glosses upon the Nietzschean antitheology. Heidegger's statement, "The slaying means the elimination of the supra-sensual world," and Sartre's allegation, "He spoke to us and now he is silent,"[41] are, for Buber, essentially correct and set the problematic for his own thinking: how to rescue the biblical God from the void into which the God of metaphysical speculation had fallen. Buber responds to the crisis of the Nietzschean death of God theology by exempting the living God of Judaism from this critique. The living God is not only self-revealing but self-concealing, Buber argues. But this self-concealment must not be misinterpreted. Since the living God is not intended by the Nietzschean attack, Buber rejects Nietzsche's attempt to bestow

[39] Martin Buber, "Religion and Ethics," in *Eclipse of God*, p. 95f.
[40] "Religion and Reality," in *ibid.*, pp. 20ff.
[41] "Religion and Modern Thinking," in *ibid.*, pp. 65ff.

upon man the divine creative freedom which would include the creation of moral values. For Buber, if values do not derive from an Absolute, they cease to be normative. "That is what Nietzsche said and it has not become any truer since then. One can believe in, and accept, a meaning or value, one can set it as a guiding light over one's life if one has discovered it, not if one has invented it."[42]

For Buber the attack upon values leads to the central contradiction of Nietzsche's thinking: the biologically based morality which leads to a doctrine of the superman espoused in Zarathustra on the one hand, and radical skepticism in regard to values on the other. Nietzsche is willing to ascribe moral value to a more originary power structure in which values were determined by a ruling class, although this view is not without its difficulties. "Underlying this view," Buber declares, "is the metaphysical conception that the life of the spirit, like all life, can be reduced to the single principle of the 'will to power.' But now Nietzsche executes a singular reversal. The 'slave morality' which turns against the will to power is identified with morality as a whole, as if the 'master morality,' of which Nietzsche approves, did not exist at all."[43] But, even if Nietzsche's description of a morality based upon the power of a noble class were accurate, and such a morality were desirable, it would, for Buber, run counter to Nietzsche's view that all moral values are the consequences of human prejudice, thus justifying moral skepticism. What is more, in Buber's view, the biologically based morality of the superman is also nullified by Nietzsche's doctrine of the eternal recurrence which Buber sees as the "eternalization of the meaningless."[44] Man is condemned to repeat and this repetition forecloses the possibility of development.[45]

[42] *Ibid.*, p. 70.
[43] "Religion and Ethics," p. 10.
[44] *Ibid.*, p. 110.
[45] Since Buber formulated his position, there has been a shift in the perspective taken on the problem of eternal recurrence. Stambough, *Nietzsche's Thought of Eternal Return*, pp. 106ff, argues that time is not something which is stretched out, ver-

But, when Buber's own thinking comes to fruition in such great personalist essays as "What is Man,"[46] his evaluation of Nietzsche shifts to a more positive assessment of Nietzsche's contribution to post-Kantian philosophical anthropology. With Kant, Buber claims, "Man has known that he is the subject most deserving of his own study."[47] But, Buber continues, "the difficulty of this concern with his own being soon overpowers and exhausts him, and in silent resignation he withdraws." For Buber, the nature of the "whole man" is destined to remain a mystery. And this is so because the whole man cannot have a nature and is, therefore, refractory to definition. Man becomes who he is only in dialogue and dialogue is an event which can never be hypostatized. That man cannot be defined Buber learns from two sources: one is Hasidism, the other Nietzsche. Buber cites Rabbi Bunam von Przysucha to this effect: "I wanted to write a book called *Adam,* which would be about the whole man. But then I decided not to write it."[48] For Buber, the questionableness of man is also Nietzsche's great theme. "Like no other previous thinker," Buber writes, "Nietzsche brings man into the center of his thought about the universe, not man as clear and unambiguous being, but rather man as a problematic being; and thereby he endows the anthropological question with an unprecedented force and passion."[49]

But Nietzsche also sees man as "something fleeting and plastic," whose goal is not preinscribed in an anterior reality. For Nietzsche man has no meaning; he must give it to himself. He

tically, backwards and forwards but recurs in the Moment. Pierre Klossowski, in "Nietzsche's Experience of the Eternal Return," in *The New Nietzsche,* pp. 108ff. sees the eternal return as "bringing on the successive realization of all identities." Bernard Magnus, *Nietzsche's Existential Perspective,* sees the eternal return both as existential imperative (each willed act being deemed infinitely worthwhile), pp. 111ff. and as countermyth, (myth opposed to the dominant Christian and Platonic myths of suprasensuality), pp. 155ff. Rose Pfeffer, *Nietzsche, Disciple of Dionysius,* pp. 145ff, sees eternal recurrence as metaphysical reality created and destroyed cyclically.

[46] In Martin Buber, *Between Man and Man,* 1955, pp. 118–205.
[47] *Ibid.,* p. 118.
[48] *Ibid.,* p. 118.
[49] *Ibid.,* p. 148.

can only find it in life; and life, it may be recalled is, for Nietzsche, a form of the will to power. This definition has two sides: a striving for the increase of power and the desire to display, employ, or practice power. But the will to power has no goal. For Buber, a will to power lacking an end leads to the avidity for power, "power which is withdrawn from responsibility, power which betrays the spirit, power in itself. It corrupts the history of the world."[50] But, if the self is reducible to the will to power in all its various guises, its masks, its personae, has Nietzsche not provided a profound, if not altogether satisfying, account of the world of It taken to the edge, at its most extreme remove from dialogue as it were? Once the fictive being of the substantive ego has been exposed, real meeting, the relational event of an encounter between a nonsolitary I and a Thou can come about. The obstacle to real meeting has been dismantled. For Buber, "Every means is an obstacle. Only when every means has collapsed does the meeting come about."[51]

[50] Buber, *Between Man and Man*, p. 153.
[51] Buber, *I and Thou*, p. 12.

THREE

American Philosophical
Reflections

Introduction

"Diversity," Professor Blau writes in the Introduction to American Philosophic Addresses, *1700–1900, "has served the end of democracy as unity never could." To exhibit this diversity so crucial to democracy has been his primary mission as an historian of philosophy in America. He has given special attention to philosophers unread today, though well known in their own day. Each of these figures in our historical community of philosophers, he believes, has said something worthy. The whole range of American thought has been within his purview. For this comprehensive scholarship all of us working today in the history of American philosophy are in his debt.*

His work in this field was begun as assistant to Herbert W. Schneider, who acknowledged him as "co-inventor" of A History of American Philosophy, *"whoever may be its author." The bibliographies he contributed to that monumental volume alone constitute a landmark in scholarship. Surely no scholar before or since has mastered the primary and secondary literature as he did.*

Following Schneider in the Deweyan tradition, Blau has not limited his attention to those who have written technical philosophy. He has seen philosophy as disciplined reflection upon all the problems of life, not merely upon intellectual puzzles. To illuminate ideas as forces in the resolution of human problems, he has made many studies of the personal, social, and intellectual settings of the works of individual philosophers. Such studies appear in the numerous books he has edited. Perhaps most notable in this regard is his Introduction to Francis Wayland's The Elements of Moral Science, *in which he explains how Wayland, a member of the "Academic Orthodoxy," modified his moral absolutism in the light of his own experience and that of his country.*

His respect for nontechnical contributions and interest in the setting of philosophical thinking have not, however, led him to treat the technical work of major figures superficially, as cultural historians often have. In

Men and Movements in American Philosophy, *a standard text*
since its publication in 1952, technical contributions are given
penetrating treatment. With good reason Max Fisch has remarked that
many of the book's "analyses of the work of major thinkers are the best in
any general history, regardless of length."

   In the essays which follow many of Blau's interests are reflected.
Edward H. Madden discusses nineteenth-century philosophers of the
"Academic Orthodoxy," an important school of philosophy little read by
professional philosophers today. Building on Blau's well known
scholarship in this area, Madden shows that there was more diversity
and much less orthodoxy among these thinkers than has hitherto been
recognized. John J. McDermott's contribution on Emerson treats the
central theme of a nonacademic philosopher with the same respect Blau
has treated many nonacademic philosophers, including Emerson.
McDermott also offers ample evidence of Emerson's importance as an
influence on classical American philosophers. In the third essay, Douglas
Greenlee, like Blau an historian in the tradition of Deweyan
naturalism, examines Santayana as an important figure in the history of
American naturalism. Greenlee's respect for Santayana's work is in no
way lessened by the fact that he seldom wrote in the manner of technical
philosophers. My own essay with Chandana Chakrabarti focuses on the
personal, social and intellectual setting of the development of James's
realism. We have attempted intellectual biography of James that we
hope resembles what Blau has done so effectively with many other
American philosophers.

   Taken together, the essays reflect the diversity in American thought
that Blau has been concerned to emphasize throughout his career.

                                                          P.H.H.

EIGHT

Asa Mahan and
the Oberlin Philosophy

EDWARD H. MADDEN

I

THE HISTORY OF American philosophy and religion from 1775 to 1850 largely centers around the reactions to Old Light Calvinism and the variations of it introduced by Hopkins and Emmons. During this period, Princeton Theological Seminary and Western Reserve College at Hudson, Ohio, remained the bastions of Calvinism. The chief reactions to it were the American Enlightenment, Unitarianism, free-will Trinitarianism, and Transcendentalism, which was essentially a move beyond Unitarianism.

Of all the reactions against Calvinism it was free-will, evangelical, revivalistic Trinitarianism which took the United States by storm from 1815 on. Almost all the denominations were affected by this Arminian surge, and its success is not difficult to understand. Church attendance had hit a low ebb even before the days of the Revolution. Many people had come to consider

This paper is a thoroughly revised and enlarged version of "The Concept of Agency in the Philosophy of Asa Mahan" read at a Conference in American Theology at Asbury College, April 1973, and subsequently printed in *The Asbury Seminarian,* 32 (1977): 36–48.

Calvinism not only theologically unsound but also morally repugnant. Equally unacceptable to most people, however, were most of the alternatives. Paine, Allen, and Jefferson seemed to miss the heart of religion. God is not simply the conclusion of a philosophical argument; the center of the religious impulse is commitment, devotion, and love. Enlightenment figures had no religious roots; Deism was primarily the religion of a momentary intelligentsia. Andrews Norton and other Unitarians also seemed to miss the heart of religion; they empirically *justified* religion and *demonstrated* the authenticity of the Scriptures (as if the Bible needed their support!) and had little to say about commitment, devotion, and love. Transcendentalism had the merit of emphasizing direct contact with God but was not widely acceptable because it wholly rejected Christian revelation. Moreover, like the Enlightenment it had no institutional base to give it continuity. Though quite differently constituted, it was the product of still another momentary intelligentsia. Free-will Trinitarianism flourished where the other alternatives did not because it satisfied a maximum of needs. It was intellectually respectable; it based its rejection of Calvinism on a rival philosophical view of human agency based primarily on the work of Thomas Reid and Dugald Stewart, supplemented, when appropriate, by the work of Kant, Cousin, Joffroy, and others; while at the same time it maintained a scriptural emphasis that made sense of revelation, commitment, and sacrifice; and all the while it stressed a close emotional tie between God and man, an element lacking in all other reactions against Calvinism. To hitherto reluctant Christians it seemed like a minor miracle to have a warm alternative to equally cold Calvinism and Unitarianism, and withal intellectually respectable!

Many of the older colleges and most of the new ones burgeoning on the frontier became, or were to begin with, free-will Trinitarian. The philosophy teachers, and the not uncommon philosopher-presidents, of these colleges constitute what has come to be called the "Academic Orthodoxy."[1] In many ways, these thinkers were not orthodox at all; they were theologically and philosophically quite radical. The actual orthodoxy of the day were the faculty at Princeton Seminary and Western Reserve College. It would no doubt have pained Professor Charles Hodge of the Seminary had he thought that Asa Mahan of Oberlin would ever be called orthodox in any sense, on any issue, by anyone! In another sense the rubric is useful, though even here it may be misleading. The free-will Trinitarians were orthodox in the sense that they had an agreed-upon view of the nature of Christianity, human agency, and consciousness, the latter expressed in an elaborate and detailed faculty psychology that was presented monolithically as "the true philosophy." There is an important element of truth in this estimate, to be sure, but in many cases, and on numerous issues, members of the so-called orthodoxy held absolutely opposite views on fundamental philosophical issues and argued against each other with great acumen as well as heat.

The Oberlin philosophers are prime examples of thinkers united in a thorough critique of Calvinistic determinism, while at the same time vigorously disagreeing among themselves.

[1] Joseph L. Blau, *Men and Movements in American Philosophy* (New York: Prentice-Hall, 1952), pp. 73–109; Herbert W. Schneider, *A History of American Philosophy*, 2nd ed. (New York: Columbia University Press, 1963), pp. 195–220; E. H. Madden, *Civil Disobedience and Moral Law in Nineteenth Century American Philosophy* (Seattle: University of Washington Press, 1968), pp. 3–84; D. H. Meyer, *The Instructed Conscience: The Shaping of the American National Ethic* (Philadelphia: University of Pennsylvania Press, 1974). The point of the phrase "free-will Trinitarian" is to set our group apart from both the Calvinists and the Unitarians. The Unitarians shared with our group an allegiance to Scottish realism and a similar attack on Calvinistic determinism, so they are usually also included in the "Academic Orthodoxy." Hence, while all free-will Trinitarians were members of the Orthodoxy, not all of the latter were members of the former. For a discussion of the Unitarians, see D. W. Howe, *The Unitarian Conscience: Harvard Moral Philosophy, 1805–1861* (Cambridge: Harvard University Press, 1970). See also W. R. Hutchison's *Transcendentalist Ministers: Church Reform in the New England Renaissance* (New Haven: Yale University Press, 1959), especially, pp. 1–51.

Mahan, Finney, and Fairchild were the first three presidents of Oberlin College, and were all squarely within the Scottish realistic tradition. Mahan always held the radical view, Fairchild the conservative one, and Finney fluttered between the two. They all defended the "doctrine of liberty" against Calvinistic determinism; Finney and Fairchild accepted Edwards' teleological analysis of true virtue, while Mahan castigated them as utilitarians and defended a deontological view close to Butler's intuitionism; Mahan and Finney extended their concept of human agency into a doctrine of Christian Perfection, Sanctification, or Holiness, which many New Light thinkers (to say nothing of the Calvinists) thought heretical, while Fairchild rejected the doctrine and was responsible for its decline at Oberlin after Mahan had left and Finney had backtracked a bit; and Mahan and Finney drew radical conclusions about social reform and civil disobedience from their view of human agency, while Fairchild was lukewarm toward activism and helped put it to sleep at Oberlin after Mahan had left and Finney again had backtracked.

I have examined in detail elsewhere the views and disputes of the Oberlin philosophers concerning the nature of true virtue and their views on social reform and their acts of civil disobedience.[2] I shall concentrate here on Mahan's view of agency and shall consider how successful he was in rebutting Edwards' determinism and how successful he was in parlaying his own view of agency into a defensible view of Christian Perfection. It will turn out that his critique of Edwards is probably more solid than his own positive view of agency and that his views of agency and perfection generate an interesting tension.

Mahan's views on agency and perfectionism are not arcane

[2] *Civil Disobedience and Moral Law,* pp. 44–84; James Hamilton and E. H. Madden, "Edwards, Finney, and Mahan on the Derivation of Duties," *Journal of the History of Philosophy,* 13 (1975): 347–60; E. H. Madden, "Oberlin Reform and Civil Disobedience," *Oberlin Alumni Magazine,* 65 (1969): pp. 9–13, 17.

topics as might be supposed. Agency, of course, is a perennially fascinating topic in philosophy, and the doctrine of sanctification has been increasingly important in American Protestantism since 1850. Mahan's writings on sanctification, influential in his day, are still read with great interest by many people today. While the Oberlin philosophers are not read by the philosophical community today, they are indispensable reading for the philosophical theologians and the laity of the contemporary holiness movement. Included in this movement—either formally by membership in the Christian Holiness Association or informally associated with this group—are such denominations as the Wesleyan Methodist Church and the Pilgrim Holiness Church (recently united as the Wesleyan Church); the Free Methodist Church; the Church of the Nazarene; the Missionary Church and the Brethren in Christ, two Mennonite groups; the Ohio, Rocky Mountain, Northwest, and Kansas meetings of the "Friends"; the Salvation Army; the Christian and Missionary Alliance; the Church of God; the Evangelical Methodist Church; and the Evangelical Church of North America (a recent merger of the Methodist and Evangelical United Brethren Churches). Presses associated with the movement have kept the works of Mahan, Finney, and John Morgan of Oberlin in print and distribute them widely, with the strange consequence that they are probably read by more people than Emerson, James, and other "stars" in American philosophy.[3]

II

Mahan's critique of determinism and his defense of the doctrine of liberty appeared in his *Doctrine of the Will,* published in

---

[3] For an excellent bibliography of the literature concerning the Holiness Movement, and for the presses associated with the movement, see the pamphlet by Donald W. Dayton, "The American Holiness Movement: A Bibliographic Introduction," (Wilmore, Kentucky: The Asbury Theological Seminary, 1971).

1845, and were summarized in his *Autobiography*, written toward the end of his life.[4]

According to Mahan, the determinist believes that any given "act of will" results from causes and that only one outcome in each case was possible. He believes that no other act of will than what actually occurred was ever possible. The events caused are various acts of the will like choosing, preferring, and intending, while the causes of such acts would be aspects of sensibility like wanting, wishing, liking, and hating. The latter as causes are lumped together as motives. The determinist, then, is claiming that all volitions are caused by motives and could not have been other than they were. Prima facie, there is no room in their world view for judgments to the effect that a person might have done other than he did, though, as we shall see, the determinist tries to make accountability and determinism compatible, efforts which Mahan is at great pains to rebut.

On the other hand, Mahan continues, the defender of the "doctrine of liberty" rejects the view that an act of will had to be what it was and could not have been otherwise. He believes that before a person decides there are various alternatives which he could have chosen. His model of conscious, voluntary acts is one of human agency rather than of motives causing volitional acts. The Will is free to choose either to follow the suggestions of Intelligence or to be determined by the sensibilities—hence it makes perfectly good sense to say that a person could have done other than he did. What a person does is not capricious; every act has a motive. However, Mahan's point is that the Will has the power to choose between motives;[5] his motives do not determine him to act the way he does. It is only when motives are conceived as direct determining factors that a person could not have done other than he did. On Mahan's view, however,

---

[4] Asa Mahan, *Doctrine of the Will* (New York: Mark H. Newman, 1845); *Autobiography: Intellectual, Moral, and Spiritual* (London: T. Woolmer, 1882), pp. 197–214. See also Mahan's *Lectures on the Ninth of Romans and Election and the Influence of the Holy Spirit* (Boston: Charles H. Peirce and Co., 1851), pp. 154–80.

[5] Mahan, *Doctrine of the Will*, pp. 84–85, 103–104.

one can say a person acted with a motive without implying the motive caused him to act the only way he could.

Mahan argued against determinism and defended "the doctrine of liberty" in various ways; the following arguments constitute only his first volley, so to speak.[6]

1. No matter what arguments are given in favor of determinism, the reports of consciousness flatly contradict them. We are all directly aware of being able to do either of two things, or, having done one, the ability to have done other than we did. More specifically, we are aware that we could have acted differently *in the identical situation.* This italicized phrase is crucial. What we are aware of when we consult our consciousness is not the belief that if our *circumstances* had been different we might have acted differently, but rather that in the very *same* circumstances we might have acted other than we did.

2. If determinism is true, men have no power whatever to will or to act differently from what they do. But in this case the idea of obligation, merit and demerit, and the consequent propriety of reward and punishment, become meaningless and inapplicable. It becomes impossible to hold anyone morally responsible for anything. The doctrine of liberty, however, salvages the notion of moral responsibility. The idea of human agency involved here makes sense of "could have done otherwise" and so provides the framework for accountability.

3. God admonishes men as sinners to stop transgressing the moral law, a command which automatically becomes meaningless on the deterministic view. On this view, God is nothing but a tyrant demanding of men what it is impossible for them to do. It likewise renders God unjust, for God must be seen on Judgment Day as eternally damning certain souls and saving others when none of the lot supposedly could have done other than they did and so merit no judgment at all. On the doctrine

---

[6] Most of the arguments in our text come from the *Doctrine of the Will,* since the later discussions tend to summarize the ones found there. There is, however, some original material in the *Autobiography* and *Lectures on the Ninth of Romans.*

of liberty, however, both human and divine legislation become legitimate, and it is no longer necessary to look upon the governments of both men and God as perfect tyrannies, and God can now genuinely be said to administer justice on Judgment Day.

4. Determinism is identical with Fatalism "in its worst form." They both affirm that man can "do as he pleases" and both agree that "man cannot but please to do as he does." The doctrine of liberty avoids fatalism by showing that man is free not only to do as he pleases but is free to do what doesn't please him.

5. If all volitions are caused, then God's as well as man's are caused and could not be otherwise. God, then, is not the first cause of anything. On the doctrine of liberty, however, God is conceivable as First Cause and can be construed thereby as the Ultimate Agent.

Mahan continued with numerous more detailed criticisms of determinism and defenses of liberty, of which the following are most important for our purposes.

6. If we attend carefully to consciousness, Mahan wrote, we can distinguish volition from the strongest desire and hence must distinguish between the separate faculties of Will as personal activity and Sensation as mere passive impression. The will is the moving force in life, and unless it can be shown that there is some necessary connection between will and sensation—which, in fact, cannot be done—then it follows that the will is free, that is, the source of personal activity. "Edwards has confounded the phenomena of the Will with those of the Sensibility which are necessary in the sense here defined. He must, therefore, hold that the characteristics of the latter class belong to those of the former." [7] At the outset, then, "Edwards stands convicted of a fundamental error in philosophy, . . . the confounding of the Will with the Sensibility." [8]

[7] Mahan, *Doctrine of the Will*, pp. 65–66.
[8] *Ibid.*, p. 213.

7. Mahan rebuts the determinists' claim that consciousness is not an adequate judge. The reason that the determinists reject the findings of ordinary experience is that they go against this doctrine. Suppose that all men were as conscious that their wills are necessarily determined as they are that only intelligence and sensibilities are. Then the determinists would honor the tribunal of consciousness just as they now eschew it. The moment the validity of the affirmations of consciousness are denied in respect to any questions in moral science, however, it becomes impossible to refer to it on any matters, an unhappy consequence even for the determinist.[9]

8. Mahan counters Edwards' effort to make sense of freedom and moral responsibility within the determinist framework.[10] According to Edwards, liberty or freedom means the power or ability to do as one pleases. One is unfree only if he is compelled to do other than he wishes. A man is not responsible for what he is compelled to do, but is responsible for what he does when not coerced. After all, in such cases *he* is the one who did as he pleased and so is responsible. Mahan objects that this argument confuses several senses of freedom and liberty. Liberty contrasted with *servitude* means that a man can do as he pleases; he is not in chains or forced by other contraints to do other than he would. Liberty contrasted with *necessity* means that a man can please (or will) to do one thing rather than another; he is under no constraint to will or choose the way he does in fact. Liberty in the second sense is what is required for the ascription of responsibility. The determinist allows only liberty in the first sense and offers it, irrelevantly, as sufficient grounds for ascribing responsibility. Mahan sums up the contrast sharply: liberty in the first sense is lost if one is put in chains; liberty in the second sense is lost only when he gives himself up to a life guided by the passions and sensibilities.

9. Edwards argues that man's free will and God's omni-

[9]*Ibid.*, pp. 55–56.
[10]*Ibid.*, pp. 75–78, 194–98.

science are incompatible and that the latter must be retained in order to maintain the absolute sovereignty of God. Mahan believes that this argument is the strongest one the determinist has and argues against it in several places. We need to be clear about Edwards' argument, which we shall formulate in our own terminology, before introducing Mahan's response.

Consider two (supposedly) alternative choices possible at t_1 by P. Call these choices a and b. Assume that if P chooses a at t_1 consequence x will follow at t_n, while if he chooses b consequence y will follow at t_n. At t_0, however, God, being omniscient, knows that x will occur at t_n; hence at t_1 P must choose a—it is the only possibility open to him since x in fact is what will be. To insist that P at t_1 can choose either a or b is to insist that the future is undetermined, open, ambiguous, and hence God himself could not know what it will be. To save God's absolute sovereignty, then, we must reject the doctrine of liberty and free will.

Mahan believes the inconsistency is only apparent and that, properly understood, man's liberty and God's foreknowledge are consistent. Quoting voluminously from Joffroy, Mahan replies that God's omniscience and man's free will are compatible concepts because God simply foresees how man will exercise his free will. God knows that x is in the future and hence that P at t_1 will choose a, but neither God's knowing how P will choose nor anything else determines, forces, or makes P choose a at t_1. "To see that effects arise from certain causes is not to force causes to produce them; neither is it to compel these effects to follow." [11] Mahan is here quoting Joffroy and heartily agreeing with him.

Mahan also replies that the determinist depends upon the erroneous assumption that God could foresee events only if they are necessitated by previous events. However, it is perfectly possible that God—though, of course, we cannot understand how—can foresee among many events, all in themselves equally

[11] *Ibid.*, p. 115.

possible now, which one in fact will occur.[12] "God has never told us that He can foresee none but necessary events. Whether He can or cannot foresee events free as well as necessary, is certainly one of the 'secret things' which God has not revealed."[13]

10. Mahan uses Kantian ideas several times in his critique of Edwards. Edwards not only confounded phenomena of the Will and the Sensibilities in his theory of agency, he also mistakenly ascribed virtue to the Sensibilities (affections) rather than to the will in his moral theory. The Will, Mahan says, must yield itself to the control of either the Sensibility or Intelligence. In all morally right acts, the Will is in harmony with the Intelligence—acting out of respect for moral obligations or duty. "Virtue does not consist in being controlled by *amiable,* instead of *dissocial* and *malign* impulses, and in a consequent exterior of a corresponding beauty and loveliness. It consists in a voluntary harmony of intention with the just, the right, the true, and the good—from a sacred respect to moral obligation, instead of being controlled by mere impulse of any kind whatever."[14] Mahan, however, also rejects what he takes to be an improper emphasis on the autonomy of man in Kant's theory of agency. He quotes Kant as saying, "A free Will and a Will subjected to the Moral Law are one and identical" and comments, "A more capital error in philosophy is not often met with than this."[15] Without divine aid, he continues, no individual has ever achieved control over his spirit. "Where is the individual that, without such an influence, can resolve upon acting in harmony with the law of pure benevolence, with any rational hope of success? To meet this great want of human nature . . . is a fundamental design of the Remedial System."[16]

11. But is not the Will itself *determined* when it *rationally*

[12]*Ibid.,* pp. 116–17.
[13]*Ibid.,* p. 117.
[14]*Ibid.,* pp. 156–57. See also pp. 194ff.
[15]*Ibid.,* p. 197.
[16]*Ibid.,* p. 198.

chooses to follow the moral law? Mahan thinks not. He admits that all events "are governed by laws" and the Will is not without law. "It is jumping a very long distance to a conclusion, however, to infer from such a fact, that Necessity is the only law throughout the entire domain of existence, physical and mental. What if, from the fact, that the Will has its law, it should be assumed that Liberty is that law? This assumption would be just as legitimate as the one under consideration." [17]

12. Calvinists claim that the doctrine of liberty undesirably exalts the nature and stature of man and tends to make him independent of the grace of God. Mahan argues otherwise: free-will trinitarianism emphasizes the Reformation view of salvation through the grace of God just as much as Calvinism. Man is sinful and deserves damnation but God graciously offers him salvation. Man is able freely to accept or reject salvation graciously offered; he is not able to achieve it on his own. Indeed, far from making man independent of the grace of God, free-will trinitarianism tends "to induce the spirit of humility and dependence upon Divine Grace." It fosters the spirit of *voluntary* dependence. "The heart is fully set upon doing the right, and avoiding the wrong, while the mind is in the voluntary exercise of *trust* in God 'for grace whereby we may serve Him acceptably.' The *spirit* of dependence, then, implies obedience actually commenced." [18]

III

How are we to interpret Mahan's views and arguments? His talk about the Will, Sensibilities, and Intelligence (1–12) is old-fashioned; such talk was largely abandoned after 1875. This faculty-psychology terminology, in fact, is misleading as far as the major emphasis of the Scottish realistic view of agency, and Mahan's, is concerned. President Jeremiah Day of Yale Univer-

[17]*Ibid.*, p. 210.
[18]*Ibid.*, pp. 199–200.

sity warned against this misleading terminology and, though he was a mild defender of watered-down Edwardsian views, gave the clearest statement of what the Scots and Mahan intended. He made a special point of warning against talking about the faculties as if they were distinct agents. "They are different powers of one and the same agent. It is the *man* that perceives, and loves, and hates, and acts; not his understanding, or his heart, or his will, distinct from himself."[19] This view of agency is essentially Aristotelian. "A staff moves a stone, and is moved by a hand, which is moved by a man."[20] The essence of this view is that motives do not directly cause actions, but that man himself initiates an action—what he does is "up to him." The truth of the matter is that this view of agency is at the heart of Reid's and Mahan's view of agency. Man chooses what motives will direct his action and hence initiates, or brings about, or determines as first cause something in the world—hence what he does is "up to him." This view of agency is again implied in Mahan's insistence that we are introspectively aware of being able to act differently in the same circumstances and not simply of being able to act differently under different circumstances (1).

This view of agency has gained favor among contemporary agency theorists like Roderick Chisholm. Mahan's distinction between a person's choosing his motives and motives determining his behavior is echoed in Chisholm's distinction between immanent and transeunt causation. "When one event or state of affairs (or set of events or states of affairs) causes some other event or state of affairs, then we have an instance of *transeunt* causation. . . . When an *agent*, as distinguished from an event, causes an event or state of affairs, then we have an instance of *immanent* causation."[21] And for Chisholm, like Mahan, human

[19] Jeremiah Day, *An Inquiry Respecting the Self-Determining Power of the Will* (New Haven, 1836), p. 40; quoted in *A History of American Philosophy*, p. 204.

[20] Aristotle, *Physics* 256a. Quoted by Roderick Chisholm, "Freedom and Action," in *Freedom and Determinism*, ed. Keith Lehrer (New York: Random House, 1966), p. 11. See also footnote 1, p. 12.

[21] Chisholm, "Freedom and Action," p. 17.

freedom is never in question but is a desideratum which any adequate system must mediate. The similarities between Mahan and Chisholm are not surprising since they drank from the same philosophical wells. Chisholm has said that he believes the works of Thomas Reid to contain more truth than that of any other philosopher.[22] Finally, Mahan's claim that a person is not determined by his motives but himself chooses among competing ones is similar to Sartre's claim that one chooses to be the kind of person one is and will be, and hence is responsible for what that kind of person does. Mahan, Chisholm, and Sartre belong to different philosophical traditions, yet they hold strikingly similar views on agency and the determinism issue. It is refreshing to see that philosophers can come to similar conclusions from widely different starting points.

Mahan's arguments that the determinist cannot make sense of accountability or God's fairness (2, 3) are standard arguments and have carried great weight. However they are inconclusive, since determinists claim that they can accommodate these notions within their own framework. Mahan later considered Edwards' effort in this direction (8) and, in my opinion, neatly destroys this effort. To do as one pleases—that is, not to be interfered with in carrying out one's choice—is a perfectly good sense of freedom and is clearly compatible with determinism, but this sense is not the one presupposed in making moral judgments. The sense needed is that a person is free to *be* as he chooses, and there is no room for this sense in Edwards' philosophy.

Edwards' strategy has been used by many later philosophers, including G. E. Moore and various contemporary naturalists. In view of how slowly this strategy dies, it seems useful to restate Mahan's point in a more precise way.

Edwards' strategy amounts to this: The sentence

---

[22] In conversation with Chisholm.

(a) He could have done otherwise

means precisely the same as

(b) If he had chosen to do otherwise, then he would have done otherwise. Since the truth of (b) is consistent with determinism (and with the sovereignty of God) and (a) and (b) say the same thing, then (a) is also consistent with determinism. Hence it is legitimate to say that the agent could have done otherwise, even though he was caused or determined to do what he did. So, after all, determinism and accountability are compatible.

Chisholm's rebuttal of this argument is almost identical with Mahan's, though it is spelled out more explicitly.

> Is the argument sound? The conclusion follows from the premises, but the catch, I think, lies in the first premise—the one saying that statement (a) tells us no more nor less than what statement (b) tells us. For (b), it would seem, could be true while (a) is false. That is to say, our man might be such that, if he had chosen to do otherwise, then he would have done otherwise, and yet *also* such that he could not have done otherwise. Suppose, after all, that our murderer could not have *chosen,* or could not have *decided,* to do otherwise. Then the fact that he happens also to be a man such that, if he had chosen not to shoot he would not have shot, would make no difference. For if he could *not* have chosen *not* to shoot, then he could not have done anything other than just what it was he did do. In a word: from our statement (b) above . . . , we cannot make an inference to (a) above . . . , unless we can *also* assert: (c) He could have chosen to do otherwise.[23]

Mahan's linking Calvinistic determinism with fatalism (4) is not wholly clear or convincing. He simply uses the terms determinism and fatalism synonymously, thereby drawing the opprobrium usually accorded the latter onto the former. However, there is a traditional distinction which Mahan ignores. Fatalism is the view that x will occur at t_n no matter whether P chooses a or b at t_1, whereas determinism is the view that x will occur at t_n because P chose a at t_1 and a leads to x. Whatever a person

[23] Chisholm, "Freedom and Action," pp. 15–16.

chooses is irrelevant to the outcome—that is the particular horror of fatalism and it plays no part in determinism.

Mahan's first-cause argument (5) is interesting but needs to be unpacked before it appears convincing. The determinist wants to say that God is First Cause but this claim is inconsistent with his commitment to the dogma that every event has a cause. God's choices are events and hence, according to the dogma, must have had a cause. But if God's will is determined, then he is no agent and initiates nothing; he is not, in short, a first cause. According to the doctrine of liberty, on the other hand, both God and man are conceived as agents and initiators of acts and God can be construed as the ultimate First Cause.

Mahan criticizes Edwards "for confusing the phenomena of the Will with those of the Sensibility" (7), and he is no doubt correct in doing so given his premises about faculty psychology. Mahan, however, was by no means the first American philosopher to accuse Edwards of this confusion. By 1845, when Mahan published his *Doctrine of the Will,* this line of criticism was already well plotted.[24] As early as 1793, the Reverend Samuel West wrote that Locke and Edwards were working with an oversimplified account of the faculties of the mind. From 1824 to 1845, there were numerous and more detailed criticisms of Edwards along similar lines. The new faculty psychology was sweeping America, and Edwards was attacked from all sides for ignoring consciousness and confusing volition and sensation. Henry Tappan of New York University, in particular, had written well along these lines (1839–41). Mahan knew Tappan's work well and had a high opinion of it.[25] It was not

---

[24]*A History of American Philosophy,* pp. 202–7. This discussion of Faculty Psychology is splendid, but it is puzzling, given what we know of Mahan by now, to read the following comments: "But Mahan, like Burton and Day, was writing as an orthodox minister defending the essentials of the Calvinist faith, and he coupled his argument for the freedom of the faculty of the will with a plea for centering the analysis, not on the will, but on 'the religious affections.' Thus, he came round in the end to Jonathan Edwards's original interest." p. 207.

[25]Mahan, *Science of Moral Philosophy* (Oberlin: J. M. Fitch, 1848, 1884).

the newness or uniqueness of this critique of Edwards that makes Mahan's *Doctrine of the Will* important but rather the way he embeds this argument in a matrix of other arguments and the fact that he drew strong conclusions about Christian holiness and social and political reform from the doctrine of liberty.

Mahan's rebuttal of the determinist's attack on consciousness (7) has some merit, though it seems more like a debater's thrust than a fundamental argument. Indeed, it is not clear that Mahan does justice to the determinist's point. He would have us think that the determinist would be happy to use the tribunal of consciousness if only it would testify for determinism rather than freedom. The determinist, rather, is rejecting in principle the adequacy of ordinary experience as a philosophical tribunal. The Calvinists had insisted repeatedly that whether consciousness of freedom exists or not is irrelevant, since *feeling* free does not establish that one *is* free. Conversely, they would have to hold that feeling unfree—should it occur—would not establish that one *is* unfree. So, after all, Mahan needs a better defense for the philosophical significance of ordinary experience.

A better defense is implicit in what his mentor Reid had to say. The commonsense judgments of mankind, what is universally concluded when consciousness is consulted without philosophical presuppositions, must reflect basic truths or they would not be so utterly pervasive—they are unavoidably implicit in our actions and have helped mold the structure of all languages. This respect for pervasiveness and communality is more trustworthy in principle than respect for contrived and parochial philosophical arguments. When philosophical arguments and positions violate what we know to be true commonsensically, so much the worse for that philosophy. The mediation of commonsense truths becomes a desideratum or requirement, so to speak, for any philosophical system. If a system does not do so, it should be eliminated.

The Joffroy-Mahan response (9) misses the heart of Edwards' argument that God's omniscience and man's free will are incompatible concepts. The point of the argument is not that God's knowing P will choose a makes him choose a, or that anything else makes him choose a, but rather that the simple fact of there being an x at t_n makes it impossible at t_1 for P to do anything except that which will bring about x at t_n. Hence there is no genuine option or alternative for P when he supposedly chooses a; he must choose a. What it is that brings about the choice of a is irrelevant to the determinist's argument.

Mahan's second argument is also unconvincing. If God at t_0 can foresee that x will occur at t_n how is it possible to say that at t_1 a and b are equally possible choices of P? If a and b are *equally possible* as Mahan claims, then the future is genuinely ambiguous as far as x and y are concerned. That future won't be decided until P in fact chooses at t_1. If the future is ambiguous until t_1—the time P decides—then at t_0 God cannot know whether x or y will occur at t_n.

Mahan's use of Kant in criticizing Edwards (10) seems consistent with his Scottish realistic principles. Virtue is a matter of Intelligence and not the Sensibilities; Kant is right and Edwards wrong. However, Mahan's subsequent dismissal of Kant for having committed "a capital error in philosophy" is perplexing. He rejects Kant on Reformation grounds: we are unable to follow the moral law if limited to our own powers; we can follow it only by freely choosing the aid God in his grace offers us. The problem is not that the rejection is wrong, given Mahan's religious views, but rather that it is not particularly appropriate or relevant. This criticism is no more appropriate to Kant than to a host of other philosophers. The reader expects a different sort of rejection, one with a special relevance to Kant. The expectation is that he will reject Kant's making a free will identical with a will subjected to the moral law. If the will is subjected to anything, how is it an ultimate agent, an initiator of action? How is Kantian self-determinism superior to Calvinistic determinism? While Mahan never rejects self-determinism in his discussion of Kant, he apparently is rejecting it later (or else is interpreting it in such a way as to make it consistent with his own doctrine of liberty) when he writes that choosing rationally does not involve any necessity (11). Mahan's use of Reformation arguments in rebutting the Calvinist view that free-will Trinitarianism exalts too much the nature of man (12) seems much more appropriate than using such arguments against Kant.

IV

Mahan, Finney, and many other free-will Trinitarians carefully distinguished between the concepts of justification (salvation) and sanctification. The former was standard Reformation doctrine: man is a sinful creature and can never merit salvation; however God, out of grace, saves some. For free-will Trinitarians it is up to each individual to accept or reject God's gracious gift; those who do so are saved, those who do not are damned. Sanctification, on the other hand, concerns man's "second birth," his "baptism of the Holy Spirit," and refers to man's capacity for following God's commandments. Man is not capable of following God's law if he is confined to his own powers. He can, however, follow God's law in specific cases, and in principle all the time, if he recognizes the need of, and freely asks for, the help of the Holy Spirit. He is "sanctified" in the sense that he acts according to God's law by the help of the Holy Spirit. Mahan and Finney used the terms "sanctification," "perfectionism," and "holiness" synonymously.

Mahan discussed his view of sanctification in numerous places, though nowhere more clearly than in his influential *Christian Perfection* and in his *Autobiography*.[26] It is loving God with all our heart, all our soul, and all our strength, and our

[26] Mahan, *Christian Perfection,* 7th ed. (Boston: Waite, Peirce, and Co., 1844), and *Autobiography*. Our special interest here is the relation between the concepts of agency and sanctification. The most useful passages for understanding this relation are: *Christian Perfection,* pp. 78, 111, 120, 126, 128, 130, 132, 134, 137, 146, 149, 152, 162, 165, 172, 186, 189; *Autobiography,* pp. 289, 290, 292, 293, 313, 325, 329, 330, 332, 340, 376, 384.

neighbors as ourselves. It implies the absence of all selfishness, the all-pervading influence of pure and perfect love, and the full and perfect discharge of our duty according to our present capacities.

Attitudes toward perfection or sanctification—whether it can be achieved on earth and how—and toward the correlative concept of justification, can be classified, Mahan avers, as antinomian, legalistic in two senses, and evangelical.[27] The Antinomian spirit "relies upon Christ for *justification* in the absence of personal holiness"; it looks to him "to be saved *in* and not *from* sin." The legal spirit in the first sense expects both justification and sanctification through the deeds of the agent himself in following the law. The legal spirit in the second sense expects justification through the grace of Jesus Christ but expects sanctification in proportion to the personal effort he puts forth. Whatever degree of sanctification he achieves falls woefully short of complete sanctification, or holiness, which can be achieved only after death. The evangelical spirit looks to Christ for both justification and sanctification: not only is man saved from his sins by God's grace but he is also sanctified by the grace of God rather than through his own effort. Through the grace of Jesus Christ man can be baptized with the Spirit of the Holy Ghost, and the result of this Pentecostal occasion is cleansing to the uttermost, or complete sanctification.

From the descriptions of the legal view in the second sense, which appear in Mahan's *Christian Perfection,* one might suppose that it insisted wholly on human effort in achieving some degree of sanctification in this world. But this is not the case; Mahan's characterization is simply inadequate. Happily in his *Autobiography,* he does more justice to this view. Here the legalistic view of sanctification is pictured as a cooperative venture between man and the Holy Ghost. Mahan writes: "Sanctification, as very commonly understood, . . . is the result of the

---

[27]*Christian Perfection,* pp. 98–100.

united action of the mind of the believer, and of the Spirit of God." [28] On the legal view sanctification is regarded "as an attainment to be reached through personal effort, aided by the Spirit of Grace." [29] However, it must not be supposed that even in the *Autobiography* Mahan makes much of the cooperativeness of the venture as envisioned by the legalist.

For the first eighteen years after his conversion, Mahan held the legal view of sanctification; for the remainder of his long Christian life he held the evangelical view. He switched because "the appropriate office of the Holy Ghost presented itself to my mind with a distinctness and interest never understood nor felt before." [30] "The great object of my being now was, to know Christ, and in knowing him to be changed into his image." [31] Mahan had had his Pentecostal experience, and he was now convinced that he held the proper view of sanctification. [32]

From Mahan's numerous descriptions of his evangelical view of sanctification, one might suppose that he insisted wholly on the agency of the Holy Spirit in achieving complete sanctification, or "cleansing from sin to the uttermost." It would be easy to fill page after page with quotations from Mahan that suggest the absence of human agency in complete santification. The following are representative examples from *Christian Perfection:* "However hard your heart may be, he can take it from you, and give you a heart of flesh in its stead. However firmly fixed your habits of sin may be, he can break them all up. However strong the power of your carnal inclinations, he can subdue them all, and give you a perfect victory over them." [33] We receive Christ as Savior "and yield up our whole being to his control, that he

---

[28] *Autobiography,* p. 290.

[29] *Ibid.,* p. 292.

[30] *Christian Perfection,* p. 186.

[31] *Ibid.*

[32] "Pentecostalism," as we know it today, must be distinguished from the American Holiness Movement. The latter takes a strong stand, e.g., against glossalalia, associated with contemporary Pentecostalism.

[33] *Christian Perfection,* p. 130.

may accomplish in us all the purposes of his infinite and special love."[34] God promises "entire freedom from all sin, and the transformation of our entire character into a likeness to his own."[35] "Hence it is said of Christians, that their 'bodies are the temples of the Holy Ghost,' and that they themselves are 'the temples of the living God.' "[36] The following examples are from Mahan's *Autobiography:* "Christ himself, through the Spirit, enters the citadel of the soul, puts to death 'the lusts that was in the members,' 'destroys the body of sin,' sanctifies to Himself 'the whole spirit, and soul, and body,' and then, under the power of the Spirit, sends the believer into the world."[37] Sanctification is "God's work just as exclusively as is the pardon of sin."[38] Man is dwarfed in power by previous sin and yet in a sanctified state is required to act with the full power he would have had had he never sinned. But this is impossible, the critic replies. "Impossible with men," Mahan replies, "but not with God."[39]

In spite of all this suggestion that in sanctification it is the Holy Ghost's agency and not man's that is operative, this view is not really Mahan's. Indeed, he must avoid it at all costs since the doctrine of the displacement of man's agency by the spirit of God was precisely the doctrine of the Oneida Perfectionists, which was so disgusting to Mahan. The Oberlin version of Christian Perfection was often confused in the public mind with the Oneida concept of perfection, and the reason for this confusion rested, no doubt, on numerous statements of the sort we have just witnessed. But Mahan, in other places, made it quite clear that human agency played an important role in the Oberlin concept of sanctification. A baptism of the Holy Ghost occurs only if a man chooses to seek it, decides to ask for its

[34]*Ibid.*, p. 132.
[35]*Ibid.*, p. 149.
[36]*Ibid.*, p. 166.
[37]*Autobiography*, p. 313.
[38]*Ibid.*, p. 332.
[39]*Ibid.*, p. 376.

bestowal as a free gift from the grace of God. In *Christian Perfection* he writes: "If you will open the door, the Son of God will enter in, and confer this blessed inheritance upon you";[40] "In his light it is your blessed privilege perpetually to walk . . . 'Ask, and it shall be given you' ";[41] "To attain to that state of sanctification myself, I had only to acquaint myself with the love of Christ, and yield my whole being up to its sweet control."[42] The point was not emphasized, however, though Mahan gave it more prominence in his *Autobiography*. There he wrote: "It is our part, as the revealed condition of receiving the blessings provided for us, to 'inquire of God to do it for us' ";[43] "by the free assent, and consent, and full choice of our heart of hearts, Christ thus dwells in our heart";[44] in justification and sanctification alike "To comply with the condition is our part in the transaction," and "the condition being complied with, our responsibility in the matter is at an end."[45]

This view of the role of human agency in sanctification, however, is quite inadequate to separate Mahan's perfectionism from the sort of Perfectionism espoused by the Oneida community. However the Spirit of the Holy Ghost enters into the heart of a man, whether by devout invitation and supplication or by breaking in, the agency of man is supplanted, according to the Oneida view, by that of the Holy Ghost, and any further sinning thereby *becomes an impossibility*. Man becomes perfect in the strong sense that it is now impossible for him to sin. Needless to say, Mahan rejects this consequence and in order to avoid it has to introduce a further role for human agency. The human being can always succumb to his previous sinful ways and thus lose the Spirit's domination of his life. Our first parents and the fallen angels were once completely pure, or entirely sanctified,

[40]*Christian Perfection*, p. 162.
[41]*Ibid.*, p. 172.
[42]*Ibid.*, p. 186.
[43]*Autobiography*, p. 325.
[44]*Ibid.*, p. 330.
[45]*Ibid.*, p. 293.

and still they were tempted and fell. "So, when we have attained to a similar state, we are subject to the same liabilities, and without watchfulness and prayer on our part, 'as the serpent beguiled Eve through his subtility, so our minds will be corrupted from the simplicity (perfect purity) that is in Christ.' "[46] A fully and wisely instructed, sanctified believer "is perfected in watchfulness, as well as in other Christian virtues, and, like the prudent general, is never for a moment off his guard."[47]

Unfortunately this move to extend man's agency in sanctification still leaves Mahan in a problematic situation. We cannot but reach this conclusion if we inquire carefully into the possible interpretations of this new move. Say that a person earnestly seeks the Divine Spirit and that it has entered his heart and is suffused through his being. Still the person is tempted just as he was before the advent of the Spirit. Now who is it that fights and triumphs, when this is the case, over these subsequent temptations and tendencies toward back-sliding? If it is the Spirit then triumph was assured at the beginning. Sanctification successfully sought at t_1 entails constant and continued sanctification through t_n. In this case, however, man's agency has really disappeared, and Mahan has not succeeded in distinguishing his kind of sanctification from the view that the agency of the Spirit literally supplants the agency of man in sanctification. Hence, Mahan must admit that it is not simply the agency of the Holy Spirit that wards off subsequent temptations and tendencies toward backsliding. A man *himself* has to be ever on guard, ever vigilant, and ever committed to walk the way of God. With this admission, however, it seems that Mahan is not at all distant from legalism in the second sense, that is, the claim that man's agency and determined effort is ineliminable in the achievement of sanctification. In effect, Mahan's position is not really a distinct one. He is either led

[46] *Ibid.*, p. 384.
[47] *Ibid.*, p. 385.

toward Perfectionism in a sense he cannot abide, or else he must agree with the legal view that man's effort is essential. However, as we have seen, man's effort need not be considered in isolation on this view. This view of sanctification can be conceived as a cooperative effort between the Holy Spirit and a human being: one tries his best and the other brings out the best that is possible in a given case. Both the Holy Ghost and man are ineliminable in this concept of sanctification.

This cooperative concept of sanctification is an interesting one and deserves detailed attention. For the moment, however, we must be content simply to state it a bit more fully. On this view, sanctification still comes through grace after man freely seeks it. Moreover, the effort put forth in the initial supplication must be constantly renewed so that the presence of the Holy Ghost can be maintained. However, it is neither simply man's effort, either initially or continually, nor simply the Spirit's agency that achieves sanctification, but rather it is a joint, cooperative effort of man and the Spirit within that makes it possible for a *person* to make progress upward on the ladder of holiness. On this view, the Spirit is always a respecter of the agency of human beings, just as the man must always open himself to the influence of the Spirit. It is certainly a more elevated concept of the Spirit to view it as helping a man help himself rather than doing everything for him.

Finally, it should be noted that this cooperative concept of sanctification has just as much right to be called evangelical as any other, because the agency of the Holy Ghost is just as ineliminable as that of a human being. Mahan misleads us by using the words "legal" and "evangelical" in persuasive and slanted ways. He so defines "evangelical" that only his view of sanctification is supposed to count as evangelical. And he usually defines "legal" in a way that would be unattractive to anyone who considered himself evangelical but could not accept Mahan's concept of sanctification. However, Mahan himself, I have argued, in his efforts to avoid Oneida Perfectionism, must himself return to the so-called legal view, but now emphatically conceived as a cooperative venture. Indeed, the cooperative view, then, becomes the *only* genuine evangelical attitude toward sanctification.

NINE

Spires of Influence:
The Importance of Emerson for
Classical American Philosophy

JOHN J. McDERMOTT

ERHAPS THE TITLE of this essay should be "Why Emerson?" as that would better reflect how I came to write this piece. It is not so much that I have had to become convinced of the singular importance of the thought of Emerson, for the writing and teaching of Joseph Blau[1] and Robert C. Pollock[2] long ago made that clear to me. Rather the query about "Why Emerson?" proceeds from my study of the classic American philosophers, especially William James, Josiah Royce, and John Dewey. Despite their differences and disagreements, often extreme in both personal style and doctrine, these powerful and prescient philosophers did have at least one influence in common—the thought of Ralph Waldo Emerson.

Another major figure of the American classical period,

[1] Joseph L. Blau, ed., *American Philosophic Addresses, 1700–1900* (New York:.Columbia University Press, 1946); *Men and Movements in American Philosophy* (Englewood Cliffs, N.J.: Prentice-Hall, 1952); "Emerson's Transcendentalist Individualism as a Social Philosophy," *The Review of Metaphysics*, 31, no. 1 (September 1977): 80–92.

[2] Robert C. Pollock, "Ralph Waldo Emerson—The Single Vision," in *American Classics Reconsidered*, ed. Harold Gardiner (New York: Scribner's, 1958), pp. 15–58.

George Santayana, seems to be a case apart. Santayana had an abiding interest in Emerson's thought and refers frequently to Emerson in his own writings. His judgments on Emerson vary from admiration and affection to pointed and even harsh criticism. I do not think that Emerson was a significant influence on Santayana. Nonetheless, his published assessments of Emerson at the beginning of the twentieth century are contextually interesting, especially as they contrast with those of James, Royce, and Dewey.

The remaining two major figures of the Classical period, C. S. Peirce and G. H. Mead [3] appear to be much less directly influenced by Emerson.

Parenthetically, however, we do find a text in Peirce about Emerson which is intriguing and perhaps merits further inquiry in another context. In "The Law of Mind," published in 1892, Peirce wrote:

> I may mention, for the benefit of those who are curious in studying mental biographies, that I was born and reared in the neighborhood of Concord—I mean in Cambridge—at the time when Emerson, Hedge, and their friends were disseminating the ideas that they had caught from Schelling, and Schelling from Plotinus, from Boehm, or from God knows what minds stricken with the monstrous mysticism of the East. But the atmosphere of Cambridge held many an antiseptic against Concord transcendentalism; and I am not conscious of having contracted any of that virus. Nevertheless, it is probable that some cultured bacilli, some benignant form of the disease was implanted in my soul, unawares, and that now, after long incubation, it comes to the surface, modified by mathematical conceptions and by training in physical investigation. [4]

---

[3] George Herbert Mead tends to speak of Emerson only in the context of Concord transcendentalism. Ironically, in lamenting the failure of the transcendentalists to develop a distinctive doctrine of American self-consciousness, Mead overlooks the powerful voice of Emerson in precisely that regard. Mead, "The Philosophies of Royce, James and Dewey in Their American Setting," in *Selected Writings*, ed. Andrew J. Reck (Indianapolis: Bobbs-Merrill, 1964), pp. 377–78.

[4] Charles Sanders Peirce, *Collected Papers*, ed. Charles Hartshorne and Paul Weiss, (Cambridge; Harvard University Press 1934), 6 (sec. 102): 86–87. Peirce also was fond of quoting and mocking Emerson's poem on the Sphinx, especially the line, "Of

The wary and tough-minded response of Peirce is not atypical of a philosophical assessment of Emerson. Indeed, even those philosophers who acknowledge their debt to Emerson lace their remarks with dubiety about his fundamental assumptions and unease about much of the rhetoric of his formulation. Nonetheless, James, Royce, Dewey, and Santayana, each in his own way, finds it necessary to evaluate the importance of Emerson in the light of their own developing position. Before turning to these judgments, it should be helpful if I sketch the Emersonian project in cultural and philosophical terms.

The central theme of Emerson's life and work is that of *possibility*. In an anticipation of the attitude of Martin Buber, Emerson believes that 'we are really able', that is, we and the world are continuous in an affective and nutritional way. It is human insight which is able to "animate the last fibre of organization, the outskirts of nature."[5] Emerson's persistent stress on human possibility is fed from two sources: his extraordinary confidence in the latent powers of the individual soul when related to the symbolic riches of nature and his belief that the comparatively unarticulated history of American experience could act as a vast resource for the energizing of novel and creative spiritual energy. The often oracular style of Emerson should not cloak the seriousness of his intention when he speaks of these possibilities. In this regard, the key text is found in his Introduction to the essay *"Nature."*

> Our age is retrospective. It builds the sepulchres of the fathers. It writes biographies, histories, and criticism. The foregoing generations beheld God and nature face to face; we, through their eyes. Why should not we also enjoy an original relation to the universe? Why

thine eye, I am eyebeam." Peirce, *Papers,* 1 (sec. 310): 153–54 and 3 (sec. 404): 252. Some unpublished material on Peirce's "boyhood impressions" of Emerson can be found in "Manuscript—296" as recorded in Richard Robin, ed., *Annotated Catalogue of the Papers of Charles S. Peirce* (Amherst, Massachusetts: University of Massachusetts Press, 1967), p. 31.
[5] Ralph Waldo Emerson, "The American Scholar," *Works,* (Boston: Houghton Mifflin, 1903–1904; reprt. AMS Publishers, n.d.), 1: 86.

should not we have a poetry and philosophy of insight and not of tradition, and a religion by revelation to us, and not the history of theirs?
Embosomed for a season in nature, whose floods of life stream around
and through us, and invite us, by the powers they supply, to action
proportioned to nature, why should we grope among the dry bones of
the past, or put the living generation into masquerade out of its faded
wardrobe? The sun shines to-day also. There is more wool and flax in
the fields. There are new lands, new men, new thoughts. Let us demand our own works and laws and worship.[6]

We of the twentieth century may not grasp the radical character of Emerson's invocation, standing as we do on the rubble
of broken promises brought to us by the great faiths of the past,
be they scientific, social, or religious. But Emerson made no
such promise and cannot be accused, retroactively, of bad faith.
His message was clear. We are to transform the obviousness of
our situation by a resolute penetration to the liberating symbolism present in our own experience. We are not to be dependent
on faith hatched elsewhere out of others' experiences, nor, above
all, are we to rest on an inherited ethic whose significance is due
more to longevity and authority than to the press of our own experience. Surely, Emerson's nineteenth century, which was
barely able to absorb the recondite theology responsible for the
transition from Presbyterianism to Unitarianism, had to blanch
at his bypassing the issue entirely, while calling for a home-
grown "revelation." The radical character of Emerson's position
at that time was given historical credence by the reception given
to his Divinity School Address, delivered two years after "Nature" and one year after "The American Scholar." Using a tone
more modest than either of those, Emerson in effect told the
graduating class of Harvard Divinity School that the tradition
they had inherited was hollow and the Church to which they
belonged, "seems to totter to its fall, all life extinct."[7] As in
"Nature", he again called for a "new hope and new revelation."[8]

[6] Emerson, "Nature," *Works*, 1:3.
[7] Emerson, "The Divinity School Address," *Works*, 1: 135.
[8] *Ibid.*, p. 151.

The upshot of this Address was that for nearly thirty years Emerson was unwelcome as a public figure in Cambridge.

Now, more to the point of the present essay is Emerson's doctrine of experience and his emphasis on relations, both central concerns of the subsequent philosophical thought of James and Dewey. In his essay "The American Scholar," Emerson points to three major influences on the development of the reflective person: nature, history, and action or experience. In his discussion of the third influence, Emerson provides a microcosmic view of his fundamental philosophy. He makes it apparent that he does not accept the traditional superiority of the contemplative over the active life. Emerson tells us further that "Action is with the scholar subordinate, but it is essential. Without it he is not yet man. Without it thought can never ripen into truth."[9] It is noteworthy that accompanying Emerson's superb intellectual mastery of the great literature of the past and his commitment to the reflective life is his affirmation that "Character is higher than intellect."[10] Living is a total act, the functionary, whereas thinking is a partial act, the function. More than twenty years after the publication of "The American Scholar," Emerson reiterated his commitment to the "practical" and to the "experiential" as the touchstone of the thinking person. In his essay "Fate" he considers those thinkers for whom the central question is the "theory of the Age." In response, Emerson writes: "To me, however, the question of the times resolved itself into a practical question of the conduct of life. How shall I live? We are incompetent to solve the times."[11] The human task for Emerson is not so much to

[9] Emerson, "The American Scholar," *Works,* 1: 95. The use of "he" and "man" in this text and in subsequent texts are to be read in the present essay as referring also to "she" and "woman."

[10] *Ibid.,* p. 99.

[11] Emerson, "Fate," *Works,* 6:3. For a similar attitude, see William James, *The Varieties of Religious Experience* (New York: Longmans, 1902), p. 489. "Knowledge about life is one thing; effective occupation of a place in life, with its dynamic currents passing through your being, is another."

solve the times as to live them, in an ameliorative and perceptive way.

Emerson's generalized approach to inquiry is clearly a foreshadowing of that found subsequently in James, Dewey, and Royce. Too often, Emerson's anticipation of these thinkers is left at precisely that general bequest, whereby the undergoing of experience is its own mean and carries its own peculiar form of cognition.[12] What is less well known is that Emerson also anticipated the doctrine of "radical empiricism," which is central to the philosophy of James and Dewey. I do not contend that Emerson's version of relations had the same psychological or epistemological genesis[13] as that of either James or Dewey. Yet, *mutatis mutandis,* Emerson did affirm the primary importance of relations over things and he did hold to an aggressive doctrine of implication. Further, his metaphors were more allied to the language of continuity than to that of totality or finality. Finally, Emerson shared that modern assumption which began with Kant and is found repeated in James and Dewey— namely, that the known is, in some way, a function of the knower.

Emerson's attitude toward implicitness, relations, and the partially constitutive character of human inquiry helps us to understand him in other ways as well. Why, one might ask, would Emerson, a New England Brahmin, have a proletarian epistemology. That is, how could Emerson write as he did in "The American Scholar," a paean of praise to the obvious, to

[12] Texts in support of this position abound in the writings of John Dewey. Among others, are *Reconstruction in Philosophy* (Boston: Beacon, 1949 [1920]), p. 91. "Experience carries principles of connection and organization within itself." And again, p. 94, "What Shakespeare so pregnantly said of nature, it is 'made better by no means, but nature makes better that mean,' becomes true of experience."

[13] For an historical and philosophical treatment of the genesis of James' doctrine of radical empiricism, see John J. McDermott, "Introduction," "Essays in Radical Empiricism," *The Works of William James,* (Cambridge: Harvard University Press, 1976), pp. xi-xlviii. Dewey's doctrine of radical empiricism is best found in *The Influence of Darwinism on Philosophy and Other Essays in Contemporary Philosophy* (New York: Holt, 1910).

the ordinary? The text, as read to the audience at the Phi Beta Kappa celebration of 1837, was startling.

> I embrace the common, I explore and sit at the feet of the familiar, the low. Give me insight into to-day, and you may have the antique and future worlds. What would we really know the meaning of? The meal in the firkin; the milk in the pan; the ballad in the street; the news of the boat; the glance of the eye; the form and gait of the body; . . .[14]

Emerson immediately provides the response to the rhetorical question posed above. For the "ultimate reason" why the affairs of the ordinary yield insight, traces to Emerson's belief that "the sublime presence of the highest spiritual cause lurks, as always it does lurk, in these suburbs and extremities of nature."[15] His version of the world is not characterized by hierarchies, nor by fixed essences, each to be known as an object in itself. Rather he stresses the flow of our experience and the multiple implications of every event and every thing for every other experience had or about to be had. Nature brings with it this rich symbolic resource, enabling all experiences, sanctioned and occasional, to retract potentially novel implications of our other experiences. The novelty is due both to the unpredictability of nature[16] and to the creative role of human imagination. Of the first Emerson writes:

> Nature hates calculators; her methods are saltatory and impulsive. Man lives by pulses; our organic movements are such; and the chemical and ethereal agents are undulatory and alternate; and the mind goes antagonizing on, and never prospers but by fits. We thrive by casualties.

[14] Emerson, "The American Scholar," *Works,* 1: III. For a richer description of the extreme variety of audience responses to Emerson's oration of 1837, see Bliss Perry, "Emerson's Most Famous Speech," *Ralph Waldo Emerson—A Profile,* ed., Carl Bode (New York: Hill and Wang, 1969), pp. 52–65. Oliver Wendell Holmes heard the oration as an "intellectual Declaration of Independence" and James Russell Lowell viewed it as "our Yankee version of a lecture by Abelard, our Harvard parallel to the last public appearances of Schelling."

[15] *Ibid.,* p. 111.

[16] Emerson, "Experience," *Works,* 6: 308, *n*1. "Everything in the Universe goes by indirection. There are no straight lines."

Our chief experiences have been casual. The most attractive class of people are those who are powerful obliquely and not by the direct stroke;
men of genius, but not yet accredited; one gets the cheer of their light
without paying too great a tax. Theirs is the beauty of the bird or the
morning light, and not of art. In the thought of genius there is always
a surprise; and the moral sentiment is well called "the newness," for it
is never other; as new to the oldest intelligence as to the young
child; . . .[17]

The malleability and novelty-prone capacity of nature feeds the
formulating and constructive powers native to the human imagination. Emerson, like James and Dewey, sees this transaction
between the open nature of nature and the "active soul" as the
necessary context for meaning. In his *Journals,* Emerson writes:

This power of imagination, the making of some familiar object, as fire
or rain, or a bucket, or shovel do new duty as an exponent of some
truth or general law, bewitches and delights men. It is a taking of dead
sticks, and clothing about with immortality; it is music out of creaking
and scouring. All opaque things are transparent, and the light of
heaven struggles through.[18]

We should not mistake Emerson's position for a flight of fancy
or for the poetic stroke in the pejorative sense of that word.
Emerson is a hard-headed empiricist, reminiscent of the Augus-
tinian-Franciscan tradition for whom the world was a temporal
epiphany of the eternal implications and ramifications of the
eternal ideas. For Emerson, "A fact is the end or last issue of
spirit."[19] Such facticity, paradoxically, comes to us only on

---

[17]*Ibid.,* p. 68. William James holds a similar position. "Notebook" entry of 1903
as found in Ralph Barton Perry, *The Thought and Character of William James,* (Boston:
Little, Brown, 1935), 2: 700. "All neat schematisms with permanent and absolute
distinctions, classifications with absolute pretensions, systems with pigeon-holes, etc.,
have this character. All 'classic,' clean, cut and dried, 'noble,' fixed, 'eternal,' *Welt-
sanschauungen* seem to me to violate the character with which life concretely comes
and the expression which it bears of being, or at least of involving a muddle and a
struggle, with an 'ever not quite' to all our formulas, and novelty and possibility forever leaking in."

[18]*The Journals of Ralph Waldo Emerson* (Boston: Houghton-Mifflin, 1909–1914), 9:
277–88.

[19]Emerson, "Nature," *Works,* 1: 34.

behalf of our grasping and formulating the inherent symbolic features of our life.

> We learn nothing rightly until we learn the symbolical character of life. Day creeps after day, each full of facts, dull, strange, despised things, that we cannot enough despise—call heavy, prosaic and desert. The time we seek to kill: the attention it is elegant to divert from things around us. And presently the aroused intellect finds gold and gems in one of these scorned facts—then finds that the day of facts is a rock of diamonds; that a fact is an Epiphany of God.[20]

The epiphanic, for Emerson, is not a result of human quietism. It is we who constitute these "facts" by our forging of relations. "Every new relation is a new word."[21] The making of words for Emerson, as for James, is the making of the world of meaning. Words are not simply grammatical connectors. As the embodiment of relations they do more than define. They make and remake the very fabric of our world as experienced. "The world is emblematic. Parts of speech are metaphors, because the whole of nature is a metaphor of the human mind."[22] This text mirrors the binary strands found in subsequent American philosophy; the idealist-pragmatic epistemology of James, Royce, Dewey, and Peirce, each with an original emphasis of one strand over another.

If we read the Emersonian project as one which focuses on the dialectic between the raw givenness of nature and the symbolic formulations of the human imagination, then we have a direct line of common interpretation from Emerson to the classic American philosophers. I grant that each of the American philosophers in question contexts this dialectic differently, yet even a cameo version reveals the similarity. The thought of Peirce, for example, exhibits a life-long tension between his acceptance of the irreducibly tychistic character of the world and of the

---

[20] Emerson, "Education," *Works,* 10: 132.
[21] Emerson, "The Poet," *Works,* 3: 18.
[22] Emerson, "Nature," *Works,* 1: 32.

inevitably fallibilistic character of human knowledge, and his extreme confidence in the method of science. And it is the tough-minded Peirce, who writes that "without beating longer round the bush let us come to close quarters. Experience is our only teacher." And "how does this action of experience take place? It takes place by a series of surprises."[23]

The philosophy of John Dewey reflects a similar tension between a confidence in empirical method and the acknowledgment of novelty and unpredictability as indigenous to the history of nature. Dewey states that "Man finds himself living in an aleatory world; his existence involves, to put it baldly, a gamble. The world is a scene of risk; it is uncertain, unstable, uncannily unstable. Its dangers are irregular, inconstant, not to be counted upon as to their times and seasons. Although persistent, they are sporadic, episodic."[24]

Still, when faced with this extremely open and even perilous version of nature, Dewey calls upon philosophy to act as an intelligent mapping, so as to reconstruct, ameliorate, and enhance the human condition. Dewey's project is Emersonian, for the affairs of time and the activities of nature are the ground of inquiry, rather than the hidden and transcendent meaning of Being. Just as Emerson broke with the theological language of his immediate predecessors and many of his peers, so too did Dewey break with the ecstatic religious language of Emerson. This break in language should not hide from us that Dewey's understanding of the relationship which exists between nature and human life, echoes that of Emerson; always possibility, often celebration, frequently mishap and never absolute certitude.

As for an Emersonian analogue in Royce, readers of that indefatigable polymath know that cameo versions of any of his positions do not come easy. Nonetheless, Royce's long speculative trek away from the absolute and toward a theory of interpreta-

---

[23] Peirce, *Collected Papers,* 5 (sec. 50, 51): 37.
[24] John Dewey, *Experience and Nature* (La Salle: Open Court, 1929), p. 38.

tion, ever reconstructed by the community, echoes Emerson's emphasis on the conduct of life. Royce was forced to abandon the doctrine of the absolute mind because he finally accepted the judgment of his critics that he could not account for the experience of the individual on either epistemological or metaphysical grounds. In his last great work, *The Problem of Christianity*, Royce has come full circle and awarded to the individual the task of formulating the "real world" by virtue of the relationship between "self-interpretation" and the "community of interpretation." Emerson wrote that "we know more from nature that we can at will communicate."[25] Similarly, Royce writes that "the popular mind is deep, and means a thousand times more that it explicitly knows."[26] In my judgment, Royce's mature thought, under the influence of Peirce, structure than we can at will communicate."[25] Similarly, Royce Although the content is Emersonian, the following passage from Royce brings a heightened philosophical sophistication.

> Metaphysically considered, the world of interpretation is the world in which, if indeed we are able to interpret at all, we learn to acknowledge the being and the inner life of our fellow-men; and to understand the constitution of temporal experience with its endlessly accumulating sequence of significant deeds. In this world of interpretation, of whose most general structure we have now obtained a glimpse, selves and communities may exist, past and future can be defined, and the realms of the spirit may find a place which neither barren conception nor the chaotic flow of interpenetrating perceptions could ever render significant.[27]

It is with William James, however, that the Emersonian dialectic between the creative and constructive character of the human mind and the apparently intransigent character of the physical world most explicitly comes to the fore. James, like

[25] Emerson, "Nature," *Works*, 1: 31.

[26] John Clendenning, ed., *The Letters of Josiah Royce* (Chicago: University of Chicago Press, 1970), p. 586.

[27] Josiah Royce, *The Problem of Christianity* (Chicago: University of Chicago Press, 1968, [1913]), p. 294.

Emerson, holds to a relationship of congeniality between nature
and human power. They both avoid the alternate interpretations, which, in turn, would stress either the complete objectivity of the meaning of nature or a completely subjective version in which nature has an existence only at the behest of the
human, or failing that, the absolute mind. In some ways, James
outdoes Emerson in his stress on the "powers" and "energies" of
the individual, although we should remember that he also emphasizes "seeing and feeling the total push and pressure of the
cosmos."[28]

William James is profoundly aware of these alternate versions
of our situation and often evokes them in an extreme way. Two
texts from *Pragmatism* stand out in this regard, and if we put
them back to back, the poles of the Emersonian dialectic are
thrown into bold relief.

> FIRST: Woe to him whose beliefs play fast and loose with the order
> which realities follow in his experience: They will lead him
> nowhere or else make false connexions.[29]
>
> SECOND: In our cognitive as well as in our active life we are creative.
> We *add*, both to the subject and to the predicate part of real-
> ity. The world stands really malleable, waiting to receive its
> final touches at our hands. Like the kingdom of heaven, it
> suffers human violence willingly. Man *engenders* truths upon
> it.[30]

Obviously, both of these texts cannot stand at one and the
same time. James was very much aware of this conflict and continued to pose it, even though he was simultaneously working
his way out of the dilemma. In an earlier entry in an unpublished notebook, he gives a reason for maintaining this conflict. "Surely nature itself and subjective construction are radi-

[28] William James, "Pragmatism," *The Works of William James*, vol. 1 (Cambridge:
Harvard University Press, 1975), p. 9.

[29] *Ibid.*, p. 99.

[30] *Ibid.*, p. 123.

cally opposed, one's higher indignations are nourished by the opposition."[31] Emerson, of course, would approve of both the "indignation" and the "nourishment." It should be noted, however, that James goes beyond Emerson at this point and develops his formal doctrine of radical empiricism to mediate this "opposition." The genesis and content of James's radical empiricism is a long and complicated story, but in his "conclusion" to his essay on "A World of Pure Experience," James sets out the dramatic presence of the knowing self in a world both obdurate and malleable.

> There is in general no separateness needing to be overcome by an external cement; and whatever separateness is actually experienced is not overcome, it stays and counts as separateness to the end. But the metaphor serves to symbolize the fact that experience itself, taken at large, can grow by its edges. That one moment of it proliferates into the next by transitions which, whether conjunctive or disjunctive, continue the experiential tissue, cannot, I contend, be denied. Life is in the transitions as much as in the terms connected; often, indeed, it seems to be there more emphatically, as if our spurts and sallies forward were the real firing-line of the battle, were like the thin line of flame advancing across the dry autumnal field which the farmer proceeds to burn. In this line we live prospectively as well as retrospectively. It is "of" the past, inasmuch as it comes expressly as the past's continuation; it is "of" the future in so far as the future, when it comes, will have continued *it*.[32]

So much for the refractions of the Emersonian dialectic in some of the classical American philosophers. At this point, the reader may well ask why I have not cited these philosophers on this central theme in Emerson? The response, alas, is quite simple. Our philosophers did not write very much on Emerson and when they did, the focus was often on other, if related, themes. I turn now to James, Santayana, Royce and Dewey on Emerson, directly.

[31] James Papers, Houghton Library, Harvard University (bMs AM 1092, box L, notebook N[2].)
[32] James, "Essays in Radical Empiricism," *Works,* 3: 42.

II

At the age of three months, William James was visited by
Ralph Waldo Emerson at the James family's home on Washington Place in New York City. This prepossessing and perhaps
burdensome presence of Emerson lasted throughout most of the
life of William James. In the decade following 1870, James
read virtually everything Emerson wrote and at one point in
1873 made the following entry in his diary:

"I am sure that an age will come when our present devotion to
history, and scrupulous care for what men have done before us
merely as fact, will seem incomprehensible; when acquaintance
with books will be no duty, but a pleasure for odd individuals;
when Emerson's philosophy will be in our bones, not our dramatic imagination." [33] Apparently, Emerson's thought had already reached the "bones" of James, for the above sentiment
about the past is shared by Emerson. In "The American
Scholar" he wrote that "I had better never see a book than to be
warped by its attraction clean out of my own orbit and made a
satellite instead of a system. The one thing in the world, of
value, is the active soul." [34]

Some thirty years after his diary entry, in 1903, James was
called upon to deliver the Address at the Centenary celebration
for Emerson in Concord. [35] This occasion caused James to reread
virtually all of Emerson's writings. Frankly, with regard to the
question of the influence of Emerson on James, the address is
disappointing. As one would expect, James is laudatory of

[33] Cited in Gay Wilson Allen, *William James* (New York: Viking, 1967), pp. 186–87.
[34] Emerson, "The American Scholar," *Works,* 1: 89–90.
[35] William James, "Address at the Emerson Centenary in Concord," *Memories and
Studies* (New York: Longman's, 1911), pp. 19–34. For a contrast of James's hagio-
graphic approach to others more critical and substantive, the reader should consult two
collections of essays; *Emerson,* ed. Milton Konvitz and Stephen Whicher (Englewood
Cliffs, N.J.: Prentice-Hall, 1962) and *The Recognition of Ralph Waldo Emerson—
Selected Criticism Since 1837,* ed. Milton Konvitz (Ann Arbor: University of Michigan
Press, 1972). It is striking that in the vast secondary literature on Emerson, distinctively philosophical considerations are virtually absent.

Emerson's person and work.[36] And, as he often did in such pieces of encomium, the text is largely made up of long passages from Emerson. Despite these limitations, an important theme runs beneath the baroque prose of James and that of Emerson as selected by James. As we might expect, it is the theme of "possibility," of the hallowing of the everyday. James is struck by the radical temporality of Emerson's vision. He offers a brief collage of that attitude: " 'The Deep to-day which all men scorn' receives thus from Emerson superb revindication. 'Other world! There is no other world.' All God's life opens into the individual particular, and here and now, or nowhere, is reality. 'The present hour is the decisive hour, and every day is doomsday.' "[37]

James cautions us that Emerson was no sentimentalist. The transformation of stubborn fact to an enhanced symbolic statement of richer possibility was an activity that James found very compatible with his own stress on novelty and surprise. Emerson had written, "so is there no fact, no event, in our private history, which shall not sooner or later, lose its adhesive, inert form and astonish us by soaring from our body into the empyrean."[38] On behalf of this and similar passages, James comments that Emerson "could perceive the full squalor of the individual fact, but he could also see the transfiguration."[39]

Aside from this important focus on Emerson's concern for "individuals and particulars," James's address is taken up with praise of Emerson's style as a literary artist. I note the irony here, for such praise of style is precisely what has taken up much of the commentaries on the thought of James, often to

---

[36] James was not always complimentary to Emerson. In *The Varieties of Religious Experience,* for example, he criticized Emerson for tending toward "abstraction" on the religious question. (pp. 32, 56.) For a discussion of James's ambivalence on Emerson, see F. O. Matthiessen, *The American Renaissance* (New York: Oxford University Press, 1941), pp. 53–54*n*.

[37] James, "Address," p. 31.

[38] Emerson, "The American Scholar," *Works,* 1: 96–97.

[39] James, "Address," p. 32. The potential capacity for "transfiguration" of fact, as

the detriment of an analysis of his serious philosophical intent. It is unfortunate that James never undertook a systematic study of Emerson, especially as directed to his notions of experience, relations and symbol. James would have found Emerson far more "congenial"[40] and helpful than many of the other thinkers he chose to examine. A detailed study of Emerson as an incipient radical empiricist is a noteworthy task for the future.

The response of Santayana to Emerson's thought was more censorious than that of James and Dewey. On several occasions, James compared the thought of Emerson and Santayana, to the detriment of the latter. In a letter to Dickinson S. Miller, James comments on Santayana's book, *The Life of Reason:*

> He is a paragon of Emersonianism—declare your intuitions, though no other man share them; . . . The book is Emerson's first rival and successor, but how different the reader's feeling! The same things in Emerson's mouth would sound entirely different. E. receptive, expansive, as if handling life through a wide funnel with a great indraught; S. as if through a pin-point orifice that emits his cooling spray outward over the universe like a nose-disinfectant from an "atomizer."[41]

We learn from a letter written by Santayana that James apparently had expressed similar sentiments to him as he had in the letter to Miller. Santayana was not pleased and in his response issues a devastating criticism of Emerson.

---

subject to human will is not a strange contention for William James, as witness his own doctrine of "The Will to Believe." Could it have some expressive origin in Emerson's "Nature"? (*Works,* 1: 76): "Build therefore your own world. As fast as you conform your life to the pure idea in your mind, that will unfold its great proportions. A correspondent revolution in things will attend the influx of the spirit."

[40] What could be more Emersonian than James's remark in his "Sentiment of Rationality" that "the inmost nature of the reality is congenial to powers which you possess"? *The Writings of William James,* ed. John J. McDermott (Chicago: The University of Chicago Press, 1977), p. 331.

[41] Henry James, Jr., ed., *The Letters of William James* (Boston: Little, Brown, 1920), pp. 234–35. For another contrast of Emerson and Santayana, see John Crowe Ransom, "Art and Mr. Santayana," in *Santayana: Animal Faith and Spiritual Life,* ed., John Lachs (New York: Appleton-Century-Crofts, 1967), pp. 403–4.

And you say I am less hospitable than Emerson. Of course. Emerson might pipe his wood-notes and chirp at the universe most blandly; his genius might be tender and profound and Hamlet-like, and that is all beyond my range and contrary to my purpose. . . . What did Emerson know or care about the passionate insanities and political disasters which religion, for instance, has so often been another name for? He could give that name to his last personal intuition, and ignore what it stands for and what it expresses in the world. It is the latter that absorbs me; and I care too much about mortal happiness to be interested in the charming vegetation of cancer-microbes in the system—except with the idea of suppressing it.[42]

Although not quite so caustic as his rebuke to James, Santayana's writings on Emerson always had a critical edge to them. In an early essay, written in 1886, Santayana comments judiciously on Emerson's optimism, which he traces more to his person than to his doctrine. Yet, Santayana's sympathetic treatment of Emerson concludes with a damaging last line: "But of those who are not yet free from the troublesome feelings of pity and shame, Emerson brings no comfort, he is a prophet of a fair-weather religion."[43]

In 1900, as a chapter in his *Interpretations of Poetry and Religion,* Santayana published his best known essay on Emerson. This piece has been frequently cited on behalf of those who are condescending to Emerson or severely critical of him. I believe this use of Santayana's essay to be a misreading. Certainly, Santayana was more indulgent of Emerson in 1900 than he was in 1911, when he published his famous essay on "The Genteel Tradition in American Philosophy." In 1911, Santayana lumps Emerson with Poe and Hawthorne as having "a certain starved

---

[42] Daniel Cory, ed., *The Letters of George Santayana* (New York: Scribner's, 1955), pp. 81–82.

[43] George Santayana, "The Optimism of Ralph Waldo Emerson," *George Santayana's America,* ed., James Ballowe (Urbana: University of Illinois Press, 1967), p. 84. Another little-known piece of Santayana on Emerson is "Emerson the Poet," a centennial contribution of 1903. Although in this essay Santayana speaks of Emerson as often bland, he praises him for self-direction and a deep and unyielding sense of personal liberty. Richard C. Lyon, ed., *Santayana on America* (New York: Harcourt, 1968), pp. 268–83.

and abstract quality." Further, their collective "genius" was a
"digestion of vacancy."

> It was a refined labour, but it was in danger of being morbid, or
> tinkling, or self-indulgent. It was a play of intramental rhymes. Their
> mind was like an old music-box, full of tender echoes and quaint fan-
> cies. These fancies expressed their personal genius sincerely, as dreams
> may; but they were arbitrary fancies in comparison with what a real ob-
> server would have said in the premises. Their manner, in a word, was
> subjective. In their own persons they escape the mediocrity of the gen-
> teel tradition, but they supplied nothing to supplant it in other
> minds.[44]

In 1900, however, when Santayana addressed Emerson's
thought directly, his evaluations are more favorable. Admitting
of Emerson, that "at bottom he had no doctrine at all," Santayana writes that "his finer instinct kept him from doing that
violence to his inspiration."[45] Santayana repeats his earlier contention that Emerson's power was not in his "doctrine" but
rather in his "temperament." And that Emersonian temperament was above all, antitradition and antiauthoritarian. Even
though he was a classic instance of the "Genteel Tradition" and
held many positions which were anathema to Santayana, Emerson neverthless pleased Santayana by his refusal to profes-
sionalize and systematize his thought. Further, Santayana, with
poetic sensibilities of his own, was taken with Emerson's style.
He writes of Emerson: "If not a star of the first magnitude, he is
certainly a fixed star in the firmament of philosophy. Alone as
yet among Americans, he may be said to have won a place
there, if not by the originality of this thought, at least by the
originality and beauty of the expression he gave to thoughts
that are old and imperishable."[46]

Still more to the point, and less known, is that Santayana

[44] George Santayana, "The Genteel Tradition in American Philosophy," *Winds of Doctrine* (London: J. M. Dent, 1913), pp. 192–93.

[45] George Santayana, "Emerson," *Interpretations of Poetry and Religion* (New York: Scribner's, 1900), p. 218.

[46] *Ibid.*, p. 233.

shared Emerson's celebration and embracing of the "common."
In 1927, as part of a chastizing letter sent to Van Wyck
Brooks, Santayana writes: "I therefore think that art, etc. has
better soil in the ferocious 100% America than in the intelligentsia of New York. It is veneer, rouge, aestheticism, art
museums, new theatres, etc. that make America impotent. The
good things are football, kindness, and jazz bands."[47] It turns
out that Santayana, like Whitman, learned something from
Emerson.

Before examining John Dewey's essay on Emerson, I offer a
brief interlude with a comment on Josiah Royce's assessment of
Emerson. Although Royce was a voluminous writer[48] and ven-
tured interpretations of an extremely wide range of problems
and thinkers, he rarely spoke of Emerson. No matter, Royce
thought far more of Emerson than we could have divined from
his publications. In 1911, Royce delivered a Phi Beta Kappa
Oration in honor of William James, who had died the previous
year. The theme of Royce's essay was that James was the third
"representative American Philosopher." It was in Royce's opening discussion of the first two candidates, that his version of
Emerson emerged:

> Fifty years since, if competent judges were asked to name the American
> thinkers from whom there had come novel and notable and typical con-
> tributions to general philosophy, they could in reply mention only two
> men—Jonathan Edwards and Ralph Waldo Emerson. For the condi-
> tions that determine a fair answer to the question, "Who are your rep-
> resentative American philosophers?" are obvious. The philosopher who
> can fitly represent the contribution of his nation to the world's treasury
> of philosophical ideas must first be one who thinks for himself, fruit-
> fully, with true independence, and with successful inventiveness, about
> problems of philosophy. And, secondly, he must be a man who gives
> utterance to philosophical ideas which are characteristic of some stage
> and of some aspect of the spiritual life of his own people. In Edwards

[47] Cory, ed., *The Letters of George Santayana*, pp. 225–26.
[48] Ignas K. Skrupskelis, "Annotated Bibliography of the Publications of Josiah
Royce," in John J. McDermott, *The Basic Writings of Josiah Royce* (Chicago: University of Chicago Press, 1969) 2: 1167–1226.

and in Emerson, and only in these men, had these two conditions found
their fulfillment, so far as our American civilization had yet expressed
itself in the years that had preceded our civil war. . . .

Another stage of our civilization—a later phase of our national
ideals—found its representative in Emerson. He too was in close touch
with many of the world's deepest thoughts concerning ultimate problems. Some of the ideas that most influenced him have their far-off historical origins in oriental as well as in Greek thought, and also their
nearer foreign sources in modern European philosophy, but he transformed what ever he assimilated. He invented upon the basis of his personal experience, and so he was himself no disciple of the orient, or of
Greece, still less of England and Germany. He thought, felt, and spoke
as an American.[49]

Again, we are left with a judgment as to Emerson's importance, notably in this case as a philosopher, but without subsequent or sufficient analysis. A search through the papers and
publications of Royce does not cast much more direct light on
this influence of Emerson. Royce's remarks do convince me,
however, that Emerson wrought more in the lives of the classical American philosophers than written evidence can sustain.

Among the Centenary addresses of 1903, we find another by an
American philosopher, John Dewey. This essay sets out to rescue Emerson from the condescension implied when he is described as not a philosopher. Dewey complains that "literary
critics admit his philosophy and deny his literature. And if philosophers extol his keen, calm art and speak with some depreciation of his metaphysic, it is also perhaps because Emerson
knew something deeper than our conventional definitions."[50]
The first of Dewey's complaints is now out of date, for Emerson
is taken very seriously as a literary artist. The second complaint,
still holds, although with important exceptions as noted above
in the work of Blau and Pollock.

In Dewey's judgment, Emerson has been misread and misunderstood. He takes as Emerson's project the submitting of ideas

---

[49] Josiah Royce, *William James and Other Essays* (New York: Macmillan, 1911),
pp. 3–4, 5–6.
[50] John Dewey, *Characters and Events* (New York: Holt, 1929) 1: 171.

"to the test of trial by service rendered the present and immediate experience."[51] Further, Dewey contends that Emerson's method is consistent with this experimental endeavor. "To Emerson, perception was more potent than reasoning; the deliverances of intercourse more to be desired than the chains of discourse; the surprise of reception more demonstrative than the conclusions of intentional proof."[52]

It is intriguing that Dewey, whose own style is anything but oracular, would praise this approach of Emerson. One might rather expect this indulgence from those reared in the language of the existentialists or of twentieth century religious thinkers, such as Buber, Berdyaev, and Marcel. A closer look at Dewey's text, however, provides some source of explanation. Similar to James's emphasis, Dewey states that the locus of Emerson's inquiry is the "possibility" inherent in the experience of the "common man." Against the opinions of other commentators, Dewey holds that Emerson's "ideas are not fixed upon any Reality that is beyond or behind or in any way apart, and hence they do not have to be bent. They are versions of the Here and the Now, and flow freely."[53]

Dewey is especially sympathetic with Emerson's attempt to avoid the "apart."[54] And he is convinced that Emerson knew, as few others, of the enervating and diluting effect often had by theory on the richness of common and concrete experience. Dewey's text on this issue is crystal-clear and can be read as well as a critique for much of what passes for philosophical discourse in our own time.

[51] *Ibid.,* p. 74.
[52] *Ibid.,* p. 70.
[53] *Ibid.,* p. 75.
[54] Dewey takes a similar position in *Art as Experience* (New York: Capricorn, 1958 [1934]), p. 11. "Theory can start with and from acknowledged works of art only when the esthetic is already compartmentalized, or only when works of art are set in a niche apart instead of being celebrations, recognized as such, of the things of ordinary experience. Even a crude experience, if authentically an experience, is more fit to give a clue to the intrinsic nature of esthetic experience than is an object already set apart from any other mode of experience."

Against creed and system, convention and institution, Emerson stands
for restoring to the common man that which in the name of religion, of
philosophy, of art and of morality, has been embezzled from the common store and appropriated to sectarian and class use. Beyond any one
we know of, Emerson has comprehended and declared how such malver-
sation makes truth decline from its simplicity, and in becoming partial
and owned, become a puzzle of and trick for theologian, metaphysician
and litterateur—a puzzle of an imposed law, of an unwished for and
refused goodness, of a romantic ideal gleaming only from afar, and a
trick of manipular skill, of specialized performance.[55]

Dewey took Emerson's task as his own. Although his prose
lacked the rhetorical flights so natural to Emerson, he too wrote
out of compassion for the common man and confidence in the
"possibility" inherent in every situation. By the time of
Dewey's maturity, the world of New England high culture had
passed. Dewey, despite being born in New England, was a
child of industrial democracy. He alone of the classic American
philosophers was able to convert the genius and language of
Emerson to the new setting. John Dewey, proletarian by birth
and style, grasped that Emerson's message was ever relevant. In
the conclusion to his essay on Emerson, Dewey captures that
message and carries it forward to his own time. I offer that we
should do likewise.

To them who refuse to be called "master, master," all magistracies in
the end defer, for theirs is the common cause for which dominion,
power and principality is put under foot. Before such successes, even
the worshippers of that which to-day goes by the name of success, those
who bend to millions and incline to imperialisms, may lower their standard and give at least a passing assent to the final word of Emerson's
philosophy, the identity of Being, unqualified and immutable, with
Character.[56]

[55] Dewey, "Emerson," p. 75.
[56] *Ibid.*, p. 77.

TEN

Santayana and the Ideal of Reason

DOUGLAS GREENLEE

THERE IS A NEED at the present time for a recovery of the meaning of philosophic naturalism as conceived by the great American philosophers of the early part of this century, George Santayana and John Dewey, not because that naturalism is an orothodoxy to which we should return, but because it is a part of our past that we should assimilate. To recover this meaning we should begin by noting that "naturalism" has been used differently in philosophic contexts than in literary contexts, where it denotes a novelistic method of precise and impartial observation. In philosophical and theological contexts, naturalism was often used in the last century to denote the combination of atheism with "materialism." Then, early in the present century, beginning with certain of the mature philosophical essays of William James and evolving with the writings of Santayana and Dewey, the term came to represent a metaphysical position most easily summed up in the vague but useful formula "man is a part of nature" or "human experience is continuous with nature at large."[1] With the last generation

The Editors wish to record, with profound sorrow, the untimely death of their distinguished colleague, Professor Douglas Greenlee, who was still able to submit this essay himself before succumbing to his fatal illness.

[1] For James see *Essays in Radical Empiricism* (New York: Longman's, 1912). In "The Thing and Its Relations" James uses the term "naturalism" to name the position he is

of philosophers, this rich sense of the term has been buried by a thinner and narrowly methodological doctrine to the effect that there is one method of knowing, the scientific, and that philosophy is continuous with science as regards this method.[2] Admittedly, the later Dewey and his followers, during the time of the high tide of logical positivism, abetted this burial, no doubt affected by the disrepute into which metaphysics had fallen.[3]

There are four major arguments against a narrowly methodological interpretation: (i) if philosophical topics such as knowledge, mind, meaning and value can be studied according to a method continuous with that of science, then it is a metaphysical (or ontological) truth that these subjects are parts of that world, generally called "nature," which is the object of scientific inquiry. And it therefore ought to be recognized that the methodological sense of "naturalism" entails the metaphysical, although it does not follow that the converse holds. (ii) The paradigmatic philosophical naturalists, apart from Aristotle and Spinoza, are Santayana and Dewey,[4] and for Santayana the methodological sense does not apply, much less constitute the whole meaning. It was Santayana who said, "My philosophy neither is nor wishes to be scientific."[5] (iii) A further consider-

---

advancing. For Santayana see *The Life of Reason, or the Phases of Human Progress,* vol. 1, *Reason in Common Sense;* vol. 2, *Reason in Society;* vol. 3, *Reason in Religion;* vol. 4, *Reason in Art;* vol. 5, *Reason in Science* (New York: 1905; 2nd ed., Scribner's, 1922). All subsequent references to the volumes of *The Life of Reason* will be to the second edition. For Dewey see *Experience and Nature* (New York: Open Court, 1925, 2nd ed., New York: Norton, 1929).

[2] Ignored here is an even more specialized use of "naturalism," in which it labels a position in ethics concerned with analyzing evaluative expressions in terms ultimately factual or descriptive or to justify certain evaluative statements (those that can be called basic) by appeal exclusively to factual statements.

[3] See *Naturalism and the Human Spirit,* ed. Y. H. Krikorian (New York: Columbia University Press, 1944).

[4] *Ibid.* The contributors to Krikorian repeatedly stress this point.

[5] *Realms of Being,* one-volume edition (New York: Scribner's, 1942), p. 827. This late statement, however, does represent a certain change in point of view. In 1905 Santayana insisted not only that rational ethics is a science (*Reason in Common Sense,* Introduction; *Reason in Science,* ch. ix) but spoke of "the rational moralist" as repre-

ation in favor of the metaphysical sense is that it serves the need of representing a great unifying theme running through the classic period of American philosophy, the period from Chauncey Wright, Peirce, and James, through Royce, to Santayana, Dewey, Mead, and Whitehead.[6] (iv) Furthermore, two of among the most original philosophic thinkers of the present day, W. V. Quine and Justus Buchler, exemplify this theme.[7] And there are other important figures in the history of American philosophy who can be well understood historically in terms of the same theme.[8]

In studying a historical tradition, the historian will be most pleased when he can find an essence to tie together a tradition and establish its unity as *a* tradition. There is always the danger of oversimplification in such an effort, especially when, in a philosophic tradition as complex as that which runs in America from Chauncey Wright to the present day, there are a number of themes that weave in and out through the period, including positivism, idealism, materialism, realism, and the much-noted pragmatism. In his comprehensive studies of philosophical thinking in America, Blau has displayed this complexity with excellent clarity.[9] As a musical composition need not have one theme in order to be a coherent composition, neither need a

senting ideals "against the chance facts." (*Reason in Science,* p. 245.) By 1922 Santayana can be found writing that "moral philosophy is not a science," (*Reason in Common Sense,* p. xii.) See below, footnote 15.

[6] Although not all of these thinkers should be called "naturalists," through them all runs an important strain of naturalism.

[7] See Quine, *Ontological Relativity* (New York: Columbia University Press, 1969), p. 26; and Buchler, *Toward a General Theory of Human Judgment* (New York: Columbia University Press, 1951), pp. 111–12.

[8] E.g., M. R. Cohen, R. W. Sellars, F. J. E. Woodbridge, J. H. Randall, Jr.

[9] See in particular *Men and Movements in American Philosophy* (Englewood Cliffs, N.J.: Prentice-Hall, 1952). Professor Blau's work is continuous with that of Herbert Schneider, to whose *A History of American Philosophy* (New York: Columbia University Press, 1946) the present essay is indebted. The present essay, however, departs from those works by de-emphasizing the poetic qualities of Santayana's thought in favor of those of systematic moral criticism.

tradition. Suffice it to note here that pragmatism, most often taken as *the* essence of the classical American philosophic tradition, omits Santayana altogether, although Santayana has indisputably earned a place central to that tradition.[10]

Though there need be no theme which is *the* theme of the classic American school, there may be an important theme that runs through the major representatives of that school. I think it can be shown that naturalism, rather than pragmatism, is just that theme.[11] Because of its importance, its elusiveness, and its continuing suggestiveness, there is a special reason to try to understand just what naturalism, in the richer, metaphysical sense, comprises. We shall turn in what follows to Santayana's naturalistic treatment of the ideal of reason—or the ideal of a life of reason—in an attempt to show what naturalism is by displaying the naturalism of one of its chief exemplars.

It was with the appearance in 1905–6 of Santayana's *The Life of Reason, or the Phases of Human Progress,* that philosophic naturalism in America came into full flower. That monumental work consists of a mixture of what may be called philosophical criticism and critical philosophy. The former is a type of moral philosophy, early exemplified by Plato's *Republic* and Aristotle's *Nicomachean Ethics* and *Politics,* in which social institutions, patterns of conduct, and human products in the most generic sense—such as types of art and political constitutions—and the values and ideals associated with them are evaluated by reference to the circumstances that make them possible and to an overarching ideal. Santayana's name for that ideal is "the life of reason." Beginning with the study of those human products which are the fundamental conceptions of common sense—such as "mind" and "nature"—the volumes of *The Life of Reason* successively study society, religion, art, and science.

[10] Thus John E. Smith, opting for pragmatism as the essence, had to omit Santayana in *The Spirit of American Philosophy* (New York: Oxford University Press, 1963).

[11] A book-length manuscript on naturalism, which will demonstrate this, is in preparation.

Critical philosophy, as understood here, is the account of the conditions of the possibilities of human ideals and achievements, including that achievement called "knowledge." The basic reason why all of the volumes of *The Life of Reason* are essays in naturalism is that all of them start, critically, from the physical and biological conditions and possibilities inherent in human nature and in the world man occupies and proceed to trace both relationships among these possibilities, and the growth of human powers from those conditions. Santayana proceeded in accordance with the program of naturalism, which aims always at exhibiting the continuity of man and nature. What Santayana wrote of his ancient Greek mentor applies equally to himself: "In Aristotle the conception of human nature is perfectly sound; everything ideal has a natural basis and everything natural an ideal development. . . . The Life of Reason finds there its classic explication."[12]

Philosophical criticism requires a conception of the sort of world in which man finds himself, for it consists of an account of what ideals are possible given the conditions which underlie human life and which limit human aims and achievements. It is a fundamental principle of Santayana's naturalistic perspective that neither human history nor the world in which that history continues is controlled, guided, or in any way influenced by a being, principle, or built-in structure of evolution that guarantees a morally desirable outcome. Nature, according to Santayana, is morally flat. No vertical order of better and worse is built into the structure of the world, and no preexisting good— no moral force or entity—stands outside of nature to provide a ground for our grand or petty hopes for moral progress and for the reduction of evil. Paying tribute to Heraclitus, Santayana described nature as the *flux*. The principle of the flux is that nature is "irrational," which is to say both that the material world is continuously and meaninglessly in motion, with everything

[12] *Reason in Common Sense*, p. 21.

gradually—or not so gradually—changing into something else, and that there is no rational providence overlooking the whole affair. Santayana's naturalism is first of all a repudiation of supernaturalism. His philosophical criticism is rooted directly in this naturalism.

II

The keynote to *The Life of Reason* lies in a prefatory remark:

> It seldom occurs to modern moralists that theirs is the science of all good and the art of its attainment; they think only of some set of categorical precepts or some theory of moral sentiments, abstracting altogether from the ideals reigning in society, in science, and in art. They deal with the secondary question, What ought I to do? without having answered the primary question, What ought to be? [13]

A large segment of ethical philosophy has, since the 1905 statement, moved even farther away from the substantive enterprise Santayana recommended to the more abstract level yet of "metaethics," the study of ethical terms and concepts and of their logical interrelations. Santayana's enterprise is the heroic one of an actual immersion in values—of the evaluation of values— heroic both because it requires an immense amount of reflection on history and an intense commitment to a point of view. [14] It requires immense intellectual strength and integrity to take a position on what is of greatest value in human life and to interpret it systematically in such a way that a perspective is sustained throughout such vast subject matters as Santayana studies in the five volumes of *The Life of Reason*. His greatest achievement there is the perspective maintained of the highest level of philosophical criticism, the level of constant attention to an ultimate ideal, while at the same time articulating that ideal in

[13] *Ibid.*, p. 30.
[14] "A great task," he called his enterprise, which no one would have the powers to perform had not "the outlines of an ideal culture" been drawn by the (ancient) Greeks. *Ibid.*, p. 32.

the account of the conditions and the appraisal of the consequences of a wide assortment of human values and achievements. It is misleading, therefore, to belittle Santayana's philosophy of the ideal of reason as "subjective" or as "personal,"
meaning thereby that it is haplessly idiosyncratic or of interest
merely as the expression of one person's taste, however cultivated that taste might be.[15] And equally off the mark is the
notion that his system is mere poetry, i.e., prose beautifully
and poetically written, although the writing shares what are
often thought of as the special effects of poetry, such as vivid
metaphors and elaborate similes.

The naturalistic character of Santayana's project is stated and
restated in many ways, such as in the capsule summary that "all
my message" (in *The Life of Reason*) is "that morality and religion are expressions of human nature; that human nature is a
biological growth; and finally that spirit, fascinated and tortured, is involved in the process and asks to be saved."[16] Or
consider his statement of his whole purpose as "to mark the *natural* origin of these improvements and their *natural* sanctions
and fate"—the "improvements" being the major categories of
the achievements of civilization which he studied.[17] To understand what the qualification "natural" means, and to break out
of the circle of defining naturalism in terms of the adjective natural, we need to turn to the subtitle of *The Life of Reason,* "the
Phases of Human Progress." Santayana held in the greatest contempt the notion of history as progress, whether as an inevita-
bility, in the style of the Hegelians, or as an evolutionary necessity, in the style of the popularizers of Darwinism, or as a
supernaturally guaranteed march, as often taught religiously.
What ran most deeply against his grain was the witless op-

[15] Santayana himself was guilty of such belittlement when he later said of *The Life
of Reason* that he might have called his work the "Romance of Wisdom," *Reason in
Common Sense,* p. vii. See also, above, footnote 5.

[16] *The Philosophy of George Santayana,* ed. P. A. Schilpp (2nd ed., New York:
Tudor, 1951), p. 23.

[17] *Ibid.,* p. 558. Emphasis in original.

timism of the belief that "historical sequence is equivalent to moral progress." [18] That his rejection of this belief concerns his naturalism is indicated in the remark that the "notion that a single universal vocation summons all mankind and even all the universe to tread a single path towards the same end seems to me utterly anti-natural. It has come into modern opinion as a heritage from religion; and I respect it in religion when it expresses the genuine aspiration of some particular race or, in the best instance, of spirit in anybody; but I cannot respect it as a view of history." [19]

Since the falsity of the belief in progress, cosmic or merely historical, is a cornerstone of Santayana's philosophy, why the subtitle of *The Life of Reason* ("the Phases of Human Progress") and how are we to understand that work as naturalistic? The answer lies in an alternative conception of progress which Santayana adopted—not the conception of it as "forward" but rather "upward," which is to say, not historical but ideal or formal. Examples could be found in the ahistorical schemes of progress of the *philosophes* of the eighteenth century, whose concerns were with schemes of ideal history—i.e., with progress in a vertical sense. A chief difference between them and Santayana, however, is that they confused the vertical with a historical sense of progress. Santayana made it entirely clear when, in *Reason in Society* for example, he distinguished among natural, free, and ideal society, that the ascent toward better embodiments of the ideal of reason in society is not historical. Progress, as he once said, could not be "universal or endless, but only episodic, divergent, and multifarious." [20] That is, progress, as the achievement of some ideal possibilities of society, art, religion, or science, is episodic. A schema, a vertical order of such possibilities, ranked according to the degree of approximation of what the ideal of reason calls for, is presented in the five vol-

[18] *Ibid.*, p. 557.
[19] *Ibid.*, p. 558.
[20] *Ibid.*, p. 559.

umes of *The Life of Reason*. Hence Santayana was not wholly accurate when he referred to his work as that of "the historian of reason" or himself as "the chronicler of human progress";[21] for it is not as a chronicler that he set out to explore progress but as a philosophical naturalist concerned to portray the conditions in the natural world which make possible the embodiment of ideals in human achievements and to make clear that the value or ideality of what is achieved depends in particular on those conditions which are human impulses or "instincts."

When Santayana said that Hegel's *Phenomenology of Mind* "set me planning my *Life of Reason,*" the response to Hegel, he confessed, is as much negative as positive. In his own work Santayana sought "a more honest criticism of progress," one "based on tracing the distracted efforts of man to satisfy his natural impulses in his natural environment."[22] With Hegel there is a guiding assumption that history and progress (specifically, world history and the progress of freedom) coincide. This assumption, according to Santayana's misinterpretation of Hegel, was accepted because the latter assumed that whatever happened to be the latest outcome of historical events was the best because it happened to be the last. However, Santayana was incorrect. Hegel identified history with progress because of the principle, equally ludicrous of course, that the consecutive outcomes of world-historical periods must be realizations of higher goods—and higher not because last but according to a rationally justifiable standard of what is better and what is worse. Yet, in comparison with those eighteenth-century notions of progress according to which a schema of stages provides a model of universal history, without regard to time, place or the particular conditions of a society or a people, Santayana stands closer to Hegel than it might at first appear.[23] Whether Santayana

---

[21]*Reason in Common Sense,* p. 8.

[22]*Ibid.,* p. xi.

[23] See, for example, Condorcet's sketch of the progress of the human mind, *Esquisse d'un tableau historique du progres de l'esprit.*

learned the principle from Hegel is not a point that could be proved one way or another, but he does share with Hegel the principle that the value of an achievement in civilization is relative to the needs, conditions, and possibilities of man as situated in the world at a time and a place. Only, unlike Hegel, the contemptuous critic of "abstract" ideals, Santayana held at the same time that there is an ideal, that of a life of reason, which is in some respect not relative and is universal.[24]

To sum up, the fundamental naturalism of Santayana's project of a criticism of progress consists, negatively, in a rejection equally of a transcendent—i.e. supernatural—guarantee and of an evolutionary guarantee of history as a progress. Positively, Santayana relates certain sorts of achievements which civilizations have realized, "episodically," to natural conditions, including actual or given human impulses.[25] We may well wonder, however, to what authority a moral critic such as Santayana can appeal if naturalism requires him to stand independently of all of the sorts of standards of progress, or of what is better and what worse, discussed. That the ideal which controls Santayana's perspective is that of reason (a life of reason) might misleadingly suggest that he had in mind an *a priori* standard which pure reason, by its own natural light, can intuit as binding. Such a standard has traditionally gone by the name of natural right or natural law. But to take Santayana as a natural law moralist could produce no interpretation falser to his naturalism. For part of the point of his naturalistic focus on the continuity of man and nature is that an ideal is desirable only because its attainment will satisfy human impulses and needs and ultimately, thereby, promote what can be called happiness.[26]

[24] There are two sides of Santayana's ethical thought, that of relativism and that of nonrelativism. See *Reason in Science,* p. 234.

[25] The expression "natural conditions" is redundant, since there are no unnatural conditions—that is, conditions not a part of nature; yet it is still useful in emphasizing the fact of the continuity of man and nature with which naturalism is concerned.

[26] See *Reason in Science,* ch. 9, for Santayana's most compact statement of his eudaemonistic conception of happiness.

III

The heart of *The Life of Reason* is the concept of a life which is "the happy marriage of two elements—impulse and ideation," or, in different words, is a "fusion of two types of life, commonly led in the world in well-nigh total separation, one a life of impulse expressed in affairs and social passions, the other a life of reflection expressed in religion, science, and the imitative arts."[27] This concept is of an ideal of a special sort; it is an idea of ideals, regulative of all other ideals. For it is the concept of an ideal economy of values in which every value (or ideal) is accorded a role in a life such that the pursuit of it leads toward a state of being called happiness. Alone, the two elements of this state of being are "monsters"; together they can combine to give human life the excellence that places it above all other animal life. The life of reason begins "with the union of instinct and ideation, when instinct becomes enlightened, establishes values in its objects, and is turned from a process into an art, while at the same time consciousness becomes practical and cognitive, beginning to contain some symbol or record of the co-ordinate realities among which it arises."[28] The separation of the two elements need not be interpreted as that between two types of persons, as if Santayana were saying only that some individuals are impulsive, others ideational. Rather, the point concerns a typical dualism in the life of each individual, who in one part of his life is predominantly impulsive, and in another predominantly ideational. The ideal of reason is the ideal of an integration of the person with respect to these two sides. This integration is completed only when, in addition to the weighing of each impulse with respect to a consideration of its possibilities of fulfillment and the satisfactoriness of its consequences, it is weighed with respect to its bearing on other impulses and possibilities, so that an overall economy of values is established which permits realization of the most fulfilling life possible.

[27] *Reason in Common Sense,* pp. 6, 5.
[28] *Ibid.,* p. 5.

Santayana's naturalism is in large part his philosophy of the continuity of impulse and reason with nature at large. In order to understand this naturalism, we shall have to proceed to an examination of his concept of nature as "the flux of existence" and, after that, trace the relation of the two elements of the life of reason to their natural setting in that flux.

IV

At the end of the first volume of *The Life of Reason* Santayana states that the main principle which the subsequent volumes will illustrate is "that nature carries its ideal with it and that the progressive organization of irrational impulses make a rational life."[29] This principle expresses in a somewhat more precise way what is to be understood by that weary formula for naturalism—which Santayana is not incapable of professing—that "man is a part of nature,"[30] or, stated more elaborately, that "human nature . . . has for its core the substance of nature at large, and one of its more complex formations."[31] What, we need to know, is the substance of nature at large, according to Santayana? The answer which suffices for the purpose of providing the ontological foundation of Santayana's philosophical criticism is "the flux of being" or, simply, "the flux."[32]

The naturalistic elements of the concept of the flux are as follows: (i) it is the sum total of what there is in existence. It is spatio-temporal nature as it is in itself, that is, spatial and temporal phenomena as whatever they are, rather than what they are just in relation to human knowledge and valuation—what they are apart from the classifications, rankings, and more or less limited perspectives of human experiencers. It need only be added that consistency in naturalism requires, of course, that

[29]*Ibid.*, p. 291.
[30]*Ibid.*, p. 288.
[31]*Ibid.*, p. 289.
[32] For the most extended treatment of the concept of the flux, see *The Realm of Matter* (Volume 2 of *The Realms of Being*), ch. v.

these perspectives, as phenomena, be included in nature.[33] (ii) In his later philosophy, when Santayana came explicitly to identify existence and matter (an identification perhaps latent in the original edition of *The Life of Reason* but not yet affirmed) and hence to systematic materialism, the flux turned out to consist of the material world, its objects and events. Thus he wrote in the preface to the second edition of *The Life of Reason,* "existing nature is a system of bodies."[34] The careful reader of Santayana will always want to bear in mind two qualifications regarding what he called his "materialism." One is that it is coupled with an epiphenomenalism concerning consciousness, described as an "emanation" of "the flux," and hence, depending on how one chooses to read the word "emanation," is either to be regarded as a nonmaterial *part* of the flux or as a nonmaterial reality which exists in addition to it. In the latter case, the concepts of "the flux" and "matter" are not, after all, coextensive, and one must understand by "the flux" nature as the system of bodies plus consciousness.[35] In what follows, "the flux" will be taken in the larger sense, inclusive of epiphenomena. The other qualification is that "existence" is not, in Santayana's ontology, coextensive with "reality" or "being." Thus in his Platonic Volume 1 of *Realms of Being, The Realm of Essence,* essences are allotted the status of being real, though existence is denied to them. Of course, the world, or "nature," in the largest sense, includes all being, and hence more than bodies. But Santayana seems to have been given to conceiving "nature" in the more limited, spatial-temporal, terms. (iii) From the standpoint of naturalism, perhaps what is most important about the concept of "the flux"

[33] "Existence is nothing if not complex, elastic, fundamentally chaotic. Perception, description and dogma over-simplify and over-regulate everything." *Realms of Being,* p. 288. Cp. 280, 292. There is hardly a more treacherous idea in metaphysics than that of reality—even of spatio-temporal reality—as it is in itself.

[34] *Reason in Common Sense,* p. viii.

[35] *Realms of Being,* p. 268. When Santayana wrote that after Descartes, "to call consciousness material would be to talk of the blackness of white," he suggested that mental phenomena are not part of the (material) flux. See *Three Philosophical Poets* (Cambridge: Harvard University Press, 1910), p. 48.

is that it represents an explicit repudiation of the Cartesian
dualism of two fundamental substances, matter and mind. According to Santayana's ontology, mind is nothing capable of existence independent of matter, and hence is not classifiable as a
separate substance. Heraclitus introduced the concept of the
flux into philosophy, Santayana notes, before remarking that
"we need but to rescind the artificial division which Descartes
has taught us to make between nature and life, to feel again the
absolute aptness of Heraclitus's expressions."[36] (iv) For Heraclitus as for Santayana, the concept of the flux is the concept of
what exists as not only in change but in a certain sort of change.
It is change with the qualification attached that rules out
change as perhaps most often conceived by philosophers and
nonphilosophers alike—i.e., change vertically, for the better or
for the worse. That which is in flux is that which is intrinsically
neither progress nor regress. It is the sheer shifting about
through time of what there is in the spatio-temporal world—
matter in motion plus matter's epiphenomena. This flux includes episodes of progress and regress, as measured by human
standards, but these episodes, as episodes, are only large-scale
events within the over-all flux, to be followed as likely as not by
episodes of the opposite sort of change or of change indifferent
to human standards. Whereas within an episode there may be
progress, the episode as such constitutes no step toward overall
progress, and is ultimately condemned to be merely another
event of the total flux. Nature is "irrational," which is not to
say unintelligible, but rather, as it stands in itself, unordered or
unstructured with regard to human values of what makes sense
morally and what is desirable.[37] The conception of nature as a
flux is a conception which denies to it *a* moral order. (v) The
flux of existence is a world intelligible scientifically. Why?

[36]*Reason in Common Sense,* p. 15.

[37]*Reason in Science,* p. 78. "Existence" is irrational and change "unintelligible." If
valuations, discriminations of ideals, human classifying and sorting are included
within nature, then "nature in itself" means merely a part of nature.

Because it is ordered in at least one very general way, and according to one very general principle, that of causality. Spatio-temporal nature, as the system of bodies plus the epiphenomena of the mental, is, in Santayana's language, "mechanical." It was Democritus, according to Santayana, who introduced, with his materialism and atomism, the conception of spatio-temporal nature as mechanical, or as causally intelligible. "Mechanism," Santayana explained, "is not one principle of explanation among others. In natural philosophy, where to explain means to discover origins, transmutations, and laws, mechanism is explanation itself." [38] Mechanism is not to be equated with the doctrine of causal relations as necessarily push-and-pull relations of mechanical contact among physical objects. It is merely the more abstract, and certainly less dubious, principle that the objects and events of the spatio-temporal world are causally related and hence causally explainable. Fundamentally, the concept of *a* mechanism is the concept of a natural regularity. To the extent that the flux contains patterns of repetitions, "to that extent it will be mechanical." [39]

The philosophy of the life of reason requires a "conception of the conditions under which man lives," [40] for the reasoned evaluation of an ideal consists in part in relating it to the conditions that make it possible, and indeed in knowing that it is possible. Certain of the conditions under which man lives coincide with those of spatio-temporal nature at large: they are circumstances that the spatio-temporal world is a flux of material objects and events mechanically explainable and mechanically reliable. This is to say that it belongs to the character of what exists that causal orders can be relied upon to persist into the future, so that what has been learned to be some particular causal sequence (in the past) can be reasonably projected into the future. The

---

[38] *Reason in Common Sense*, p. 17.

[39] *Realms of Being*, p. 81. Since anything is like anything else in some respect, it is not immediately clear what a regularity is. Santayana neither addressed himself to this matter nor to an analysis of causality.

[40] *Reason in Common Sense*, p. 28.

point (which is not to be confused with a response to Hume's problem of induction) is merely that it is *in fact* one of the conditions of rational life that the world man occupies is this way—the way, namely, of containing causal relations learned in the past that are projectible into the future. It is not a project of Santayana's ontology to justify the common-sense assumption that this projectibility is *in fact* a feature of nature. It is enough for him to take note of its being such a feature. Nor did Santayana address himself to the puzzle of the projectibility of "predicates" (i.e., properties) that has received much attention by the recent generation of logicians. Quite clearly many, if not all, of the ideals which the philosophy of reason should take into account for its task of philosophical criticism depend for their status as ideals for human life on this feature of nature. For an ideal is an idea of a possible perfection of human life in some respect, relating conditions and consequences. The task for the philosophy of reason is "not to construct but only to interpret ideals, confronting them with one another and with the conditions which, for the most part, they alike ignore."[41] Heraclitus and Democritus provided the conception of nature for this task, a conception, Santayana noted, "such as all later observation, down to our own day, has done nothing but fill out and confirm."[42]

(vi) Finally, the conception of existence as the flux rules out any such principle as Leibniz's notion of sufficient reason, a principle according to which there is a reason for everything discernible—including the existence of the nature or flux with which we find ourselves confronted rather than some other, pos-

---

[41]*Ibid.*, p. 32.

[42]*Ibid.*, p. 29. An ambiguity exists in Santayana's conception of the flux—whether "the flux" designates the immediate flux of human sensations and feelings or existence at large. I take for granted the latter alternative. But there is textual evidence for the former, as in the treatment of Heraclitus, who is said to be describing "the immediate." (p. 23). But even "the immediate" is ambiguous, since Santayana may intend by using it things as they are apart from value discriminations, classifications, and, in general, human mediation.

sible, nature. To equate existence and the flux is to insist that nature is contingent, in the sense that ultimate reasons why the spatio-temporal world and its fundamental mechanism are what they are cannot be given. "The flux is itself absolute and the seat of existence."[43] Existence is irrational in more ways than one, and one of those ways is the limitation of the principle of sufficient reason to phenomena within the world. Mechanism holds within nature but not for the explanation of nature as such. Thus: "At the foundation there is one total groundless reality, breaking in upon nothingness with an overwhelming irrational force."[44]

V

One "later observation" that fills out and confirms the conception of the spatio-temporal world presented by Heraclitus and Democritus is of special significance for Santayana's naturalism. Santayana was a member of the generation whose growth to intellectual maturity coincided with the period of intellectual and emotional assimilation of Darwin's demonstration of the principle that human life is to be accounted for according to the same principles which account for the emergence of any form of life. It is to be expected, therefore, that Santayana's naturalism is a response to the Darwinian bombshell that made a decisive impact on the philosophical awareness of the later nineteenth and early twentieth centuries. Santayana is to be counted with Wright, James, Peirce, Dewey, Mead, and Whitehead as an American naturalist whose naturalism is an assimilation of Darwinism. To Heraclitus and Democritus, then, Santayana might have added the name of Darwin, whose work constitutes one of those later observations—and for naturalism a peculiarly important one—which have filled out the picture of nature sketched by those early Greek cosmologists. Santayana recog-

[43] *Realms of Being,* p. 277.
[44] *Ibid.,* pp. 846–47.

nized that "Darwin . . . did more than any one since Newton
to prove that mechanism is universal,"[45] and explained that
what is "scientific or Darwinian in the theory of evolution is
. . . an application of mechanism, a proof that mechanism lies
at the basis of life and morals."[46] In ontological terms we are
told that the theory of evolution "reintroduced flux into the
conception of existence,"[47] and did so in two ways, the first of
which was by destroying the Aristotelian doctrine of fixed and
perpetual species. What Darwin showed, as his title, *The Origin of the Species,* expresses, is that even the species are not permanent fixtures of nature but part of its flux. The second way
was by showing that neither final causes, a transcendent provi-
dential agency, nor a natural order of values is responsible for
the emergence of that "highest" form of life called human, and
that this form is subject to the same principles of mechanism
and to the same fortuitous circumstances as those of any other
sort of natural being.

The naturalistic import of Darwinism, and the meaning of
"the flux" it filled out, may be summed up in the paradox that
the world, after Darwin, was revealed as at once less rational
and more rational. There are two ways in which the world is
understood to "make sense," or to be intelligible, (i) as a moral
order and (ii) as containing patterned orders of phenomena recurring according to regularities of recurrence. The latter kind
of order is that with which scientific inquiry is concerned. The
former is that with which beliefs in natural justice and variously
in such conceptions as those of fate or of divine providence are
concerned. To say of the world that it is irrational may be to
charge it with the lack of either one of these two sorts of order.
A world irrational morally is one in which there is no ultimate
justification of evil. It is, of course, the world as it is in fact experienced to be, one in which the most appalling tragedies as

[45] *Reason in Science,* p. 98.
[46] *Ibid.,* p. 108.
[47] *Reason in Common Sense,* p. 270.

often as not find no compensation. But for naturalism there can be no problem of evil:

> If a younger son asks why he was not born before his elder brother, that question may represent an intelligible state of his feelings; but there is no answer to it, because it is a childish question. So the question why it is right that there should be any evil is itself perverse and raised by false presumptions. To an unsophisticated mortal the existence of evil presents a task, never a problem. Evil, like error, is an incident of animal life, inevitable in a crowded and unsettled world, where one spontaneous movement is likely to thwart another, and all to run up against material impossibilities. While life lasts this task is recurrent, and every creature, in proportion to the vitality and integrity of his nature, strives to remove or abate those evils of which he is sensible.[48]

But for anyone there can be the feeling of moral unintelligibility, which will be felt by whoever has experienced an unexpected disaster, and which is felt by anyone sensitive enough, when he takes the time, to contemplate the actual evils which are the lot of those who choose to stay alive, and which sometimes make life intolerable. Traditionally philosophy, like religion, has probably been more concerned with making sense out of the moral chaos of nature than in studying its patterned sequences of phenomena. Examples abound: Plato with his form of the Good, Aristotle with his teleologically ordered universe of natural ends leading up to a highest end called the Prime Mover, Leibniz and his best of all possible worlds, or even Spinoza's desperate attempt to convince himself and others that what is, is divine and hence justified.[49] Nineteenth-century romantic philosophies, pulling out all the stops and discarding all philosophic scruples, went off on a wildly illusory tangent of moral justification. Hegel, for example, optimistically justified the course of world history by proclaiming its inevitable,

---

[48]*Character and Opinion in the United States* (New York: Scribner's, 1924), pp. 106–7.

[49] Spinoza held officially that moral concepts do not apply to nature at large, or apart from human interests. Yet his doctrine of the intellectual love of God does express an acceptance of nature as morally justified.

glorious outcome. Royce—one of Santayana's teachers—in a typically idealistic effort, attempted to justify evil morally. Herbert Spencer—the immensely popular English philosopher whose influence may, in a negative way, have been formative of Santayana's naturalistic conclusions—espoused an evolutionary optimism. Santayana's category of the flux is designed to express a denial of any of the moral idealisms of the above sort. Since existence is morally neutral, all progress is *human* progress, not "natural" progress, or progress measurable by any standards other than those of human happiness. Thus Santayana could say that "thought is essentially practical in the sense that but for thought no motion would be an action, no change a progress."[50]

The fundamental naturalistic argument behind Santayana's philosophical criticism is that if man is a part of nature, and if nature is the natural order of the flux of existence, then man is a part of that order. What this inference amounts to is that there are universal principles which apply equally to that order and to the order of human life. Put another way, nature is the flux of existence, and man, as part of nature, is an "eddy" in that flux, no less subject to the principle of mechanism than is any other part of that flux.[51]

Finally, how do impulse and reason fit into the flux? To begin with impulse, we should note that it differs from preference in requiring no discrimination between one object and another.[52] Often Santayana uses "instinct" in place of "impulse," and it may help to comprehend his concept of human impulse to think of it as instinct, so long as a none too technical sense of "instinct" is insisted upon. Impulses, or instincts, in man do not fuel fixed modes of behavior. Santayana, although writing at the beginning of the century, was well aware of the fact, made much of by such twentieth-century anthropologists

---

[50] *Reason in Common Sense*, pp. 213–14.
[51] *Ibid.*, p. 283.
[52] See Stephen C. Pepper, "Santayana's Theory of Value," in *Philosophy of Santayana*, ed. Schilpp, pp. 219–39.

as Malinowski, that one of the conditions of an efficacious faculty of reason in man is "an animal body of unusual plasticity" with "instincts" that are "volatile." [53] There is such a thing as a human nature, according to Santayana, but it is variable.[54] Man's ability to adapt his behavior according to what he has learned would be of little use were his behavior determined by innately fixed responses. "To be born half-made is an immense advantage." [55] We may best think of Santayana's concept of impulse, then, as the concept of a drive toward a satisfaction either more or less specific. Other terms sometimes used are "passion," "demand," and "interest," but none of these terms is intended to be technical. So Santayana allows that "interest" may refer to the "source of value"—impulse in the sense of a nonspecific drive—or to the "goals of aspiration." [56]

To be alive is to possess a mechanism, or a complex of mechanisms, which arises when "the flux manages to form an eddy and to maintain by breathing and nutrition what we call a life." [57] Man is a particular sort of eddy distinctive in possessing impulses the least determinate among those of the animal species and something else, called reason. These impulses and the capacity called reason are themselves products, or organizations, of that part of the flux man composes. "Men, like all things else in the world, are products and vehicles of natural energy"; accordingly, "their conscious will, its moral assertiveness, is merely a sign of that energy and of that will's eventual fortunes." [58] Every impulse has a biological source, according to Santayana, for every "theme or motive in the Life of Reason expresses some instinct rooted in the body and incidental to natural organization." [59] The function of reason is to rationalize or harmonize the demands of the human organism. But it is not

[53] *Reason in Common Sense*, p. 40.
[54] *Ibid.*, ch. xii.
[55] *Reason in Society* (New York: 1922), p. 36.
[56] *Philosophy of Santayana*, ed. Schilpp, pp. 577–78.
[57] *Reason in Common Sense*, p. 42.
[58] *Ibid.*, p. 216–17.
[59] *Reason in Science*, p. 177.

the function of reason, nor could it be, to create these demands. "Nature dictates what men shall seek and prompts them to seek it." [60] By "nature" one may read "mechanisms of the flux." It is Santayana's version of naturalism, his sense of "man's essential continuity with other natural things," that lies behind these statements; for once this continuity is appreciated, we are told, "there could be no ground for doubting that similar principles (could they be traced in detail) would be seen to preside over all man's action and passion." [61] What is the evidence for this position? Santayana's answer is,

> A thousand indications, drawn from introspection and from history, could be found to confirm this speculative presumption. It is not only earthquakes and floods, summer and winter, that bring human musings sharply to book. Love and ambition are unmistakable blossomings of material forces, and the more intense and poetical a man's sense is of his spiritual condition the more loudly will he proclaim his utter dependence on nature and the identity of the moving principle in him and in her. [62]

The burden of this remark is that the evidence lies copiously at hand in our common sense fund of information about that particular vortex of the flux which we happen to inhabit. But though common sense can be invoked to justify the view that man's place in the order of nature is in no way privileged by exemption from the principle of mechanism that rules equitably throughout the flux, science cannot be invoked. "Physics cannot account for that minute motion and pullulation of the earth's crust of which human affairs are a portion." [63] The reason is the customary one: there is a gulf in our explanatory powers. We can explain the relatively simple mechanisms that are those of particles and bodies of matter in motion, but we cannot explain in an equal degree of detail the complex mechanisms which

[60] *Reason in Common Sense*, p. 222.
[61] *Reason in Science*, p. 74.
[62] *Ibid.*, pp. 74–75.
[63] *Ibid.*, p. 75.

compose life, and especially human life. Yet "what all practical reason must assume and what all comprehended experience bears witness to" is that a "cosmos . . . underlies the superficial play of sense and opinion."[64]

What Santayana did not but should have added is that a distinction may be drawn between the thesis that mechanisms—of whatever sort—pervade all portions of nature and the thesis that the mechanisms of the flux are, specifically, physical in character. According to the first view, the mechanisms may be biological, sociological, economic, and so on, as well as physical. According to the second, either all other mechanisms are reducible to the physical or there are no mechanisms but the physical. The second view, in either form, is materialism; and we must note in passing that Santayana's naturalism included what he called "materialism," understood neither as a reductionistic nor eliminative account of the mental, but rather an epiphenomenal account.[65] Fundamentally, materialism meant for Santayana the position (i) that mechanism (mixed, perhaps, with some not very important element of chance-spontaneity) is the rule in every portion of the flux, and (ii) that the causal side of the cause-and-effect linkage that constitutes a mechanism is always material in character.[66]

A certain vagueness seriously mars Santayana's naturalistic account of human impulse. Although our task here is not to assess critically Santayana's naturalism but to expose it, one needs to take note of this vagueness in order to complete that exposure. The problem of his vagueness is that it is not clear what it means to say that impulses have a biological source. Does it mean that they have no other source? If so, then, in addition to vagueness, there will be the problem of incorrectness. For

[64] *Ibid.*, p. 76.
[65] Said in many places. See, for example, *Realms of Being*, p. 292.
[66] *Ibid.*, pp. 845–46. Santayana's epiphenomenalism introduces a fundamental incoherence into his naturalism. For (i) reason is in one respect rendered discontinuous with its biological roots and (ii) the function of reason in achieving ends is rendered unaccountable.

human needs are determined by many different sorts of factors, including social influences and even including such consequences of reason as the gaining of knowledge. For example, by gaining a knowledge of music, one may develop a need for music. Part of the problem lies in the knotty issue of epiphenomenalism. Suffice it to note that if indeed a function of reason is to harmonize and rationalize the impulses, then reason must be capable of modifying impulses. The difference between modifying or changing an impulse and creating it is not, however, clear. For a changed impulse can be regarded as a new impulse and when changed by reason then new because of the work of reason—in short, created by reason. Or, if this is not "creation," we need to know why not.

Summing up the arguments for Santayana's version of the naturalistic thesis that man is a part of the flux and subject to a principle fundamentally like that of any other part—the principle of mechanism—we have found two arguments. (i) There is copious evidence of a common-sense sort (the indications drawn from introspection and from history) for the conclusion that human behavior is the product of more and less complicated mechanisms, and (ii) acceptance of such a principle is rationally required because it is regulative of practical reason. Were we not to assume the universality of mechanism we would have no ground for projecting what we have learned in past experience about the conditions (both internal to us and external) that have to be met in order to realize the ends we shall pursue in the future, and in that case we should have no reason to attempt to live rationally and to take seriously an enterprise such as that of philosophical criticism. To these arguments it can be replied that a small dose of indeterminacy is compatible with what we know on the basis of common sense and what we can reasonably generalize on the basis of the scientific knowledge we have. One may recall that one of Santayana's mentors, Lucretius, posited such an indeterminacy, and did not even find it incompatible with a materialistic cosmology. But Santayana himself recognized that a margin of unpredictable variation in the mechanism of the flux is not incompatible with what experience bears witness to and what the principle of mechanism requires,[67] and so he would have considered the reply no objection.

Where does reason fit into the flux? To ask this question is to open up a nest of questions and problems, including one of the most vexatious in Santayana's systematic thought. This is the problem of how reason can be efficacious given the epiphenomenalism Santayana found to be required by an honest assessment of man's place in nature. To begin with, we must keep in mind two senses of "reason," that of a human capacity and that of an ideal, the ideal of a rational life. What we are now concerned with is reason as a capacity. This capacity is not to be identified with consciousness; there may be intense consciousness in madness.[68] But clearly it requires consciousness. It also requires memory and imagination, for it depends on the ability to hold in attention (that is, to represent) what is not present, whether past or future, and whether spatially near or remote. And it requires the ability that Santayana calls "reflection."

> So soon as man ceases to be wholly immersed in sense, he looks before and after, he regrets and desires; and the moments in which prospect or retrospect takes place constitute the reflective or representative part of his life, in contrast to the unmitigated flux of sensations in which nothing ulterior is regarded. . . . To the ideal function of envisaging the absent, memory and reflection will add (since they exist and constitute anew complication in being) the practical function of modifying the future.[69]

To live the life of reason is to "adjust all demands to one ideal and adjust that ideal to its natural conditons."[70] Reason, as a human ability, is a negotiator or mediator; it mediates among impulses, and among impulses and the conditions of their satis-

[67]*Ibid.*, p. 412.
[68]*Reason in Common Sense*, p. 5.
[69]*Ibid.*, p. 2.
[70]*Ibid.*, p. 267.

faction. Reason represents no interest itself except a "formal interest in harmony, in which peace is made within the irrational chaos or flux of impulses given by the fortuitous circumstances of heredity and environment."[71]

If the possibility of serving such an interest is to exist, the human organism must be able to operate upon its impulses and to adjust them in the light of the over-all ideal of a rational life. There must be, in short, mechanisms which permit this sort of adjustment. Some impulses will have to be trimmed down, others cultivated.[72] Santayana recognized that "before we can convince ourselves that a Life of Reason, or practice guided by science and directed toward spiritual goods, is at all worth having, we must make out the possibility and character of its ultimate end."[73] To make out this end, we must be able to conceive the harmony and cooperation of impulses mentioned. And for there to be any point to such conceiving, we must be able to do something about achieving that harmony and cooperation. Santayana's naturalism is nowhere more compelling than when he forgot his epiphenomenalism and proceeded to develop the theme of the efficacy of reason. This efficacy is explicitly related to the problem of the relation of mind and body. Naturalistically, and nonepiphenomenalistically, Santayana began his original chapter advancing epiphenomenalism ("How Thought Is Practical", ch. 9 of *Reason in Common Sense*) with the statement that the relation of mind to body is simply that

> when bodies have reached a certain complexity and vital equilibrium, a sense begins to inhabit them which is focused upon the preservation of that body and on its reproduction. This sense, as it becomes reflective and expressive of physical welfare, points more and more to its own persistence and harmony, and generates the Life of Reason. Nature is reason's basis and theme: reason is nature's consciousness; and from the point of view of that consciousness when it has arisen, reason is also nature's justification and goal.[74]

[71] *Ibid.*
[72] *Ibid.*, p. 259.
[73] *Ibid.*, p. 256.
[74] *Ibid.*, p. 205.

The efficacy of reason, this remark makes clear, is not limited to mediation among impulses. It extends outward to the modification (through the body, of course) of the physical environment. Santayana thus defined art as "that element in the Life of Reason which consists in modifying its environment the better to attain its end."[75] Both industrial and fine art attest to the efficacy of reason, the former being a modification of nature in which mechanisms are noted and rendered useful and the latter being a modification which "consists in the activity of turning an apt material into an expressive and delightful form."[76]

Santayana's naturalistic account of the continuity of reason with the natural conditions which give rise to it is summed up as follows:

> Reason was born, as it has since discovered, into a world already wonderfully organized, in which it found its precursor in what is called life, its seat in an animal body of unusual plasticity, and its function in rendering that body's volatile instincts and sensations harmonious with one another and with the outer world on which they depend. . . . Reason has thus supervened at the last stage of an adaptation which had long been carried on by irrational and even unconscious processes.[77]

Once reason had supervened upon life, it had a contribution to make to the human struggle for survival. It could perform such useful feats as "distinguish events pertinent to the chosen interests," "compare impulse with satisfaction," and contribute to the improvement of conduct by presiding "over the formation of better habits, habits expressing more instincts at once and responding to more opportunities."[78]

The account of Santayana's naturalism must stop here. Enough has been said to show the basic elements of that naturalism. It was not without internal problems of incoherence and inconsistency, raised largely by Santayana's materialism and epiphenomenalism. But despite those problems it constitutes a

---

[75] Reason in Art (New York: 1922), pp. 16–17.
[76] Ibid., p. 33.
[77] Reason in Common Sense, p. 40.
[78] Ibid., pp. 62–63.

compelling philosophical perspective, or systematic point of view, of man's place in nature, and one that had immense influence on subsequent philosophic reflection in America even though there have been few, if any, specific teachings of Santayana's naturalism that have been taken up by that subsequent thought.

The intrinsic importance of Santayana's naturalistic philosophy of the life of reason—that is to say, the intellectual gain it has to offer, does not lie in a set of doctrines that can be detached from his system of thought, consigned to textbooks or to papers in books and journals, and taught one by one, with appropriate objections and replies. Nor does its informativeness lie in new arguments invented or new puzzles unearthed and solved. It lies instead in the conceptual perspective—the framework of concepts and ideals it interprets in its survey of the great categories of human achievements. The value of this criticism is to be found in the integrity of the whole moral and metaphysical perspective communicated. The intellectual gain afforded will include an increase in one's powers of appreciating the roles, limitations, and possibilities of the ideals studied for a well-lived human life. It is, perhaps, the sort of intellectual gain that has the fairest claim to that carelessly used honorific, "wisdom," and most certainly is part of what the ancient Greeks had in mind by *sophia*. Of all philosophers, Santayana is one who can be said (with attention to the etymology of the word) to be among the most "philosophical."

ELEVEN

The Development of William James's Epistemological Realism

PETER H. HARE
AND
CHANDANA CHAKRABARTI

IN A CHAPTER of *The Thought and Character of William James* entitled "From Idealism to Phenomenalism," Ralph Barton Perry says that, "concerning empirical or Berkeleyan idealism, James was long of a divided mind, and it was only towards the end of his career that he could pronounce unequivocally in favor of realism."[1] Perhaps influenced by Perry, Max Fisch, in his general introduction to the widely used *Classic American Philosophers*, remarks that James "was originally an idealist after the fashion of George Berkeley and of John Stuart Mill; then a phenomenalist in Renouvier's sense according to which subject and object are complementary aspects of every 'phenomenon'; and only late in life a 'radical empiricist.' "[2] This sort of characterization of the development of James's epistemology seems to us seriously misleading, if not altogether false. Perry and Fisch fail to appreciate that, often, the change

---

[1] Ralph Barton Perry, *The Thought and Character of William James* (2 vols., Boston: Little, Brown and Co., 1935), 1: 573.

[2] Max H. Fisch, ed., *Classic American Philosophers* (New York: Appleton-Century-Crofts, 1951), p. 21.

was more in James's *attitude* toward his own realistic view of perception than a change in the view of perception itself.

We shall defend the contention that epistemological realism was implicit in James's thought from the beginning of his philosophical career. In our defense of this continuity thesis we hope to provide answers to such questions as: Why did James for many years not publish an explicit defense of epistemological realism? Why did James say in 1885—when he published "The Function of Cognition," which he later insisted was realistic epistemology and included in *The Meaning of Truth* (1909)—that it was only descriptive psychology without a solution of the problem of self-transcendence? Why in "The Function of Cognition" did James not use the neutrality idea even though he had long since developed it as a way of coping with the problems of realistic epistemology? Why in his publications between 1885 and 1892 was James unwilling to present his already elaborately developed use of the notion of neutral or pure experience in dealing with the problems of epistemological realism? Why, when he published "The Knowing of Things Together," in 1895, which contains all the essentials of what he later insisted was realistic epistemology, did James say, in response to questions about the nature of "things," that he could "only make the answer of the idealistic philosophy"?[3]

Before we can answer these questions and support our continuity thesis, we must sketch James's epistemological realism as it was explicitly presented in publications of 1904 and thereafter. One of us, in collaboration with Edward H. Madden, has elsewhere published a detailed account of James's mature realism in response to A. J. Ayer's charge that James was a phenomenalist.[4] Here we shall reiterate only those points needed to provide background for the defense of our continuity thesis.

[3] *The Writings of William James: A Comprehensive Edition*, ed. John J. McDermott (New York: The Modern Library, 1968), p. 154.

[4] Edward H. Madden and Chandana Chakrabarti, "James' 'Pure Experience' versus Ayer's 'Weak Phenomenalism,'" *Transactions of the Charles S. Peirce Society* 12 (1976): 3–17. A similar charge has been made still more recently by Bruce Kuklick in *The*

According to the doctrine Ayer calls "strong phenomenalism," the meaning of any proposition which asserts that a
material object exists can be analyzed *without remainder* into
statements about sense experience. "Weak phenomenalism" is
the view that material objects are hypothetical and theoretical
constructions for interpreting our sense experience but are not
constructions out of sense experience. James, however, was neither sort of phenomenalist. Repeatedly he referred to himself as
a "natural realist," an epistemological realist, and a defender of
common-sense ontology. In 1907, for example, he moaned:
"with epistemological realism at the very permanent *heart and
centre* of *all* my thinking, it gives me a queer 'turn' to hear you
[C. A. Strong] keep insisting that I shall and must be treated as
an idealist [i.e., phenomenalist]."[5] Earlier in 1907 he had written Strong: "Schiller, Dewey, and I are all (I, at *any* rate!) epistemological realists—the reality known exists independently of
the knower's ideas, and *as* conceived, if the conception be a true
one. I can see that some bad parturient phrases of my radical
empiricism might lead to an opposite interpretation, but if so
they must be expunged."[6] Treating "natural realism" as synonymous with "epistemological realism," James, in his later writing, insisted that he was a natural realist in the sense that he
took the view that objects exist independently of the perceiver
and can be known as they are. Objective reference is present,
not in any "messenger" sense as in representative realism, but in
the sense that nonatomistic particulars of direct awareness are of
everyday physical objects. He rejected the dualistic view of

Rise of American Philosophy: Cambridge, Massachusetts, 1860–1930 (New Haven: Yale
University Press, 1977). For comment see the review of Kuklick's book by Edward
H. Madden and Peter H. Hare, *Transactions of the Charles S. Peirce Society* 14 (1978):
58–60. For those unfamiliar with the history of epistemology it may be useful to
point out roughly the difference between "phenomenology" and "phenomenalism."
Phenomenology is a method of descriptive analysis of subjective processes without
any claim as to what does or does not exist, whereas phenomenalism does say what
claims of existence amount to.
[5] Perry, *Thought and Character*, 2: 549.
[6] *Ibid.*, p. 536.

knowledge that posits subject and object as discontinuous entities, where knowing involves conquering the discontinuity.
Knowledge does not involve "a chasm and a mortal leap." [7] In
so far as "common-sense theories" of knowledge suppose there
to be a gap between knower and known, a gap our mind is able
to clear "by a self-transcending leap," common sense is mistaken. [8] He defended common sense in its insistence that some
of our experiences are genuinely cognitive of independently existing objects but rejects the common-sense view that this cognition is accomplished by a self-transcending leap. [9] In other
words, he supports common sense's identification of the cases of
genuine cognition but rejects common sense's assumptions
about *how* these cognitions are possible.

He describes his natural realism as an "ambulatory" theory of
knowledge, as opposed to the "saltatory." [10] "Cognition, whenever we take it concretely, means determinate 'ambulation,'
through intermediaries, from a *terminus a quo* to, or towards, a
terminus ad quem. As the intermediaries . . . fall wholly within
experience . . . we need use, in describing them, no other
categories than those which we employ in describing other natural processes." [11] This "ambulation" he thought of as a kind of
mediation between knower and known but mediation of a different kind from that found in *representational* realism where
sense data are said to mediate by representing the known to the
knower. Representation implies a discontinuity that James was
at pains to deny.

Such an epistemological realism was, James recognized, compatible with *metaphysical* idealism. "One of pragmatism's
merits," he said, "is that it is so purely epistemological. It must
assume realities, but it prejudges nothing as to their constitution, and the most diverse metaphysics can use it as their foun-

[7] William James, *The Meaning of Truth: A Sequel to Pragmatism* (Cambridge: Harvard University Press, 1975), p. 68.
[8] *Ibid.*, p. 61.
[9] *Ibid.*, p. 14.
[10] *Ibid.*, p. 79.
[11] *Ibid.*, p. 81.

dation." [12] Consequently, the question of whether James was a panpsychical idealist in metaphysics is not relevant to an understanding of his epistemology. Any metaphysical inclination James had toward idealism in no way undermined his commitment to epistemological realism. Similarly, his commitment to metaphysical pluralism was in no way incompatible with his *epistemological* monism. His denial of any dualism of subject and object in the process of cognition left him free to affirm pluralism otherwise. It must be stressed that we are attributing to James only *epistemological* realism and monism.

II

In the early 1870s, James wrote—but did not publish—a criticism of Chauncey Wright entitled "Against Nihilism," which contains the germ out of which developed his distinctive brand of epistemological realism in the form of an attack on Wright's atomistic phenomenalism.

> Thus the truth of a perception or conception depends on its objectivity—this is equivalent to "it is meant that we should *so* perceive or conceive, not otherwise." . . . They [objective thoughts] stand in a peculiar relation to our general capacity for feeling, a relation difficult analytically to express, but which as familiarly felt is clearest and simplest of our elementary representations—the relation of reality, which implies not only that we feel so and so, but that we *should* feel so, that we are meant to feel so, that there *is* something outside of the feeling itself as an instant conscious existence. [13]

As Perry says, James thought Wright's positivism (i.e. nihilism or phenomenalism) was "repugnant to common sense and contrary to metaphysics; and in pointing this out he made it quite evident that his sympathies were with 'common sense and metaphysics.' " [14]

Though James early felt in his bones the truth of epis-

[12] *Ibid.*, p. 115.
[13] Perry, *Thought and Character*, 1: 527.
[14] *Ibid.*, 1: 524.

temological realism, he continued his struggle with idealism and phenomenalism in unpublished notes. In a note on idealism written in 1884, he reviewed the arguments pro and con and found himself unable to reach a conclusion.[15] In another unpublished note apparently written in the same year he used Charles Renouvier's idea that subject and object are complementary aspects of "the phenomenon" as a way of salvaging epistemological realism by eliminating the gulf between subject and object.

> The synthetic construction of objectivity and subjectivity may mean that even in the most rudimentary sensation there is a dim duality, a duplex aspect: what one may call an "immanent" side (which constitutes the fact that it *is* actually a sensation), and a transcendent side (which is the reference to something as known through the sensation). . . . I myself incline more and more to some such view as this.[16]

The neutrality idea he later used in his mature epistemology as another way of eliminating the epistemological gulf appears in an unpublished note, apparently also written in the early 1880s: "I should say the *rudiment* of thought was always of an object, in the logical sense; but in the material sense, something in which the discrimination of sub- and ob- ject had not yet been affected—a neutral experience, a phenomenon."[17]

Perry's two volumes again and again indicate that there were many philosophers James studied and corresponded with throughout his career who used either a neutrality idea or a double aspect idea like Renouvier's. His familiarity and sympathy with these two ways of coping with the subject-object relation is a thread running through his entire career. Very early he saw ways one could avoid the dualistic view of knowledge where knowing involves conquering the discontinuity between subject and object.

[15]*Ibid.*, 1: 578.
[16]*Ibid.*, 1: 580–81.
[17]*Ibid.*, 1: 582*n.*

If James had always been committed to natural realism and early saw how to avoid a dualistic view of objective reference, why did he delay publicly declaring himself an epistemological realist for so long?

One reason he did not declare himself earlier was that he associated natural realism with the Scottish realists. As his notes amply show, James was interested in, and very familiar with, Scottish philosophers, but by the 1870s they had been thoroughly discredited. Though in our own day such leading philosophers as Roderick Chisholm and Keith Lehrer have come to have enormous respect for the Scottish school, the best American minds in James's time had come to think of the Scottish school as pedantic traditionalism and edifying eclecticism.[18] Many of the members of that school in the United States (e.g. his seniors Andrew Preston Peabody and Francis Bowen in the Harvard Philosophy Department) seemed a stuffy, pedestrian and uninspiring lot. The consensus of Anglo-American philosophy in the late nineteenth century was that philosophical progress lay in other directions.

Another reason for delay was that in the period 1870–1900 the most logically acute epistemology was being done by antirealists of one kind or another. Such figures as J. S. Mill and Chauncey Wright were rigorously arguing antirealism from an empiricist point of view (i.e. phenomenalism) and such figures as F. H. Bradley and Josiah Royce were rigorously arguing antirealism from a neo-Hegelian point of view (i.e. absolute idealism)—not to speak of the variety of neo-Kantians on the continent. Herbert Spencer, who was at the height of his fame in the 1870s, defended a "hypothetical" realism, but James regarded him as a hopelessly sloppy thinker. Especially before 1900, James was very concerned to be scientifically rigorous in his

[18]*Ibid.*, 1: 464. James shared with the Scottish philosophers their nonskeptical attitude and their view that philosophy should account for common-sense beliefs instead of explaining them away. However, he felt that the Scottish philosophers did not make systematic and rigorous use of common sense.

thought. In his early work he thought of himself primarily as a scientist and felt insecure in his role as a philosopher. He thought that the truth was on the side of natural realism but found too many arguments by the most brilliant, most "scientific" minds on the other side.

Another reason, we suggest, why James did not earlier proclaim himself a natural realist was that, from the beginning, he favored an empiricist but *experimental* epistemology,[19] in which the knowing mind *initiates* ideas which it submits to existence. From his earliest work he was voluntaristic in his theory of knowledge and belief, and traditional natural realism conceived of knowing as a *passive* process. Knowing as active was associated with idealism (i.e. the doctrine that the existence of the object known is not independent of the knower), and it took James a long time to become confident that he could consistently be both realistic and experimentalistic or voluntaristic in his epistemology. It was no easy matter to shake off the conventional view that a realistic epistemology *must* conceive knowing as entirely passive. In his early work, such as "The Function of Cognition," when he succeeded in making realism compatible with experimentalism, he naturally worried about whether this was *really* epistemological realism, and hesitated to claim he had realistically solved the problem of objective reference. Only with the development of his pragmatism was he able to look back on "The Function of Cognition" and see that the sole important difference between the 1885 view and the later one was that there was less emphasis on resemblance and more on functional adaptation in the latter. Having developed a pragmatic epistemology, he saw that pragmatism required willy-nilly a realistic epistemology. Thus, there was no holding back. James's earlier motivation was revealed in a remark made to Warner Fite in 1906: "The pragmatist in my eyes *must be a natural realist.*"[20] Pragmatism required a way of getting prosperously from

[19]*Ibid.*, 1: 454.
[20]*Ibid.*, 2: 392.

one part of our experience to another through intermediaries; such ambulation was precisely what he had earlier described in "The Function of Cognition" and "The Knowing of Things Together" as the way to avoid dualism between subject and object. It became obvious to James that pragmatism's prosperous, continuous movement within concrete experience was no more than another way of stating a realistic account of cognition. He had already gone to the barricades to defend pragmatism, so he could hardly avoid going to the barricades in defense of the realistic theory of perception he thought an integral part of pragmatism.

One must also keep in mind that, after 1900, the epistemological climate changed drastically. For many reasons, the ablest philosophers lost sympathy with idealism. The "young Turks" were especially fed up with it. Rigorous minds like those of D. S. Miller, C. A. Strong and R. B. Perry were eager for some alternative. And, in England, G. E. Moore published his landmark, "The Refutation of Idealism," in 1903. Idealism had run its course, and the philosophical community was receptive to other approaches. We believe that if idealism had run its course fifteen years earlier when James published "The Function of Cognition" his readers would have seen it, as they did later, as a realistic alternative. James, in the context of such receptivity, would have proclaimed himself a realist then and there. Unfortunately, the time was not ripe, and James kept his realistic epistemology largely to himself.

In 1903, James wrote to Schiller: "The times are fairly crying aloud for it [a philosophy of pure experience]. I have been extraordinarily pleased at the easy way in which my students this year assimilated the attitude, and reproduced the living pulse of it in their examination and other written work."[21] But earlier, instead of getting that sort of encouragement for his realistic epistemology, he was discouraged by people like Royce, with

[21]*Ibid.*, 2: 376.

whose logical power he was still vastly impressed. In 1895, he wrote Bradley: "Years ago in a paper on Mind (the Function of Cognition) I described it [intending, pointing] as now in this paper ["The Knowing of Things Together"]—relation through a context. Then Royce beat me out of it; but further pondering has bro't me back to wallow in the same mire."[22]

Perry says of "The Knowing of Things Together" that "he specifically anticipated some of the central ideas of his radical empiricism. He still professed idealism of the Berkeleyan type, but it was clear that his thought was already disloyal to that creed."[23] Perry's interpretation is unfortunate. James never really did more than profess idealism in an empty sort of way; he never *believed* it as a "creed"; idealism was merely an interpretation he reluctantly gave to his realistic views. It is true that in "The Knowing of Things Together" James said:

> What, then, do we mean by "things"? To this question I can only make the answer of the idealist philosophy. . . . Whenever we speak of a thing that is out of our mind, we either mean nothing; or we mean a thing that was or will be in our mind on other occasions; or, finally, we mean a thing in the mind of some other possible receiver of experiences like ours.[24]

First it should be noted that James said he could "only" give an idealistic answer—a clear indication of reluctance. More important, after he had publicly declared himself an epistemological realist, he reprinted the crucial part of "The Knowing of Things Together" as "The Tigers in India" in *The Meaning of Truth*. He simply deleted the part of the article which contained the reluctant acceptance of idealism quoted above. Obviously, after 1904, he could see nothing idealistic in the major part of his earlier article just as he could see nothing idealistic in "The

---

[22] J. C. Kenna, ed., "The Unpublished Letters from William James, 1842–1910, to Francis Herbert Bradley, 1846–1924," *Mind* 75 (1966): 313.

[23] Perry, *Thought and Character*, 2: 364.

[24] *The Writings of William James*, p. 154.

Function of Cognition," which he also reprinted in *The Meaning of Truth*.

It is also misleading for Perry to say that James "was a recent convert from idealism and lapsed readily into its habits of speech."[25] We concede only that James wavered on the matter of whether he was *entitled by the arguments* to consider his doctrines realistic. He always *believed* in natural realism, but in his earlier work often doubted that he could convincingly marshal arguments in support of that position. He was constantly being thrown into doubts about the force of the realistic arguments by volleys of criticism from antirealists like Royce.

Also important to keep in mind is that around 1900 James resolved to devote himself to working out a comprehensive system of philosophy. It was obvious to him that laying his realistic cards on the table would be essential in any such system. In the *Principles* (1890), he had said that he had a monistic philosophy in reserve. Commentators usually say that he did not present his metaphysics there because he wanted to explicate his psychology first, did not want to confuse the psychology he was working on, and because he did not feel he had satisfactorily worked out his system of epistemological monism. These comments are accurate as far as they go, but these commentators (e.g. R. B. Perry) do not adequately appreciate the other factors involved. It will not do to say simply that he was primarily a psychologist before 1900. After all, he had published "The Function of Cognition" in 1885 and had taught philosophy, including epistemology and metaphysics, for many years.

It is true that the relative emphasis on philosophical issues increased as time went on; however, it should not be overlooked that by 1900 his philosophical interest took the form of a demand for a *systematic* philosophy in which there would obviously be no way to keep his doctrine of pure experience "in reserve." His system demanded a dredging up of all the arguments he

[25] Perry, *Thought and Character*, 2: 388.

had used in the 1890s in defense of a realistic epistemology in terms of pure experience. It is inaccurate to say that, in 1900, when his interests became almost exclusively philosophical, he worked out for the first time the details of his realistic epistemology. If one examines the 1904 articles published in *Essays in Radical Empiricism,* there is not much that he had not worked out long before. It was just that his new demand for system (along with the other reasons already mentioned) required him now to present publicly those old ideas in order to flesh out a system. It should also be noted that in those 1904 articles he does not present much detailed, technical argument of the sort one finds in his earlier notes. To say that his new philosophical interests led him, in the 1904 articles, to work out epistemological details for the first time is nonsense. Indeed, he left out most of the technical details!

Another factor to be noted in connection with his new interest in a systematic philosophy is that, before 1900, he feared that any discussion he might offer of the philosophy of pure experience would seem to be wildly unscientific psychology. However, when he became committed to the outline of a systematic philosophy, he became much less shy about including some speculative theory of mind. What mattered most was that this theory was an integral part of a comprehensive system. Also, before he became committed to the development of a system, he worried whether his philosophy of pure experience committed him to panpsychism—a view Anglo-American philosophers (including James) tended to associate with bizarre and weak metaphysics. He always felt a little guilty about his attraction toward panpsychism; but once he was committed to systematic philosophy, the risk of a bizarre metaphysics of panpsychism was a price worth paying in order to achieve a comprehensive philosophy.

Attention should also be given to the important role that James's intellectual conscience played in delaying his public declaration of epistemological realism. In a real sense, the history of James's epistemological realism is a monument to his intellectual honesty and capacity for self-criticism. Although reading "The Will to Believe" has convinced many that James was inclined to credulity, that view seriously misrepresents him in many ways. Qualms of intellectual conscience appear throughout his writings, especially his writings on epistemological issues. As Perry says in connection with "The Will to Believe," James "was not credulous, but *suffered from incredulity.*"[26] When, in the 1870s, James discussed the ideas of G. H. Lewes, Lewes was, as Perry remarks, "applauded as one who followed empiricism without falling into skepticism or nihilism. His method of avoiding those alternatives was also similar to that of James: both men affirmed identities and continuities where other empiricists found only manifoldness and irrelevance. But James felt that Lewes won his victory too cheaply."[27]

In the 1870s and 80s, James read deeply and talked with a number of philosophers who used either a double aspect device or neutrality idea to present a realistic empiricism. However, his intellectual conscience made him take the view that he could not legitimately declare a victory and pronounce himself until he was sure that an invincible array of genuinely *empiricist* arguments were logically lined up on the side of realism. James told Hodgson in 1885 that he thought Hodgson's double aspect idea was just a *postulate* and did not have an adequate general empiricist epistemology and metaphysics to back it up. It would be a serious mistake to confuse this exercise of intellectual conscience with his ever actually adopting an idealist creed. He was not yet confident that he could rebut with solid empiricist argument the idealistic arguments that came at him thick and fast. It was not until he wrote the Epilogue to *Psychology: A Briefer Course,* published in 1892, that his conscience allowed him to use the neutrality idea in print at all,[28] and it was not until the 1904 articles that he publicly used the doctrine of

---

[26] *Ibid.,* 2: 211.
[27] *Ibid.,* 1: 592.
[28] William James, *Psychology: Briefer Course* (London: Collier-Macmillan Ltd., 1962), p. 461.

pure experience in the service of realism. By that time he had found the needed empirical arguments in his comprehensive functional and relational theory of consciousness.

His reactions to Royce offer another illustration of how he came to delay declaring himself an epistemological realist. For moral reasons, as well as epistemological ones, he was never inclined to accept Royce's speculative hypothesis; for some years, however, he felt he had to find out precisely and in detail what was wrong with Royce's idealistic arguments before he could pronounce himself a realist. Though it took him a long while to break the force of Royce's argument, his sympathies remained with realism. And even after he had satisfied himself that he could point to the faults in Royce's arguments, he still did not publicly announce his realism for the various other reasons we have mentioned.

Related to his later commitment to systematic philosophy is another consideration: he was concerned, even before he made such a commitment, about the relations between a realistic solution of the problem of perception and all the other major problems of philosophy. He was acutely aware of how interconnected all the major philosophical problems are, and since he had not in the 1880s and 90s been able yet to work out his views on the other problems in epistemology and metaphysics, that was yet another reason to hesitate to affirm realism publicly. He saw that a philosopher like Royce could fit his theory of perception within a comprehensive metaphysics. Although he found Royce's system repugnant in important respects, he believed that he could not legitimately declare himself a realist until he had a comparable comprehensive system to propose as an alternative. He wanted somehow to achieve unity and comprehensiveness in his philosophy without the paralysis of morality found in Royce's system. Although in the 1880s, and certainly in the 1890s, he had all the ideas about continuity and neutrality as a way of dealing with the subject-object relation within realism, he still lacked a general theory of consciousness to back it up. He was not able to start work on such a theory of consciousness to act as underpinning for his radical empiricism until about 1895–96. James needed to satisfy himself that he had systematically treated all the interrelated metaphysical issues before his realism could be more than the cheap victory he had criticized in other realists.

Finally, it should be mentioned that James worried that his version of epistemological realism might not be commonsensical after all. Common sense seemed to him to give *"stable* elements," while his pure experience hypothesis seemed to be "afflicted by a restlessness which is painful to the mind." [29] Common sense also seemed to assume a discontinuity between subject and object that he had been at pains to deny in his doctrine of pure experience. It took time for James to reconcile himself to the sacrifice of parts of common sense in the interest of vindicating the crucial commonsensical assumption that knowledge of independent objects is possible.

We conclude that there was more continuity in the development of James's epistemology than Perry and others allow, and that the causes of the genuine discontinuities were more complex than usually supposed. The discontinuities were not a consequence of James's adopting different epistemological "isms" successively. Rather, the discontinuities were primarily in his attitude toward what was a remarkably continuous commitment to realistic epistemology.

[29] Perry, *Thought and Character,* 2: 370.

FOUR

The Teacher As Moral Agent

Introduction

Joseph Blau's essential career is in scholarship and criticism. Yet, inevitably for him, scholarship has never been merely scholarly and research never morally neutral. In that he reflects the impress of Columbia's philosophic naturalism and its theory of human knowledge: the point of inquiry has always been the free mind finding itself in a free society and a free society building itself in free minds. The failure of inquiry is to close down the question when an answer, always and only temporary, has been found. Knowledge itself, then, is a type of social ethics. This Deweyan inspiration breathes life into the work of Joseph Blau.

The essays in this final section illustrate his social and ethical concerns. Each is drawn from a different tradition: critical Christian scholarship, classic American pragmatism, a new and still forming intersection of Platonism and humanistic psychology. And each represents a different intellectual generation, a different deposit of learning. Finally, each represents a different end in view and a different perception of the realities which generate such ends and are served by them. And yet, for all these differences—indeed because of them—we become aware of a common and significant universe of discourse. All are "post-enlightenment," all reflect a democratic inspiration, and all are committed to liberalism. It is the support and advance of such a universe of discourse, as against other modern options which never intrigued Blau—less rational, more enamored of authority, more distrustful of persons—that was and is the "mission" which enformed Blau's work.

Blau did not develop a complete, systematic social philosophy. However, we may readily perceive the presence of an abiding social ethic as the organizing principle of his scholarship, teaching, and criticism. That, finally, is what the essays in this section exemplify.

H.B.R.

TWELVE

The New Censors of Science

PAUL KURTZ

I

THE FREEDOM of scientific research, a basic principle essential for scientific inquiry, is undergoing considerable criticism in contemporary society. Indeed, so sustained has the assault become in some areas that we may be reaching a situation of clear and present danger in which the very viability of the scientific enterprise is thrown into question. Accordingly, it is important that the ethical justification of scientific research be clarified, particularly since the new censors usually claim the right to restrict scientific research on ethical grounds.

Many of us grew up believing that science and the quest for truth were positive goods. We assumed, moreover, that the growth of scientific knowledge was progressive and that in time we would be able to extend significantly the boundaries of our understanding of nature and life. Indeed, this attitude has characterized the outlook of wide sections of the educated classes for the past three centuries. The scientific revolution of the sixteenth and seventeenth centuries, first developed in physics and astronomy, was later applied to chemistry and biology, and in the nineteenth and twentieth centuries to the social and behavioral sciences. Many of us were educated in a climate that was highly favorable to the scientific approach, which held the belief that scientific research ought to be pursued unencumbered by political, religious, economic, or social pressures. This point of view involved the conviction that reason and science ought to be applied to human affairs and that, with the growth of universal learning and education, we would be able to solve the problems besetting humankind and contribute to the common good.

The development of the scientific outlook was not made without opposition from many quarters. There was the notorious conflict between science and the established ecclesiastical forces at the beginning of the modern era and when Bruno and Galileo were made martyrs to the cause of free inquiry. Physics and astronomy were eventually vindicated by their demonstrated success in explaining a wide range of previously inexplicable phenomena. Even in the twentieth century, biologists who proposed theories of evolution to account for the origin of species had to contend with opposing religious doctrines of creation; and the rise of behavioristic psychology precipitated an outcry in some quarters that it had destroyed the soul. Similar objections were voiced against Freudian theories of psychoanalysis. By and large, however, these religious objections eventually dissipated—or at least we thought so—and most educated people were willing to accept the findings of the sciences.

Demands for the censorship of science historically have come from other quarters as well: political and economic repression is familiar. Vested interests have often found scientific discoveries dangerous; totalitarian regimes, in particular, have sought to impose an ideological straitjacket on creative scientific inquiry and have proscribed scientific theories if they were contrary to the prevailing status quo. Nazi racial doctrines made non-Aryan science *verboten,* and Lysenkoian environmentalism inveighed against genetics. One cannot perform scientific research if there is fear of reprisal. The principle is, or at least it was until recently, well understood in democracies. Even dictatorships have recognized that if their scientists are to be effective they must be allowed some degree of autonomy.

II

It is disturbing therefore, to find that there are today new calls for the limitation of scientific research. Indeed, much to the surprise of scientists in many fields of inquiry, their investigations increasingly are being condemned, and all sorts of pressures are being brought to bear to police, stifle, even prohibit their research. The paradox is that the great hue and cry is not made on religious or political grounds—blasphemy or sedition—but rather on alleged ethical grounds. The indictment usually is that some areas ought *not* to be inquired into, are intrinsically evil to know about, or that the research will have harmful consequences to individuals or to society. The new censors of science today are, above all, moralists. One might say that the censor has always been a closet moralist in disguise; today he is out in the open and his sense of moral righteousness has become intensified.

We may ask if scientific research is ethically justifiable and if so under what conditions. Is the quest for truth less important than the attainment of justice, virtue, or goodness?

It is clear that scientific research is no longer simply the work of the isolated individual in a secluded study or laboratory, but has wide social implications. Accordingly, we are told that what the scientist does must be carefully regulated by society. If the medieval church opposed research on human cadavers, modern moralists have their own "Thou Shalt Nots." Usually, they insist that legal restrictions be enacted to enforce their moral concern. Since scientists often need governmental or foundation support, regulation at the source becomes especially threatening to the kinds of research that they wish to pursue. There is an ever-increasing catalogue of projects that various groups seek to proscribe.

Many moralists a generation ago condemned physicists for their work on nuclear energy. The development of nuclear weapons, and their attendant capacity for the destruction of life on this planet, was attributed by some to a lack of social conscience.

More recently, biologists and geneticists have been seriously criticized for engaging in genetic engineering. This is considered to be dangerous. Geneticists are opening up a Pandora's Box, we are told, by cloning, by interfering with the natural processes of evolution, or by participating in DNA recombinant research—which, we are warned, could unleash highly resistant strains of E Coli bacteria and destroy humankind. In some cases this has reached the proportions of moral hysteria. The public outcry is growing: city councils, state legislatures, the Congress, even some concerned scientists are outdoing themselves in seeking to regulate this research.[1]

Geneticists have also been attacked by some groups for focusing on the hereditary factors in behavior and minimizing environmental conditions. This is said to be "conservative" or "reactionary," for it undermines efforts at social reform. Similar charges have been leveled against sociobiologists.

Astronomers have been cautioned about bringing back virulent strains of life from other planets. Some have said that efforts to communicate with extraterrestrial intelligences by means of radio astronomy could also be of detriment to the human species. Why inform possible hostile forces in the universe about our presence?

Medical researchers have also been censured for various forms of human experimentation and drug therapy. Many disciples of the "right to life" have sought to prohibit any form of fetal research, and, in fact, the federal government banned fetal research for several months pending the recommendations of a Commission set up to investigate its "morality."

Psychiatrists have come in for heavy indictment for engaging in "brainwashing," performing lobotomies, implanting electrodes, or for seeking to control and thus "dehumanize" person-

[1] The Carter Administration, indeed, recently proposed legislation which would give the Secretary of HEW the power to license and regulate research projects doing the controversial genetic studies. Violators of the licensing or other provisions of the law could be assessed penalties of up to $5,000 and as much as a year imprisonment. (*Chronicle of Higher Education*, April 11, 1977, p. 3.)

ality. Psychologists have also received their share of criticism. Some critics have maintained, for example, that it is wrong to investigate the subject of IQ and race, or to publish findings that may be injurious to certain racial or ethnic groups. Jensen and Eysenck have been called racists for their work in this area. Extreme critics of the behaviorists have characterized them as "totalitarian oppressors," objecting to their use of behavior modification, or to their "depersonalized" approach to human subjects. New regulations governing the study of human subjects have been issued which are restrictive and require the establishment of special ethical review boards.[2] Research involving prisoners has been made very difficult, if not virtually impossible; the same restriction has been applied to children, who cannot grant informed consent, and to retarded and handicapped persons.

Some have objected strenuously to research with animals. There is a development movement for the protection of animal rights. Frederick Wiseman recently produced a film, widely shown on educational television, portraying scientists studying the sexual behavior of primates as questionable; and Peter Singer, the philosopher, in a much discussed book on *Animal Liberation,* has criticized the use of animals for scientific research. The antivivisectionists believe that animal rights should transcend the interests of the scientist in research.

I have only touched on some of the recent efforts to limit

[2] Congress has enacted legislation to regulate research on human subjects in order to protect their rights. And the National Research Act and the Public Health Service Act charges HEW with responsibility for such regulations:

"The Secretary shall by regulation require that each entity which applies for a grant or contract under this Act for any project or program which involves the conduct of biomedical or behavioral research involving human subjects submit in or with its application for such grants or contract assurances satisfactory to the Secretary that it has established (in accordance with regulations which the Secretary shall prescribe) a board (to be known as "Institutional Review Board") to review biomedical and behavioral research involving human subjects conducted at or sponsored by such entity in order to protect the rights of human subjects of such research." *Federal Register,* 40, no. 50, part II, Protection of Human Subjects, Technical Amendments (March 13, 1975), p. 11854.

research. There are many other illustrations that could be offered. The merits of each of these cases need to be discussed in detail and in its own terms, something that I cannot attempt to do here. What I wish to identify, however, is an emerging trend. We may, indeed, have passed a critical turning point in society's appraisal of the ethical case for scientific research.

III

Clearly, at present, the public has a very deep mistrust of certain aspects of science. This distrust is shared by the communications media, some intellectuals, and some scientists. It has assumed many dimensions.

There is a profound apprehension that science and technology are responsible for many of the serious problems of the contemporary world. It is believed that, since the results of scientific research are often harmful rather than beneficial, society needs to regulate what scientists do. This antiscience attitude must, of course, be put in proper perspective; there is also a deep appreciation for the positive uses of science and technology by modern society, and the whole structure of industry rests upon scientific research. The critique of scientific research on moral grounds must be related to two other disturbing trends.

There appears to be a growing breakdown of the conviction that there are objective scientific criteria for judging the truth. This argument assumes many forms but, taken in its extreme, it claims that knowledge, in the last analysis, is "subjective." This view is prevalent in the current generation of college students, who often call upon us to justify the scientific method itself. Many people today fail to understand even the most elementary canons of inquiry—for example, they believe that merely to formulate a speculative hypothesis (e.g., von Daniken's "chariots of gods," or Uri Geller's psychokinesis) is sufficient to make it true without the need either for additional supporting evidence, or for satisfying the criteria of logical consistency. Clearly, this attitude is symptomatic of a broader mood in society, a mood that usually has two contradictory aspects. In its extreme forms it is held that we ought to be tolerant of different points of view and that since one view is as good as the next, no one is entitled to criticize a contrary view. Or, contrariwise, that one's system of beliefs or values are absolutely true and immune to criticism (a view generally held by the various cults of unreason). The point is, we have failed here to define the tentative and hypothetical, yet objective, character of scientific inquiry.

Unfortunately, this rejection of objectivity has had its counterpart among some of the most sophisticated philosophers of science, who (following Kuhn, for example) argue that the logical positivistic view of science is mistaken, that there are no clearly definable criteria of the logic of scientific validation, but that the methods by which we judge theories and the models themselves are a function of social and historical forces. These are very serious criticisms. Certainly we cannot deny the sociohistorical context of scientific research. Yet scientific inquiry, if nothing else, rests upon a set of epistemological assumptions. If one abandons these, then one really throws the scientific program into serious jeopardy, for there may then seem to be little reason to assume that science is any truer than religion, art, poetry, or feeling. If the scientific program is to succeed, we must recognize that there are at least *some* objective standards of verification and validation, however much we may quibble about certain aspects of these criteria.

Science is also criticized today by those who would reject its naturalistic or materialistic "world view." We are told by many critics that scientists are biased because they automatically exclude data that do not fit their preconceived categories. These critics maintain, for example, that scientists neglect to consider a whole range of paranormal phenomena that transcend the usual boundaries of evidence and logic. Telekinesis, remote viewing, clairvoyance, astral projection, precognition, preception, and other kinds of experience are said to give us glimpses of the "new vision of reality." There are those who claim to be doing "hard research" in these areas—though I am extremely skeptical about their rigor and find that their activities more often than not border on pseudo-science. In any case, many of the concepts of behavioristic science have been discarded. I might add that the recent developments in physics and astronomy and the frequent inability of physicists and astronomers to interpret their theories on the frontiers of knowledge—black holes, antimatter, quarks, and charms—invites speculation about the possible "psychical" implications of their findings. Similarly, the probability that there are other forms of intelligent life in the universe invites to science-fictional extravagance. My response to all of this is, of course, that science is not unalterably committed to any world view per se—whether materialist, mechanist, or naturalist. Science is, however, committed to the use of the hypothetical-deductive method as a way of verifying its hypotheses, and it should be open to any and all new theories that are proposed.

Whatever the reasons, this is the age in which there has been a proliferation of unsubstantiated claims: faith healing, exorcism, astrology, auras, fortune telling, transcendental meditation, and the resurgence of fundamentalism are all symptomatic of a spiritualist-psychic world view that has descended upon us. One might ask: are we "opening up to a new dimension of reality," as the proponents of the paranormal claim; or are these signs that the scientific revolution which began in the sixteenth and seventeenth centuries is reaching an end and that we shall be overwhelmed by new forms of irrationalism? I don't mean to be overpessimistic. One cannot predict historical trends. In a sense the future is not fixed, but depends upon what we will do. Perhaps what we have been witnessing is simply a return to the normal state of human credulity in which gullibility and the will to illusion prevail; every age needs to develop critical intelligence as therapy against nonsense, and perhaps we have been failing in that endeavor.

Nevertheless, one should not simply minimize or dismiss the significance of what has been happening in the past decade. Science is basically an affair of a relatively small percentage of the total population. Even those who claim to be scientists may be narrow specialists in their fields, failing to understand the nature of scientific intelligence or the scientific outlook and not extending it to other domains.

Whatever the causes, a strong antiscience mood seems to have developed. Today, the scientist is considered in some circles to be a kind of moral monster who, if left to his own devices, is likely radically to alter human beings or to destroy the world. Doomsday prophecies abound. Much of the indictment is against technology; scientific research has given us powerful tools for understanding and controlling nature, but the same research has had harmful fallouts (e.g., ecological pollution, environmental carcinogens, the dangers of biochemical and nuclear warfare). What is often taken for granted is that scientific technology has provided many boons to humankind: the green revolution, the marvellous therapies of medical science, the increase of learning, literacy and education, improved communication and travel, the electronic and computer revolution, and so on.

All of this brings me back to my original theme. The assault on science has not only involved skepticism about its methodology, its worldview (if there is such a thing), and the deleterious effects of an uncontrolled technology, but free scientific research itself.

IV

Should scientific research be limited on ethical grounds, as its critics maintain? That is, are there certain things that we should not inquire into or know because it would be evil to do so? Or, should we insist upon the principle of free research without infringement by external controls? Can an ethical case be made for scientific freedom? An unfortunate aspect of recent discussions is the impression that there is an opposition between ethics and scientific research; often it is assumed that scientists are *a*ethical and the burden of proof is thus placed upon *them* to show why they should be allowed to investigate in a field where the rights of others are at stake.

Another illustration of the prevalent tendency to cut off research is seen in the *Report and Recommendations: Research Involving Prisoners,* recently published by The National Commission for the Protection of Human Subjects of Biomedical and Behavioral Research.[3] The Report recognizes that "since the 1960's, the ethical propriety of participation by prisoners in research has increasingly been questioned in this country. . . . Eight states and the Federal Bureau of Prisons have formally moved to abandon research in prisons." Following this the Health Subcommittee of the Senate Committee on Labor and Public Welfare held hearings in late 1973. In 1975 the House Subcommittee on Courts, Civil Liberties, and the Administration of Justice held hearings on whether to prohibit medical research in federal prisons or in prisons of states receiving federal grants. After these hearings, the Director of the Federal Bureau of Prisons mandated that "continued use of prisoners in any medical experimentation should not be permitted" and he ordered that such participation be phased out.

With this as background, the Commission was called upon to make recommendations. It concluded: "In the course of its investigations and review of evidence presented to it, the Commission did not find in prisons the conditions requisite for a sufficiently high degree of voluntariness and openness, notwithstanding that prisoners currently participating in research consider, in nearly all instances, that they do so voluntarily and want the research to continue."[4]

The Commission therefore recommends that research be conducted, but only if certain restrictive standards are met. The

[3] Bethesda, Maryland, October, 1976.
[4] *Ibid.,* p. 12.

Report states: "Compliances with these requirements must be certified by the highest responsible federal official, assisted by a national ethical review body. The Commission has concluded that *the burden of proof that all the requirements are satisfied should be on those who wish to conduct the research.*"[5] (Italics mine.)

The Report then recommends that a number of requirements be satisfied: studies of the causes and effects of incarceration, studies of prisons, and studies improving the health or well-being of individual prisoners can be carried on provided they present minimal or no risk to the subjects. The Commission then recommends that any other type of research involving prisoners should *not* be conducted unless: (a) "the type of research fulfills an important social and scientific need, and the reasons for involving prisoners in the type of research are compelling;" (b) "the involvement of prisoners in the type of research satisfies conditions of equity;" (c) "a high degree of voluntariness . . . and openness . . ." and other provisions, such as "provisions for effective redress of grievances," are fulfilled. It is a further recommended that "the head of the responsible federal department or agency should determine . . . the competence of the investigator."[6] Moreover:

> All research involving prisoners should be reviewed by at least one human subject review committee or institutional review board *comprised of men and women of diverse racial and cultural backgrounds* and that includes among its members prisoners or prisoner advocates and such other persons as community representatives, clergy, behavioral scientists and medical personnel not associated with the conduct of the research or the penal institution.[7] (Italics mine.)

One may ask why there should be equal board representation on a quota basis and why community representatives and clergymen, who have no scientific qualifications, should serve? Unfortunately, what is often alleged to be an ethical issue becomes

[5]*Ibid.*, p. 13.
[6]*Ibid.*, pp. 16, 20.
[7]*Ibid.*, p. 20.

politicized and is taken up as part of an ideological battle. The concern for prisoner's rights—as important as it is—has become for some groups basically a political, not ethical, issue. Prisoners have become the folk heroes of society, oppressed because of class or race; critics ask, in effect, "how dare the establishment experiment with the poor victims of society?" Even if prisoners themselves voluntarily agree to participate in research (which is almost always the case) the paternalistic moralists, claiming to believe in the right of individual consent, will not permit it.

Clearly, prisoners' rights should not be violated nor should prisoners be harmed. The Report indicated two basic ethical principles to safeguard prisoners: (1) "the principle of justice," which required that prisoners and groups be treated fairly, and (2) "the principle of respect for persons," which requires that the autonomy of prisoners be promoted and protected. I disagree with neither of these; it is merely a question of emphasis.

Public interest lawyers have argued that prisoners cannot really give free and informed consent because of the constraints implicit in their incarceration; therefore, one should not be allowed to conduct medical, social, or psychological research on prisoners. But actually prisoners often stand greater risks in the prison yard from other inmates or guards than from research projects. It is absurd to allow a narrow application of the risk-benefits principle to prohibit research. Raymond B. Cattell argues that had we used this principle at the time of Columbus, we would not have approved funding for his voyage to America because of the dangerous risks suffered by certain Portuguese seamen.[8]

Those who argue for drastically restricting research offer moral arguments. The following statements, for example, appear in the Appendix to the Report, and are illustrative of the case against research: "Scientific progress is grand, but even it must bow before the altar of human rights; scientific progress is

[8] Raymond B. Cattell, A New Morality from Science: Beyondism (New York: Pergamon, 1972).

progress only if it legitimately respects the value and dignity of persons."[9]

"Experimentation with prisoners is not scientifically necessary for the good of society. . . . To continue experimentation with prisoners under the present circumstances would violate and erode our sense of what we are as a society; a community constituted by mutual regard for other's equal, intrinsic dignity."[10]

But may we not question, on a more fundamental level, the lower priority given to another basic ethical principle: that the right to free inquiry ought to prevail in society? What we have are competing principles and rights. Which ones ought to prevail?

Often the principle of informed consent, if pushed to an extreme, can become ridiculous in its interference with bona fide research, as Bernard Davis of Harvard Medical School points out:

> An example of silly interference has arisen in connection with some research on cell genetics in man that depends on cultivating human cells in test tubes. . . . A convenient source is foreskins from newborns, a byproduct of circumcision. This material has been used now for a number of years. An investigator at MIT recently had his regular supply of foreskins from the Boston Women's Hospital cut off . . . because the doctor was afraid that he would have to have written informed consent from both the father and the mother. He didn't know what some Massachusetts prosecutors might do.[11]

It is sometimes even necessary today to have written informed consent in order for scientific investigators to use waste products of a patient that are collected in the hospital.

But there are many less amusing incidents of repression. John

[9] Cornell West, "Philosophical Perspectives on the Participation of Prisoners in Experimental Research," in *Report and Recommendations,* pp. 2–14.

[10] Roy Branson, "Philosophical Perspectives on Experimentation with Prisoners," in *Report and Recommendations,* pp. 1–28.

[11] Bernard Davis, "The Scientific Versus the Adversary Approach in Bio-Medical Research," in *The Ethics of Teaching and Scientific Research,* eds. Sidney Hook, et al. (Buffalo, New York: Prometheus Books, 1977), p. 168.

L. Horn, professor of psychology at the University of Denver, relates how a research proposal that he submitted in 1974 to the Small Grants Section of the National Institute of Mental Health was rejected. The proposal was "to construct tests that would be more nearly culture-fair than existing tests and yet would measure important aspects of intelligence." Involved in the project was the analysis of data that had been gathered by another investigator some five years earlier concerning 624 middle-class urban white children and 209 lower-class rural black children. Although the SGS Review Committee that had evaluated the proposal judged it to be adequate on scientific grounds, it was rejected for reasons concerning "the ethics of research." According to the letter of rejection, the reasons were as follows:

> 1. The reviewers were seriously concerned about the potential risks both to the subjects in the study and to the classes of persons represented by the subjects. In regards to the former, *no information was given in the proposal that the childrens' parents gave consent to have their children's test performance used for research purposes of this kind.* . . .
> 2. Even more seriously, the reviewers felt that this study was *liable to potential social and political misuse.* They were aware that you had intentionally confounded race and class in an attempt to prevent invidious comparisons between groups, but given today's climate, the reviewers were not sure that any precautions could be successful in that respect. . . .[12]
> (Italics mine.)

Both of these reasons are highly suspect. To require researchers to obtain informed consent from parents for possible use of the data by other researchers at some future date would make research cumbersome, if not impossible. No one can foresee all of the secondary analyses which will be made of their studies.

To extend the notion of risk beyond the individuals originally involved in the study to a "class or group risk" is equally dubious. It is an impossible burden to ask that the scientist antici-

---

[12] John L. Horn, "The Ethics of Research: A Case History and its Lessons," in *The Ethics of Teaching and Scientific Research*, p. 137.

pate all of the social consequences of his inquiry, and whether
the results might be used adversely against some group at a
later date.

Horn relates that not only was his proposal rejected, but that
a government official wrote to his university about the proposal,
suggesting ethical improprieties on Horn's part—a subtle form
of coercion.

V

I submit that we need to recognize the freedom of inquiry as
a general *prima facie* ethical principle that ought to be respected
by society. Such a principle serves as a guide for decision. Can
this principle be justified, and on what grounds?

There are many arguments which can be adduced in its favor.
First, the quest for truth is among the highest of human values,
expressing an enduring human interest and the intrinsically
worthwhile nature of the search for knowledge. People have
always cherished new discoveries about nature and life. They
have wished to ferret out what is genuine from what is false, to
understand the cause of things, to unravel and comprehend
their complexity.

In this regard, science has emerged as the most powerful tool
invented to reveal causal relationships. The search for knowledge is unending. It requires constant care and attention,
nourishment, and cultivation. No one can anticipate what new
ideas will emerge or new hypotheses will develop. There are
always surprises that arise in the course of inquiry.

If the creative "mind" of man is to proceed, it requires conditions of freedom. Fear of sanction or reprisal will destroy the
quest for truth. Thus, a society which prizes knowledge and
allows its scientists, philosophers, humanists, poets, artists, and
ordinary people to live and breathe in a context of freedom is
more likely to come closer to discovering it. Truth is hard to
come by. We cannot add to the fund of knowledge if the censor

or moralist is permitted to prohibit the free expression of our cognitive talents.

In the tradition of Western civilization, the use of our rational capacities has been considered to be the highest good and a significant source of happiness. Perhaps this tradition has underestimated the emotional satisfaction of other needs essential to the good life. Nevertheless, the rational life (as broadly interpreted) is among the deepest expressions of human power, and that which distinguishes humans, in some sense, from other forms of life on earth.

Accordingly, the first observation to be made here is that perhaps the quest for knowledge needs no justification. This quest is ethically significant in its own terms as the most developed expression of our potentialities, the most eloquent source of enrichment, the noblest fulfillment of human excellence.

We need not apologize because we are curious, inquisitive, or wish to find what is the case and why. Those who oppose the continuing human search—for whatever lofty moral principles—are, in the last analysis, the enemies of humankind. These persons seek to suppress our deepest inclinations to know. It is they, not those who seek knowledge, who are behaving unethically.

There is also a second argument in support of free scientific inquiry: its utilitarian justification. Knowledge is an instrument of action and of life. Basic research can be applied in practice and can stimulate invention and technology; it can help to cure suffering and disease, eliminate poverty, and create a better life for humanity.

One never knows beforehand what the full consequences of scientific research will be. Hence, to seek to limit any area of inquiry on the basis of present-day knowledge is to cut off the possibilities of new applications which may be beneficial to humankind. We cannot anticipate the results of free inquiry; however, we must encourage continuing investigation. A progressive society is one in which innovation and ingenuity, imagination and intellect, should have free play.

Hence, even though there may be some abuses in the quest for knowledge, the long-range advantages of free inquiry far outweigh any immediate disadvantages. We need to balance possible short-range dangers with long-range results. We may thus maintain that "the right to knowledge and the free use thereof" has, overall, long-range utility for the good of society at large. No doubt, there will be hazards and mistakes, but it is far better to risk possible abuses than to adopt a policy of short-sighted censorship.

In arguing on both intrinsic and consequential grounds that the "right to free scientific research" is a *prima facie* principle that ought to prevail, I do not wish to assume the mantle of the absolutist. No right is absolute and there may be exceptions to the application of general ethical principles. We are, in general, opposed to killing, yet in some situations—for example, in self-defense, or in cases of euthanasia—killing may be ethically justifiable. A *prima facie* duty is not an absolutely binding one. We ought, in general, to keep our promises, but we can imagine cases in which we are released from an obligation to do so, particularly if keeping a promise would have destructive consequences. Thus, although one ought to recognize the general right of scientists to seek the truth, we may in certain situations reluctantly, and only as a last resort, decide to limit the application of that right.

But the salient point is that *the burden of proof should be upon those who wish to restrain the quest for knowledge, and not on those committed to seek it.* I fear that what is happening now is that scientists are increasingly being put on the defensive and being called upon to vindicate their commitment; the public is becoming suspicious of their motives and goals. However, it is precisely those groups which wish to abrogate the right to knowledge that need to justify their call for constraints, and their reasons must be compelling. There must be an overwhelmingly clear and present danger which would allow us to restrict such inquiry.

We may add to this still another consideration: the freedom

of scientific research ought to be explicitly protected as a First Amendment right. I cannot understand why censors in recent years have transgressed this right with impunity. It should have full Constitutional protection. Perhaps, some one should make a case against the Secretary of HEW and the new "Boards of Inquisition" now being established. The right to scientific research is intrinsically related to freedom of belief, speech, and publication—as is academic freedom. And we are well aware that many disciples of virtue have attempted in the past to abrogate academic freedom; inquisitional Congressional committees and militant disruptions of classrooms and speakers are recent instances of such abrogation. The committees and the militants have also violated First Amendment rights.

I am not unaware of the distinction between knowledge and action. I concede that, although society ought not in principle to limit knowledge, it can in some situations restrict actions, especially where such actions invade the rights of others. In a sense, this distinction is false, for all knowledge is a form of behavior, not an inner "mentalistic" state. Still, a distinction can be made in degree if not in kind. However, knowledge, even if it involves no overt action, may have consequences which someone may interpret to be "harmful." It is on the basis of these considerations that some have called for a moratorium on research on IQ and race for fear of injuring minority groups. But if we were to argue in this way, then Linus Pauling should not be permitted to publish his findings about the alleged benefits of Vitamin C. Nor should the proponents of Vitamin E be allowed to publish their research until the evidence is conclusive, because of possible hazards to a class of users. But clearly, in an open society, all points of view should contend; if someone's views are mistaken this can be pointed out by their critics. To restrict any and all knowledge which may be "harmful" is excessive moral zeal, which in the last analysis is counterproductive, and, if generalized, would make the attainment of truth virtually impossible.

Nevertheless, I think that a democratic society *can* limit certain forms of technology. Many products of industry are so noxious to health and to the environment that it is perfectly within the jurisdiction of the community to establish standards to prohibit their production. There should be, of course, sufficient evidence for these decisions. The fact that the products of technology and industry need greater scrutiny and control is surely not at issue here. The right to knowledge does not mean in all cases the right to manufacture goods that will poison the atmosphere or pollute the streams. (Though I would here take a libertarian position, and I would allow, wherever possible, individuals to have the free choice to purchase products that may harm them, so long as these products are properly labelled.)

The very process of conducting scientific research may, in some instances, have overt public consequences. This seems to be the case with recombinant DNA research (though I might add that I am not convinced of the clear and present danger to public safety which the opponents of DNA research have portrayed). Thus, the scientific researcher does not always passively view his subject; indeed, he may manipulate, change, even harm it. When should he be allowed to do that?

I would, however, suggest the following guideline: the right to inquire should be respected. It is so intrinsically and instrumentally valuable that it should be curtailed only after critical, reflective inquiry. I reiterate: the person who wishes to suppress inquiry—not those devoted to it—should ultimately be required to demonstrate his case.

Still, one cannot say that the scientist is immune to the laws governing society. Nazi doctors did experiment with their patients, tortured them, and violated their rights. There is the unfortunate Tuskegee study, in which researchers withheld treatment from some black patients with syphilis. Scientists who perform such acts cannot expect to occupy a privileged place in society, immune from jurisdiction. Scientists do not have a right to place in excessive risk the health and well being

of subjects under study—unless the subjects agree. The right to
seek the truth does not mean that scientists are entitled to kill
or maim subjects in the process. But I fear that the principle of
informed consent can be construed in such a way as to impair
legitimate scientific research.

The principle of informed consent should not be interpreted
as universally binding. If we were to permit this interpretation,
we might seriously impede much research that can be highly
significant for society. Indeed, some kinds of research may be
invalidated if the subjects being tested are aware of that fact.
Withholding some information may be necessary—surely not to
injure or harm subjects, but in order accurately to investigate
their behavior, without their pre-established attitudes interven-
ing.

Similarly, there are many kinds of tests, in schools or other
institutions, which we should be able to do with children—
without their consent or that of their parents being required.
Bureaucracies—whether police departments, hospitals, corpora-
tions, government agencies, churches, or schools—are notoriously cautious. There seems to be developing a generalized
apprehension that, since certain forms of research might be ad-
verse to the institution's reputation or to the subjects involved,
the institution should not participate in it. There is a growing
fear by administrators and scientists of possible adversary legal
proceedings being brought against them.

My chief concern here, however, is not the topic of informed
consent. I have used it only by way of illustration. I am concerned, I reiterate, with the broader question: the undermining
of scientific research in general, of which this is only one aspect.
That is why I have argued that we need to be aware of our
obligation to it as a general ethical principle.

VI

I think it important that we now call a halt to the encroach-
ments of governments and other external bodies which wish to

regulate scientific research. We should instead allow for responsible peer review by those within the profession. It is true that professionals may disagree, and moral choices are often difficult to make. Nonetheless, it would be mistaken for scientists to look outside for political or legal adjudication, any more than they should seek religious sanction for what they do. To move in the direction of government control will set an unfortunate precedent and may hopelessly impair future scientific investigation. The danger is that scientists will barter away their creativity to unqualified review boards, which are being asked to pass on the merits of an inquiry or the competence of the researchers and may destroy daring innovations and discoveries. Such boards may hamper research, functioning instead as inquisitional bodies. If such boards had existed in the days during which Freud developed his theories of psychoanalysis, they might have prohibited publication of case studies about patients (without their consent) as a violation of their right to privacy (or as sexually prurient). They might have condemned Galileo's experiments as immoral for unsettling religious beliefs. Marx's inquiries might have been censored as having bad social consequences, because they would lead to violent revolution and harm some individuals in the process. These boards might have forbidden the work of such scientists as Pasteur, Ehrlich, and Koch and would have made difficult the discoveries of vaccines for yellow fever, poliomyelitis, or other dread diseases. The entire field of nuclear research, like recombinant DNA today, might have been enjoined because of the possible dangers of nuclear contamination.

In the current context, I believe that scientists are faced with an urgent problem: to make clear to themselves and to society the humanistic character of their enterprise. Scientists must demonstrate that, far from there being an opposition between science and ethics, science is among the highest of human endeavors, and that to seek to restrict or prohibit it is a most drastic step that itself requires justification. There is today within society an excessive, brooding, pessimistic fear of the unknown that we might unmask. Yet, only by intensified research can we hope to discover not only new and exciting forms of truth, but the safeguards that can also be applied in the process of research. To close the door to research is to prevent not only positive results from being known, but also the means of guarding ourselves against possible misadventures.

In the last analysis, the best safeguard against the undermining of scientific research is an informed, intelligent public. The larger task facing scientists is to help educate the public about the nature of the scientific method and the roles of science and research in human progress. We have been failing to accomplish this task, and the rising tide of subjectivism and the assault on scientific research likewise is symptomatic of a failure by the broader public to appreciate how society has benefited from the untrammelled search for knowledge.

The freedom of scientific inquiry ultimately depends upon a public enlightenment that must be nurtured not only in the schools but through every media of communication. The task is heavy and unremitting and seems sometimes like the labors of Sisyphus. But it must be shouldered by all who have faith that human freedom can be furthered by the arts of intelligence.

THIRTEEN

Equality and Excellence in the Democratic Ideal

DAVID L. NORTON

IN HONORING Joseph L. Blau I will concentrate on what he has identified as "perhaps the most serious question about democracy that we can raise,"[1] and my own wrestling here will be an attempt to expand upon a clue given by him to answer this question.

Concerning the "most serious question about democracy," Blau says, "There is certainly a sense in which any striving to excel—to be better than others in whatever doings one shares with them—is on the face of it destructive of equality, leading perhaps, to the Orwellian *Animal Farm,* where 'all animals are equal, but some animals are more equal than others.' On the other hand, where no one strives to excel, so that all animals are *equally* equal, we shall surely witness the apotheosis of mediocrity, leading to a static and unprogressive and moribund society."[2] The problem, then, concerns the relationship of excellence and equality in the democratic ideal. Is it a tension or a contradiction? If it is a tension, it can infuse working democracy with the aspiration to excellence which the democratic ideal univer-

---

[1] Joseph L. Blau, "Ethics, Equality, and Excellence," address to the *New York Society for Ethical Culture* (19), unpublished typescript, p. 11.

[2] *Ibid.,* pp. 11–12.

salizes. But if it is a contradiction, then the democratic ideal is self-contradictory and unactualizable, and what passes for working democracy is irremediably crippled by self-contradiction.

What I referred to as the clue to the answer is given by Blau in the following lines. "How can each person be made to realize that excellence consists in doing well whatever one is able to do, reaching out for the maximum expression of one's talents, rather than in trying to do what one is not fit for and, of course, doing it poorly? Perhaps the way is to be found by a stress on the equivalence—the equal value—of all occupations as opportunities for serving human needs. Perhaps we need to reemphasize a factor in our definition of success that has always been there but that we have given less stress than it deserves—that success includes being satisfied doing whatever we can do as well as we can do it."[3]

In due course I shall develop this clue, but first let us discern the full force of the question. For this I turn, not to theorists of democracy, but to democracy's profoundest adversaries.

The dilemma is roughly this: if human excellence is exceptional, then to distribute authority equally, as by the principle "one man, one vote," is to ensure the sovereignty of mediocrity by rendering it authoritative. Worse, by the truth in the adage, "A person cannot see over his own height," and because mediocrity has overwhelming strength of numbers, something akin to Gresham's Law works to extinguish excellence altogether.

Historically the dilemma has prompted either of two moves by which to commensurate excellence and equality. One is to employ the concept of "proportional" rather than "arithmetic" equality. The former obtains when the holdings of each person (to use distribution for our example) are proportional to his or her personal excellence or merit. First formalized by Plato and Aristotle,[4] the concept of proportional equality is denounced by egalitarians as an apologetic of privilege. The idea of propor-

[3] *Ibid.*, p. 13.
[4] See Plato, *The Republic*, bk. 9; and Aristotle, *Nichomachean Ethics*, Bk. V.

tional equality, it should be noted, sets strict limits to entitled holdings (for Aristotle and Plato, injustice obtains no less in cases of too much as too little) and thereby precludes extreme disparities of wealth, education, and honor, such as we countenance today.

The other measure is to construe equality as "equality of opportunity." In this case what accrues to individuals through exercise of opportunity is regarded as earned by them, and therefore possessed with entitlement. The rationale for this is that because "human being" is originally mere potentiality, excellence can only be achieved by exercise of opportunity. A great problem, to be sure, lies in what can be attained by cheating and ruthlessness, for these, too, are exercisings of opportunity.

Friedrich Nietzsche offered the truly formidable argument that equality of opportunity inevitably produces the triumph of mediocrity; it behooves the friends of democracy to give careful attention to this argument. As a partisan of excellence, Nietzsche is a eudaimonist. For eudaimonism, human being is metaphysically distinctive as incomplete or unfinished, with responsibility for completing the work of its own making. It possesses an original, innate inclination to its self-completion (in Plato and Aristotle, "desire for the good"; in Nietzsche, "will-to-power" understood as will to self-surpassing or growth; in Jean-Jacques Rousseau, "natural goodness"). But the indeterminacy of human beings deprives this original inclination of necessity and couples it with the opportunity of its own denial. Human being is thus problematic being; it is a radical equivocation—in Nietzsche's terms, between "Yea-saying" and "Nay-saying"—and human freedom devolves upon the irreducible choice between self-affirmation and self-negation. Yea-saying is affirmation of original inclination and, as such, active and constructive. Nay-saying, or denial of original inclination, is reactive and destructive. Nietzsche maintained "that, in man's historical development, the reactive, destructive propensity is certain to become dominant." This view summarizes the major argument against democracy raised by critics from Plato to Jose Ortega y Gasset. By our resolve to meet democracy's opponents in their strength, we shall discover one profound friend of democracy who did likewise, and sought to reformulate the ideal of democracy—John Stuart Mill.

According to Nietzsche the reactive, destructive propensity is certain to predominate because of *ressentiment*.[5] Enactment of innate, affirmative inclination comes first, but it requires initiative. Exercise of initiative never occurs uniformly in a population but always originates with a few persons. However, the few who first exercise initiative at self-determination will before long begin to benefit from the achievements of such exercise. (For we are here speaking of *art*—action disciplined by will and guided by knowledge—which, as Santayana says, "is the principle of benefit, and without art the freer a man is the more miserable he must become."[6]) These benefits are of three sorts; excellence in the products of labor, intrinsic rewards in the labor itself, and transformation in the person of the laborer through self-actualization.

Meanwhile the majority, having as yet not exercised comparable initiative themselves, are in the position of witnesses to the benefits of the few. They desire them for themselves but cannot appropriate them, for as individuals the persons of the majority lack the acquired strength of the few. (These persons are not yet organized as a collective.) As desire for others' benefits becomes envy when it remains ungratified, so envy which cannot express itself directly is internalized as the much deeper and more pervasive phenomenon of *ressentiment*. *Ressentiment* remains will-to-power, but must express itself by devious means

[5] See notably Friedrich Nietzsche, *On the Genealogy of Morals,* trans. Walter Kaufmann and R. J. Hollingdale (bound with *Ecce Homo*), (New York: Vintage Books, 1969), esp. First Essay, Section 13ff.

[6] George Santayana, "On Self-Government," in *Dialogues in Limbo* (New York: Scribner's, 1925), p. 95.

(hence Nietzsche's use of insidious images, e.g., the spider). It gains the upper hand in the only way open to it: by a subjective, moral transvaluation which sanctions weakness and docility and by inventing a God who prefers this. And in so doing it supplies the self-justification which is the precondition of its organization into a collective movement, destined to succeed by weight of numbers. The new "good" declare themselves to be "the just," and what they desire they declare to be the "triumph of justice." They adopt what Nietzsche terms the "slogan of *ressentiment*"—"supreme rights of the majority." [7]

The movement in question has been named by Jose Ortega y Gasset "the revolt of the masses." By weight of numbers it achieves "the sovereignty of the unqualified individual, of the human being as such." [8] In an analysis closely resembling Nietzsche's, Ortega says that the characteristic of the movement "is that the commonplace mind, knowing itself to be commonplace, has the assurance to proclaim the rights of the commonplace and to impose them wherever it will." [9] It effects a transvaluation by asserting a morality of the commonplace in which what is common to all persons is normative—"real," "good," "beautiful"—and what is exceptional is pretentious, false, unnatural.

It is important to notice that the antidemocratic arguments of Nietzsche and Ortega do not derive, as did Plato's and Aristotle's, from the elitist premise that, by birth, only rare individuals are equipped with the potentiality for excellence. This is clear in Ortega, for he repeatedly condemns hereditary aristocracies whether of class, of intellect, or of talent. On the contrary, he says, "We distinguish the excellent man from the common man by saying that the former is the one who makes great demands upon himself, and the latter the one who makes

[7] Nietzsche, *Genealogy of Morals,* p. 54.
[8] Jose Ortega y Gasset, *The Revolt of the Masses,* trans. anonymous (New York: W. W. Norton & Co., 1932), p. 23.
[9] *Ibid.,* p. 18.

no demands on himself, but contents himself with what he is, and is delighted with himself."[10] And Ortega believes that whether to make great demands upon oneself, or minimal demands, or no demands, is a choice which is open to every individual.

Nietzsche has frequently been identified as an elitist in the above sense, but this view is mistaken. For Nietzsche the essential, irreducible essence of human being is will-to-power. Will-to-power is inherently teleological. It can enact itself as "self-surpassing" only because it contains its end implicitly within it. This end is the *Ubermensch*—the completed, noble, excellent individual. Therefore, according to Nietzsche, to be a human being is to possess potential excellence and the moral responsibility to actualize it. Nietzsche's position, like Ortega's, is that all persons, by virtue of their nature, are capable of manifesting excellence; inevitably, however, the majority will not develop their potential.

The ideal of democracy is not the sovereignty of mediocrity but the widespread cultivation of excellence. This concept is expressed by R. H. Tawney: "The well-being of a society is likely to be increased if it so plans its organization that, whether their powers are great or small, all its members may be equally enabled to make the best of such powers as they possess."[11] It is likewise given expression in these words by Ralph Barton Perry: "In democracy it is not a question of giving room and authority to the genius which has already declared itself, and of sacrificing thereto the residual mass of mediocrity, but one of tapping new sources, and discovering genius in obscure and unsuspected quarters. By giving light and air to the hitherto buried masses of mankind, democracy hopes to enrich human culture in the qualitative, and not merely in the quantitative sense."[12] Logically, the democratic ideal requires the

[10]*Ibid.,* p. 63.

[11] R. H. Tawney, *Equality,* 4th ed. (London: Allen & Unwin, 1952), pp. 35–36.

[12] Ralph Barton Perry, *Puritanism and Democracy* (New York: Harper Torchbooks, 1964), p. 453.

postulate that potential excellence is possessed by all persons. Nietzsche and Ortega are forceful advocates of this postulate. Therefore, the unworkability they find in the democratic ideal is not logical (self-contradictory), but practical. It is incumbent upon serious supporters of democracy to acknowledge that democracy has not been successful at eliciting excellence from the "hitherto buried masses of mankind." Indeed, this aim, which we here identify as the democratic ideal, is today apt to be greeted with cynicism by advocates of democracy themselves. But the viability of democracy is the viability of this ideal. What is today urgently needed is to demonstrate that this failure of democracy* is owing to contingent and remediable factors, and is therefore not inevitable.

John Stuart Mill, a strong supporter of democracy, recognizes the great force of the antidemocratic arguments. To begin with, Mill is no less a partisan of excellence than Nietzsche or Ortega (or Plato or Aristotle), and in company with them he believes that the nurture of excellence is the highest purpose of government. In his words, "The first element of good government, therefore, being the virtue and intelligence of the human beings composing the community, the most important point of excellence which any form of government can possess is to promote the virtue and intelligence of the people themselves." [13] Of paramount concern, then, is the influence of forms of government upon the character of the people governed. But this question, Mill says, "really depends upon a still more fundamental one, viz., which of two common types of character, for the general good of humanity, it is most desirable should predominate—the active or the passive type: that which struggles against evils or that which endures them; that which bends

---

*It is imperative to acknowledge the failure to be a failure, for if it is not, then the implication is that life as we know it in our democracy is ideal. In this case our widespread discontent is given notice that nothing more is to be expected from democracy, and aspiration must find other ideals.

[13] John Stuart Mill, *Considerations on Representative Government*, ed. by Currin V. Shields (Indianapolis: Bobbs-Merrill, 1958), p. 25.

to circumstances or that which endeavors to make circumstances bend to itself." Mill next observes that "The commonplaces of moralists, and the general sympathies of mankind, are in favor of the passive type." (On the following page he adds that institutional religion likewise prefers the passive type as "being more in harmony with the submission due to the divine will.") "Yet," he says, "nothing is more certain than that improvement in human affairs is wholly the work of the uncontented characters, and moreover, that it is much easier for an active mind to acquire the virtues of patience than for a passive one to assume those of energy." [14]

The evident resemblance to Nietzsche's two fundamental types of character (active, value-actualizing; and reactive, value-destroying) becomes closer still when Mill proceeds to generate reaction out of passivity. "There are, no doubt, in all countries really contented characters who not merely do not seek, but do not desire, what they do not already possess, and these naturally bear no ill will toward such as have apparently a more favored lot. But the great mass of seeming contentment is really discontent combined with indolence or self-indulgence, which, while taking no legitimate means of raising itself, delights in bringing others down to its own level." [15] Later he adds, "In proportion as success in life is seen or believed to be the fruit of fatality or accident, and not of exertion, in that same ratio does envy develop itself as a point of national character." [16]

Mill also recognizes, in common with the partisans of excellence, that all excellence represents actualization by individuals of potentiality, and is therefore available only to the active, as against the passive, type of character. He uses the example of contentment, pointing out that where it is worthy of approval it is *acquired,* and involves "an ability to do cheerfully without what cannot be had: a just appreciation of the comparative value

[14]*Ibid.,* p. 47.
[15]*Ibid.,* p. 50.
[16]*Ibid.,* p. 49.

of different objects of desire and a willing renunciation of the
less when incompatible with the greater." [17] We shall return to
this insight.

Mill judges representative democracy the highest form of
government for two basic reasons. The first is that by calling for
participation of all citizens in government it encourages the active temperament, thereby conducing to improvement of the
quality of life of citizens. The second is that the kind of participation thus encouraged—i.e., participation in political life—is
calculated to replace the narrowly self-regarding sentiments
which predominate in private life ("It is not sufficiently considered how little there is in most men's ordinary life to give any
largeness either to their conceptions or to their sentiments." [18])
with thought and feeling which aims at benefiting the public.
Accordingly, politics is, for Mill, the "school of public
spirit." [19]

It is worth noting that Mill here ratifies the place ascribed to
politics for the development of individuals by Aristotle. For
Aristotle, moral development involves three levels of living:
self-interested private or economic life, which of itself holds no
aretai (virtues); political life, the domain of the moral virtues;
and philosophical life—the highest level, the region of the intellectual virtues. Aristotle identifies man as *zoon politikon,* not
simply because he is inherently social or sociable, but because
political activity is the exclusive instrumentality by which the
"moral virtues" are elicited. [20]

I believe that there is profound truth in what I shall term the
Aristotle-Mill thesis; however, there is also something amiss in

[17] *Ibid.,* p. 50.
[18] *Ibid.,* p. 53.
[19] *Ibid.,* p. 54.
[20] Aristotle, *Politics,* bk. 7, chs. 1–3, 13; *Nichomachean Ethics,* bks. 6 & 10. Appli-
cability of the concept of economic man to Aristotle's political thought is suggested
by C. B. Macpherson, *The Political Theory of Possessive Individualism* (London: Oxford
University Press, 1964), and by Leo Strauss, *Natural Right and History* (Chicago: University of Chicago Press, 1953), ch. 5. I thank Professor Stephen G. Salkever, Bryn
Mawr College, for calling this to my attention.

this concept. To begin with the latter, the "participation" upon which Mill places such heavy reliance is in fact limited, with respect to national political life, to voting and jury duty. At the local level, this participation is restricted to service on "parish counsels" (the English counterpart to our representative bodies of state, city, and town). But the sanctity with which Mill invests voting and jury duty are scarcely discoverable today. Indeed, as Steven Lukes points out, "Research into voting behavior—who votes, how and why? who does not vote and why not?—would seem to have confirmed abundantly the old impressionistic conservative arguments about the 'bovine stupidity' and the 'heavy, lumpish acquiescence' of the mass electorate and to have shown the democratic hope to be a mere delusion, based on false intellectualist assumptions about human nature."[21]

Concerning participation in local government, it would seem that such widespread participation as Mill seeks would diminish the significance of each individual almost to the token level represented nationally in voting and jury duty. Moreover, it appears clear today that Mill did not sufficiently take account of the distinction between thinking *in* the public interest and thinking *of* the public interest. Doubtless, political participation educates participants at recognizing collective desires, interests, apprehensions, and so on. But, participation in the political process may also generate contempt for these desires and interests. And, with disheartening frequency, politics shows itself to be a schooling in ways to employ this new knowledge for personal gain.

In commending politics as a "school of public spirit" Mill relied upon two other conditions which require comment. It is a school, Mill held, where the teaching is by example. As Mill explicitly recognized, this requires, that in all branches of political life there are to be found at work some experienced individuals of intellectual, practical, and moral excellence; and that

[21] Steven Lukes, *Essays in Social Theory* (London: Macmillan, 1977), p. 34.

there exist what Mill termed "deference" on the part of newcomers—the ability to recognize superior performance and character, and the desire to emulate it. Concerning the omnipresence of experienced persons of excellence in political life, Mill was perhaps no more ready than we to take it for granted. He sought to secure it by extending the franchise, ensuring to every interest some representation. He strongly recommended adoption of the system of the single-transferable vote, designed by Thomas Hare, because he believed it to ensure better quality in candidates for office.[22]

These reforms are central to Mill's program to counteract what he terms "the general tendency of things throughout the world . . . to render mediocrity the ascendant power among mankind."[23] But the question is, where is Mill to find the incentive to effectuate his program? Of "mass man" Ortega y Gasset says, "feeling himself 'common,' he proclaims the right to be common, and refuses to accept any order superior to himself."[24] The result is what Ortega terms the "characteristic of the hour . . . that the commonplace mind, knowing itself to be commonplace, has the assurance to proclaim the rights of the commonplace and to impose them wherever it will."[25] In this case "deference" does not exist, and Hare's system has no chance of adoption. The common man acknowledges the superiority of no other, and wants to be represented by persons just like himself. Nor does it seem that our "hour" is different in this respect from Mill's, for (in a presumably despairing moment) Mill observes that the common man no sooner ceases to be servile than he turns insolent.[26]

The proposition that politics is the necessary mediating struc-

[22] Mill offers a good synopsis of Hare's system in *Considerations*, pp. 109–26.

[23] John Stuart Mill, *On Liberty*, ed. Currin V. Shields (Indianapolis: Bobbs-Merrill, 1956), p. 80.

[24] Ortega y Gasset, *Revolt of the Masses*, p. 133.

[25] *Ibid.*, p. 18.

[26] See Michael St. John Packe, *The Life of John Stuart Mill* (New York: Capricorn Books, 1970), p. 298.

ture for the cultivation of the moral virtues was labeled above the Aristotle-Mill thesis, but space allows only a word on Aristotle. Identifying the moral virtues as habits, Aristotle took them to be elicited in conformity to positive law. ("Lawgivers make the citizens good by inculcating good habits in them."[27] "What produces virtue entire are those lawful measures which are enacted for education in citizenship."[28]) But those who take a dim view of Aristotle's "paternalism" will argue that obedience (in this case, to law) cannot be the means to cultivate the autonomy and self-determination which moral virtues presuppose. Moreover we do not share Aristotle's confidence in the rectitude of law, and are disinclined to encumber the law with the function of moral pedagogy. Finally, Aristotle's moral pedagogy relies upon the supposition that habituation in the semblance of the virtues will eventually generate the virtues themselves. But it seems more likely that what is generated by mimicry of the virtues is habitual mimicry of the virtues.

If we conclude, as I think we must, that political participation is not reliable (much less indispensable) for the cultivation of excellence in citizens, the question becomes—is there another way? I think there is, and I shall devote the remainder of this essay to it, explicating (in a way for which I alone am responsible) Blau's suggestion that "excellence consists in doing well whatever one is able to do."

What is profound in Aristotle and Mill, as well as in Nietzsche, Ortega y Gasset (and likewise in John Gardner, whom Blau cites), is the presupposition that excellence is innate in personhood as potentiality. The indispensable presupposition of the democratic ideal, I contend, is the supposition that potential excellence is universally distributed, but rarely actualized. Our contemporary notion that potential excellence is sparsely distributed is an aberration produced by the trans-individual nature of culture. The spontaneous, productive activity of certain

[27] Aristotle, *Nichomachean Ethics,* bk. 2, ch. 1, 1103b, 3–5.
[28] *Ibid.,* bk. 5, ch. 2, 1130b, 24–26.

individuals living in the past eventuates in objective outcomes ("products") which are recognized by the community to be of value. These values then become severed from their foundation in the subjectivity of individuals (innate inclination, aspiration, "love of the good") and are held before subsequent generations as obligatory ends of activity. These objective ends, in turn, define "excellence" as the specific talents suited to these ends, and it is a foregone conclusion that the number of persons of potential excellence, with respect to these ends and these talents, will be few. Meanwhile, other potential excellences with their corresponding talents and ends are overlooked. Persons who are "other" in this sense are judged to be, and taught to regard themselves as, without potential excellence, irredeemably ordinary.

In other words our aberration centers in applying the term excellence to products of labor exclusively or primarily, disregarding the labor itself and the persons whose labor it is. But the vitality of the democratic ideal will only be regained when product-excellence is reconnected to its roots and taproot, to be found respectively in the work and the person.

In this crucial respect the Greek term *arete* is gratifyingly concrete. Formerly, it was usually translated as "virtue." However, this term—under the influence of religion and conventional morality cited by Mill and Nietzsche—connotes passivity, not the "strength" of the Roman *virtus*. For this reason some current translators opt for "excellence" as the English equivalent of *arete;* but, because of the aforementioned preoccupation with products, "excellence" can also mislead. Despite awkwardness, Martin Ostwald's persistent translation as "virtue or excellence" has the merit of conveying the humanistic Greek recognition that all consideration of excellence must be grounded in the question of excellence in persons.

My thesis is that the democratic ideal is viable and vital when "equality" is understood as equal opportunity of individuals to manifest the individual excellence which is theirs innately, by the nature of personhood. The key to the question of how personal excellence is to be cultivated lies in the recognition that the *aretai* are not tools for the attainment of excellent products; rather, they refer to excellence in persons. Bear in mind that product-excellence is not our core problem, but is derivative. Our core problem is personal excellence. This consists, as has been recognized since classical times, in the "virtues or excellences"—justice, love, honesty, courage, wholeheartedness, fidelity, resourcefulness, highmindedness. Is it not clear that whatever may be the native differences of individuals as determined by the "natural lottery of birth" (and they are certainly many), *personal* excellence as defined by the *aretai* is within the reach of everyone? As Seneca said, "Virtue [excellence] closes the door to no man: it is open to all . . . the freeborn, the freedman, the slave and the king. . . . neither family nor fortune determines its choice; it is satisfied by the naked human being."[29] Or in John W. Gardner's words today, "Human dignity and worth should be assessed only in terms of those qualities of mind and spirit that are within the reach of every human being."[30]

Politics is not the indispensable cradle of the moral virtues; there is another way. The *aretai* are the natural expression of the engagement of individuals in the distinctive sort of productive work which by nature is theirs to do. In the interest of cultivating excellence in persons (and the derivative excellence in products) the *social* task is that of providing the conditions under which individuals qua individuals are given the best possible chance to find the distinctive kind of productive work which is theirs by their nature to do, the work which they love to do, and in which they experience intrinsic rewards.

To show the generation of the *aretai* from meaningful work

[29] Cited in Stanley I. Benn, "Equality, Moral and Social," *The Encyclopedia of Philosophy* (New York: Macmillan, 1967), 3:39.

[30] John W. Gardner, *Excellence: Can We Be Equal and Excellent Too?* (New York: Harper & Row Perennial Library, 1961), p. 95.

we shall begin with one for which Aristotle and Mill emphasized the necessity of political life, the "virtue or excellence" of
generosity. For Plato and Aristotle the primal moral force in the
world is love of the good, but it first arises in individuals, not
as love of the abstract, universal good, but as love of one's own
good. This "self-love," as Aristotle stresses, must be distinguished from vanity.[31] Vanity precludes love of others; self-love
is the precondition of it. Vanity is love of one's actual self
which, as such, is devoid of a dynamic of growth. In eudaimon-
istic self-love the object of love is the ideal self, and love is
moral aspiration, the incentive to become the worthier person
one can be by fulfilling one's innate potentiality. The worth one
hereby actualizes is objective, which is to say it is *of* worth, not
to oneself alone or primarily, but in principle to all persons, and
in practice to such persons as fulfill the conditions of appreciation and utilization of the *kind* of worth manifested by a given
individual. To see this we need only ask whether Beethoven's
Ninth Symphony, or Newton's *Principia,* or Henry Ford's
Model T, or the Golden Gate Bridge of Joseph B. Strauss (its
chief designer) were of worth exclusively or primarily to their
creators. That these individuals are widely held to be geniuses
in their respective arts must not mislead. Our "geniuses" are
not a species apart, but serve to exemplify the potential creativity in all persons. (In its original Latin meaning *genius* was
possessed by all persons, and likewise for the *daimon* of the
Greek.)

When personal worth is recognized to be the objectification
of subjectivity, then the long-neglected current of generosity in
meaningful work will be disclosed. It has always been apparent
that persons who love their work are personally invested in the
products of that work. By this self-objectification they are giving of themselves to others, and the effort of self-actualization is
their endeavor to be sure that what they thus give to others is

[31] Aristotle, *Nichomachean Ethics,* bk. 9, ch. 8.

the best of which they are capable. When treated collectively
the theme we touch here is termed culture, and our argument is
that a profound generosity is intrinsic to culture. This has been
obscured in modern life by the elevation of economics over both
politics and morality, an elevation which inverts the three-
tiered Aristotelian pattern of human development and fixates
human life at the level of competition for subsistence. A tragedy
of modern life is that when one is being perpetually set upon by
thieves, one cannot be generous, nor is one ready to affirm the
worth of other persons.

Consider now the important virtue we have termed "wholeheartedness." It is the unqualified investment of one's whole self
in the enterprise at hand. Its contaminants can be termed *distractions,* and they are of two basic kinds, external and internal.
The primary internal distractions are ambivalence, and the
choice "with reservations." The choice "with reservations" is
epitomized in the languid cynicism which judges the world to
be a place in which nothing is found that warrants wholehearted
commitment. But this judgment misses the point. The function
of wholeheartedness is not to approve the world but to improve
it, and in this work priority attaches to ourselves. Each individual has the responsibility for actualizing his or her potential
worth (which demands wholeheartedness), and here languid
cynicism has the same effect as ignorant self-satisfaction. On the
other hand, ambivalence means that the individual in question
is never wholly where you find him; a part of him is elsewhere,
and the "elsewhere" is not commensurate with his "here" (for
thus does ambivalence afford the shelter which is its attraction).
This means that the ambivalent individual is in contradiction
with himself, and cannot effectively move.

Elimination of external distractions is a prominent part of our
nationwide program to teach "good study habits" in our secondary schools, a program which is symptomatic of our misunder-
standing of the virtues generally. The program is conducted

through remedial clinics attached to our high schools, where deficient students are taught a list of do's and don't's—choose an isolated setting, set up good lighting, go to the bathroom first, see to it that others will answer the phone, choose a chair that is neither too comfortable nor too uncomfortable, periodically check reading comprehension, establish a routine. What thwarts this enterprise is, first, that there is nothing intrinsically interesting about good study habits; hence, of all possible studies, the study of *them* is unlikely to encourage students to pursue knowledge with zeal. Second, students who pass through these clinics predictably learn, not to study, but to study themselves studying—a distraction from study itself.

Our mistake here reflects our basic error regarding the "virtues or excellences" as a whole. They are not to be taught abstractly, as standardized parts which are to be bolted on to individuals and enterprises indifferently. Rather, the "virtues or excellences" are individual potentialities, to be elicited by associating individuals with the appropriate circumstances. We can see that this is so with wholeheartedness, beginning with "good study habits."

Among every individual's variety of activities are apt to be some, or at least one, which are intrinsically rewarding. At these activities an individual will manifest a longer attention-span, more acutely focussed, than at the others. Here the discipline has already begun by which to attain the concentration which is the fundamental characteristic of "good study" as it is of wholeheartedness generally. Indeed, the individual who loves the work he does exhibits the disciplined power of attention of a master of Raja Yoga. We begin to teach good study habits by making the student aware of the very self-discipline which his interest has compelled him to work out for himself. The remaining task is to help him extend and supplement it, and to discover that what he has taught himself here is applicable to any other endeavor to which he chooses to apply it. In sum, wholeheartedness, like generosity, is the natural product of the engagement by individuals in their preferred activities, activities they find intrinsically rewarding.

It will be unnecessary to repeat the argument for each of the virtues in turn. Concerning honesty, for example, I think it will be clear that the individual who loves his work and reveres the vision of perfection which serves him as the ideal limit of his enterprise will not contaminate either by investing them with deceit. Honesty also traces to the profounder virtue of integrity. The person who has something important to do abandons lying because he recognizes it to be incredibly time-wasting. If I fail to keep an appointment with you and lie about the reason, I shall be forced to keep in mind what I told you for weeks, months, and perhaps even years, in order to remain consistent with it. And on each occasion in which I think or act in consonance with the lie, I am inconsistent with the truth, *my* truth.

Here also is the key to the insidious corrosives of both excellence and democracy according to Mill and Nietzsche—envy and *ressentiment*. As Socrates long ago advised, injustice harms the perpetrator more than the victim.[32] Envy and *ressentiment* are, as Nietzsche warns, a very costly indulgence.[33] They are given up by individuals who have something important to do, because such individuals recognize that they cannot afford them. They become "a point of national character" (Mill's term, but my thesis) where the ordinary run of human beings are made to believe that they have no potential excellence and nothing important to contribute. In our time John Cowper Powys writes, "Conceit seals up the exploring antennae of your free sensibility. Malice and hate distract you and waste your life-energy. Possessions make you a fussy super-cargo."[34]

[32] Plato, *Gorgias,* 469.

[33] Nietzsche, e.g. *Ecce Homo* (bound with *Genealogy of Morals*—see note 5), all of "Why I am so Wise," but see esp. p. 231.

[34] John Cowper Powys, *The Meaning of Culture* (New York: Norton, 1929), pp. 260–61.

As John Gardner advises, the danger to the democratic ideal lies not in paucity of potentiality for excellence among individuals, but in the problem of motivation. Gardner rightly identifies in our paragons of personal excellence the qualities of "drive," "sense of purpose," and "indomitability."[35] These qualities can, of course, be generated reactively, by hatred or fear, and in the service of bad ends, constituting fanaticism. But, they are available within every individual to serve the work of value actualization. The "problem of motivation" is one which perplexes us today, and we attribute our bewilderment to the complexity of the problem itself; in fact, it betokens our mistaken perspective. Seeking to correlate motivation with environmental factors, we are off on an endless goose-chase in which the geese multiply geometrically by a dazzling display of autogenesis. The problem of motivation is really a problem of persons. Persons are individuals, which in this context means that for each person there are countless kinds of valuable work which this person, as an individual, prefers not to do. Of the many kinds of valuable enterprises, every individual is highly selective in the matter of the work which he finds intrinsically rewarding. The "problem of motivation" is not bewilderingly complex; it is the problem of aligning individuals with the value-producing activities which they as individuals love to do, are rewarded intrinsically by doing, and prefer to do over all other activities as well as over doing nothing at all.

The vitality and viability of the democratic ideal depend upon our taking this problem seriously. We do not take it seriously by merely affording to individuals freedom in the "private sector," for when we couple the native selectivity of individuals in the matter of their loved work with the great diversity of types of work to be done in so complex a culture as ours, such freedom is reduced to little more than the opportunity to flounder hopelessly. For this reason libertarian ("classical lib-

---

[35] Gardner, *Excellence,* p. 115.

eral") advocates of exclusively "negative" freedom are, in practical effect, dooming the democratic ideal. It is imperative that
"equal opportunity" be understood not merely as guaranteed
freedom from coercion, but as including entitlement to those
conditions of autonomy and self-responsibility which persons cannot
reasonably be expected to provide for themselves. We must understand equal opportunity to mean, in the expression of R. H.
Tawney, "equal enablement."[36] It is our social responsibility to
provide to individuals improved chances of discovering their
loved work. What we speak of here is termed, eudaimonis-
tically, self-discovery. What is needed is a logic of discovery
and the cultural programs to put self-discovery into practice.

Together with this, the vitality of the democratic ideal
requires that we capture the regenerative potentiality of culture.
As morphologists of culture (Vico, Spengler, Toynbee) recognize, cultures follow the cycle of individual organisms; they are
born, they ascend in vitality and growth, they wane, and they
die. But in so doing they follow no inexorable law of nature (the
morphologists are mistaken in this). In the first place, while
cultures are biological entities, they are also ideal. Moreover, as
noted earlier, cultures are trans-individual, and therefore possess
the opportunity to invest themselves with the regenerative
power which is available in the succession of individuals by new
individuals, the succession of generations by new generations.
Cultures wane and die because they do not incorporate into
themselves this regenerative power. They outlive their original
inspiration, becoming worn-out, exhausted. This "entropy" will
be counteracted when we learn to treat new individuals as the
original persons they in fact are, and help them to find the original inspiration which subsists as slumbering potentiality within
each. It is the contrary practice of requiring individuals of later
generations to fit themselves to "roles"—the husks of the original inspirations of ancestors—that accounts for entropy in cul-

[36]Tawney, *Equality,* pp. 35–36.

ture. The waning of our own democratic inspiration is told in
our preoccupation with excellence in products (or lack of it) in
disregard of excellence in persons. This is a role-dominant orientation in which the ideal of democracy appears as nothing but
a husk.

FOURTEEN

Toward a Post-Enlightenment Doctrine of Human Rights

ROGER L. SHINN

IN THE worldwide turmoil over human rights today, a few things are clear. The cry for rights arises in most nations. Systems of communication and international organizations, both voluntary and intergovernmental, send those cries throughout the world. Yet human oppression is blatant and cruel. More than ever before, nations are embarrassed to admit violations of human rights. But prisoners and torture, suppression of free speech and press, denial of the right to emigrate, racist and sexist discrimination, and economic exploitation flourish.

Champions of human rights have trouble finding effective ways to act. For example, President Carter no sooner decided in 1977 on a policy of supporting human rights around the world than he ran into a triple embarrassment: he found it risky to affront some dictators whose support he needed for foreign policy; his outspoken accusations angered the USSR; and the offended nations pointed to the crippling of human rights in his own country. These difficulties did not silence President Carter, but they certainly removed some of the bravura from his declarations.

It is my thesis that the modern belief in human rights is in large degree a legacy from the eighteenth-century Enlightenment in Western Europe and North America, that the legacy is not adequate to the contemporary world, and that the formulation of a post-Enlightenment doctrine of human rights is a difficult but important task of our time.

This thesis does not imply that human history is primarily the result of intellectual movements. Political institutions are the consequences of many human experiences, struggles for power, and thoughts and passions. Doctrines are often the rationalizations of what has already happened. They may be ideological weapons of people trying to maintain or to grasp power. But I assume that ideas—including the idea that ideas are only a superstructure over a material process—have consequences. And I assume that the clarification of ideas has value, both on intrinsic and on utilitarian grounds. Hence my concern is for the idea and the practice of human rights.

The Novelty of the Enlightenment

It was the triumph of the Enlightenment that it enunciated human rights with an unprecedented power and universality. The Declaration of Independence is a good example of the faith of the Enlightenment. Historians often point out that it represented a wide consensus in its time, and Thomas Jefferson himself acknowledged that his critics said that the Declaration was largely taken from John Locke. However, if the basic themes of the Declaration were not unusual in their cultural setting, the culture itself was making a novel and radical set of affirmations:

> We hold these truths to be self-evident, that all men are created equal, that they are endowed by their Creator with certain unalienable Rights, that among these are Life, Liberty and the pursuit of Happiness.—That to secure these rights, Governments are instituted among Men, deriving their just powers from the consent of the governed,—That whenever any Form of Government becomes destruc-

tive of these ends, it is the Right of the People to alter or to abolish it, and to institute new Government, laying its foundation on such principles and organizing its power in such form, as to them shall seem most likely to effect their Safety and Happiness.

In most eras of history any such doctrine would appear startling and unreal. The recognition of a full humanity, with its inherent rights, has usually been limited to a quite particular peer group. The customary limitations can be described as both horizontal and vertical.

The horizontal limitation usually defines an in-group, geographically and socially cohesive, affirming itself in relation to outsiders. Anthropologist Ruth Benedict has said: "All primitive tribes agree in recognizing this category of the outsiders, those who are not only outside the provisions of the moral code which holds within the limits of one's own people, but who are summarily denied a place anywhere in the human scheme." Furthermore, she states, "so fundamental a human trait" is not limited to primitive tribes but persists in modern civilization.[1]

The vertical limitation is inherent in the hierarchical arrangement of most human societies. An elite exercises rights not available to all people. Systems of slavery, castes, racial distinction, and social or economic class mark off ranks within hierarchies. The assumption is that people have the rights appropriate to their status.

The Declaration of Independence, verbalizing the faith and dream of the Enlightenment, broke both the horizontal and vertical barriers. That the rhetoric outran the practice and the intention of the signers is an important fact that haunts their descendants—and that must concern us later in this essay. For the moment, however, it is enough to notice the radical innovation.

A comparison with classical culture shows the point. Plato

---

[1] Ruth Benedict, *Patterns of Culture* (New York: Penguin Books, Inc., 1946, [1934]), pp. 6, 7.

and Aristotle took for granted the horizontal limitation; they distinguished between Greeks and barbarians. They took for granted also the vertical limitation; they accepted slavery and gradations of worth and status among free citizens. They might lament that the powerful were often not worthy of their power, but they did not doubt that some men—those born and trained to be "Guardians" or to exercise command—had dignity not inherent in other men and women.

There were, of course, other roots of Western culture that contributed to the Enlightenment vision of a universal human dignity. The first dramatic assault upon both the horizontal and the vertical limitations on human rights came from the Hebrew prophets. In the tenth century B.C. the prophet Nathan, accusing David of treachery to Uriah because of David's lust for Bathsheba, asserted the rights of commoners against kings (2 Samuel 12:1–4). In the ninth century Elijah denounced Ahab for seizing the vineyard of Naboth, even though Ahab had offered "a better vineyard" in exchange, or "its value in money" (1 Kings, 21). Amos, the first of the great literary prophets, in about 760 announced God's denunciation of the wealthy and powerful, who "trample the head of the poor into the dust of the earth and turn aside the way of the afflicted" (Amos 2:6–7).

These prophets and their eloquent successors were not devising political philosophies or constitutions and legislative-judicial systems in the manner of the modern world. But they were asserting fundamental ethical convictions that could become sources for political philosophies and systems.

The breakthrough of the horizontal limitation was even more momentous. The Hebrew people in the conquest of Canaan took it for granted that their God was conferring certain privileges on them at the cost of the Canaanites. Deuteronomy 20 is about as complete an illustration as anyone could ask of Ruth Benedict's thesis about "outsiders." In an act of remarkable daring the prophets set themselves against this tradition:

"Are you not like the Ethiopians to me,
    O people of Israel?" says the Lord.
"Did I not bring up Israel from the land of Egypt,
    and the Philistines from Caphtor and the Syrians from Kir?"
                                                        (Amos 9:7)

The New Testament declaration of the coming Kingdom of God renewed the same double theme. The breach of the vertical limitation on human worth came in Jesus' mission "to preach good news to the poor" and "to set at liberty those who are oppressed" (Luke 4:18). The breach of the horizontal limitation came in the faith that in Christ, God was reconciling "the world" (the Cosmos), not just some limited race or church, to himself (2 Cor. 5:19).

However, neither Judaism nor Christianity did what the Enlightenment was to do much later in enunciating human rights. Judaism remained the belief of a small group of people, often conquered and oppressed by imperial powers. Christianity began as a tiny community within the powerful Roman empire. Within the church, Christians broke the horizontal boundaries by including people of many races and languages; they broke the vertical boundaries by including all classes of people. But they did not try to change the public institutions of the vast empire. That was not a promising opportunity for a people themselves persecuted. They waited for God to complete his Kingdom at the end of history. By the fourth century, when a Roman emperor (Constantine) actually became a Christian, the church had no thought of radically changing the system. As an example of its political inefficacy, the church did not try to eliminate the secular institution of slavery, even though it might make a slave a bishop. One other movement in the ancient West, Stoicism, had a potential appreciation of universal human rights. Its affirmation of human dignity transcended horizontal and vertical boundaries. In a world where people might assert, "I am a Greek," "I am a Roman," "I am a Carth-

aginian," the Stoic said: *"Homo sum*—I am a human being."
And one of its greatest writers, Epictetus, was a slave.

Through Seneca, Cicero, Marcus Aurelius, and others, Stoicism had some direct influence on political philosophy and practice—as it had on the theological ethic of the Apostle Paul and Augustine of Hippo. But its doctrine of human worth had rather little political effectiveness. One reason was its historical fatalism, related to a cyclical conception of history.

Throughout centuries of Western history, therefore, Christianity and Stoicism contributed to the dignity of individuals, but did little to change social institutions that were destroying human rights. Even worse, they let themselves be co-opted by social systems (for example, medieval feudalism) and used to reinforce the hierarchical arrangement of society. The Stoic doctrine of natural law, often absorbed within Christian teaching, was more often used as a vindication of the existing order than as a call for change.

Occasional movements beginning in the Middle Ages related the religious vision of a transformed future to the pains of the lower social classes. These included the Waldensians (from about 1170 on) in Italy, Wyclif (c. 1320–1384) and the Lollards in England, Jan Hus (1369–1415) and the Hussites in Bohemia. Contemporary with Martin Luther, Thomas Münzer (1488?–1525) led the Peasants' Revolt in Germany, and many pacifist sects echoed the New Testament affirmation of the poor, usually in apolitical ways. The regnant powers of church and state generally repressed these movements or sealed them off from the main currents of society. Judaism kept alive a memory of the prophetic ethic, but Christendom was not interested in learning from the Jews. By the seventeenth century, however, left-wing Puritanism and a variety of sectarian movements (Baptists, Levellers, and Diggers) in England were making insistent demands for what today are called human rights. Society had to take notice.

Against this historical background the Enlightenment intentionally and self-consciously set out to do two things. First, it took the dreams once regarded as eschatological and supernatural, and it tried to institutionalize them in society. Those dreams became programs for the overthrow of kings, the establishment of new nations, the writing of constitutions and bills of rights. Second, it detached the expectations from any particular religious tradition. Sometimes (as often in France) it stated its philosophy in atheistic terms. Sometimes (as usually in Great Britain and the United States) it remained more or less Christian, modifying the Christian traditions in the direction of a rationalistic theism or deism, independent of any specific revelation. It might, as in the case of the Declaration of Independence, appeal to "the Laws of Nature and Nature's God."

Simultaneously the Enlightenment, often without realizing it, recovered and modified one ancient biblical theme. It was the belief that history is not a static order but has about it an openness and dynamism that make possible a new and different future. The Bible had told of a God who led his people into a promised land or a promised era, who was bringing into being his kingdom. Puritanism renewed something of that spirit of expectation. The Enlightenment secularized it and turned it into the peculiarly modern idea of progress.

To many people in the eighteenth century the new faith was overwhelmingly persuasive. It required no suspension of reason, no deference to ecclesiastical authorities. It promised human liberation and a brighter future. It was, at least in theory, accessible to everyone. It was a matter of "self-evident" truths. The belief in "unalienable rights" as an endowment of "all men" had a kindling effect upon human imagination.

That effect is still evident in this final quarter of the twentieth century. But it has run into obstacles that the eager and confident voices of the Enlightenment could not have imagined.

A Troubled History and a Contemporary World

The history of the nineteenth and twentieth centuries is a commentary, both pathetic and sardonic, upon the high hopes of the Enlightenment. Britain, "mother of Parliaments," also became ruler of the greatest empire of all history—an empire which eventually faded as subject peoples demanded the rights enunciated in the British Enlightenment. In North America, the Continental Congress that adopted the Declaration of Independence went on to wage a successful war of Independence. The new nation then enacted a constitution enshrining some of the philosophy of the Declaration. But not even a century had elapsed before that nation fought a bloody Civil War in order to institutionalize some of the "self-evident truths" proclaimed in its Declaration of Independence but denied by its Constitution. France carried out its revolution, made its own Declaration of the Rights of Man (1789), and had its Reign of Terror; then the French set out upon the Napoleonic conquests, which led eventually to the Congress of Vienna, which effectively muted the hopes of the Enlightenment for some time to come.

The twentieth century has been a painful era for those committed to the human rights celebrated by the Enlightenment. The Soviet Revolution proclaimed its version of human rights and went on to the terrors of Stalinism. Nazism brought its own devastating assault on human rights. The Chinese Revolution is too young for even the preliminary assessments to be in, but its sense of the relation of the individual to society is noticeably different from the articulations of the British, American, and French revolutions. In a world of post-Enlightenment societies, South Africa stubbornly tries to live as though there had never been an Enlightenment, even though it embraces the Industrial Revolution that followed the Enlightenment. The United States, with its far-flung economic and military involvements, finds itself accused of neoimperialism and domestic injustice inconsistent with the innocent idealism of its origins.

In intellectual history the minds that have contributed most to the twentieth century are curiously related to the brave and simple reasoning of the Enlightenment. Charles Darwin developed ideas of nature radically different from the earlier faith in "the Laws of Nature and Nature's God"; and the Social Darwinism that followed him echoed something of the liberty but nothing of the equality of the eighteenth-century idealists. Karl Marx sought to emulate Darwin in developing a science of history, but his social thought was a refutation both of Enlightenment individualism and of Social Darwinism. Friedrich Nietzsche came to a fervent rejection of the doctrine of progress, a refutation of belief in equality, and a disdain for the utilitarianism of the nineteenth-century heirs of the Enlightenment. Sigmund Freud, in some ways as relentless a rationalist as any of the leaders of the Enlightenment, disclosed aspects of human nature far removed from Locke's notion of the human mind as like "white paper, void of all characters";[2] his ideas about the relation of civilization to the individual were far from the hopeful beliefs of the Declaration of Independence.

Hence, the faith of the Enlightenment has come to this late twentieth century in a sorely battered state. Yet many of its hopes have seized the imagination of humanity more impressively than ever before.

An obvious example is the United Nations Universal Declaration of Human Rights, adopted without dissent by the General Assembly on December 1, 1948. The document both continues and modifies the thinking of the Enlightenment. It even echoes and plays variations on the language of the American Declaration of Independence. Its preamble refers to "the equal and inalienable rights of all members of the human family."[3] Article 1 reads:

> All human beings are born free and equal in dignity and rights. They are endowed with reason and conscience and should act towards one another in a spirit of brotherhood.

[2] John Locke, *Essay Concerning Human Understanding*, bk. 2, ch. 1, sec. 2.

In our pluralistic world nobody can assume that all people are "created" equal; but the General Assembly can vote its conviction that they are "born" equal. If it is impossible to declare that people "are endowed by their Creator" with anything at all, it is still possible to say that "they are endowed with reason and conscience." There can be no agreement about "the Laws of Nature and Nature's God"; but there can be the affirmation of "inalienable rights." Instead of metaphysical proclamation about the nature of things, there is moral exhortation as to how people "should act." There is also pragmatic acknowledgment that recognition of human rights "is the foundation of freedom, justice and peace in the world."

The intention of this language is a little obscure. The signers

[3] The Preamble to the Universal Declaration of Human Rights reads as follows:

"WHEREAS recognition of the inherent dignity and of the equal and inalienable rights of all members of the human family is the foundation of freedom, justice and peace in the world,

"WHEREAS disregard and contempt for human rights have resulted in barbarous acts which have outraged the conscience of mankind, and the advent of a world in which human beings shall enjoy freedom of speech and belief and freedom from fear and want has been proclaimed as the highest aspiration of the common people,

"WHEREAS it is essential, if man is not to be compelled to have recourse, as a last resort, to rebellion against tyranny and oppression, that human rights should be protected by the rule of law,

"WHEREAS it is essential to promote the development of friendly relations among nations,

"WHEREAS the people of the United Nations have in the Charter reaffirmed their faith in fundamental human rights, in the dignity and worth of the human person and in the equal rights of men and women and have determined to promote social progress and better standards of life in larger freedom,

"WHEREAS Member States have pledged themselves to achieve, in cooperation with the United Nations, the promotion of universal respect for and observance of human rights and fundamental freedoms,

"WHEREAS a common understanding of these rights and freedoms is of the greatest importance for the full realization of this pledge,

"NOW THEREFORE The General Assembly proclaims

"THIS UNIVERSAL DECLARATION OF HUMAN RIGHTS as a common standard of achievement for all peoples and all nations, to the end that every individual and every organ of society, keeping this Declaration constantly in mind, shall strive by teaching and education to promote respect for these rights and freedoms and by progressive measures, national and international, to secure their universal and effective recognition and observance, both among the peoples of Member States themselves and among the peoples of territories under their jurisdiction."

of the American Declaration of Independence were, with all
their limitations, issuing a political manifesto, for which they
pledged, as they said, "our Lives, our Fortunes and our sacred
Honor." The UN Declaration, according to Eleanor Roosevelt,
who chaired the Commission of Human Rights, "does not pur-
port to be a statement of law or of legal obligation."[4] Yet
something in the climate of our time has led the nations of the
world to endorse it. In some important sense the Enlightenment, with its philosophy of human rights, is enthroned as
never before.

The curious situation today is a combination of three phenomena: the philosophical basis of the Enlightenment has been
eroded by modern skepticism and pluralism; the human rights
affirmed by the Enlightenment are nevertheless more widely
acclaimed around the world than in any past era; governments
often neglect or deliberately suppress the rights that are so
widely acknowledged.

The Waning Authority of
the Enlightenment

Unsurprisingly, the human rights affirmed by the Enlightenment were always controversial. Every old regime had power
blocs that resisted it. Wherever the Enlightenment prevailed,
there were reactions to the new trends. Such is still the case
today.

The newer situation is the erosion of the authority of the
Enlightenment among those who share much of its idealism.
Advocates of human rights today must come up with more persuasive reasoning than they inherit from the Enlightenment.
Deep fissures rend the foundations of human rights. People may
still struggle for human rights even though they cannot give
their reasons with the clarity of Locke or Jefferson. But when

[4] UN General Assembly, *3d Session, 1st Part, Official Records, Plenary,* 180th
Meeting, New York, p. 860.

conflicts arise—sometimes even among fervent advocates of human rights—it becomes important to get back to reasons for the rights.

The fact is that the Enlightenment doctrines have lost their authority. And nothing has replaced them. There are several reasons for the faltering of the Enlightenment:

THE ENLIGHTENMENT HAD A WEAKNESS FOR RHETORIC.

It did not dare examine some of its proudest assumptions. It disbelieved some of its most ringing pronouncements. For example, when the Declaration of Independence announced that "all men are created equal," it said more than it intended. All *men* did not include women; and *all* men did not include slaves or native Americans Indians.

The silence about slavery was a matter of embarrassed controversy in the Continental Congress. Jefferson's draft of the Declaration included, among the condemnations of King George, this one: "He has waged cruel war against human nature itself, violating its most sacred rights of life and liberty in the persons of a distant people who never offended him, captivating and carrying them into slavery in another hemisphere, or to incur miserable death in their transportation thither."[5] That line had to be excised before the Congress would adopt the Declaration. The ensuing Constitution, in the most cynical of its entries, provided for the counting of three-fifths of the slaves for purposes of representation in the House of Representatives, although the slaves could not vote (Article 1, Sec. 2).

Much of the turmoil about human rights in the twentieth century has been caused by tardy efforts, both within Western nations and around the world, to make good the unmet promises of the eighteenth century.

[5] See Carl Becker, *The Declaration of Independence* (New York: Vintage Books, 1958), p. 212.

THE ASSUMPTIONS OF THE ENLIGHTENMENT,
ALTHOUGH INTENDED AS BULWARKS AGAINST TRADITIONAL
CREDULITY, SOON CAME TO BE QUESTIONED.

The skeptical strain within the Enlightenment turned against the Enlightenment itself. The creators of the Enlightenment thought that their empiricism was clearing away inherited metaphysical deadwood and religious dogma, some of which was simply cumbersome and some of which was hostile to human rights. The rather gentle skepticism of Locke and the more radical skepticism of others were good instruments for this attic-cleaning. But it was not long before skepticism would turn against the legacy of belief that persisted in the British and American Enlightenments. The Enlightenment thought that it was empirical. Later, more radical empiricism would undermine its latent rationalism and its inherited doctrines.

Thus the Enlightenment intended to appeal to universal human experiences, not the particular experiences of specific historic communities. The Declaration of Independence invoked not the God of the Hebrews but "Nature and Nature's God." Some of the signers could not guess that later empiricists would find "Nature's God" as incredible as a God who spoke from Mount Sinai.

The twentieth century is looking for a foundation of human rights in a world where no truths are self-evident. Radical empiricism and cultural pluralism have done their work.

The UN Universal Declaration of Human Rights repeatedly edges up to the problem. Obviously it could not explore the issue in depth—not if it wanted to get a document voted within less than a century. Its preamble, without quite saying so, looks to three kinds of authority. One is functional: recognition of "equal and inalienable rights" is held to be "the foundation of freedom, justice and peace"—as though the latter were any more firmly founded than the former. A second is expressed in such phrases as "the conscience of mankind" and "the highest aspiration of the common people." The document cannot pause to ask what empirical evidence there is for a "conscience of mankind" or whether the aspirations of "common people" may not often be for the land and property of other common people. A third is the appeal to the Charter of the United Nations— which is like quoting oneself as an authority.

It may be better for human history that no sophisticated linguistic analysts shared in the drafting of the Declaration of Independence or the UN Universal Declaration of Human Rights. Such participants might have immobilized both assemblies. Some kinds of philosophy are luxuries for those who do not have to do the world's work. But all who would be both doers and thinkers must sometimes ask the reasons for their conduct. It is harder in the present cultural situation to give persuasive reasons for human rights than it appeared to be in the eighteenth century.

THE ENLIGHTENMENT HELD AN INDIVIDUALISTIC DOCTRINE OF THE HUMAN SELF.

It neglected the social aspects of personality. It is a symbolic coincidence that 1776 was the year both of the Declaration of Independence and of Adam Smith's *The Wealth of Nations.* The two documents assume an individualistic conception of selves interacting beneath "Nature's God" or an "invisible hand." More important is the deep reliance of the Enlightenment and the Declaration upon the doctrine of the social contract as the basis of government.

The idea of the social contract, whether meant literally or symbolically, was useful as an answer to claims of the divine right of kings. Although the notion of the social contract could, as in Thomas Hobbes, lead to an authoritarian political philosophy, it could also lead to philosophies of popular sovereignty and personal rights. Hence it served an effective polemical function. And it had some persuasiveness when, as in the forming of the Constitution of the United States, delegates of the states actually came together to establish the rules of a federal government.

But the social contract assumed an unreal individualism. Historically, government appears to be as old as individuals. At any rate, community is as primordially human as individuality. A century of scholarship—sociology, cultural anthropology, and social psychology—has made the point. Philosophers like George Herbert Mead, John Dewey, and Martin Buber have pondered its meanings for selfhood. Selves that are recognized as human—that is, selves with language and all the other gifts that a culture offers to individuals—are as much products of community as communities are assemblies of selves. Individuals may in rare cases choose to leave communities and live as hermits—although not until culture has nurtured them through a long infancy and childhood in which they have internalized much of the culture.

It remains true that the individual needs protection from the tyrannies, whether cruel or benign, of culture. And it remains true that individuals can enter into political associations and change operations of government. All that the Enlightenment saw well, and the twentieth century needs to see it. But the relation between individual and community—and there is no community without government—is far more mutual, complex, and subtle than the Enlightenment realized.

THE ENLIGHTENMENT STOPPED SHORT OF SOME HARD QUESTIONS ABOUT HUMAN RIGHTS.

Hence it was silent on many issues that now trouble the world. It showed courage in taking on a sizable agenda. But the gaps in its doctrine of rights were immense. For example, Locke's *Letters on Toleration* show a refreshing and humane openness after the religious wars of Britain and continental Europe. They might still bring a refreshing spirit into contemporary religious strife (for example in Ireland and Lebanon).

But their boldness suddenly pales when Locke explains that the state should not tolerate religious doctrines that "undermine the foundations of society." Examples are churches with allegiance to foreign jurisdictions (the transubstantiation of Roman Catholicism does not bother Locke, but the papacy does) and atheism, since it dissolves "promises, covenants, and oaths."[6]

A century later the United States' Bill of Rights goes considerably farther than Locke in its guarantees of freedom of speech and religion. But the twentieth century has seen far more litigation on those subjects than the preceding century, as courts try to decide whether pornography (including exploitation of children), Nazi parades, and racial defamation are constitutionally protected.

A second example of contemporary perplexity that did not trouble the Enlightenment comes in the area of economic rights. One theme of the UN Universal Declaration of Human Rights is conspicuously absent in our own Declaration of Independence and Bill of Rights:

> Everyone has the right to a standard of living adequate for the health and well-being of himself and of his family, including food, clothing, housing and medical care and necessary social services, and the right to security in the event of unemployment, sickness, disability, widowhood, old age or other lack of livelihood in circumstances beyond his control.
>
> (Article 25, Section 1)

The sweeping statement says little about the translation from intention to enactment, but it comes close to the heart of many controversies about human rights today. The Enlightenment gave attention to the right to own property; apart from that, it knew little about human economic rights.

Bertrand Russell has said: "Locke's political philosophy was, on the whole, adequate and useful until the industrial revolu-

---

[6] John Locke, "The Spirit of Toleration," in *Locke: Selections*, ed. Sterling Lamprecht (New York: Scribner's, 1928), pp. 49–50.

tion. Since then, it has been increasingly unable to tackle the important problems." [7] The irony is that the Industrial Revolution had much to do with the spread of the Enlightenment around the world. The inheritance of the Enlightenment was helpful to colonized peoples rebelling against colonial powers, which were often the nations where the Enlightenment originally flourished. The legacy of the British Enlightenment, proved more useful to India in its struggle for freedom from Britain than in its subsequent struggle against hunger— although the resistance to Indira Gandhi's dictatorial policies showed that the values of the Enlightenment have persisted there. China has taken (via Marxism) that strain of the Enlightenment which sought widespread happiness as a secular human goal, but is not interested in most of the Enlightenment's political values.

Where the Enlightenment flourished, governmental interventions in social and economic life have expanded. In politics, "liberalism" once meant the effort to limit the powers of government, in the tradition of the Enlightenment. Since Franklin Roosevelt and the New Deal, conservatives in America have taken the old "liberal" line.

THE ENLIGHTENMENT HAD TOO SIMPLE AN UNDERSTANDING
OF HUMAN NATURE.

It sought to pit reason against foolishness and prejudice, sometimes with admirable courage, but with little sense of the ecstatic or demonic possibilities of human beings. Alfred North Whitehead has said of the Enlightenment: "It was the age of reason, healthy, manly, upstanding reason; but of one-eyed reason, deficient in its vision of depth." [8] And Carl Becker qualifies his admiration of Thomas Jefferson by writing: "One would like more evidence that the iron had some time or other

[7] Bertrand Russell, *A History of Western Philosophy* (New York: Simon and Schuster, 1945), p. 640.
[8] Alfred North Whitehead, *Science and the Modern World* 2d ed (New York: Macmillan, 1947), p. 86.
[9] Carl Becker, *The Declaration of Independence*, pp. 218–19.

entered his soul, more evidence of his having profoundly reflected upon the enigma of existence, of having more deeply felt
its tragic import, of having won his convictions and his optimism and his felicities at the expense of some painful travail of
the spirit."[9] Becker concludes that the faith of the Enlightenment was "a humane and engaging faith," but a faith that
"could not survive the harsh realities of the modern world."[10]

One can read long in the writings of the Enlightenment
without finding any clue that human beings are male and fe-
male; that their personalities include those qualities that would
later be labeled (more or less adequately) ego, superego, and id;
that the purported "laws of Nature and Nature's God" are
frequently the habits of particular cultures, and that people find
their identity as much in culture as in nature. There are few
clues to what in retrospect seem so obvious: that the Age of
Enlightenment would inevitably provoke a Romantic Era. Ro-
manticism would prove to be a poor, often disastrous, creator of
political philosophies. And some people in the twentieth century would find themselves flying the banners of the Enlightenment alongside those not of the Enlightenment, in gales that
threatened to shred all such banners.

Toward Reconstruction

In the years ahead, I expect, there will be many efforts to
reconstruct a doctrine of human rights. Some of us will aspire to
the improbable goal of some international consensus on human
rights that will do for our time what the Enlightenment did for
a small region in its time.

HUMAN RIGHTS MUST STAND ON SOME RECOGNITION OF
BOTH PLURALISM AND CONSENSUS.

Without pluralism, forced conformity denies human rights.
Without some consensus, society is impossible. At least since

[10]*Ibid.*, pp. 278, 279.

Herodotus, some people have been sensitive to the pluralism of cultures and subcultures. But the more typical practice has been to assume that one's own ethos is normative and to impose it on others. The Enlightenment saw itself as far more appreciative of diversity and dissent than the Middle Ages or the period of religious wars. But it assumed too easily that all reasonable people could recognize common moral principles.

Radical pluralism means that there are no self-evident truths. Yet a society must concur on some values and rules—at a minimum, on methods for resolving some disagreements, allowing others to flourish, and deciding which ones must be resolved and which may flourish.

With today's weapons a world must find some consensus if civilization is not to perish.

Furthermore, contemporary pluralism must recognize that people find their identities in various collective groups—tribal, ethnic, national, and religious—which are far more particular than the human race. The Enlightenment knew something about persons both as individuals and as samples of the human race. It thought that common rationality could transcend historic particularities. The twentieth century is more aware that persons are social, within particular cultures.

There are terrible dangers in this notion of the social self. It can lead to Hegelian nationalism, to creeds of blood and soil, to such travesties of humanity as Nazism, to racism. Advocates of human rights must struggle against these distortions of humanity. But they will not help their struggle by failing to notice that even the most cosmopolitan human spirits are quite particular in their social identities. Racial and ethnic minorities, for example, often recognize the "universalism" of the dominant races as one more particularism bent on wiping out the particularism of minorities. Hence the minorities often want to reassert their ethnic heritages, sometimes in the face of long suppression of their own "roots."

In the United States advocates of human rights, who once

sought to be "color-blind," have more recently heightened their sensitivity to color in an effort to redress past wrongs. The UN Universal Declaration of Human Rights states that "higher education shall be equally accessible to all on the basis of merit" (Article 26). But is that ideal best realized by ignoring race and color, or by "affirmative action" programs that set "goals"— possibly "quotas"—for university admissions and faculty appointments? On such a question the Enlightenment has little to say.

Likewise in the international sphere it is easier to advocate an abstract liberty and equality for all individuals than to say precisely what these rights mean for Israelis, Palestinian Arabs, Lebanese, and Egyptians. Justice is harder to define and more subtle in its meaning than the Enlightenment thought. Somehow a doctrine of human rights today must take account of individuality, group identity, and universalism as it addresses the issues of pluralism and consensus.

HUMAN RIGHTS MUST BE WORKED OUT WITHIN A DIALECTIC OF FREEDOM AND COERCION.

That dialectic is more intricate than traditional doctrines have supposed. Since the most coercive society allows some personal freedoms and the most libertarian society imposes some obligations, advocates of human rights may simply try to tip the balance toward the side of freedom. But that picture falsifies the complex relations between freedom and coercion. More freedom sometimes requires more coercion.

The right to education is an interesting case in point. The UN Universal Declaration of Human Rights (Article 26) says: "Everyone has the right to education. Education shall be free, at least in the elementary and fundamental stages. Elementary education shall be compulsory." The combination of the words "free" and "compulsory"—as well as the unstated proposition that "free" education usually requires compulsory taxation—is a clue to the paradoxical relations between freedom and coercion.

Industrial civilization has brought increasing governmental regulation in the common life. Traffic controls on roads and in the air, rules about food and drugs, laws about collective bargaining, prohibitions of monopolies—these are a few cases of compulsion for the sake of freedom and safety. The consumers' movement in the United States—a form of human rights movement—has increased government regulation. It may be that regulation is sometimes excessive today; that does not deny the point that there is a dialectic of freedom and coercion.

So long as the civil rights movement sought some elemental political freedoms—elimination of compulsory segregation, the right to vote, etc.—the tradition of the Enlightenment served it well. The coercion necessary to secure such rights was relatively small and clearly definable. As the movement went on to such issues as cultural deprivation and access to jobs—as indeed it had to do, if human rights were to be meaningful—far more intricate agencies of coercion became necessary.

When Franklin D. Roosevelt defined the Four Freedoms, three of these—freedom of speech and religion, freedom from fear—rested firmly in the Enlightenment tradition. The fourth—freedom from want—recognized a quite different human right. For many of the world's people a free press is less important than access to food. Hence they may relate human rights to an authoritarian socialism rather than to an individualistic democracy. It is easy to say that human rights should include both political and economic rights. But to relate the two kinds of rights and work out the relation between freedom and coercion in both is a task that challenges the best of human wisdom.

Even more difficult problems lie ahead. Some of these are connected with the ecological limits on human society. Others come out of new technologies that make possible the reconstruction of the human genetic constitution. For example, do all human beings have a right to reproduce? And do human beings have a right to reproduce as much as they want? A heritage of human rights from the Enlightenment (among other things) has made it harder for India to restrain population growth than for China, which lacks such a heritage.

The issue of the dialectic between freedom and coercion will be prominent on the agenda of human rights for as long as anybody can foresee.

HUMAN RIGHTS WILL REQUIRE FIRMNESS OF COMMITMENT
COMBINED WITH EXPERIMENTALISM OF DESIGN, BOTH
IN UNPRECEDENTED DEGREE.

These two attitudes, the one often associated with ethical absolutism and the other with relativism, are not easily combined. Yet their combination is essential. Commitment will be in some ways harder to sustain than it was for the Enlightenment, because it does not have so many obvious forces going for it. The Enlightenment could claim the support of rationality, self-evident truths, "the Laws of Nature and Nature's God," the progress of history. In today's pluralistic world all these are questioned. Those who believe in human rights must struggle for real institutional change without assurances of quick or enduring success. Frustration and defeat are as characteristic of the human story as is victory.

In an interesting way the UN Universal Declaration of Human Rights touches on this theme. In many respects its philosophy is a secularization of the philosophy of the Declaration of Independence, which is already a secularization of preceding traditions. Yet the UN Declaration, reaching for a word that Jefferson did not need, refers to "faith" in human rights. The word is appropriate, because faith usually refers to a venturing beyond empirically grounded certainties and a commitment beyond empirical assurances of success.

Faith, however, as the Enlightenment knew it, was often associated with dogmatic rigidities hostile to the experimental institutional devices needed today. No fixed codes, whether inscribed on tablets of stone or on parchment, are adequate to the securing of human rights today. It is sometimes said that our time needs new social inventions, as innovative as representative parliaments once were. Whether such inventions will come, nobody knows. But clearly, experimentalism in the social process, combined with firmness of commitment, is needed.

Reinhold Niebuhr has suggested the combination:

> Every society needs working principles of justice, as criteria for its positive law and system of restraints. The profoundest of these actually transcend reason and lie rooted in religious conceptions of the meaning of existence. But every historical statement of them is subject to amendment. If it becomes fixed it will destroy some of the potentialities of a higher justice, which the mind of one generation is unable to anticipate in the life of subsequent eras.[11]

It is not likely that this generation will find a formulation of human rights so definitive and satisfying as a select segment of humanity found in the Enlightenment. Any venture involving the earth's nations, races, cultures, and social classes is bound to be far more difficult than the more limited venture of the intellectuals of the Enlightenment. But the world has entered an era when tremors of discontent and injustice resonate far more widely than ever before. The consequent opportunities and perils are plain. The search for a conscience of humanity and a realization of human rights must continue.

[11] Reinhold Niebuhr, *The Children of Light and the Children of Darkness* (New York: Scribner's, 1944), p. 176.

FIFTEEN

Schooling and the Search for a Usable Politics

HOWARD B. RADEST

I

TODAY, UNFORTUNATELY, philosophic naturalism [1] is seldom taken seriously. Except for a vulgar identification of the pragmatic with the practical and opportunistic, naturalism, the philosophic movement native to the American scene, seems to be only an item in the history of ideas. By looking at one of its outcomes, progressivism in education, we may be able to illustrate naturalism's unrealized and still relevant virtues. This, it seems to me, is particularly appropriate in celebrating Joseph Blau whose career is rooted in America's naturalistic traditions.

I want to address myself to progressivism in education precisely because schooling, here and abroad, is in terrifying disarray and, hence, is truly one of the "problems of men." More and more people are in schools of one kind or another while schoolmen and women at the same time confess their helplessness. Partisans argue the benefits of "basics" or "bilingualism"

---

[1] There are, of course, many variations within naturalism and pragmatism, nor are these terms synonymous. However, for purposes of a short essay, the finer distinctions can probably be ignored.

or "vocationalism" or a "return to the liberal arts." In the midst
of this clamor, illiteracy increases and is further encouraged in
its growth by resort to whatever is latest in "gimmickry"—
which usually turns out to be useless. Education budgets grow.
Perversely, it seems that educational effectiveness decreases almost in precise degree to which investment increases.

More generally, educational excitement is vanishing. The
days of "relevance"—the mad, sentimental, romantic wildness
of the 1960s—are over; the quiescent days of a "silent generation" are upon us. But that silence barely masks anger and frustration. Beneath the calm, there grows an anxiety of culture, a
culture that has grown so shapeless and even so bizarre as to
jeopardize its defensible goals. It is not surprising, then, that
schooling should be mystified and mystifying, for it is a puzzle-
ment indeed in the present circumstance to know what to teach,
to whom, how, where, and above all, for what reasons.

This is all the more problematic for liberals. Liberal society,
we know, tends to rely on "education" as a method, if not *the*
method, of politics. Schooling, like liberal politics, has a long
history. Characteristically, while revolution surged through the
streets of Paris, Condorcet was introducing legislation for public
education to the nascent French Republic. In America, liberal
policy still turns to the schools—whether to assimilate immigrants into an American culture or to respond to a Soviet
"challenge" by investing in "post-Sputnik" scientism. To be
sure, such more recent turns to schooling reflect inherited cultural habits and even a renewed faith in magic—above all,
perhaps, a confession that nothing else seems to work. Rather
than making a critical decision to commit to schooling as a progressive political method, modern liberal policy, then, often
reflects its own vacuousness. For want of better alternatives or in
fear of radical politics, liberal culture turns to the schools again
and again—but without ideas. Alas, the schools become thereby
a hiding place for helplessness or for political disingenuousness.
A further loss of confidence in liberal society is, then, not

surprising, since the schools seem to serve merely as "dumping" grounds for unresolved problems or, more cynically, as agencies of "co-optation."

If liberal social policies today often seem to be blind and even vicious, the progressivism which was shaped in philosophic naturalism was not. So, education as political method developed from it out of a new view of the possibilities of human nature for growth and of society for democratic development. Above all, schooling conceived as the method of democracy was being given a new psychological content and social mission. To be sure, schooling had been connected with a variety of social ethics. Thus, both Greek *paideia* and Tory "character formation" relied on schooling to enform persons with perennial values that were interpreted as social and cosmic.

Progressivism, however, represented a departure from such personalistic and aristocratic commitments and moved, instead, toward inclusive schooling as the ground of a participatory politics. In this context, politics was not in the first instance a matter of parties, laws, governments, or candidates. Rather, it was conceived as empowering human agents capable of shaping themselves and their worlds. Schooling as politics rested on the claim that moral agency could be rational and instructed and need not be merely sentimental or willful, that politics could be intended for the general welfare and not just for particular goods, and that any moral agent could benefit from learning the activities of other agents, past or contemporary. Politics was indeed an "architectonic" discipline, as Aristotle had it—form-giving and society-constructing. As it was connected inextricably with moral judgment, politics was value-filled and never merely prudential.

Progressivism, unlike its more conservative relatives, proposed that both persons and societies were ever incomplete and so politics was always an opening toward a future. Most radically of all, the fulfillment in part of that future, but never the entire determination of it—for progressives were not perfec-

tionists—was within the grasp of all persons who were able to
shape themselves, their culture, and even their universe. This
commitment to radical human agency represented and represents still the relevant point of entry for another look at educational progressivism.

Commitment to human agency in this progressive context
must be distinguished from the utter voluntarism of modern ex-
istentialism with its focus on the defiant act. Less dramatic and
soulful, progressively agency was for its proponents a feature of
"organized intelligence" taking social forms as scientific inquiry, democratic polity, and progressive education. It was not
then egoistic but sociable. With its roots in Western classicism
and its sources in eighteenth-century rationalism, progressivism
was a ready victim of the terrifying realities of the middle of the
twentieth century. Against the apparently overwhelming evidence of human viciousness and the irrationality of modern mass
violence, the claims of human intelligence and of the possibilities of rational morality and coherent policy seemed irredeemably optimistic. Indeed, the common criticism of progressivism—as of its parent, naturalism—was its failure to meet the
experience of the twentieth century, a drastic indictment indeed
of a philosophy which claimed to be a philosophy of experience.

We may notice too that the attack on progressive schooling
was an attack on the presumed ability of schooling to be socially
critical. Thus, from the left, schooling was understood as inevitably a function of class interest. Along with other "bourgeois"
institutions, schooling was but another vehicle of "false consciousness." On the political right, education as "basic" education was still linked to essential and eternal truths. Hence, it
could not properly create anything novel but could only "recall"
the permanent. By left and right, then, schooling was taken as
a dependent activity with its content derived from external
sources. Teachers, students, and parents were merely transmit-
ters and receivers of messages located elsewhere in their sources
and going elsewhere in their ends. Schooling was thus not a

politics of agency at all, but, in some general sense, always and only a preparation for life elsewhere.

Ironically, the liberal center today appears to agree with the notion that the function of schooling is merely preparatory—indeed a failure of nerve. Vocationalism, an appropriate successor to the scientism of the Sputnik era, is typical of this thinking. The "value" of education is to be measured by its effectiveness in training people for careers. Thus, unwittingly, the center validates the critiques of left and of right. Since the marketplace as seen from the left is inevitably exploitive, so schooling by serving it must be inevitably corrupt. On the right, the marketplace is seen as self determining, so schooling except for training is pointless. The center, having surrendered its point of view, thus ceases to be intelligible as a center. This utter failure of intelligibility, with unconscious satire, is called "pragmatic," which thereby becomes a mere name for moment-to-moment reactions guided by pseudo-ends like the "bottom line." Perhaps out of a guilty conscience, the center talks of "excellence" too—not as a general and generous development of human talents but as the location of some new and more deserving elite.

To be sure, a careless use of language among the classicists of naturalism seems—but only seems—to justify saddling progressives with this modern outcome. So, Dewey's "instrumentalism" invites practicalism and James's "cash value" seems to sanction the worst forms of a market mentality. The serious question, however, is substantive and not editorial: is a postmodern progressivism possible in education?

II

The key to schooling as usable politics lies in the notion of "reconstruction."[2] Unlike "reform" or, more pallidly, "social

[2] I am aware that "reconstruction" is used in a special way by Theodore Brameld and others. My own usage in this essay is, I trust, more general although that does not necessarily mean that I reject Brameld's social democratic views.

change," reconstruction stresses the constitutive role of persons in the active building up of culture and society. It identifies the fact that no building up ever starts from virgin ground; it is always a reconstruction. By contrast, "contract" theories, a different source for a different center now enjoying some popularity, are not to be confused with progressivism. Such theories rely on some putative original moment, a "state of nature," whether in Hobbesian or Rawlsian form. Progressivism, reflecting its naturalistic roots, always begins in the middle of things and denies the possibility or value of searching for or postulating some abstract beginning.

Reconstruction takes its meaning from its presence within a democratic situation; i.e., reconstruction entails participation. It is impossible, on naturalistic grounds, to designate *a priori* some finite set of persons as uniquely qualified to be agents. To do so would require an extra-experiential vision of nature and human nature derived, let us say, from some variation on Plato's gold, silver, and bronze souls. By contrast, human events teach the nonpredictably good and not so good in any person. For naturalism, human nature is itself a theme of active inquiry and not a term of cosmology. We are to learn who we are by what we are able and enabled to do. Reconstruction thus represents the reformulation of a Jeffersonian "revolution" made permanent. As a democratic politics, reconstruction is proposed as an alternative to stasis (against liberalism) or to periodic wars of each against all (terrorism).

It is no accident, then, that the idea of reconstruction in a variety of ways is central to progressivism which, as a theory of radical rational human agency, requires a tutored social intelligence. This rests in the hypothesis that, for the human animal, habits replace instinct and so human conduct is naturally open and corrigible. Unlike pedagogies of preparation, however, for which schooling is a present activity for the sake of some future effectiveness, progressive methodology sees present activity always within presented and actually present goals. So experienced, ways of dealing with every present become available as ways of learning personal capacities in the midst of social possibilities. The connection between method and end, then, is not mechanical or causal—in the sense, let us say, of temporal sequence—but organic and implicative. Learning arises within events that by nature are simultaneously means and ends and as such are a present "having" and also a "leading out." All experience is educationally potent just as all education is in itself a worthwhile experience.

It is in the context of corrigibility that schooling appears at the center of democratic politics from the beginning. It is also for this reason that progressivism once represented a next step, a step from the pastoral into the industrial world. Clearly, this is quite a weight to put on schooling. It would seem more sensible, at first glance, to rely more directly on what we ordinarily call politics itself. But this would miss the point of a progressive criticism of "realism" in politics; such politics represents the failure of intelligence just because it aims directly at issues of power per se. Where this is not the case, as in Aristotelian politics and ethics, a complementary organicism appears, a theory of human nature and nature as both source and outcome of what is by nature normative activity. In short, progressivism seized anew a classical inspiration as against varieties of Machiavellianism. Progressivism was not thus modernist at all and indeed from a certain point of view might even be judged counter-modern in its rejection of positivism and other primitive empiricisms.

For progressivism, sociability is the way human beings take their means and their ends. Social forms thus mediate means and ends generally so that, for example, means do not attach to machinery while ends attach to cosmos. The mere "self," the "old individualism" as it was called, really leads us away from democratic reconstruction even while pretending to be democratic value incarnate. In educational form, as so-called self-education, it is only an "ego" activity, as appears quite clearly in today's notions of "self fulfillment" which are often utterly asocial and certainly idiosyncratic. Such a misnamed "self" both avoids and voids all sociality. Arising in a "negative" interpretation of what it means to be free, even were it possible, such a "self" in principle is without any polity at all—it is not democratic, aristocratic, totalitarian, or even anarchic since all of these imply some form of sociability. An individualist schooling is then delusional. Where "self" refers to a rejection of the world, it does not require schooling at all but rather "disciplines" for meeting unavoidable demands as in some types of mysticism. Here, "self" education is misnamed. Clearly what is intended is not schooling at all but an experience of the extra-mundane which is also extra-egoistic. A "school," however, is any locus of learning and is then a necessary outcome of the notion of schooling as a form of sociability. So, for example, "deschooling" society carries with it the self-contradictory directive to desocialize society as well. It is an invitation not to anarchism but to chaos, which is another matter entirely.

Why, however, the progressive reliance on schooling rather than on more traditional social forms like family or church? Certainly, the family serves to mediate means and ends, as for example in relations between generations, in social rituals, and the like. Yet, precisely where family is strongest it must set itself apart from and even on occasion be hostile to all other socialities. For example, where family values are most impressive the distinction between "Greeks and barbarians" is most sharply drawn. This, of course, is the paradox of community, its negative condition so to speak. Family introduces a separation of persons by restricting who may and who may not count as its participants. Nor is this merely a fact, since "kinship" is by no means dictated by biology. On these grounds, family cannot be the mediating form of democratic society—any more than the "individual" can be. This is, of course, counter to democratic common sense and suggests the critical importance of progressive analysis. On the other hand, this does not deny the importance of familial values, as for example a human experience of particularisms and intimacies. Just because other institutions cannot do, however, the school as a "public" schooling does not appear for progressivism as an imperative of the "melting pot" or some other historic accident. The school is an implication of democratic reconstruction itself having to do with a *res publica,* with a general and never only with a particular good.

This view of schooling, however, raises a troubling question. How can we expect a social form appearing as an institution within a society to be "marginal"—i.e., critical and independent of its own society and culture. Yet, if schooling is to serve reconstruction, it cannot be entirely within the culture it is intended to reconstruct. Certainly, in practice if not in theory, ordinary politics shapes the school much more than it shapes politics. Teachers and students already are tutored by the particularisms of class and caste before they enter the school. Reliance on schooling then might seem only a further demonstration of progressive naïveté and of the inadequacy of its theory. The requirement of marginality turns in a sense then into a crucial question: what are the conditions and possibilities of marginality?

We are, in effect, trying to find out what counts as a school and why. There are, to be sure, institutions called "schools" which do social training and others which serve as apologists for culture or subculture. However, as a mediating institution, the school properly so called is committed to corrigibility for both persons and the culture itself. Failing that it is not a school at all. Its function thus takes it to the margin over and over again. It is at the same time implicated in its society as one of its institutions and yet required by its own imperative to provide a critical reflection on its society. Even in pretending only to transmit social values, schooling interprets—it never simply replicates as it mediates between generations, classes, and castes. Its very function then forces attention to alternatives even where the legitimacy of all alternatives to what exists is denied.

That is why teaching is, per se, a "subversive" activity and why cultures defend themselves by trying to substitute trainers for teachers when they can. And, that is why, on principled grounds, "automated" teaching and the like is a contradiction in terms since teachers always bring with them a history, a politics, and a subjectivity in addition to some announced curriculum. Robots cannot be subjects in this sense and cannot therefore be teachers.

It might be suggested, by way of contrast, that the church, unlike the school, is by its nature more available as a marginal institution. Its transcendent reference—whether to some cosmic truth or humanistic ideal—would always seem to take it part of the way out of its culture. But precisely because of this transcendent reference the church can be itself and yet be utterly uninterested in social reconstruction; it can quite reasonably "render unto Caesar" without being dishonest to itself. So, while its marginality might be admitted, its sociability need not be.

Of course, more than transcendence disqualifies the church for reconstruction. Historically and sadly, successful churches notoriously succumb to stasis which is why they need the periodic uprooting of prophecy and heresy. But this uprooting need not be sociable at all. The school like the church may surrender to stability too. But its heresies cannot properly ignore sociability. This suggests that religious marginality is "vertical." Religion has a different reference and, at least logically, need not seek to sanctify the secular world at all. Churches, finally, as legitimate forms of faith are particularized even when they are not corrupted, as today, into merely private enclaves. In that sense, under the best of conditions, they cannot be and at the same time only be representative of some "common faith." Hence, their very strength and legitimacy disqualifies them as agents of reconstruction. So, in a sense, for want of other traditional alternatives, progressivism properly came to rely on schooling.

The question of marginality thus becomes: what is necessary in order for schooling to be what progressives say it intends to be?

III

If the function of schooling is self-consciously reconstructive and never just replicative, then marginality entails a need for independent standpoints from which to establish legitimate cultural criticisms and social actions. From a progressive point of view, this marginality is a requirement of all schooling as such—even where more conservative schoolmen do not admit to it. For progressivism, the problem of marginality developed when its view of schooling's "social" nature was misleadingly interpreted by some progressives and by their critics as meaning that progressivism was based always and only within its culture. But progressive discussion had recognized an independent standpoint for the school against the cultural and social values of its location. So, for example, John Dewey[3] commented about teachers:

> The sum of the matter is that the times are out of joint and that teachers cannot escape, even if they would, some responsibility for a share in putting them right. They may regard it, like Hamlet, as a cursed spite or as an opportunity. But, they cannot avoid the responsibility. Drifting is merely a cowardly mode of choice. I am not trying here to tell teachers with which of the antagonistic tendencies of our own time they should align themselves—although I have my own conviction on that subject. I am trying only to point out that the conflict is here and that as matter of fact they are strengthening one set of forces or the other. The question is whether they are doing so blindly, evasively, or intelligently and courageously. If a teacher is conservative and wishes to throw in his lot with forces that seem to me reactionary and

[3] Since John Dewey was the naturalist most committed to the place of schooling in progressive theory, I shall rely on his formulations from time to time as illustrative of a forgotten progressivism. However, as I trust will be clear, Dewey was by no means the only naturalist who developed the inhering connection between philosophy and progressive pedagogy.

that will in the end, from my point of view, increase present chaos, at all events let him do it intelligently, after a study of the situation, and a conscious choice made on the basis of intelligent study. The same thing holds for the liberal and radical.[4]

It is by no means inconsistent, as Dewey illustrates, for progressivism to reject mere relativism. Indeed, a review of progressivism in its classic form, as an emergent feature of philosophic naturalism, demonstrates its continuing search for reliable sources of critique that meet the double requirement of independence of culture and avoidance of dualism—in the progressive search for scientific "laws," an "objective" psychology, etc.

I cannot here solve the epistemological and metaphysical problems I am now going to raise as a reminder of our lost progressivism. It is clear enough, however, that "inquiry" itself interacts (or "transacts") with objects that are independent of inquiry, i.e., a world in some sense that is not reducible only to some psychosocial world. Misinterpreted as the notion that naturalism holds that things are just what they seem to be, this transactional view has been described as "naïve" realism and so dismissed by persuasive name calling. Nevertheless, "objects" in an "object world" are necessary if inquiry is to be anything more than an exercise in inward reflection and self-delusion. That, after all, was the heart of a naturalistic criticism of the subjectivism of earlier empiricisms and it was the basis of its own "radical" empiricism. Unfortunately, the notion of "intersubjectivity," which played such a significant role in naturalistic logic, misled us. A shared culture world, for example, could indeed be intersubjective without having to make any reference to other features of existence at all. Charles Peirce, in describing a community of inquiry as the convergence over time toward singular validated knowings, was most explicit but not alone in

[4] John Dewey, *Philosophy and Education* (Problems of Men) (Totowa, New Jersey: Littlefield Adams and Company, 1966), p. 71.

denying such a purely cultural and hence relativistic epistemology as an interpretation of intersubjectivity. Yet, in its anxiety to clarify its method and in order to attack traditional dualisms, naturalism surrendered too quickly the possibilities of a critical ontology. This, in turn, forced progressivism as a politics of reconstruction into a philosophic dilemma.

The particular reality for schooling is the person as such who is not only a creature of culture and society; i.e., progressivism was grounded in a psychobiological realism. Unfortunately, the debate on this point developed in politicized discussions of human nature, as in the endless and indeterminate debates between proponents of "nature" and "nurture." To be sure, a "real" person is not merely some mechanical sum of biological endowment and environmental influence in continuing interactivity; the person was in part always external to culture although personhood was not therefore genetically fixed. Deny the elusiveness of personhood, for example, and the endless variations of the personal within any culture would be utterly unintelligible. Again, Dewey illustrates this reach for a philosophic psychology and shows that progressivism did not have to presume the absolute maleability of persons, anything like the "blank tablet," or the unfettered flowering of a preexistent but blocked innate human stuff. Later progressivism, unfortunately, seemed to advocate one or another of these views, some variation on environmentalism and sentimentality. So, by contrast, Dewey commented on the child in school as follows:

> There are those who see no alternative between forcing the child from without or leaving him entirely alone. Seeing no alternative, some choose one mode, some another. Both fall into the same fundamental error. Both fail to see that development is a definite process, having its own law which can be fulfilled only when adequate and normal conditions are provided. Really to interpret the child's present crude impulses in counting, measuring, and arranging things in rhythmic series involves mathematic scholarship—a knowledge of mathematical formulae and relations which have, in the history of the race, grown out of just such crude beginnings. To see the whole history of development

which intervenes between these two terms is simply to see what steps the child needs to take just here and now; to what use he needs to put his blind impulse in order that it may get clarity and gain force.[5]

Along with an ontological and biological realism, a third independent reference sustaining the possibility of marginality is found in an objectivity of values. Again here, tradition is misleading for such a claim is often put in terms that embed values in the cosmos itself. If true, of course, that would turn value inquiry into a form of physics. The opposing view—in the name of liberation—defended the position that values were "nothing but" reflections of a particular set of culture choices, a kind of elaborated conventionalism. Certain liberal virtues seem to follow, varieties on the theme of toleration which came to be justified, as well, by the paraphernalia of the social sciences—e.g. comparative culture study. However, if values are only culture-reflections, it follows that only within any given culture is it possible to make a moral claim, and it would never be possible to make a moral claim against a culture. Values would thus be reducible to descriptions and, perhaps, to typological tables which might help to identify kindred cultures or to locate common cultural roots. As between cosmos and culture, the claim that values are independently real in some sense was defended by progressives although only partially and with increasing difficulty. So, for instance, Dewey argued for "funded experience," and naturalism generally did not find a language of "ideal" possibilities—natural possibilities that transcended the social and cultural past—alien to it.

In short, for schooling to be a usable politics it needs references to extra-cultural and extra-social realities; and it can find them in progressivism. We might even put the question in Kantian form by asking, how is schooling possible—and so propose the eventual search for a Kantian "deduction." Natural-

<hr />

[5] John Dewey, *The Child and the Curriculum* (Chicago: University of Chicago Press, 1956), p. 17.

ism, traditionally, has located just such an object world(s) although often without being explicit about it for tactical reasons. Such worlds, however, show again how closely naturalism as a general theory and progressivism as a theory of education are tied to each other and to critical philosophy, as in a theory of inquiry, a theory of human development, and a theory of values. To be sure, these central features of naturalism which gave coherence to progressivism were lost when the latter turned from a philosophic to a merely empirical psychology. A concentration on second-order virtues appeared—on toleration, openness, comparative study—which led to near denial of first-order virtues like goodness and truthfulness. Unlike "state of nature" liberalisms, however, progressivism's claims for human autonomy and of a real world out there did not rest on an abstract device like the "social contract." Instead, progressivism relied both on its Hegelian roots in a view of human history as "natural" history and on the generic meanings of science. So, for example, "history" became one form and "science" another in which extra-cultural and extra-social reality could be grounded and from which reconstruction could be advanced. Naturalism then has its relevant traditions in critical theory which made and make marginality for the sake of reconstruction a rational possibility. Progressivism then need not be confounded with a reductive theory of culture or an absolutist theory of society.

IV

A usable politics based in an "independent" reality is quite intelligible to progressives. I suggest, moreover, that the need to emphasize this independence—in intelligence, self-hood, and value—is peculiarly apt in a post-modern world. Independence, in other words, is much more an issue for us today than when the progressive struggle was against another opponent, i.e., moral absolutism and metaphysical dualism, and so when comparative study, and toleration, seemed more germane strategically. Progressivism today, however, is undermined more by an uncritical liberalism than by "forces of reaction."

The modern liberal temptation is an appalling subjectivism, and with it a deliberate rejection of organized intelligence. Motivated, no doubt, by dreams of freedom, this contemporary corruption of progressivism is in its unrecognized import far more destructive of liberating than of conservative values. So, when moral and other judgments of value are reduced to mere "matters of taste"—or, which is the same thing, to acts of isolated egos—we do not really threaten traditionalist moral agencies at all. They, after all, expect that of liberalism and indeed are even strengthened by such a chaos of privatism. It is understandable, too, that we should approach the sciences skeptically. Too often, scientists have succumbed to the calls of scientism and the luxuries of the marketplace by playing political games of grantsmanship and the like. It is quite another thing, however, to foster cynicism when, like Pilate, we wash our hands and by asking "what is truth" deny that there is any such thing. Having surrendered both independent values and critical intelligence, it is no wonder either that liberation comes paradoxically to rely on power itself and encourages a new authoritarianism as in the search for "charismatic" leaders.

Reconstruction requires that we set before ourselves, by contrast, the genuine possibility of the good, the true, and the beautiful—although the progressive formulation of these will not be absolutist but developmental and participatory. This is, moreover, quite in tune with naturalistic thought, although quite alien to the modern deteriorated forms of liberalism we are used to. For example, in commenting on an already visible degradation of progressivism, Dewey once remarked:

> Now such a method (the classroom as a *laissez-faire* classroom) is really stupid. For it attempts the impossible which is always stupid and it misconceives the conditions of independent thinking. There are a multitude of ways of reacting to surrounding conditions and without some guidance from experience, these reactions are almost sure to be casual, sporadic, and ultimately fatiguing accompanied by nervous strain. Since

the teacher has presumably a greater background of experience, there is the same presumption of the right of a teacher to make suggestions as to what to do as there is on the part of the head carpenter to suggest to apprentices something of what they are to do.[6]

The independent ground is thus no doubt uncomfortable to the contemporary liberal temperament but by no means foreign to progressivism as such. The danger, of course—which is why an earlier generation was so hesitant—is that such an independent ground may tempt us unwittingly back into dogmatism. That suggests the need for great care in formulating judgments of value. For example, we dare not retreat to the intellectualist error of thinking that the most careful "saying" is a way of corroborating and "doing." We notice thus that the notion of experience reappears, not as passively "had" as in today's sensualism but as shaped, deliberated, and envalued active "havings." So, taste too, properly understood, does permit legitimate distinctions between instructed and brute preferences as between actively chosen and merely possessed events.

In describing the features of an independent ground for valuing and human action, we must not underestimate the strength of the habits arrayed against us from the liberal side. It is popular, for example, to interpret scientific activity itself under the rubrics of subjectivism although in more sophisticated and not overtly subjectivist languages. Current discussions of scientific "paradigms" emerge from a legitimate recognition of the contributions of history and culture to inquiry. But, such discussions move quite rapidly in circles that should know better toward a vicious relativism so that science ceases to deal with worlds and instead comes to deal only with itself.[7]

Naturally, this makes science liable to the accusation of being

[6] John Dewey, *Intelligence in the Modern World*, ed. Joseph Ratner (New York: Modern Library, 1939), pp. 623–24.

[7] For example, see the by now classic discussion of this theme in Thomas S. Kuhn, *The Structure of Scientific Revolutions* 2d ed. (Chicago: The University of Chicago Press, 1970). Kuhn, however, is much more sophisticated scientifically on the matter than many of his readers and is not given to an uncritical subjectivism. Unfortunately, others have seized upon his notion of "paradigms" and corrupted his intention.

an ideological apologia—merely another form of interest politics. So, from the left-liberals we get the ready agreement that all politics—including science perceived as ideology—is to be understood as self-serving, a way of elevating what are only interests into falsely objectified powers. There is sufficient evidence in post World War II experience to give superficial credibility to this view. Science, after all, has been a too-willing servant of other powers, and politics has too often spoken the language of virtue while practicing the advantage of interests. But, while this surely warrants radical criticism, it does not justify the surrender of the scientific enterprise itself.

Nor are liberals any the less unintelligible when they speak to human nature or to moral values. Talk of morals deteriorates into a concern for usage or conventionality or feeling. What this invites, although unintentionally, is a final admission that values are really only "epiphenomenal." And, as in the recent debate over IQ, a sentimental and anxious environmentalism among liberals blinds judgments about variation and confuses identity with equality. In short, critical intelligence which might contribute to a reasoned and objective development of egalitarian policy is silenced. To postulate an independent reality as a necessary condition of progressivism, in other words, is to reject at the same time much that goes by the name of modern liberalism and at the same time to deny classical Marxism and an equally classical Toryism.

Schooling then is not only required to engage in an affirmative politics. It is at the same time a critical politics too. In this double sense, schooling is not merely a technology, i.e., morally neutral. A school's members must have some common allegiance to common values and ends. Participants in schooling who denied the existence of independent "objects" of inquiry—the possibility of finding truths that are not reducible to mere mental projections—would have subverted their participation. Their subjectivity, becoming an environmentalism without an environment, could only be reducible to the impress of culture and so make schooling as an intentional activity redundant.

They would join with those who, committed to some fixed human nature, make schooling pointless. Taken seriously, both of these views also make it impossible to be a teacher, for they deny that what I know can or need have any possible authority for anyone else. The subjectivist, ironically, putting himself forward as the proponent of freedom, must finally rely on some type of imposition or manipulation of others since no external reference can be legitimate. Behaviorally, then, he becomes indistinguishable from his alleged absolutist opponent.

Progressive schooling then is not at all eclectic in its values nor is it merely the arena of tolerations. The school as a usable politics needs its self-given rules and its own ethic as they emerge from the mission of marginality itself. This imperative does not, however, sanction intrusions into schooling, as in statutory punishments for "disloyalty" to the state. We are not after all denying "civil" liberty but identifying the conditions under which schooling can be schooling. Confusion arises when we permit coercive social practices like state loyalty oaths to become surrogates for common intellectual and professional responsibilities. Subjectivism which denies professional community and toleration which denies meaningful community invites this invasion from authority. What is sanctioned by our view of schooling is the development of communal disciplines and a public ethic. That we have, in effect, almost dismissed these in the name of contemporary liberalism and in an understandable but indefensible reaction to recent authoritarianism reveals how far we have come from progressivism and also, paradoxically, explains the intrusions into schooling by political and state powers. Progressivism then calls us back to an independent view of schooling which requires us to make judgments, accept risks, and exercise powers.

V

We have been seeking the conditions that would return schooling to its mission as a usable politics. These were developed, in fact, within the progressive tradition. We notice too how much of that tradition has been surrendered even while the language and, on occasion, the forms of progressivism are sustained. Its remains only to comment on yet a further term of disrepute, the idea of progress itself. Interpreted as a sentimental illusion—that the course of history is ever onward and upward and that the world is finally perfectible—progress would deserve to be viewed with contempt. So treated, however, progress is only a distorted reflection of progressivism's intention.

Again, we may understand why progress has been a ready victim of both deterioration and slander. Leaving aside the naïveté of a vulgar belief in an ensured and beneficient outcome to history, we may understand the modern world as counter-progressive because so much of modern experience is filled with the barbaric. Hence, it is little wonder that we opt for what seems a more "realistic" pessimism and even in a perverse way seem to enjoy our despair. This contemporary elation of misery admits the horrors we have perpetrated as a species and even helps turn the guilt we feel into self-serving emotionalism.

If a usable politics is to make any sense, however, then progress too must make sense—else the effort to reconstruct person and sociability is a pointless exercise at best and more often than not only foolish. In some meaningful senses, then, reconstruction must assume the continuing possibility of the better in experience. From that point of view, progress is a political *stance,* another expression of marginality, and not a cognitive claim. Hence, it is misleading to talk of progress as a reading of history or as the moral or other advancement of the race or of civilization or what have you. Nor is progress found by insisting that the present is by that fact alone superior to the past. A progressive view, instead, identifies some actual events as steps forward—whenever they occur—and finds in them suggestions for yet other steps to be taken. And "forward" has here certain concrete references to experience, e.g. as increase of health or of participation, or generally of some enrichment of experience.

Progress is then, to put it another way, the heuristic principle of a usable politics.

Once it is admitted, then, that there is at least some legitimate and not just sentimental or self-serving meaning for progress, it becomes possible to ask critically whether a mood of pessimism is any more coherent than eighteenth-century optimism. Is it necessarily and always the case that things must happen badly? Asked in this way, it rather quickly becomes clear that today's pessimism, like Enlightenment optimism, is a point of view and not a demonstrable hypothesis. Moreover, as a guide to perception, pessimism is at least as likely to contribute to a certain moral blindness as its equally uncritical partner. Thus, at a rather simple level, there would seem to be some intuitive warrant for regarding reduction in infant mortality, increase in human longevity, wider opportunity for travel, and the like as prima facie goods. To add that each of these brings with it its own difficulties is not to deny what is achieved, the temptation of pessimism, but to suggest the ground for further achievements. More significantly, each instance under a progressive perception is progressive not in its particularity alone but because it consists also in an enlargement of the ascriptions we assign to human events, as for example we enlarge the norm of healthfulness (e.g. life's quality) by expanding the meanings and possibilities of birth and even death.

Seen in this way, progress is not so much a name for optimism as another name given to criticism. There is no history as "it really was" but only as an interpreted field of events and choices. A sense of history then is never only backward-looking—some abstract replication of a putative past. History is by nature implicated in future events and it is the outcomes of those events which warrant or defeat our interpretations. To "learn" from history is only meaningful, as with any other knowing, when put to tests of experience to come. But that is also to admit that history is not a finished subject matter. This essential presentation of history as progressive history is reflec-

ted, by way of example, in a comment Joseph Blau made recently on "rootlessness":

> We need roots. We moderns need, as Simone Weil pointed out nearly a
> quarter of a century ago, to grow new roots to replace those that we
> have lost. Uprootedness has become a central phenomenon of the spirit
> of the modern world. Re-rooting cannot take place by the simplistic ex-
> pedient of merely returning to the land, for although uprooted-ness
> may originally have been a development of urban life, by now it is a
> malaise prevalent in the countryside as well. And so the two processions
> pass each other—the uprooted and alienated populations of the cities
> naively seeking to find roots by returning to the land—the uprooted
> and alienated populations of the countryside seeking to find roots by
> moving to the cities. Both are naive because human roots grow not in
> the soil but in the soul.[8]

Progress as a critical term is a sign of the always-possible
moral potency in activity. So, for example, where the "realist"—for which here read pessimist—is content, even joyous,
to rehearse the disappointments of human experience and to
point out in them a recurrence of the human pattern of failure,
the progressive insists that recurrence is not destiny because it is
failure. For example, the recurrent "realism" of Machiavellianism in politics only tells us that reliance on it guarantees future
failure. In a sense then, *realpolitik* is inevitably a helpless politics, an endless round of palace revolutions and not the effective
method we conceive it to be. At the same time, since progress
entails the possibility of intentional change, we are directed to
search out what does in fact lead to change. In that sense, progressivism is far more realistic than pessimism, which can only
leave us to mourn our fate as we repeat our errors.

Progress as a generic standpoint is a way of asserting that the
preferable is always a present possibility. That then, finally, is
its potency for reconstruction. It justifies individual capacities
in ways that have been denied to persons in recent history. The

---

[8] Joseph L. Blau, "Religion and The Newer Forms of Consciousness," *The Journal
of The Ancient Near Eastern Society of Columbia University,* 5, (1973).

desertion of progressivism then may be understood not as a warranted judgment at all but as a reflection of a prior despair of events. And it is true that were we only to look within society and culture in the present as all that there is—only to the internal forms of a presented sociality—despair might indeed be justified as responsive to the modern experience.

The justification of schooling as a usable politics is found finally thereby when we realize that the locus of experience is never entirely within the presented moment or the given sociality. It is instead ever infused with the passing generations which only the blind or deliberately obtuse would believe to be merely duplicates of ourselves. Marginality, therefore, rests not only in independent metaphysical, cognitive, and valuational notions but in the very membership of schooling itself. In that sense, schooling is always an existential center of organized social disequilibrium introduced by its ever-renewing populations. Progressivism recognizes this—if not always self-consciously—when it joins theory, politics, and pedagogy. When that alliance is fractured and thus separated from a legitimate "child-centeredness," then theory retreats to abstractness, politics surrenders to realism, and pedagogy turns into mere expertise. With this, progressivism loses its spirit and gives birth to the empty liberalism of our post-modern age. But, fortunately, the infusion of new life continues and forces new attentions even when we are existentially fatigued. It is precisely that which turns schooling into a form that cannot escape its marginality in experience, no matter how interpreted theoretically, and is thus the existential warrant for a progressive interpretation of all schooling. Joseph Blau noticed this in a typical progressive expression to a group of teachers:

> When we ask ourselves—as we must—what we hope our children and
> all the children of our communities may derive from the long and costly
> educational process, surely the minimum answers can be no less than
> this: that we hope each child will develop, as far as in him lies, the
> power to use his mind; the ability to manage his own affairs and to help

in the management of the affairs of the community; an interest in the companionship of others whether or not they are of his own ethnic, religious, or economic group; a capacity to appreciate at least some of the forms of artistic excellence; and a sensibility to the rights of others or, at least, as Edmund Cahn has so well put it, "a sense of injustice." . . . There is no private property in this garden of children, for children are the future and it is the future even more than the past that is our common heritage.[9]

Of course, this need not turn progressivism into a travesty, a "children's crusade." The young cannot lead us so much as demand of us. To confuse that demand with wisdom was an error made obvious in the 1960s—but also evident much earlier. We lost our way again when we confused commitment to schooling as commitment only to the young, and then transformed commitment itself into a type of cognitive theory. So, we became "child-centered" in a strange and disastrous way. Progressivism revisited, then, is addressed not to the child alone but to the adult, and not the adult playing social roles but to the adult as person even against the social role. To retake that ground—as well as all the other ground of a lost progressivism—would be the legitimate development of a prematurely deserted American naturalism, "a solid basis," as Joseph Blau put it in describing naturalism, "for further speculations."

[9] Joseph L. Blau, "Ethics, Experience, and Education," in *The Ethical Culture Movement Today*, 1962, p. 90.

Joseph L. Blau: A Bibliography

SAM DeKAY

The majority of entries are arranged topically, in accordance with the major divisions of the Festschrift. *However, many of Blau's writings reflect historical interests which extend beyond these divisions. I have placed such works within a broad category, "General History of Ideas." There are also a few writings which elude classification; these constitute a "miscellaneous" group of materials.*

Books, articles, pamphlets, and addresses are arranged alphabetically, by title. Reviews are listed alphabetically, by the name of the author of reviewed materials.

Philosophy of Religion

ARTICLES AND ADDRESSES

"A Man Who Counted—J. H. Leuba." Review article of J. H. Leuba. *The Reformation of the Churches.* In *The Standard,* 38 (February–March 1952): 95–99.

"Are You an Atheist?" *The Christian Register,* 130, no. 3 (1952): 14–16.

"God and the Philosophers." In *The Idea of God: Philosophical Perspectives,* ed. E. H. Madden, Rollo Handy, and Marvin Farber, pp. 139–63. Springfield, Illinois: Charles C. Thomas, 1969.

"In the Age of Shadows, Does Liberal Religion Have a Future?" In *A Lively Connection: Intimate Encounters with the Ethical Movement in*

America, ed. Cable Neuhaus, pp. 157–174. New York: Ethica Press, 1978.

"Martin Buber's Religious Philosophy: A Review Article." *The Review of Religion*, 13 (1948): 48–64.

"Religion and the Newer Forms of Consciousness." *The Journal of the Ancient Near Eastern Society of Columbia University*, 5 (1973): 17–22.

"Religions Facing the Modern World." *Dharma World*, 3 (April 1976): 10–13.

"Religion Today." *The Humanist*, 37 (January-February 1977): 42–43.

"Reply to Commentators." In *The Idea of God: Philosophical Perspectives*, eds. E. H. Madden, Rollo Handy, and Marvin Farber, pp. 173–78. Springfield, Illinois: Charles C. Thomas, 1969.

"Resurrection and the Mysteries." *The Graduate Faculties Newsletter*, Columbia University, Spring 1968, pp. 5–6.

"Roots and Relatives of Twentieth-Century Humanism." *Religious Humanism*, 10 (Autumn 1976): 146–152. [This article was reprinted, with additional notes, in *Ethical Perspectives* (1977), a publication of the New York Society for Ethical Culture.]

"The Roundness of the World." An Address at the New York Society for Ethical Culture, July 12, 1959.

"Toward a Definition of Humanism." In *The Humanist Alternative*, ed. Paul Kurtz, pp. 38–40. Buffalo, New York: Prometheus Press, 1973.

REVIEWS

Argo, Waldemar. *The Case for Liberal Religion*. Lloyd Morain and Mary Morain. *Humanism as the Next Step*. Eugene Kohn. *Religion and Humanity*. In *The Review of Religion*, 20 (1956): 216–18.

Bari, Eugenio. *G. Pico della Mirandola. Sincretismo Religio-Filosofico, 1463–1494*. In *The Journal of Philosophy*, 34 (1937): 556.

Braden, Charles S. *The Scriptures of Mankind*. Homer W. Smith. *Man and his Gods*. Edmund Davison Soper. *The Religions of Mankind*. Paul J. Williams. *What Americans Believe and How They Worship*. In *Jewish Social Studies*, 15 (1953): 77–80.

Buber, Martin. *Mamre. Essays in Religion*, trans. Greta Hart. In *Jewish Social Studies*, 10 (1948): 397–400.

Dunn, William P. *Sir Thomas Browne: A Study in Religious Philosophy*. In *The Standard*, 38 (1951): 343.

Ebner, Ferdinand. *Das Wort und die geistigen Realitäten*. In *Erasmus: Speculum Scientiarum*, 11 (1958): 330.

Eliot, Samuel Atkins, ed. *Heralds of a Liberal Faith*. Vol. 4: *The Pilots*. In *Jewish Social Studies*, 16 (October 1954): 385–86.

Ferm, Vergilius, ed. *Forgotten Religions: A symposium*. In *The Standard*, 36 (March 1950): 279–81.

—— *What Can We Believe?* In *The Standard*, 35 (1938): 118–20.

Heschel, Abraham. *Die Prophetie*. In *The Review of Religion*, 2 (1938): 484–85.

Möller, Joseph. *Existentialphilosophie und Katholische Theologie*. In *Erasmus: Speculum Scientiarum*, 7 (1954): 523–24.

Samuel, Herbert A., et al. *Religion in the Modern World*. In *Jewish Social Studies*, 18 (January 1956): 66–67.

Stromberg, Roland N. *Religious Liberalism in Eighteenth Century England*. In *The Review of Religion*, 20 (1956): 236–37.

Temple, Sidney A., Jr. *The Common Sense Theology of Bishop White*. In *The Review of Religion*, 11 (1947): 302–5.

Thomas, Wendell. *On the Resolution of Science and Faith*. In *The Journal of Philosophy*, 48 (1951): 110–11.

Wieman, H. N., et al. *Religious Liberals Reply*. In *The Journal of Philosophy*, 45 (1948): 78–79.

REVIEW NOTES

Einstein, Albert, et al. *Voices of Liberalism, II*. In *The Journal of Philosophy*, 47 (1950): 79.

Hook, Sidney. *Religion in a Free Society*. In *The Humanist*, 28 (July-August 1968): 26.

Gibran, Kahlil. *Secrets of the Heart*, trans. Anthony Rizcallah Ferris, ed. Martin L. Wolf. In *The Journal of Philosophy*, 45 (1948): 137.

Hutchison, John A. and James A. Martin, Jr. *Ways of Faith: An Introduction to Religion*. In *The Review of Religion*, 19 (1954): 98.

Schoen, Max. *Thinking About Religion*. In *The Journal of Philosophy*, 44 (1947): 50.

History and Philosophy of Judaism

BOOKS

Essays on Jewish Life and Thought, presented in honor of Salo W. Baron (The Baron Festschrift). Joint editor, with Philip Friedman, Arthur Hertzberg, and Isaac Mendelsohn. New York: Columbia University Press, 1959.

The Jews of the United States, 1790–1840; A Documentary History. Co-editor with Salo W. Baron. 3 volumes. New York: Columbia University Press; Philadelphia: The Jewish Publication Society of America, 1963.

Judaism in America: From Curiosity to Third Faith. Chicago: University of Chicago Press, 1976.

Judaism: Postbiblical and Talmudic Periods. Joint editor with Salo W. Baron. New York: Liberal Arts Press (Library of Religion, no. 3); Indianapolis: Bobbs-Merrill, 1961.

Modern Varieties of Judaism (American Lectures on the History of Religions, no. 8). New York: Columbia University Press, 1966.

Reform Judaism: A Historical Perspective. Edited with an Introduction [by J. L. B.] New York: Ktav, 1973.

The Story of Jewish Philosophy. New York: Random House, 1962. Reprint, Ktav, 1971.

ARTICLES AND REPORTS; PAMPHLETS

"Albo, Joseph." Article in *The Encyclopedia of Philosophy,* 1:66–67. New York: Macmillan, 1967.

"Alternatives Within Contemporary Judaism." In *Religion in America,* eds. William G. McLoughlin and Robert N. Bellah. Boston: Houghton, Mifflin (The Daedalus Library, no. 12), pp. 299–311.

"An American-Jewish View of the Evolution Controversy." *Hebrew Union College Annual,* 20:617–34.

"Bahya b. Joseph ibn Paquda." Article in *The Encyclopedia of Philosophy.* 1:242–43. New York: Macmillan, 1967.

"Cabala." In *ibid.,* 2:1–3.

"Comment" on Hourani's "Israel, the Arabs, and Ethics." *The Humanist,* 29 (1969): 18–19.

"The Confrontation of Cultures." [Preface and first two sections of chapter 6 of *The Story of Jewish Philosophy*]. *Recall,* 2 (1961): 14–22.

"Cordovero, Moses b. Jacob." Article in *The Encyclopedia of Philosophy,* 2: 223. New York: Macmillan, 1967.

"Dialogue with Joseph Blau." In *Let Us Reason Together,* ed. William Berkowitz, pp. 191–204. New York: Crown, 1970.

"The Historic Quest." In *Essays on Jewish Life and Thought,* [the Baron *Festschrift*], pp. vii–xi. New York: Columbia University Press, 1959.

"Ibn Zaddik, Joseph b. Jacob." Article in *The Encyclopedia of Philosophy,* 4:110. New York: Macmillan, 1967.

Introduction to *Jewish Theology, Systematically and Historically Considered*, by Kaufmann Kohler. New York: Ktav, 1968.

Introduction to "Christian Traveler in the Holy Land: Selections from a 19th Century Journal," by John Lloyd Stevens. *Commentary*, 27 (March 1959): 252–55.

"Israeli, Isaac b. Solomon." Article in *The Encyclopedia of Philosophy*, 4: 224. New York: Macmillan, 1967.

"The Jewish Day School." *The Reconstructionist*, 24, no. 14 (1958): 29–32.

"Jews in the Western World Since the Renaissance." Richmond, Virginia: Richmond Jewish Community Council. (Scholar-in-Residence Program at University of Richmond, April, 1967).

"Kaplan, Mordecai Menahem." Article in *The Encyclopedia of Philosophy*, 4:324–25. New York: Macmillan, 1967.

"Mukammas, David b. Merwan al." Article in *ibid.*, 5:411.

"On the Supposedly Aristotelian Character of Gabirol's *Keter Malkut*." In *Salo Wittmayer Baron Jubilee Volume*, pp. 219–28. Jerusalem: American Academy for Jewish Research, 1974.

"Pilgrims to Zion—Activists for Zion." (The Abba Hillel Silver Lecture, no. 10, for 1973.) *Jewish Social Studies*, 36 (1974): 95–105.

"Problems of Modern Jewish Thought: Tensions Between Particularism and Universalism." *Journal of Reform Judaism*, (Fall 1978): 47–62.

"A Proposal for a Professional Association." In *The Teaching of Judaica in American Universities: The Proceedings of a Colloquium*, pp. 89–92. New York: Association for Jewish Studies/Ktav, 1970.

"Recent Philosophic Importations." In *Freedom and Reason: Studies in Philosophy and Jewish Culture in memory of Morris Raphael Cohen*, eds. by S. W. Baron, E. Nagel, and K. Pinson (Jewish Social Studies Publications, no. 4), pp. 87–96. New York: Conference on Jewish Relations, 1951.

"The Red Heifer: A Biblical Purification Rite in Rabbinic Literature." *Numen: International Review for the History of Religions*, 14 (1967); pp. 70–78. [A condensation of this article was published in the *Proceedings* of the XI International Congress of the International Association for the History of Religions, 2:82–84. Leiden: E. J. Brill, 1968.

"Robert Burton on the Jews." *Jewish Social Studies*, 6 (1944): 58–64.

"A Roundup of Religious Thought." Group review of Norman Lamm, *Faith and Doubt*. Eli J. Gottlieb, *The Inescapable Truth*. Samuel S. Cohen, *Jewish Theology*. Samuel Sandmel. *Philo's Place in Judaism*, and *Two Living Traditions;* James E. Wood, Jr., ed., *Jewish-Christian Relations in Today's World.* Milton R. Konvitz, *Judaism and Human Rights.* W. Robertson Smith, *The Religion of the Semites. In Jewish Bookland,* October 1962, pp. 1, 4.

"Saadia b. Joseph." Article written for *The Encyclopedia of Philosophy,* 7:273–74. New York: Macmillan, 1967.

"Salo W. Baron: Historian of the Jews." *Jewish Heritage,* 11 (Summer 1969): 43–45.

"Schnitzler Had World Wide Following." *American Hebrew,* 129 (1931): 531–34.

"Scholarly Works on Jewish Philosophy and Religion." In *Jewish Book Annual, 5728, 1967–68,* 25:148–54. New York: Jewish Book Council of America, 1967.

"Some Historical Facets of Jewish Affiliation." *Jewish Social Studies,* 31 (1969): 242–52.

"Some Notes on the History of Humanistic Judaism." *Humanistic Judaism,* 1 (Winter 1968): 13–18.

"The Spiritual Life of American Jewry, 1654–1954." In *American Jewish Year Book,* 56:99–170. New York: The American Jewish Committee, 1955. [This article was reprinted in *The Characteristics of American Jews.* New York: Jewish Education Committee Press, 1965, pp. 61–132.]

Summary of Address [by J. L. B.] at the Reconstructionist Conference. *The Reconstructionist,* 11 (November 16, 1945): 19.

"Tradition and Innovation." In *Essays on Jewish Life and Thought* [the Baron Festschrift], pp. 95–104. New York: Columbia University Press, 1959.

"What is Jewish about Jewish Philosophy?" *Recall,* 2, no. 4 (1962): 3–7.

"What's American About American Jewry?" *Judaism,* 7 (1958): 208–18.

REVIEWS

Agus, Jacob B. *Modern Philosophies of Judaism. A Study of Recent Jewish Philosophies of Religion.* In *The Review of Religion,* 6 (1942): 421–31.

Baron, Salo Wittmayer. *Bibliography of Jewish Social Studies, 1938–39. proceedings* of the American Academy for Jewish Research. Vol. 10 (1940). In *The Review of Religion,* 6 (1941): 56–59.

Bokser, Ben Zion. *The Legacy of Maimonides.* Philip David Bookstaber,

The Idea of Development of the Soul in Medieval Jewish Philosophy. In *The Standard*, 38 (1951): 346–47.

Buber, Martin. *Tales of the Hasidim. Vol. 2: The Later Masters.* In *The Review of Religion*, 14 (1950): 425–26.

——. *Two Types of Faith* and *The Way of Man According to the Teachings of Hasidism.* In *Jewish Social Studies*, 17 (1955): 83–84.

Cohen, Morris Raphael. *A Dreamer's Journey.* In *Jewish Social Studies*, 12 (1950): 257–58.

——. *Reflections of a Wandering Jew.* In *The Journal of Philosophy*, 48 (1951): 169–70.

Finkelstein, Louis. *The Jews: Their History, Culture, and Religion.* In *The Review of Religion*, 17 (1952): 51–54.

Glanz, Rudolf. *The Jew in Early American Wit and Humor.* In *Jewish Bookland*, October 1973, p. 7.

Goldman, Solomon. *The Book of Books.* Vols. 1 and 2. In *Jewish Social Studies*, 12 (1950): 392–96.

Goldstein, Israel. *Toward a Solution.* In *Jewish Social Studies*, 4 (1942): 181–82.

Goodman, Abraham Vossen. *American Overture. Jewish Rights in Colonial Times.* In *The Review of Religion*, 12 (1948): 233–34.

Jacobson, David. *The Social Background of the Old Testament.* Louis Wallis, *The Bible is Human. A Study in Secular History.* In *The Review of Religion*, 7 (1943): 278–82.

Kallen, Horace M., ed. *"Of Them Which Say They Are Jews," and Other Essays on the Jewish Struggle for Survival.* In *Judaism*, 4 (1955): 365–67.

Kaplan, Mordecai M. *The Meaning of God in Modern Jewish Religion.* In *The Review of Religion*, 2 (1938): 361–64.

Karff, Samuel E., ed. *Hebrew Union College—Jewish Institute of Religion at One Hundred Years.* In *American Jewish Historical Quarterly*, 67 (March 1978): 271–73.

Karp, Abraham J., ed. *The Jewish Experience in America.* In *Jewish Social Studies*, 33 (1971): 59–61.

Kohn, Eugene, ed. *American Jewry: The Tercentenary and After.* In *The Reconstructionist*, 21, no. 2 (1955): 29–32.

Lassen, Abraham L., ed. and trans. *The Commentary of Levi ben Gerson (Gersonides) on the Book of Job.* Edward J. Kissane, *The Book of Job, Translated from a Critically Revised Hebrew Text with Commentary.* In *Jewish Social Studies*, 9 (1947): 259–61.

Lewisohn, Ludwig. *The American Jew: Character and Destiny.* In *Jewish Social Studies*, 13 (1951): 83–85.

Loewe, Raphael, ed. *Studies in Rationalism, Judaism, and Universalism in Memory of Leon Roth*. In *Journal of the History of Philosophy*, 7 (1969): 322–23.

Marcus, Jacob R., ed. *Critical Studies in American Jewish History. Selected Articles from American Jewish Archives*. In *Jewish Social Studies*, 34 (1972): 273–74.

Morgenstern, Julian. *As a Mighty Stream. The progress of Judaism through history. And Reform Judaism. Essays by Hebrew Union College Alumni*. In *The Standard*, 38 (1951): 344–45.

Müller, Ernst. *A History of Jewish Mysticism*. In *The Review of Religion*, 13 (1949): 303–6.

Rudavsky, David. *Emancipation and Adjustment: Contemporary Jewish Religious Movements; Their History and Thought*. In *Jewish Bookland*, February 1969, p. 7.

Scholem, Gershom G. *Major Trends in Jewish Mysticism*. In *The Review of Religion*, 8 (1943): 67–77; also in *Jewish Social Studies*, 5 (1943): 187–92.

Sérouya, Henri. *La Kabbale: Ses origines, sa psychologie mystique, sa métaphysique*. In *The Journal of Philosophy*, 45 (1948): 51–52; new edition reviewed in *The Journal of Philosophy*, 58 (1961): 828.

Silver, Daniel Jeremy. *A History of Judaism*, Volume 1, *From Abraham to Maimonides;* and Volume 2, *Europe and the New World*, by Bernard Martin. In *Judaism*, 24 (1975): 495–99.

——. *Judaism and Ethics*. In *Union Seminary Quarterly Review*, 26 (1971): 435–36.

Sjöberg, Erik. *Gott und die Sunder im Palästinischen Judentum nach dem Zeugnis der Tannaiten und der apokryphisch-pseudepigraphischen Literatur*. In *The Review of Religion*, 4 (1940): 334–36.

Sklare, Marshall. *Conservative Judaism: An American Religious Movement*. In *The Review of Religion*, 20 (1956): 183–86.

Stonehill, C. A., Jr., ed. *The Jewish Contribution to Civilization* [A Bookseller's Catalogue.] In *The Review of Religion*, 5 (1941): 191–94.

Trachtenberg, Joshua. *The Devil and the Jews. The Medieval Conception of the Jew and its Relation to Modern Antisemitism*. In *The Review of Religion*, 8 (1944): 396–400.

——. *Jewish Magic and Superstition: A Study in Folk Religion*. In *The Review of Religion*, 4 (1940): 456–60.

Tresmontant, Claude. *A Study of Hebrew Thought*, trans. Michael Francis Gibson. In *Jewish Social Studies*, 27 (1965): 118–20.

Ussher, Arland. *The Magic People.* In *Jewish Social Studies,* 14 (1952): 275–76.

Viterbo, Egidio da. *Libellus de litteris hebraicis: Scechina.* In *Renaissance News,* 14 (1961): 263–66.

Warrain, Francis. *La théodicée de la Kabbale.* In *The Journal of Philosophy,* 48 (1951): 613–17.

REVIEW NOTES

Adler, Cyrus. *I Have Considered the Days.* In *The Review of Religion,* 6 (1942): 347–48.

Agnon, S. Y. *Days of Awe.* In *The Review of Religion,* 14 (1950): 209.

Auerbach, Leo, ed. and trans. *The Babylonian Talmud in Selection.* In *The Review of Religion,* 9 (1945): 322.

Bokser, Ben Zion. *From the World of the Cabbalah: the Philosophy of Rabbi Judah Loew of Prague.* In *Bibliography of Philosophy,* 1 (October–December 1954): 48–49.

——. *The Wisdom of the Talmud.* In *The Review of Religion,* 17 (1952): 84.

Buber, Martin. *Hasidism.* In *The Journal of Philosophy,* 46 (1949): 731.

——. *Israel and the World: Essays in a Time of Crisis.* In *The Review of Religion,* 14 (1950): 426.

Cahn, Zri. *The Rise of the Karaite Sect: A New Light on the Halakah and Origin of the Karaites.* In *The Review of Religion,* 2 (1938): 242.

Crook, Margaret, et. al. *The Bible and its Literary Associations.* In *Jewish Social Studies,* 1 (1939): 376–77.

Elmslie, W. A. L. *How Came Our Faith. A Study of the Religion of Israel and its Significance for the Modern World.* In *The Review of Religion,* 16 (1952): 209–10.

Feldman, Abraham J. *A Companion to the Bible.* In *The Review of Religion,* 4 (1940): 367–68.

Gaster, Theodor, Herzl. *Passover: Its History and Traditions.* In *The Review of Religion,* 14 (1950): 209.

Glatzer, Nahum N., ed. *Hammer on the Rock, a Short Midrash Reader.* In *The Review of Religion,* 15 (1950): 93.

——. *In Time and Eternity. A Jewish Reader.* In *The Review of Religion,* 11 (1947): 432–33.

Goldstein, Morris. *Thus Religion Grows: The Story of Judaism.* In *The Review of Religion,* 1 (1937): 325–26.

Goodman, Philip. *The Purim Anthology.* In *The Review of Religion,* 15 (1951): 208–9.

Grayzel, Solomon. *A History of the Jews from the Babylonian Exile to the End of World War II.* In *The Review of Religion,* 13 (1949): 213.

Gregorovius, Ferdinand. *The Ghetto and the Jews of Rome.* In *The Review of Religion,* 14 (1950): 208.

Hadas, Moses, ed. and trans. *Aristeas to Philocrates (Letter of Aristeas).* In *The Review of Religion,* 17 (1953): 192–93.

Halkin, Abraham S., ed. *Moses Maimonides' Epistle to Yemen.* In *The Review of Religion,* 17 (1953): 193.

Hamblen, Emily S. *The Book of Job Interpreted.* In *The Review of Religion,* 5 (1941): 371–72.

Helfgott, Benjamin W. *The Doctrine of Election in Tannaitic Literature.* In *Jewish Bookland,* May 1955, p. 6.

Heschel, Abraham Joshua. *The Earth is the Lord's.* In *The Review of Religion,* 17 (1952): 85–86.

Hodes, Aubrey. *Martin Buber: An Intimate Portrait.* In *Jewish Bookland,* February 1972, p. 2.

Kadushin, Max. *The Rabbinic Mind.* In *The Review of Religion,* 18 (1953): 103–4.

Kaplan, Mordecai M. *The Purpose and Meaning of Jewish Existence: A People in the Image of God.* In *Jewish Bookland,* (October 1964), p. 1.

Kayser, Rudolf. *The Life and Time of Jehudah Halevi.* In *The Journal of Philosophy,* 47 (1950): 478.

Krakowsky, Levi I. *The Omnipotent Light Revealed: The Luminous Tegument to Unite Mankind into One Loving Brotherhood.* In *The Review of Religion,* 5 (1940): 115.

Lichtigfield, Adolf. *Twenty Centuries of Jewish Thought.* In *The Review of Religion,* 3 (1939): 498–99.

Maimonides, Moses. *The Guide of the Perplexed,* trans. Shlomo Pines. In *Jewish Bookland,* October 1963, p. 3.

Marcus, Jacob Rader. *Memoirs of American Jews, 1775–1865.* 3 vols. Vols. 1 and 2. In *The American Historical Review,* 61 (April 1956): 656–57. Vol. 3 in *ibid.,* 62 (October 1956): 231–32.

Marx, Alexander. *Essays in Jewish Biography.* In *The Review of Religion,* 14 (1949): 106.

Meyer, Michael A. *The Origins of the Modern Jew.* In *Jewish Bookland,* March 1968, p. 1.

Minkin, Jacob S. *The Shaping of the Modern Mind: The Life and Thought of the Great Jewish Philosophers.* In *Jewish Bookland,* September 1964, p. 3.

Pinson, Koppel S., ed. *Essays on Antisemitism.* 2nd ed. In *The Review of Religion,* 12 (1948): 346.

Reider, Joseph. *The Holy Scriptures: Deuteronomy, with Commentary.* In *The Review of Religion,* 3 (1939): 229.

Reines, Alvin Jay. *Maimonides and Abrabanel on Prophecy.* In *The Journal of Religion,* 53 (1973): 504–5.

Rotenstreich, Nathan. *Jewish Philosophy in Modern Times.* In *In Jewish Bookland,* February 1970, p. 7.

Roth, Cecil. *The House of Nasi: The Duke of Naxos.* In *The Review of Religion,* 14 (1950): 424.

Schoeps, Hans Joachim, ed. *Jüdische Geisteswelt: Zeugnisse aus Zwei Jahrtausenden.* In *The Review of Religion,* 19 (1955): 208–9.

Scholem, Gershom G. *Major Trends in Jewish Mysticism.* In *The Review of Religion,* 12 (1948): 447.

Scholem, Gershom G., ed. *Zohar: The Book of Splendor.* In *The Review of Religion,* 16 (1951): 90.

Segal, Samuel M. *The Sabbath Book.* In *Jewish Social Studies,* 4 (1942): 279.

Sharot, Stephen. *Judaism: A Sociology.* William E. Kaufman, *Contemporary Jewish Philosophies.* In *The JWB Circle: Jewish Bookland,* April–May 1977, p. 3B.

Solis-Cohen, Emily, Jr., ed. *Hanukkah: The Feast of Lights.* In *The Review of Religion,* 3 (1938): 110–11.

Vajda, Georges. *Introduction à la Pensée Juive du Moyen Age.* [Introduction to Medieval Jewish Thought] In *The Journal of Philosophy,* 48 (1951): 650–51.

Vishniac, Roman. *Polish Jews: A Pictorial Record.* In *The Review of Religion,* 13 (1949): 214.

American History and Philosophy

BOOKS

American Philosophic Addresses, 1700–1900. New York: Columbia University Press, 1946.

Cornerstones of Religious Freedom in America. Boston: Beacon Press, 1949. [A revised and enlarged edition of this book, with a new introduction, was published in 1964 by Harper & Row.]

Francis Wayland: The Elements of Moral Science. [With an introduction by J. L. B.] Cambridge: The Belknap Press of Harvard University, 1963.

Men and Movements in American Philosophy. New York: Prentice-Hall,

1952. [Several foreign language editions of this book have been published: Spanish translation, *Filósofos y Escuelas Filosóficas en los Estados Unidos de America*. S. A.: Editorial Reverté, 1957. Hindi translation, Allahabad: Leader Press, 1958. Korean translation, Seoul: Sasang Ge Sa, 1957. Italian translation, *Movimenti e Figure della Filosofia Americana*. Florence: La Nuova Italia, 1957. German translation, *Philosophie und Philosophen Amerikas*. Meisenheim/Glan: Anton Hain, 1957.]

William James: Pragmatism and Other Essays. [With an Introduction by J. L. B.] New York: Washington Square Press, Inc., 1963.

ARTICLES, PAMPHLETS, AND LECTURES

"Abbot, Francis Ellingwood." Article in *The Encyclopedia of Philosophy,* 1:2–3. New York: Macmillan, 1967.

"The Age of Revolution and Reason: The Origins of Ethical Humanism in the American Tradition." *The Humanist,* 36 (1976): 26–34.

"American Philosophy." Article written (in English) for the Teluga encyclopedia, Vijnana Sarvasvamu, volume 7, "Darsanamulu-Matamulu" (Philosophy and Religion), pp. 255–260. Madras, India, 1962.

"American Religion: From Cosmos to Chaos." *The Humanist,* 34 (1974): 31–33.

"American Values in World Perspective." *The Philosopher's Newsletter,* no. 35 (1959), pp. 1–2.

"Chauncey Wright: Radical Empiricist." *New England Quarterly,* 19 (1946): 495–517.

"The Christian Party in Politics." *The Review of Religion,* 11 (1946): 18–35.

"Church and State in the United States." *The Plain View,* 6 (1951): 146–153.

"The Cooperative Commonwealth as Secular Apocalypse." *Transactions of the Charles S. Peirce Society,* 12 (1976): 209–22.

"Darwin, Dewey, and Beyond." *The Christian Register,* 128, no. 10 (1949): 19–21, 39.

"Emanuel Haldeman—Julius (1889–1951)." *The Humanist,* 11 (1951): 205–8.

"Food for Middle Western Thought." In *The Heritage of the Middle West,* ed. John J. Murray, pp. 177–97. Norman, Oklahoma: University of Oklahoma Press, 1958.

" 'The Freeborn Mind': a Review Article." *The Review of Religion,* 9 (1944): 31–41.

"Freedom of Prayer." *The Review of Religion,* 14 (1950): 250–69.

"Hickok, Laurens Perseus." Article in *The Encyclopedia of Philosophy,* 3:495–96. New York: Macmillan, 1967.

"The Influence of America on the Mind": Notes Toward a Philosophy of American Culture. Public lectures delivered at the University of Arkansas, October 4 and 18, November 1 and 15, 1950. [The four lectures are: (1) "Religion in American Life—The Emotional Center," (2) "The Importance of Science—The Intellectual Method," (3) "A National Literature—The Transmission Belt," (4) "Democratic Social Order—The Climate of Free Culture."]

"The Influence of Darwin on American Philosophy." *Bucknell Review,* 8 (1959): 141–53.

"Jacob Henry 'On Religion and Elective Office.' " In *An American Primer,* ed. Daniel J. Boorstin, 1:219–26. Chicago: The University of Chicago Press, 1966.

"James, Henry [the Elder]." Article in *The Encyclopedia of Philosophy,* 4:239–40. New York: Macmillan, 1967.

"Joel Barlow, Enlightened Religionist." *Journal of the History of Ideas,* 10 (1949): 430–44.

"John Dewey and American Social Thought." *Teacher's College Record,* 61 (1959): 121–27. [A condensation of this article was published in *The Education Digest,* 25 (1960): 89–100.]

"John Dewey's Democratic Theory." *The Reconstructionist,* 25 (October 30, 1959): 7–14.

"John Dewey's Theory of History." *The Journal of Philosophy,* 57 (1960): 89–100. [A Japanese translation of this article was published in *Americana,* 6 (December 1960): 70–80.]

"Jonathan Boucher, Tory." In *History 4,* pp. 93–109. New York: World Publishing Company, 1961.

"Kant in America, I. Brownson's Critique of the *Critique of Pure Reason.*" *The Journal of Philosophy,* 51 (1954): 874–80.

"The Lesson of the Past." *The Nation,* 174 (January 12, 1952): 30–33.

"The Maryland 'Jew Bill': A Footnote to Thomas Jefferson's Work for Freedom of Religion." *The Review of Religion,* 8 (1944): 227–39. [A condensation of this article was published in *Religious Digest,* 17 (1944): 41–44.]

"Mather, Cotton." Article in *The Encyclopedia of Philosophy,* 5:213. New York: Macmillan, 1967.

"A Nation of Nations." In *Forum: Religious Faith Speaks to American Issues. A Bicentennial Discussion Stimulator,* ed. William A. Norgren,

pp. 11–14. New York: Friendship Press; and New York and Para-
mus, N.J.: Paulist Press, 1975.

Nature. By Ralph Waldo Emerson. ed. J.L.B. New York: The Liberal
Arts Press, 1948. [This pamphlet was reprinted in 1961 by Bobbs-
Merrill Company, Inc.]

"The North American as Philosopher." In *Naturalism and Historical
Understanding. Essays on the Philosophy of John Herman Randall, Jr.,*
ed. John P. Anton, pp. 134–46. Buffalo: State University of New
York Press, 1967.

"Porter, Noah." Article written for *The Encyclopedia of Philosophy,* 6:
412–13. New York: Macmillan, 1967.

"Pragmatism." Article written (in English) for the Teluga encyclopedia, Vijnana Sarvasvamu, volume 7, "Darsanamulu-Matamulu" (Philosophy and Religion), pp. 721–24. Madras, India,
1962.

"The Recovery of Thomas Paine." *The Critic and Guide,* 5 (1951):
57–60.

"Religion and Culture in America." *The Ethical Outlook,* 46 (1960):
198–202.

"Religion and Politics in Knickerbocker Times." In *The Knickerbocker
Tradition: Washington Irving's New York,* ed. Andrew B. Myers, pp.
51–64. Tarrytown, N.Y.: A Sleepy Hollow Restorations Book,
1974.

"Religion and Religiosity in the United States." *Ararat,* 8 (Spring
1967): 2–8.

"Religion and the Two Faces of America." In *The Search for Identity:
Essays on the American Character,* pp. 28–38. New York: The Institute for Religious and Social Studies, 1964.

"Royce's Theory of Community." *The Journal of Philosophy,* 53 (1956):
92–98. [A Japanese translation of this article was published in
Americana, 3 (1957): 61–68.]

"Sellars, Roy Wood." Article in *The Encyclopedia of Philosophy,* 7:
348. New York: Macmillan, 1967.

"Tayler Lewis: Classicist and Conservative." In *Tayler Lewis, Class of
1820,* ed. H. A. Larrabee (Union Worthies, no. 11), pp. 9–13.
Schenectady, N.Y.: Union College, 1956.

"Unfettered Freedom." *Transactions of the Charles S. Peirce Society,* 7
(1971): 243–58.

"Urian Oakes' The Soveraign Efficacy of Divine Providence." [Fac-
simile Reprint, with an Introduction by J. L. B.] Los Angeles: The
Augustan Reprint Society, 1955.

"Wayland, Francis." Article in *The Encyclopedia of Philosophy,*
8:280–81. New York: Macmillan, 1967.

REVIEWS

Atkins, Nelson F. *Philip Freneau and the Cosmic Enigma: The Religious
and Philosophical Speculations of an American Poet.* In *Modern Language Notes,* 66 (1951): 131–33.

Bowers, David F., ed. *Foreign Influence in American Life: Essays and
Critical Bibliographies.* In *The Journal of Philosophy,* 41 (1944):
669–71.

Brown, Stuart Gerry, ed. *The Social Philosophy of Josiah Royce.* In *Political Science Quarterly,* 66 (1951): 468–70.

Childs, John L. *American Pragmatism and Education.* In *The Journal of
Philosophy,* 58 (1961): 784.

Cohen, I. Bernard. *Some Early Tools of American Science.* In *American
Quarterly,* 2 (1950): 282–284.

Fisch, Max H., ed. *Classic American Philosophers.* In *The Journal of Philosophy,* 48 (1951): 536–37.

Foner, P. S., ed. *The Complete Writings of Thomas Paine.* Howard Fast,
The Selected Works of Tom Paine Set in the Framework of His Life. In
The Journal of Philosophy, 44 (1947): 191–92.

Freidel, Frank. *Francis Lieber, Nineteenth-Century Liberal.* In *The Journal of Philosophy,* 46 (1949): 564–66.

Gabriel, Ralph Henry. *The Course of American Democratic Thought.* 2d
ed. In *The Journal of Philosophy,* 58 (1961): 828–29.

Herrick, C. J. *George Ellett Coghill, Naturalist and Philosopher.* In *The
Journal of Philosophy,* 47 (1950): 276–78.

Hofstadter, Richard. *Social Darwinism in American Thought,
1860–1915.* In *The Journal of Philosophy,* 42 (1945): 191–93.

Hopkins, Vivian C. *Spires of Form: a Study of Emerson's Aesthetic Theory.*
Sherman Paul. *Emerson's Angle of Vision; Man and Nature in American Experience.* In *The Journal of Philosophy,* 50 (1953): 195–96.

Hudson, Winthrop H. *The Great Tradition of the American Churches.*
In *The Review of Religion,* 19 (1954): 96–98.

Johnson, F. Ernest, ed. *Wellsprings of the American Spirit.* In *The Journal of Philosophy,* 45 (1948): 719.

Keeton, Morris T. *The Philosophy of Edmund Montgomery.* I. K. Ste-
phens, *The Hermit Philosopher of Liendo.* In *The Journal of Philosophy,*
48 (1951): 727–31.

Kuklick, Bruce. *Josiah Royce: An Intellectual Biography.* In *American
Historical Review,* 79 (1974): 597–98.

LeBoutillier, Cornelia Geer. *American Democracy and Natural Law.* In *The Journal of Philosophy,* 48 (1951): 198–99.

Lehmann, Karl. *Thomas Jefferson: American Humanist.* In *The Journal of Philosophy,* 45 (1948): 275.

MacIver, R. M., ed. *Unity and Difference in American Life. A Series of Addresses and Discussions.* F. Ernest Johnson, ed., *Foundations of Democracy, A Series of Addresses.* Liston Pope, ed., *Labor's Relation to Church and Community.* In *The Journal of Philosophy,* 45 (1948): 216–20.

Mosier, Richard D. *Making the American Mind.* In *Modern Language Notes,* 63 (1948): 362.

Murphey, Murray G. *The Development of Peirce's Philosophy.* In *American Quarterly,* 14 (1962): 511–12.

Nathanson, Jerome. *John Dewey. The Reconstruction of the Democratic Life.* In the *New York Herald-Tribune* Books Review, November 11, 1951, p. 8.

Newlin, Claude M. *Philosophy and Religion in Colonial America.* In *Union Seminary Quarterly Review,* 19 (1963): 61.

O'Neill, James M. *Catholicism and American Freedom.* In *The Humanist,* 12 (1952): 87–88.

Patterson, R. L. *The Philosophy of William Ellery Channing.* In *The Journal of Philosophy,* 52 (1955): 759–60.

Persons, Stow. *Evolutionary Thought in America.* In *The Journal of Philosophy,* 49 (1952): 48–51.

—— *Free Religion—An American Faith.* In *The Review of Religion,* 12 (1948): 216–21.

Runes, D. D., ed. *The Selected Writings of Benjamin Rush.* In *The Journal of Philosophy,* 45 (1948): 52–55.

Vogt, V. Ogden. *Cult and Culture: A Study of Religion and American Culture.* In *The Journal of Philosophy,* 50 (1953): 393–95.

Wakefield, Eva Ingersoll, ed. *The Letters of Robert G. Ingersoll.* In *The Standard,* 38 (October 1951): 29–30.

Werkmeister, W. H. *A History of Philosophical Ideas in America.* In *American Quarterly,* 1 (1949): 376.

White, L. D. *The Federalists.* In *The Journal of Philosophy,* 45 (1948): 615–16.

Winn, Ralph B., ed. *American Philosophy.* In *The Journal of Philosophy,* 58 (1961): 827–28.

REVIEW NOTES

Atkins, Nelson F. *Philip Freneau and the Cosmic Enigma. The Religious and Philosophical Speculations of an American Poet.* In *The Journal of Philosophy,* 47 (1950): 362.

Carpenter, Frederic Ives. *Emerson Handbook.* In *The Journal of Philosophy,* 50 (1953): 702–3.

Clark, Henry Hayden, ed. *Thomas Paine. Representative Selections.* In *The Journal of Philosophy,* 41 (1944): 420.

Cotton, J. Harry. *Royce on the Human Self.* In *Bibliography of Philosophy,* 1 (1954): 54–55.

Foote, Henry Wilder. *Thomas Jefferson—Champion of Religious Freedom—Advocate of Christian Morals.* In *The Journal of Philosophy,* 44 (1947): 362.

Holloway, Mark. *Heavens on Earth: Utopian Communities in America, 1680–1880.* In *The Review of Religion,* 17 (1953): 200–201.

Horton, Rod W. and Herbert W. Edwards. *Backgrounds of American Literary Thought.* In *The Journal of Philosophy,* 50 (1953): 703–4.

Larrabee, H. A., et al. *Laurens Perseus Hickock (Class of 1820).* In *The Journal of Philosophy,* 45 (1948): 274–75.

Levy, Babette M. *Preaching in the First Half Century of New England History.* In *The Review of Religion,* 11 (1946): 102–3.

Miller, Fide Wolfe. *Christopher Pearse Cranch and his Caricatures of New England Transcendentalism.* In *The Journal of Philosophy,* 49 (1952): 22–23.

Miller, Perry. *The New England Mind: From Colony to Province.* In *The Review of Religion,* 19 (1955): 217–18.

Norlin, George. *The Quest of American Life.* In *The Journal of Philosophy,* 42 (1945): 554.

Richardson, R. D. *Abraham Lincoln's Autobiography.* In *The Journal of Philosophy,* 45 (1948): 224.

Ryan, Alvan S., ed. *The Brownson Reader.* In *Bibliography of Philosophy,* 2 (1955): 44.

Sweet, William Warren. *Religion in the Development of American Culture, 1765–1840.* In *The Review of Religion,* 18 (1953): 109.

White, L. A., et. al. *Lewis Henry Morgan (Class of 1840).* In *The Journal of Philosophy,* 44 (1947): 53.

Ziegler, H. J. B. *Frederick Augustus Rauch: American Hegelian.* In *The Journal of Philosophy,* 52 (1955): 760.

Social Philosophy

BOOKS

Social Theories of Jacksonian Democracy: Representative Writings of the Period 1825–1850. New York: Hafner Publishing Company, 1947. [Reprint 1952, New York: The Liberal Arts Press; reprinted 1961, Indianapolis: Bobbs-Merrill.]

ARTICLES AND ADDRESSES

"A Philosophic View of the City." *American Quarterly,* 9 (1957): 454–58. [Reprinted in Hennig Cohen, ed. *The American Culture. Approaches to the Study of the United States,* pp. 312–17. Boston: Houghton-Mifflin, 1968.]

"'Bellamy's Religious Motivation for Social Reform: A Review Article." *The Review of Religion,* 21 (1957): pp. 156–66.

"Conscience and Compassion." [Commemoration Address for Dr. Felix Adler and Dr. John Lovejoy Elliott.] *The Ethical Outlook,* 44 (November–December 1958): 196–99.

"Democracy and Parochial Schools." *Jewish Frontier,* 21, no. 4 (1954): 10–15.

"Emerson's Transcendentalist Individualism as a Social Philosophy." *The Review of Metaphysics,* 31 (September 1977): 80–92.

Letter to the Editor, *Saturday Review of Literature,* January 19, 1946, p. 25. Concerning Mortimer J. Adler's review of Benjamin Fine, *Democratic Education.*

"Mordecai M. Kaplan as a Philosopher of Democracy." In *Mordecai M. Kaplan: An Evaluation,* eds. Ira Eisenstein and Eugene Kohn, pp. 243–61. New York: Jewish Reconstructionist Foundation, Inc., 1952.

"Planning and Democracy." [Abstract of a paper read at a meeting of the Eastern Division of the American Philosophic Association, December 27, 1946.] *The Journal of Philosophy,* 43 (1946): 677.

"Ralph Barton Perry's Social Philosophy." *The Reconstructionist,* 12, no. 14 (1946): 18–21.

"Reading the Signs." An address delivered April 30, 1961, at the Assembly of The American Ethical Union.

"Reflections on Anarchism." *The Standard,* 36 (October 1949): 25–29.

"Remote Control and the 'New Authoritarianism.'" *The Standard,* 36 (April 1950): 300–306.

"Science and Social Progress." In *Philosophy and the Civilizing Arts. Essays Presented to Herbert W. Schneider on his Eightieth Birthday,* eds. Craig Walton and John P. Anton, pp. 166–77. Athens, Ohio: Ohio University Press, 1974.

"Social Planning Appropriate in a Democracy." *The Humanist,* 9 (1949): 110–16.

"Some Suggestions for Implementing a Cooperative Philosophy of Education." *Harvard Educational Review,* 14 (1944): 221–31.

"Tayler Lewis: True Conservative." *Journal of the History of Ideas,* 13 (1952): 218–33.

"The Three R's: A Teacher's Faith." *The Ethical Outlook,* 43 (September–October 1957): 157–59.

"Utopia." An address delivered at the regular Sunday morning meeting of the New York Society for Ethical Culture, July 10, 1960.

"We Don't Want Prayer in the Schools." [Identical with " 'Are You an Atheist?' "] *The Standard,* 38 (April–May 1952): 111–16.

"What Is the Ethical Movement Today?" *The Ethical Outlook,* 45 (1959): 185–90.

REVIEWS

Bailyn, Bernard. *Education in the Forming of American Society.* In *The Ethical Outlook,* 47 (1961): 209–10.

Ewing, A. C. *The Individual, The State, and World Government.* Sidney Hook, and Milton R. Konvitz, eds. *Freedom and Experience.* In *Jewish Social Studies,* 11 (1949): 315–18.

Henderson, Stella Van Petten. *Introduction to the Philosophy of Education.* In *The Journal of Philosophy,* 45 (1948): 249.

Hollingworth, Harry L. *Psychology and Ethics, A Study of the Sense of Obligation.* In *The Journal of Philosophy,* 47 (1950): 259–63.

Kallen, Horace M. *Cultural Pluralism and the American Idea.* In *Congress Weekly,* 25 (June 1958): 15.

—— *The Liberal Spirit.* In *The Journal of Philosophy,* 47 (1950): 78–79.

—— *Modernity and Liberty.* In *The Journal of Philosophy,* 44 (1947): 694–95.

Kurtz, Paul, ed. *Moral Problems in Contemporary Society: Essays in Humanistic Ethics.* In *Religious Humanism,* 4 (1970): 92.

Moehlman, Conrad H. *The Wall of Separation Between Church and State.* In *The Standard,* 38 (October 1951): 30–32.

—— *The Wall of Separation Between Church and State.* V. T. Thayer, *The Attack upon the American Secular School.* John L. Childs, *Education and Morals. Moral and Spiritual Values in the Public Schools*

(Washington, D.C.: Educational Policies Commission). Henry P. Van Dusen, *God in Education: A Tract for the Times*. In *The Humanist*, 11 (1951): 183–85.

Pfeffer, Leo. *Church, State, and Freedom*. In *The Humanist*, 14 (1954): 101–3.

—— *The Liberties of an American: The Supreme Court Speaks*. In *The Reconstructionist*, 23 (November 1, 1957): 23–25.

Stanton, William. *The Leopard's Spots: Scientific Attitudes Toward Race in America, 1815–59*, In *American Anthropologist*, 63 (1961): 174–75.

Volkart, Edmund H., ed. *Social Behavior and Personality. Contributions of W. I. Thomas to Theory and Social Research*. In *The Journal of Philosophy*, 49 (1952): 479–81.

REVIEW NOTES

Lecler, Joseph. *The Two Sovereignties; a Study of the Relationship Between Church and State*. In *The Journal of Philosophy*, 50 (1953): 705.

Roemer, Lawrence. *Brownson on Democracy and the Trend Toward Socialism*. In *The Review of Religion*, 19 (1954): 93–94.

Titus, Harold H. *Ethics for Today*. 2d ed. In *The Journal of Philosophy*, 44 (1947): 644.

Zabel, Orville H. *God and Caesar in Nebraska. A Study of the Relationship of Church and State, 1854–1954*. In *The Review of Religion*, 22 (1957): 98–99.

General History of Ideas

BOOKS

An Introduction to Contemporary Civilization in the West. 2 vols. Rev ed. [J. L. B. was co-editor with several others.] New York: Columbia University Press, 1954.

Chapters in Western Civilization. 2 vols. Co-editor with Justus Buchler and George T. Matthews. New York: Columbia University Press, 1948. [A revised edition of this book was published by Columbia University Press in 1954.]

The Christian Interpretation of the Cabala in the Renaissance. New York: Columbia University Press, 1944. [Reprint 1966, New York: Kennikat Press]

Man in Contemporary Society. Vol 1. [J. L. B. was co-editor with several others.] New York: Columbia University Press, 1955.

ARTICLES

"Browne's Interest in Cabalism." *PMLA,* 49 (1934): 963–64.

"The Diffusion of the Christian Interpretation of the Cabala in English Literature." *The Review of Religion,* 6 (1942): 146–68.

"Magic and Kabbala." *Hemispheres,* 2, no. 5 (1945): 55–59.

"The Philosopher as Historian of Philosophy: Herbert Wallace Schneider." *Journal of the History of Philosophy,* 10 (1972): 212–15.

"Robert Burton on Voice and Speech." *Quarterly Journal of Speech,* 23 (1942): 461–64.

"Rosmini, Domodossola, and Thomas Davidson." In *Atti del Congresso Internazionale di Filosofia Antonio Rosmini,* pp. 427–436. Firenzo: Sansone, 1957. [A revised version of this article was published in *The Journal of the History of Ideas,* 18 (1957): 522–28.]

"The Scope of Perennial Philosophy." *The Standard,* 37 (November 1950): 77–81.

"An Unpublished English Translation of Justinian's Life of Columbus." *Columbia Library Columns,* 13 (May 1964): 9–20.

REVIEWS

Bergman, Samuel Hugo. *The Philosophy of Solomon Maimon.* In *Journal of the History of Philosophy,* 7 (1969): 470–71.

Boas, George. *Essays on Primitivism and Related Ideas in the Middle Ages.* In *The Journal of Philosophy,* 46 (1949): 720–21.

Brod, Max. *Franz Kafka, a Biography.* Angel Flores, ed. *The Kafka Problem.* In *Jewish Social Studies,* 10 (1948): 197–99.

Coburn, Kathleen, ed. *The Philosophical Lectures of Samuel Taylor Coleridge.* In *The Standard,* 36 (January 1950): 184–85.

Cone, Carl B. *Torchbearer of Freedom: The Influence of Richard Price on Eighteenth Century Thought.* In *The Review of Religion,* 17 (1953): 185–87.

Diekhoff, J. S. *Milton's Paradise Lost.* In *The Journal of Philosophy,* 44 (1947): 695–96.

Fairley, Barker. *A Study of Goethe.* In *The Standard,* 36 (December 1949): 138–39.

Feuer, Lewis S. *Spinoza and the Rise of Liberalism.* In *The Ethical Outlook,* 45 (March–April 1959): 66–68.

Fisher, Mitchell Salem. *Robert Boyle—Devout Naturalist. A Study in Science and Religion in the Seventeenth Century.* In *The Review of Religion,* 12 (1947): 71–73.

Gross, Feliks. *European Ideologies.* In *Jewish Social Studies,* 11 (1949): 318–19.

Hayes, J. H. *Christianity and Western Civilization.* In *The Humanist,* 14 (1955): 196–97.

Holmes, S. J. *Life and Morals.* In *The Journal of Philosophy,* 46 (1949): 82.

Hook, Sidney. *The Paradoxes of Freedom.* In *Jewish Social Studies,* 27 (1965): 262–63.

Hopper, Vincent Foster. *Medieval Number Symbolism: Its Sources, Meaning, and Influence on Thought and Expression.* In *The Review of Religion,* 4 (1940): 206–8.

Jaccard, Louis Frédéric. *Blaise Pascal.* In *Erasmus: Speculum Scientiarum,* 8 (1955): 324–25.

Kurtz, Paul, ed. *Sidney Hook and the Contemporary World.* In *Jewish Social Studies,* 31 (1971): 214–15.

Larrabee, Harold A., ed. *Bentham's Handbook of Political Fallacies.* In *The Standard,* 40 (May–June 1954): 106–8.

Lauth, Reinhard. *Die Frage nach dem Sinn des Daseins.* In *Erasmus: Speculum Scientiarum,* 11 (1958): 332–33.

Lindblom, Joh. *Die Jesaja-Apokalypse.* In *The Review of Religion,* 3 (1939): 314–17.

Lovejoy, Arthur O. *Essays in the History of Ideas.* In *The Standard,* 36 (November 1949): 89–91.

Morgan, Arthur E. *The Philosophy of Edward Bellamy.* In *The Journal of Philosophy,* 43 (1946): 331–34.

Price, Richard. *A Review of the Principal Questions in Morals,* ed. D. D. Raphael. In *The Journal of Philosophy,* 46 (1949): 733–34.

Ratner, Sidney, ed. *Vision and Action. Essays in Honor of Horace M. Kaplan on His 70th Birthday.* In *Jewish Social Studies,* 17 (1955): 168–69.

Rosenberg, Alfons. *Die Seelenreise. Wiedergeburt, Seelenwanderung oder Aufstief durch die Sphären.* In *Erasmus: Speculum Scientiarum,* 8 (1955): 709–10.

Rosenthal, Erwin I. J. *Law and Religion (Judaism and Christianity,* vol. 3). In *The Review of Religion,* 4 (1940): 200–202.

Siwek, Paul, *Au coeur du Spinozisme.* [The Essence of Spinozaism]. In *Erasmus: Speculum Scientiarum,* 7 (1954): 199–200.

Wade, Gladys I. *Thomas Traherne, A Critical Biography.* In *The Journal of Philosophy,* 41 (1944): 642–44.

Wallis, Wilson D. *Messiahs, Their Role in Civilization.* In *The Review of Religion,* 8 (1944): 289–91.

REVIEW NOTES

Briggs, Arthur E. *Walt Whitman, Thinker and Artist*. In *The Journal of Philosophy*, 50 (1953): 704–5.

del Vecchio, Giorgio. *Philosophy of Law*. Translated by Thomas Owen Martin. In *Bibliography of Philosophy*, 1 (1954): 43.

Dunham, Barrows. *Man against Myth*. In *The Journal of Philosophy*, 44 (1947): 445.

Dunner, Joseph. *Baruch Spinoza and Western Democracy: An Interpretation of his Philosophical, Religious and Political Thought*. In the *Bibliography of Philosophy*, 2 (1955): 54–55.

Finegan, Jack. *The Archeology of World Religions*. In *The Review of Religion*, 18 (1953): 102–3.

Lévi, Eliphas. *Transcendental Magic: Its Doctrine and Ritual*, trans. Arthur Edward Waite. In *The Review of Religion*, 3 (1939): 244–45.

Raglan, Lord. *The Hero: A Study in Tradition, Myth, and Drama*. In *The Standard*, 36 (May 1950): 378–79.

Whyte, A. Gowans. *The Story of the R. P. A.* [Rationalist Press Association]. In *The Journal of Philosophy*, 47 (1950): 363.

Wieler, John William. *George Chapman—The Effect of Stoicism upon his Tragedies*. In *The Journal of Philosophy*, 47 (1950): 363.

Miscellaneous

"The Fallacy of the Abused Premise." *The Critic and Guide*, 5 (1951): 74–76.

"A Fantasy." [A poem.] *New York Times Magazine*, (October 24, 1943), p. 24.

"Foreshadowings of Phonetics." *The Spoken Word*, 3, no. 2 (1935): 11–13.

"The Function of Drills in the Teaching of Speech." *High Points*, 21, no. 5 (1939): 26–31.

Letter, including a poem, "A Rose by Any Other Name Would Smell." *Saturday Review of Literature*, August 31, 1946, p. 12.

"Lippmann's 'Vital Center.'" *The Standard*, 36 (February 1950): 223–27.

"On the Celebration of Christmas." *Columbia University Report*, (Christmas 1964–New Year 1965), pp. 3–6.

"Public Address as Intellectual Revelation." *Western Speech*, 21 (1957): 77–83. [Reprinted in *Essays on Rhetorical Criticism*, ed.

Thomas R. Nilsen, pp. 18–28. New York: Random House, 1968.

"The Roundness of the World." [Address delivered at the New York Society for Ethical Culture, July 12, 1959.] In *The Ethical Platform*.

"Three Poems." In *Columbia Poetry, 1931,* p. 4. New York: Columbia University Press, 1931.

"Vanitas Vanitatum." In *Best College Verse, 1931,* ed. Jessie Rehder, p. 70. New York: Harper, 1931.

"What Lets the Light Shine Through." *The Standard,* 30 (1944): 224–25.

Index

Notes on Contributors

Though most of the participants in this Festschrift *have published a considerable number of books and articles, the editors, to maintain a unity of form, have decided to list only two or three of each contributor's most important publications.*

SALO W. BARON, Professor of Jewish History, Literature and Institutions on the Miller Foundation, Emeritus, Columbia University, is the author, among many other works, of the monumental 17-volume *A Social and Religious History of the Jews.*

DAVID R. BLUMENTHAL, Co-Editor, is Jay and Leslie Cohen Professor of Judaic Studies, Emory University, and author of *The Commentary of Hoter Ben Shlomo to the Thirteen Principles of Maimonedes,* and editor, *Understanding Jewish Mysticism: A Source Reader.*

JUSTUS BUCHLER, Distinguished Professor of Philosophy, State University of New York at Stony Brook, is the author of *Nature and Judgment,* and *Metaphysics of Natural Complexes.*

RAYMOND F. BULMAN, Assistant Professor of Theology and Philosophy, St. John's University, New York, is the author of "Theonomy and Technology," and the forthcoming *A Blueprint for Humanity: The Structure of Tillich's Theology of Culture.*

CHANDANA CHAKRABARTI, Senior Research Fellow in Philosophy, Jadavpur University, Calcutta, is the author of "The Identity Theory and James" and co-author, "James' 'Pure Experience' Versus Ayer's 'Weak Phenomenalism.' "

SAM DEKAY, Secretary, is former Assistant Professor of Religion and Philosophy, Adrian College, Michigan, and former Adjunct Assistant Professor of Religion, Baruch College, City University of New York.

DOUGLAS GREENLEE, late Professor of Philosophy, Temple University, is the author of *Peirce's Concept of Sign,* and late editor of the forthcoming complete edition of the semiotical writings of C. S. Peirce.

JAMES GUTMANN, Professor and Chairman, Emeritus, Department of Philosophy, Columbia University, is the editor and translator of Fichte's *The Vocation of Man* and Schelling's *Of Human Freedom.* He also served as Director of Columbia's University Seminar.

PETER H. HARE, Co-Editor, is Professor of Philosophy, State University of New York at Buffalo, and Editor, *Transactions of the C. S. Peirce Society: A Quarterly Journal in American Philosophy,* and co-author, *Evil and the Concept of God;* and *Causing, Perceiving and Believing: An Examination of the Philosophy of C. J. Ducasse.*

PAUL O. KRISTELLER, Frederick J. E. Woodbridge Professor of Philosophy, Emeritus, Columbia University, is the author of *Renaissance Thought* and *Eight Philosophers of the Italian Renaissance.*

PAUL KURTZ, Professor of Philosophy, State University of New York at Buffalo, is editor of *The Humanist,* and author of *Existence: A Philosophy of Happiness,* and *The Fullness of Life.*

JOHN J. McDERMOTT, Professor and Chairman, Department of Philosophy and Humanities, Texas A & M University, is the author of *The Culture of Experience: Philosophical Essays in the American Grain;* and editor, *The Writings of William James.*

EDWARD H. MADDEN, Professor of Philosophy, State University of New York at Buffalo, is the author of *Civil Disobedience and Moral Law in Nineteenth Century American Philosophy,* and co-author, *Causal Powers.*

JAMES A. MARTIN, Jr., Co-Editor, is Professor of Religion, Columbia University, and author of *The New Dialogue Between Philosophy and Theology,* and *Empirical Philosophies of Religion.*

JACOB NEUSNER, University Professor of Religious Studies and Ungerleider Distinguished Scholar of Judaic Studies, Brown University, is the author of *A History of the Mishnaic Law of Purities* and *Development of a Legend: Studies on the Traditions Concerning Yohanan ben Zakkai.*

DAVID L. NORTON, Professor of Philosophy, University of Delaware, is the author of *Personal Destinies: A Philosophy of Ethical Individualism.*

HOWARD B. RADEST, Co-Editor, is Director, Ethical Culture Schools, and Professor of Philosophy (on leave), School of American Studies, Ramapo College, New Jersey, and author of *Toward A Common Ground;* and editor, *To Seek A Humane World,* and *Ramapo Papers.*

STEVEN C. ROCKEFELLER, Associate Professor of Religion, Middlebury College, Vermont, is completing a book on the religious dimension of John Dewey's life and thought.

HERBERT W. SCHNEIDER, Professor of Philosophy, Emeritus, Columbia University, is the author of *A History of American Philosophy* and *3 Dimensions of Public Morality.*

WILLIAM M. SHEA, Associate Professor of Religion, Catholic University, Washington, D.C., is the author of "Santayana on Knowing and Being" and "Task of the Foundational Theologian."

ROGER L. SHINN, Reinhold Niebuhr Professor of Social Studies, Union Theological Seminary, New York, is the author of *Man: The New Humanism,* and *Wars and Rumors of Wars.*

MAURICE WOHLGELERNTER, Editor, is Professor of English, and Chairman, Religion and Culture Program, Baruch College, City University of New York. He is the author of *Israel Zangwill: A Study;* and *Frank O'Connor: An Introduction;* and of the forthcoming *Joseph Wood Krutch: Humanist.*

EDITH WYSCHOGROD, Associate Professor of Philosophy, Queens College, City University of New York, is the author of *Emmanuel Levinas: The Problem of Ethical Metaphysics;* and editor, *The Phenomenon of Death: Faces of Mortality.*